3/5/77

Romanticism

A volume
in
THE DOCUMENTARY HISTORY
of
WESTERN CIVILIZATION

ROMANTICISM

edited by
JOHN B. HALSTED

WALKER AND COMPANY
New York

Library of Congress Catalog Card Number: 68-27378.

Printed in the United States of America.

Published in the United States of America in
1969 by Walker and Company, a division of the
Walker Publishing Company, Inc.

Published simultaneously in Canada by
The Ryerson Press, Toronto.

Volumes in this series are published in association
with Harper & Row, Publishers, Inc., from
whom paperback editions are available in Harper
Torchbooks.

Contents

Introduction

We all feel we know what "romantic" means: the word conveys notions of sentiment and sentimentality, of a visionary, idealistic lack of realism, of fantasy and fiction. It has been associated with distant places and times—the island of Bali, the world of the *Arabian Nights*, the age of the troubadours. Advertising links it with the effects of lipstick, perfumes, and soap. Such a range of implication causes little trouble in common parlance, but scholars have been quarreling over the meaning of "Romanticism" for nearly 150 years. The editor of a volume of documents illustrating such a subject cannot avoid implicitly imposing his definition upon his choice of documents. I will seek in this Introduction to suggest some of the considerations which have guided my choices, indicating thereby my view of Romanticism. I feel definition should serve as a heuristic device, and hence, for a variety of purposes, a variety of definitions of Romanticism might prove most illuminating. In the present instance, my concern is to exemplify major aspects of an era in the intellectual life of Europe. Therefore it does not seem to me particularly useful to follow some leading scholars in identifying Romanticism as one of the two, or one of the very few, permanent dispositions of the human spirit and "Romantic eras" as those wherein that disposition became dominant. We lose thereby the advantages of a distinctive name for a unique epoch in the history of ideas, the period from about 1780 to about 1850. "Romanticism" in this sense may serve as a concept for a period, as does the term "Enlightenment."

The term "Romantic" gained currency during that time—1780 to 1850—although a wide variety of meanings were attached to it. The very variety of such meanings makes it the more legitimate, I think, for later students of the period to attempt some greater coherence of definition and to try to make the terms "Romantic" and "Romanticism" match more closely the traits we find a large number of intellectuals in that era had in common—or what many of them seem to have felt they had in common. This intention leads me to prefer a scope of meaning similar to "general world view" or "a way of answering the main questions men face," which would give the terms "Romanticism" and "Enlightenment" a comprehensiveness like that of "Humanism." This broad sense allows us to include and to go beyond the traditional usage of "Romanticism" as a name simply for a type of art and of artistic taste, usually contrasted to "classicism." A narrow definition of this latter sort would, I believe, shape the readings in such a way that the complex reality of an era in the history of ideas would be lost.

I will restrict use of the phrase "Romantic movement," as is normally done, to the arts, where in Germany and France at least there was conscious and coordinated effort to effect change. Though in revolutionary and religious sects such efforts also occurred, they were not coordinated with the arts, and there seems no way to view them all together as one movement. In the wider sense in which I wish to use it, Romanticism is a name for interrelated and similar ideas and attitudes—and related and derivative forms of behavior—in the whole range of intellectual concerns, in the arts, of course, but with equal import and novelty, I suggest, in religion, history, and politics.

To speak of a "Romantic era" is to identify the period, *circa* 1780 to 1850, in which these ideas and attitudes arose and had currency and in most areas of intellectual concern became fully dominant. But it is not to suggest that older ideas disappeared or ceased to exert influence. As we shall note, Romantic ideas arose both as implicit and explicit criticisms of leading eighteenth-century views; they were adumbrated largely out of a sense of the inadequacy of the dominant ideas of the Enlightenment and of the society which produced them—or what Romanticists identified as "those" ideas and "that" society. As time went on, Romantic ideas appeared in conflict against the inheritance and the inheritors of the Enlightenment—or again, what Romanticists took them to be. Our problem of defining Romanticism and identifying Romanticists is made easier by the effort Romanticists made to distinguish themselves—and their key ideas—at first from the classicists and *philosophes*, and later from philistines, economists, and the rest. Despite changes that evolved throughout the period, we can point to considerable similarities and considerable consistency, which allow us legitimately to use a broad class term such as Romanticism for the period 1780 to 1850.

Romanticism was the new thought, the critical ideas, the creative or despairing efforts to cope with the insufficiency of old ways of confronting experience. The Romanticists were the proponents, exemplars, and followers of the newly emphasized ideas and patterns of behavior that arose in the period following 1780.

The Romantic era was one in which there was a widespread sense of crisis, a sense evident even before the outbreak of the French Revolution that the old order was coming to an end. And once the Revolution had broken out, the activities of intellectuals gained in urgency as fear of *political* disaster spread—fear of the Terror, of Napoleonic armies, of the chaos in internal and international politics as war continued for twenty-five years. Then the coming of the Industrial Revolution, already begun in Britain and spreading to the Continent after 1820, added *social* concerns. There were now new urban masses affected by the factory system, and the French Revolution had revealed some of their political potentialities and provided the model for visions of class war. The rapid growth of manufacturing wealth in a competitive market spread fear that egoistic individualism might enhance the *sauve qui peut* attitude already too evident among the fearful or the politically uninvolved, which many believed threatened political order, unity or progress. Egoism, materialism, unconstrained freedom, these ideas now had their theoretical and propagandizing advocates. All seemed likely outgrowths of the dissolution of old disciplines and traditional political forms and hence raised the threat of *moral* disaster.

Men faced the need to build new systems of discipline and order, or to reshape old ones. The era was prolific in important and innovative ideas and art forms. Theory proliferated (often under the stress of intense emotion) to come to terms with rapid, apparently unmanageable, change. Of course, much of the theory, many of the ideas were mere transfers, or reinterpretations, of old theories and ideas. But such has ever been the way theories grow and change. For example, Burke and other conservatives feared and disdained "the swinish multitude," which was believed to have generated the "excesses of the Revolution." Subsequently, their views of revolutionary mobs helped shape the

treatment of the denizens of the new urban slums after indus-
trialization spread. Classical economic thought incorporated into
the analysis of the market the old political liberal doctrine of
rational self-interest and the physical notion of equilibrium.

Such transference and use of old doctrines in new contexts, of
old forms of understanding to comprehend novelty, should force
us to keep in mind how slow and incomplete are revolutions in
thought and how strongly the past persists. We will not find in
the documents presented here clear breaks between eras of
thought.

In the midst of what has been called a Romantic era, an era
often portrayed as devoted to irrationality, the most purely rational social science, classical economics, carried on the Enlightenment tradition. Enlightenment rationalism continued to be expressed in political liberal and radical doctrines. Bentham's radical-
skeptical critique of traditional politics became an active political
movement among the philosophic radicals, and Chartist politics
was full of Jacobinism. The Continental left and much of socialism reflected in full clarity an Enlightenment heritage.

Nor should we be misled about the sharpness of the distinction
between Enlightenment and Romanticism by the needs and desires of intellectuals to assert their own novelty by exaggerating
how much they differed from their predecessors. That we identify
traits or ideas as "Enlightenment" rather than as "Romantic" is
itself a consequence of the period under study. For the early
Romanticists defined the Enlightenment as something to which
they were opposed and exaggerated its unanimity. They were
aided in this by the earlier efforts of the *philosophes*, who had
formed a conscious coterie and put up a common front to the
world to help promote a militant ideology despite a good deal of
disagreement among themselves. Rousseau for instance was a
philosophe, yet certainly not fully so, for his works were blamed,
or credited, with beginning the Romantic era. The *philosophes*
oversimplified. Enlightenment thought was not a simple and
clearly identifiable thing. What has often been identified as the
Enlightenment has at best a superficial similarity to the reality
that seems to have existed. Just as Jacques Barzun showed, a
generation ago, that Romanticism was the creation of quite diverse real men trying as best they might to face a disrupted world
with all their human capacities—quite practical men seeking

practical solutions to life's problems—so now Peter Gay is engaged in demonstrating that the misjudgments and unfair charac-
terizations of the *philosophes* by their successors attribute to
those eighteenth-century figures too much unanimity and fail to
apprehend that they were largely quite practical and realistic
men seeking practical solutions to life's problems in the terms
then available to them.

And it is perfectly true that the successors of the *philosophes*
were often unfair to the thought of the eighteenth century, failing
to recognize how much they shared with it, how much of it they
carried over into their own ideas, how much of what they thought
revolutionary was not so at all. In so doing they were like the
Humanists who were similarly unfair to the Middle Ages. The
Humanists invented a Middle Ages to define themselves against,
and they thereby enhanced both their own self-evaluation and
their prestige, while foisting error on later generations. Their
error lay in their evaluation of the past as well as in their simple
failure to apprehend or even show interest in facts about the
Middle Ages. Both aspects of the error are important. As in the
case of the Romanticists, it shows first how men make an identity
for themselves—as sons do against their fathers—by defining an
enemy, making clear what they oppose, making life a battle to be
fought, their own success the winning of it. Second, it is evident
that factual, accurate, subtle understanding makes the enemy mere
men like ourselves: Diderot begins to look like a Romanticist instead of a staunch *philosophe*.

Even before the Revolution, Romanticists opposed the super-
ficiality of the conventions of an artificial, urban, aristocratic society quite as much as the ideas the conventions were taken to
embody. They blurred distinctions between its decadent, fashionable Christianity or unemotional Deism and the theoretical irreligion or passionate anti-clericalism of the *philosophes*. The *philosophes*, experts in defining themselves in conflict with their enemy
the Church, helped to create the mythical ungodly Enlightenment the Romanticists opposed.

But it was during the Revolution and in the succeeding sixty
years that opposition to the Enlightenment became clarified, and
myth was given form. The vision of the Enlightenment that
emerged probably had no true living type, yet the myth has dominated the image of the eighteenth century until our own time.

While the myth was being worked out (we will sketch it in a moment), polarizations that fitted the problems faced by some men proved insufficient for others. The enemy could hardly remain the same through sixty or more years and through all the diversity of European culture. Romanticism came to oppose, as time went on, not just the Enlightenment but also ideas derived from it and the men influenced by it—its inheritors.

These were times of active war, revolutionary combat. Violence and partisanship seemed most normal. Increasingly Romanticists rejected those aspects of the French Revolution, the Terror, and the Napoleonic régime that were felt to have been inspired by the *philosophes*. But for some people neither the *ancien régime* aristocrats, nor French revolutionary armies, nor natural rights and constitutionalism represented real enemies—especially after 1815. Metternich might find quite adequate the old polarization of presumptuous intellectuals against an ordered state. But for many, especially of the younger generations, the terms of the contest shifted, although the revolutions 1848 demonstrated how dominated they remained by the old terms of opposition. But new contests were afoot too: where earlier aristocratic urban society had been rejected, now Romanticists combatted the heartlessness of a middle-class laissez-faire, urban, industrial society,—its soulless individualism, its economic egoism, utilitarian and materialistic. That society now came under attack from new critics, Utopian socialists and early communists, but it was also attacked by many we unequivocally class as Romanticists—Disraeli, Carlyle, Mazzini—men who saw the threat of egoism as the chief danger of their times, as dominating the bourgeoisie, especially in France and Britain, to the deprivation of all "higher" virtues and social concerns. And it was the same identification of an enemy that found the artists and intellectuals attacking the "philistinism" of the bourgeoisie—their lack of taste and their lack of any exalted moral qualities. Documents drawn from the Romantic era will reveal, besides the persistence of Enlightenment thought, both the Romanticists' definition of themselves and the gradual transfer of their animus to new opponents.

This shift of opposition reminds us that the Romanticists were eclectic, sometimes consciously, sometimes unintentionally. Neither the Enlightenment nor Romanticism was a monolithic ideology, everywhere the same. Ideas seldom move as systems. Men are brought up in particular historical moments and geographical locations that we must take account of. Our labels too readily let us forget that past ideas form the context in which intellectuals innovate and that their innovations are usually recombinations of what they have learned. These contexts differed from state to state despite the dominance of French culture in the eighteenth century. Both Germany's *Sturm und Drang* and Scotland's moral philosophy were independent cultural developments. And national variations were enhanced further when, under the impress of wars, boundaries were closed and the comparatively easy international interchange of ideas of the cosmopolitan eighteenth century was inhibited. It was inhibited not merely by closed frontiers but also by profound antagonism and by the newly learned desire to build autonomous cultures, which formed so large a part of the new nationalist ideology. And within each state, institutional and social differences helped provide limits to any generalized assimilation of a clearly defined set of ideas or even of incidental novelties. In France, for example, the academies were strong and, at least in the Napoleonic period, censorship was quite effective. Artists and intellectuals were actively prevented from innovating or adopting novel views. Elsewhere, what was new and different found a readier audience—Goethe's Weimar is a famous example. The structure of society, the character of educational forms (the dominance of universities in Germany laid a heavy academicism upon German Romantic thought), and other institutional traits affected the possibility of learning or of expressing new thought. Most important, I think, were the progressive change in the potential audience artists and intellectuals faced and the developing dependence of many upon that audience. Where the audience was very small—as in largely illiterate aristocratic states, e.g., Austria, parts of Germany—the results were sometimes extreme, either great openness to novelty or rigid conservatism. Where the audience was steadily growing, as in France and Britain, and the process of urbanization and the growth of a literate middle class were transforming the whole social position and the expectations of the artist or the intellectual, there was room for experiment, innovation, and often for disastrous failure. Instead of dependence upon aristocratic patronage, popularity among newly powerful classes became a survival test. The discomfort of this situation is evident in the continual attacks upon the tasteless and unreceptive philistine bourgeoisie. A free press and careers open to talent provided possibilities of competitive innovation in overcrowded fields and led to new efforts to train audiences to be receptive to the productions of artists and intellectuals, while hacks produced popular potboilers for the masses.

All these characteristics of the societies of the several states of Europe placed limits that cannot be ignored upon the activities of intellectuals. In fact, they often exerted pressures that can be identified as clearly causative of the novelties of Romanticism. Even more obviously causative were the great events experienced by the youth (those whose ideas were still not settled into rigid molds) of the various states of Europe. The Revolution and the Napoleonic wars were universal phenomena that influenced directly an entire European generation. Those who were young after the Revolution felt a chasm dividing them from the generation that had lived through it. Those who had seen Bonaparte seemed different and felt different from those who were too young to understand. The difference lay in a great discrepancy in the quality of their experience, the more so in that such great international events gave identity to generations and made them feel as one. So, in consequence, the qualities of thought and behavior of 1790 vary immensely from those of 1820, and reformulations and reorientations occur. As the readings to follow indicate, in the Romantic era men felt these temporal and experiential differences intensely and consciously. Obviously, too, only after Bonaparte could the cult of the hero and of genius take full form—for then the great example was known. And only after 1815 could youth complain that their time no longer offered opportunities for heroism such as their predecessors had known.

The importance of national differences should be kept in mind here too. It is not merely the moment itself—the experienced event or events—that has importance. *Where* the moment was experienced can be crucial also, as might be anticipated if we consider for instance the possible effect of participation in a major Napoleonic battle upon a Bonapartist Italian youth, in contrast to its likely effect upon a young German nationalist in 1813.

A final warning about generalization in the history of ideas. All men accept from their intellectual environment probably far more than they think. And we departmentalize our thought, relying readily upon accepted authorities in areas other than our chief interests. To be sure, there was less specialization around 1800 than there is now; yet, despite the wide range of interests revealed by Romanticists, in many areas they could neither be fully innovative nor even up to date on the latest views. One obvious way in which thought persists is as the habitually accepted. It is a fact too that men can survive a lot of self-contradiction: they can be captured by their conceptual categories so that their views are less novel than they believe, and they sometimes, especially when young, adopt in a rather experimental way fads and poses, which may show strongly in our evidence without constituting an expression of profound belief of commitment.

These warnings and qualifications should be kept in mind in reading the documents in this volume. Each may reveal much of interest which is idiosyncratic, expressive of distinctive national or generational traits, or of traditional thought, besides expressing some aspect or aspects of Romanticism.

It is hardly crucial that no men were perfect exemplars of the type "Enlightened" or of the type "Romantic," or that no perfectly typical documents exist.[1] What is important is that we recognize that we can *build* such constructs, that we do so consciously (as the Romanticists seldom did), and that we use them with full awareness of their inadequacy to comprehend fully the variety of materials and men we address them to. The version of the Enlightenment I offer derives originally from the *philosophes* themselves, and it incorporates much of the Romanticists' view of that which they rejected. The presentation of such a set of interrelated ideas of course intentionally simplifies the complexity of eighteenth-century thought and risks the perpetuation of oversimplifications and distortions, many of which have persisted since the Romantic era. It will give us, however, the compensating advantage of clearer definition of the complex of ideas making up Romanticism by emphasizing the sharp contrasts stressed by many Romanticists themselves. The Enlightened and Romantic notions sketched below can most usefully serve as a suggestive guide with which to approach the documents, a means of naming

[1] The very brief selections at the end of the volume seem to me to come close to exemplifying Romanticism, but of course they fail in comprehensiveness.

and classifying, a set of identifying traits to distinguish the more-or-less "Enlightened" from the more-or-less "Romantic."

For both the Enlightenment and for Romanticism, nature was pointed to as a standard, the "natural" constituted a standard for beauty and natural behavior a standard in morality. The Enlightenment view of nature was Newtonian: the physical world was seen as orderly, symmetrical, and regular, essentially repetitive and maintaining a static equilibrium. It was a nature subject to laws that could be stated with mathematical exactitude. That which was most worth knowing about it was just such general laws as described (or determined) its operation. Universal truths (like universal natural rights) were the object of science and philosophy. And the uniformity and regularity of nature permitted just that sort of knowledge which was so rapidly accumulating in consequence of men's rational capacity and the use of scientific techniques to penetrate what otherwise might be the mysteries of nature.

The Enlightenment defined human knowing in a Lockean sense as sensationalist and associationist—an environmentalist psychology, wherein men knew only what their sense impressions allowed their reason to work upon. And the Enlightenment was rationalist, glorifying reason and desirous of making it play a larger part in human affairs. Reason was looked on variously: as the power of analysis that breaks down experience into comprehensible parts, as the power of associating like experiences in order to generalize about them inductively, or as the power of deducing particular applications or logical consequences of either self-evident truths or truths held *a priori*. Reason was taken to be a common human possession, held by all men alike. All men, even visiting primitives from the American wilds, possessed such power to know the universal truths of nature. Hence, the emphasis upon common sense; it offered a groundwork for an anticipated common morality. As nature was studied to discover its universal aspects, so for men what was most worth knowing, what was taken to be most valuable was what they had in common. Society became an object of science, either of inductive analysis or of a deductive science derived from self-evident truths about men's common human nature or their self-evident natural rights. Social and political thought was individualistic and atomistic. Ready analogies were made between physical nature and the social order—the most obvious being

that the world of man was seen as made up of discrete atoms, as
was the material universe, and the action of the force of rational
self-interest was seen as analogous to gravity. And as the material
universe was ultimately machinelike, so social organization could
best be modeled upon a machine. From physics was also borrowed
(or unconsciously assimilated) a belief in the advantages of a kind
of static equilibrium of forces (as in Montesquieu's and Madison's
views of the balance of powers).

Science might pronounce what society ought to become in view
of men's natural needs. Such needs were not being fulfilled by
old, existing collectivities; these irrational residues of the past—
the old corporate bodies of medieval and early modern Europe—
were the Englightenment's enemies, for they inhibited rational
progress. Since Enlightenment psychology was largely environmentalist, so was much of its impulse to political reform. The
desire was to change institutions, in order to shape men and to
produce a better society—to construct a universally applicable constitutional mechanism. For immediate reformist purposes, it was
important to point out what men had in common and to emphasize
this against divisive forces, especially religious fanaticism. The
intention was cosmopolitan and humanitarian.

Much the same sorts of ideas were preached regarding art and
beauty but without a similar urge to reform. A neoclassical for-
malism, rigidly bound by Aristotelian unities in drama and
equally rigid rules elsewhere, was taken to resemble the orderly
and rule-bound character of nature itself. Above all, symmetry
and order were stressed. And just as common reason might comprehend (as Condorcet anticipated) the conclusions of science,
just so the common taste of literate mankind could serve as an
aesthetic standard. The conservative implications are fairly obvious, especially the implicit conclusion that what is beautiful for
one time and place (e.g., ancient Greece) is equally so for all
times and all places. Aesthetics in this view was universalist, cosmopolitan, and ahistorical. Most of the important truths had been
discovered by the ancients, and little more needed to be done to
ascertain the rules for art.

Romanticists felt that such views, along with some important
truths, contained very dangerous errors and oversimplifications.
Romanticism may be seen as a critique of the inadequacy of what
it held to be Enlightenment abstractions and tendencies.

The discussions of the five categories of documents will suggest (and the documents themselves exemplify) some of the positive Romantic assertions that accompanied the critique. Here should be added a few words about Romantic views of nature, of human nature, and of knowledge, which serve as often unstated assumptions underlying more specific Romantic ideas.

Romanticism as a critique of Enlightenment ideas can be seen as a new study of the bases of knowledge and of the whole scientific enterprise. It rejected a science dominated by physics as inadequate to describe the reality of experience and turned to the life sciences for more fully satisfactory insights and analogies. The universe Romanticists believed in was an expanding, evolving universe; their concern moved from physics to biology and from planets to plants.

It was Romantic thought that first offered the escape from what seemed to many an oppressive mechanism. It did so by returning God to nature, reviving, in fact, the unseen world, the supernatural, that which is not amenable to scientific procedures, that which mystical thought and medieval man had believed in. These aspects of Romanticism are most strikingly exemplified in the popularity of the Gothic novel. Nature for some became divinity; pantheist ideas can be found in Wordsworth, Heine, and Schelling. God in nature is one version of nature's beneficence.

Nature came to be viewed historically—a developing world, continual process, and continual growth could only be understood by historical thinking. The shift to such modes of thought, the seeking of origins and the inclination to relativism, is the single most revolutionary aspect of Romanticism.

Oscar Wilde suggested in *The Decay of Lying* that artists shape our views of nature. The new views of nature were adumbrated by artists (as Whitehead showed in *Science and the Modern World*) and anticipated the efforts of scientists and philosophers, who by the end of the nineteenth century were inclined to a genetic vitalism in contrast to the earlier positivist mechanistic materialism.

An admiration for all the potency, fecundity, the diversity of living nature superseded a concern for the discovery of its universal traits. The elements Romanticists felt worth knowing or noting or representing as beautiful in nature were no longer its abstract universal laws, but nature's glorious diversity of detail and especially its moral or emotional relation to mankind. Romantic artists showed a new concern for accuracy in presenting that detail. The persistence of these ideas later helped inspire the great fact-collecting impulse that developed by the mid-nineteenth century. In the course of the century, collecting easily became linked to the belief in the spiritual beneficence of communion with nature; week-end hikes became botanizing expeditions. The modern week end and vacation as escape from the city both express the same originally Romantic anti-urban impulse. Nature unsullied by man was seen as full of spiritual value; and those peasants who lived in it (or the yeoman whose revival was so urgently sought) were believed to be spiritually superior to city men.

In a central and constantly repeated figure that dominates Romanticism's criticism of its predecessors, the rationalism of the *philosophes* was characterized as cold, like the mechanical universe they believed in, as unfeeling, without the warmth the Romanticists admired. This warmth was of the heart, expressed in enthusiasm and usually enhanced by communion with nature. Much as we may now admire the human warmth of Voltaire or Franklin, much as we may approve the liberality and generous cosmopolitanism of many other eighteenth-century minds, they did not share in the cult of the heart, which is a key conception for understanding Romantic views both of man and of his knowing.

Romanticists, with Pascal, felt that the heart has reasons that the reason knows not of. The heart was held to be a source of knowledge, the location of innate ideas. Intuition was equated with that which men feel strongly. Men could learn not just through experiment and induction, or by logical processes, but in intuitive flashes, by trusting their instincts. Romanticists tended to distrust calculation and stressed the limitations of scientific knowledge. It was held that the rational counters of scientific abstractions fail to apprehend the variety and fullness of reality, that the process of rational analysis destroys the integrity of naïve experience of the stream of sensation and in this violation misleads the knower into error.

One power possessed especially by the artist, a power Coleridge asserted was distinct from and superior to reason, namely imagination, might apprehend the essential reality—and create art in accord with it. And the further belief that the untutored and uncultured (i.e., primitives and peasants) know not merely differently but best is an example of Romanticism's reinterpretation of the irrational. The Romanticists did not merely reassert that there were irrational ways of knowing, they rejected materialism and utilitarianism as types of personal behavior besides rejecting them as philosophic positions. They sought the sense of regeneration the religious convert has, and they favored selfless enthusiasm which was not a product of calculation but a pursuit of ideals, an expression of faith. Actions prompted by pure emotions came to be glorified irrespective of consequences.

Romanticism's reassessment of the irrational was not exclusively approving. There was also much traditional Christian pessimism about the dangerous role of the passions, much fear of their ability to overcome reason, a pessimism about man's ability to control either his environment or himself, much real disillusionment after the optimism of Enlightenment thought. Both views emerge clearly in Romantic political speculation. But, whether optimistic or pessimistic, the main force and tendency of the new interpretation of nonrational experience was to note the importance of the heart, of feeling, of emotion, of passion, and often to contend that, in contradiction of Enlightenment views, these were good, or potentially so; to note man's irrational weakness, but to glory in his potentiality. Where the Enlightenment had stressed the universal character of common sense, Rousseau and others now stressed the universal character of common feelings and built moral systems upon the basis of feelings of sympathy and empathy. Pity and the importance of sentiment often produced sheer sentimentality, as in much of the glorification of children or pity for the fallen woman who was pure of heart.

It became possible to affirm general moral codes on the basis of common sentiments, but it also became possible to affirm the superior morality of those with superior sentiments—the cult of the heart was available both to moral democrats and to moral aristocrats, and the importance among those aristocrats of unique, divergent, special feelings was asserted as a justification for a wide variety of eccentric behavior. Where men might be comforted that tradition and custom irrationally shaped the irrational morality of the masses, a higher virtue for the few could be expressed in the revival of the chivalric code or in the new noblesse oblige of a declining aristocracy, in patriotic codes of military heroism or of civic duty, in a new cult of the hero, or, finally, in hedonism and dedication to art among bohemian intellectuals. Among Romanticists the common feelings of the heart were probably less significant and interesting than what distinguished men from one another. Élitist moral codes and emphasis on the distinctive quality of imagination and the unique creative attribute of genius suggest that, just as to Romanticists particulars in nature were more fully true than their inadequate representation in abstractions, what was most worth knowing about men was the particular. Men's traits were seen historically, relativistically, as uniquely dependent upon circumstances. Their distinguishing characteristics were most fully theirs; the most fully real and admirable was the most distinctly different, either in individuals or in groups. There might be any number of general features of individuals or groups a Romanticist would find quite uninteresting. What would interest him are the traits that distinguish one individual or group, one nation or era, from others. The *characteristic* aspects of men and nature received emphasis in the arts, which served as the dominant expression of Romanticism. To them we turn next.

Aesthetics

As the Revolutionary era began, there was a widely held conviction that old religions and old political and social forms were outworn or outdated and needed replacement or reinvigoration. So, too, in the arts, with which the term Romanticism is most usually associated. There was a sense that old forms, old rules, old styles, old tastes were insufficient, and a host of major pronouncements upon the arts appeared in the Romantic era, dealing, as the documents to follow suggest, with such questions as: What in nature is worth portraying in art? What are suitable subjects? What styles should be employed in the several arts? Old models no longer seemed to fit. New artists treating new subjects felt there should be new models, or no models.

Older aesthetics had viewed classic art as a model for modern art—and had conceived of the prime beauties of that art as its universality and timelessness. Now came the new emphasis upon the unique, the particular, that which was historically localized, whence came the search Hugo points to for the *characteristic* detail, the traits related to time and place. Even if art were to be simply representational, still the possibility that the full diversity of reality or a fuller selection from its diversity might serve as suitable subject matter was explored. The grotesque was newly valued, and contrast, apparent "natural" disorder—as in new tastes in gardening—was now approved. New subjects, new models and styles [2] were drawn from a variety of hitherto unappreciated sources. One of the most thoroughly mined was the Middle Ages: a source for folk art, a model for Gothic architecture and Gothic novels.

Medievalism was a striking trait among the group of young German writers who first adopted the name Romantic for their own work around the turn of the nineteenth century. Under the leadership of A. W. von Schlegel and his brother Friedrich, the journal the *Athenaeum* became a vehicle for the aesthetic theory of the movement, expressed and exemplified in the art of such writers as Novalis (Friedrich von Hardenberg) and Ludwig Tieck. For this Romantic School—and to a lesser degree for young French artists of the 1820's—it seems legitimate and meaningful to speak of a "Romantic movement," for they engaged in a conscious collective effort in the arts.

The Schlegels proclaimed an art suitable to the modern age. Their view was both historical and relativist. They sought an art which would fit an age widely different from the classic era that had dominated European ideas of art for centuries; an art which would fit its present locale and its producers. They urged that modern art, the art of the modern Romantic era which they defined as beginning with the triumph of Christianity, must comprehend its Christian medieval inheritance as well as that of classic era.

The classical world, already reinterpreted in the poetry of Hölderlin, revealed far less of its traditionally glorified austere simplicity, far more of the Greeks' close association with nature and

---

[2] Obvious examples from literature are the decline of the heroic couplet in English poetry, the widespread increase in the popularity of the lyric, the battle over verse drama in France, and the immense development of the novel.

what Nietzsche later depicted as their Dionysian traits. A further element of importance introduced through this Romantic School was the use of nonclassical and pre-Christian mythology and folklore as subject matter for art. Such mythology and folklore had thrived in the Middle Ages, and it found its first great modern popularity when the Scots poet Macpherson invented the Ossian poems (a legendary Gaelic cyle) in the late eighteenth century.

The Schlegels immensely impressed Mme. de Staël, daughter of the ill-fated French finance minister Jacques Necker. Refusing to cooperate with the Napoleonic régime, she spent considerable time in Germany, and a major consequence of her visit and her acquaintance with the Schlegels was her book *Germany*, which sought to introduce the new thought of Germany to Frenchmen, whom she felt were excessively parochial in their lack of awareness of and respect for cultures other than their own, which had successfully dominated Europe since the days of Louis XIV. In the second half of the eighteenth century an authentic indigenous literature had arisen in Germany in the hands of Lessing, Schiller, and, finally and especially, Goethe. It was against the background of such a literature that the Schlegels and their young Romantic followers were able to argue for a new *German* literature. Mme. de Staël's book was cosmopolitan in intent (and the first significant attempt at a sociology of literature). But the literature (as well as the philosophy and religious speculation) she dealt with was at least incipiently nationalist, expressing a desire to assert the autonomy of German culture against the French, for it rejected the cosmopolitanism that had often served as an unconscious apology for French cultural dominance and for the universal applicability of French neoclassic taste.

Mme. de Staël helped popularize German letters in France; first Coleridge and later Carlyle served the same role in England. But in neither country was there any simple adoption of new doctrines from the Germans. There were already well-developed tendencies in both England and France that met and coalesced with the tenets of the first Romanticists. To some degree, also, they all drew from similar sources. There was, for example, widespread reinterpretation of Shakespeare, whose violation of unities, grotesquerie, blending of comedy and tragedy were once again acceptable. It was no accident that A. W. von Schlegel translated Shakespeare into German, or that Hugo saw Shakespeare

as the greatest figure of modern letters, while Coleridge and Haz-
litt were reassessing his genius for the English. The Gothic revival was another common interest. Horace Walpole's *Castle of
Otranto*, Mrs. Radcliffe's novels, the work of Matthew "Monk"
Lewis at the start of the century, and other English writings
were matched in France by Chateaubriand's very Gothic, aesthetic Catholicism. Primitivism as the glorification of the peasant
mentality was the possession of no single national literature, nor
was its combination with the glorification of traditional, religiously
sanctified virtues among knights and fair maidens.

The primitivist idea that purer art and deeper truth might
come from the uncultured persisted in the continuing interest in
untutored genius, natural genius not blunted by civilization. The
glorification of folk art, of the nameless builders of Gothic cathedrals, of the nameless authors of medieval lays or primitive
epics became common and helped promote the revival of folk
literatures. It also promoted the view that even civilized artists
were better off if they did not strain over their work but produced
almost unconsciously—as we find Shelley advocating. The fact
remains, of course, that the memorable artists of the era in literature and the plastic arts were also masters of their crafts. They
showed no tendency to turn the arts over to the uneducated. Even
among the uneducated, their interest was chiefly in the unique
individual, the natural genius, or in the individuality of collective
folk art. In either case, they were confronting a significant issue
for cultivated artists: how to free their perceptions and their creations from the force of convention without totally casting aside all
the skills and techniques artists had been developing for centuries. We find Hugo embarrassedly wrestling with the persistent
problem of whether or not the developing artist should rely upon
models, concluding only that true genius would transcend imitation. Wordsworth makes clear the difficulty of effectively imitating
folk speech, a lesson learned also by the forgers of invented folk
literature. Such questions formed but one aspect of the highly self-
conscious reassessment of themselves Romantic artists engaged in.

Artists and critics of several nations shared in the era's social
transformation and the breakdown of the old order. Their writing
expresses a new and profound concern for the role and function of
the artist in those processes, though their statements show little
unanimity. They are concerned about what he is able to do, and

what he should do. Old doctrines, such as those that presented art as representational and the artist as copier, did not disappear— Hugo's idea of the artist as mirror recalls them. The changing subject matter of art, however, gave respectability to the artist's feelings, which many believed it was his special function to resurrect or recreate. And insofar as the artist was taken to have uniquely sensitive feelings, he had a distinctive and special mirror quality. Something of this is to be seen in Wordsworth's idea of the artist's more profound expression of more profound (but not different) feelings than those experienced by common men. The artist was taken to be a seer, able to perceive and to present a deeper, truer reality, able to commune more fully with the nature the Romanticists venerated. The artist expressed his genius by feeling more deeply and creating more truly. His imagination, the power permitting him to do this, set him apart from other men, made him an outsider, but it also made him potentially a creator and shaper of reality, matching in art what Bonaparte's imaginative genius had accomplished in politics and war. To create art became increasingly to originate beauty and a new, truer understanding of the world, to introduce novelty, not merely to represent existing beauties.

These theories added luster to the position of the artist, making him a special sort of man. Such specialty could be comforting or distressing, could serve to rationalize the distance felt by artists from the increasingly bourgeois society they lived in, where they were increasingly unaided by aristocratic patronage yet desired the distinctions of an aristocratic world. It could account for failure to communicate with dissimilar men or justify a wide variety of experiments for fuller and more perfect expression of the perceptions of genius (such as Wordsworth's search for a new poetic language, Delacroix's extension of the range of the painter's palette, or Berlioz's increasing the size of the orchestra); above all, it posed in novel terms the problem of the relation of the artist to his fellow men.

The artist, clearly, is motivated to produce his art, but on what terms? With what end in view? The temptation was to feel that the mere creation of beauty—whether judged so by others, whether appreciated or not—was not sufficient in itself. It was still felt to need philosophic if not social buttressing. Keats's conviction that Beauty and Truth must be one is of such sort. Most artists, as

Wordsworth and Shelley reveal, were wrestling with the problem of their social function. The terms of debate over the role of the artist were being set out in an age when only the independently wealthy artist could be confident that he could define his role without threatening his livelihood. Artists in general were dependent; often they were just on the fringes of powerful social groups, such as the new urban social leadership. The audiences they sought for their work were new masters, masters toward whom they themselves often felt superior, whom they criticized as philistines without culture or taste. Some found it necessary to appeal to the existing standards of the growing audience for art; some were quite untroubled in doing so. Others felt a truly moral impulse to elevate this audience to a higher civilization or to such fuller experience of reality as could be achieved only through art.

That the artist might serve as a potential savior was one of Romanticism's answers to an age when faith was disrupted, as it was at the end of the eighteenth century. The cult of the artist as genius-creator anticipated a religion of art, which flowered only at the end of the nineteenth century when cynicism and disillusionment over the possibility of finding meaning outside oneself had grown immensely. In the Romantic era it was affirmed that the uniquely sensitive genius—or the uncultured primitive— might apprehend the truly essential reality. Romantic art itself served to express, and to propose ways of filling, the spiritual needs of the era. Medievalism offered examples of true religiosity and the close presence of the supernatural. Similarly, the new interest in Nordic and Celtic mythology and folklore, the reinterpretation of Hellenic paganism, the vaguely pantheistic spiritualizing of nature—all these asserted the contemporary desire to deny mere mechanism.

Religion

Efforts to revitalize both Protestantism and Catholicism had preceded the outbreak of the French Revolution. Rousseauists had sought a middle way between the intellectualized Deism of some of the *philosophes* (rejecting the atheism and materialism of such as d'Holbach and Helvétius) and the rustic Catholicism of much of Europe's peasantry. They produced (with Rousseau's Savoyard Vicar as spokesman) a Romantic religion of the heart, aclerical rather than anti-clerical, incipiently Protestant, and perhaps more important, incipiently ecumenical. For in rejecting theology, they rejected what seemed to them the points of issue over which fanatics had contended for centuries.

But they did not reject feeling. In fact, enthusiasm came into good odor again after a century of decorum. The Wesleyans in England and the Pietists in Germany represented this revival of emotional involvement, the new approval of intense, unintellectualized religious experience. The feeling, the emotional conviction of the converted soul overrode any theology—again with primarily Protestant implications that threatened both traditional Anglicanism and established Lutheranism. The potentially ecumenical implications of these movements, of religion reinterpreted as a private emotional experience, were exemplified in the spread of similar ideas outside the originating sects.

Feeling as a way of knowing—of apprehending reality—was taken to be the mode of understanding employed by children, primitives, peasants, the people, the *Volk:* the unlettered, the uncultivated, the uncivilized. They were seen as closer to reality, able to apprehend it more fully and truly because their apprehension was undistorted by analytic understanding and the forms of reason. The characteristic form of understanding among the peasantry was of course religious—and a religion quite unsullied by theology. Those supposedly happy irrational peasants seemed, to jaded urban intellectuals, to suffer not at all from doubts about the meaning and value of life. Intellectuals, regretting (probably not wholeheartedly) their culture, envied and aped children and primitives (doubtless enjoying all the while the consciousness that they were doing so). Others, such as Schleiermacher, sought to express the important truths implicit in these views. A major social-psychological discovery was in fact being formulated about the role of habitual, irrational, and religious elements in society by men troubled about their perception that the world (or their circle) was losing its faith. The variety of forms these perceptions took showed how pressing the problem seemed. For abstract analysis scarcely occurred. Instead, the era was prolific with religious reforms and the invention of surrogate faiths.

The French Revolution was especially productive of religious change. Rationalism and anti-clericalism among the *philosophes* were felt to have led inevitably to the Revolution's attacks upon the Church, as in the acquisition of Church lands and the Civil Constitution of the Clergy. Anti-clericalism was feared as fanatical in its turn. There grew up a wide concern for the possible destruction of all old, established Christian faiths, not simply through rational critique, but through the revolutionary action of militant irreligion. Many of those most threatened by the Revolution expressed their intense concern for the "moral," i.e., political, consequences of a loss of faith among the masses, by which they often meant the loss of priestly discipline and consequent social upheaval. But the conservatives' fears were not all selfish and hypocritical—fear of anarchy and blood baths is seldom so. There was real and widespread concern over the danger to the spiritual well-being of the mass of mankind in this life and in the life to come. Opponents of the Revolution found, as among the Vendée peasantry, that popular Catholicism was a power that could aid in their cause, enhancing their desire to reinforce the waning authority of the Church. The Romantic Chateaubriand contributed to such a revival by painting Catholicism as a beautiful religion of the heart. In the era after 1815, admittedly, the social and political implications of anti-revolutionary Catholicism were most in evidence, especially in the union on the French right of kings, nobles, and clerics, but these often bespoke, as we shall see, a thoroughly Romantic conception of the social needs of men.

The dangers of violence from mobs without religion were a concern to revolutionaries as well, even those most certain of the natural virtuousness of the people. Revolutionary sects, Robespierre's cult of the Supreme Being, Rousseauist civil religion, the new revolutionary nationalism encouraged forms of religious behavior that echoed sentiments of earlier proponents of a religion of the heart. These were new revolutionary faiths, which could promote heroic action—uncalculating, unselfish, idealistic.

The upheaval seemed so great that the opinion grew apace that a new epoch in the religious history of mankind was under way. Attacks upon the churches aroused a new conservative ultramontanism, as with de Maistre; the conviction that the Church's defeats demonstrated its day had passed called others to view this historical moment as another turning point in the history of Christendom, an analogue to the era of Rome's decline, a time wherein, by extrapolation from the past, they might predict and assist into being the next stage of development. Such were the hopes of Novalis, and of Alexander I of Russia in the first proposal of the Holy Alliance, who desired a new ecumenical Christianity to counteract the egoism of the present by bringing faith again into accord with practice (and suffusing practice with faith) as they believed medieval Catholicism had done. Lamennais, breaking with the Church, turned to the future and preached a Christianity of the common man, a universal faith democratized in accord with revolutionary principles, which could provide the needed universal religious transformation.

Even the un-Christian in the Revolutionary era tended to retain belief in some divinity, such as the apotheosized "Humanity" adored by a whole sequence of thinkers from Condorcet to Comte, including the Saint-Simonians and Mazzini; and they tended to retain the forms and language of their religious heritage, especially the Messianic belief that their time—lacking, in its disunity and egoism, the ties of faith—was big with the next great development for mankind, the step beyond Christianity, into new forms of community and association.

The Romantic view of nature was drawn upon to reinforce existing faiths or novel creeds. It appears in Chateaubriand and Schleiermacher. A pantheist strain is clear in Schelling, can be seen in Heine, and appears in Wordsworthian nature worship, which affected a whole generation of English students. But belief in the spiritual qualities of nature, like a private religion of the heart, appears to have influenced many while satisfying the religious needs of few: far more characteristic of the era is the efflorescence of new faiths and the reinvigoration of the old in the face of the widespread belief that the evils to the revolutionary years demanded a faith and a church—whether new or old—for their cure.

There was much fanaticism among the proponents of new faiths; witness the intransigence of much of the new nationalism. But tolerance, too, was implied by the growing relativism, which emphasized the value of private religious experience, which argued with Schleiermacher for the values of a variety of religious expressions, in diverse groups, sects, and churches. And the religious developments of the French revolutionary era and its aftermath helped develop those social-psychological insights that stressed the emotional and affective life of mankind and the centrality of religious experience in comprehending and dealing with social affairs. That is to say, religious thought in this era was highly political. Just so was Romantic political thought deeply concerned with the importance of religion.

Politics

The political aspects of Romanticism were most evident in nationalism and conservatism. There was, of course, a thoroughly un-romantic conservatism best exemplified by Metternich and Gentz: a conservatism motivated to a large extent by fear, which urged the utility of faith and religious discipline, which supported the new anti-revolutionary alliance of monarchs, nobles, and churches for quite pragmatic reasons, i.e., the retention of rights and powers and privileges against the new political threat of other social groups. Monarchy was given a new mystique, but the mystique was often used by utterly practical men who were meeting the need to convince others in the conflict of opinion. Old anti-monarchial doctrines, such as the need for a balance of elements in the state, the need for powers of estates, and local privilege to resist centralization, were also revived. Feudal privilege or the advantages of the guilds could be used in argument against the middle class and laissez faire. They did not require ardent Romantic faith. Yet few who found such ideas useful remained totally unconvinced, and many came ardently to favor them.

All the Romanticists felt the need for the preservation or reassertion of ties among men, of which the religious were taken to be the most important. And while the moral benefit of faith as it affected the individual was important to them, in political affairs it was the associative consequence they most desired. Their politics was a politics of groups, against the egoistic theories they opposed.

Burke's opposition to the mechanistic atheist philosophy of the

Enlightenment is an influential example of such concern for religion. He wrote, "We know, we feel inwardly, that religion is the basis of civil society." Religious ties were to him the most important ties that bound men together. In an era that seemed to him and to others anarchic, faced with theories that glorified an atomistic rationalist individualism, he reasserted the importance of custom and tradition, of that drapery and illusion, of those symbols which produce irrational and habitual deference and idealistic patriotism—what Carlyle later called government by shams. Men behave in civil society, Burke tells us, not so much rationally as emotionally. Hence he distrusted rule by lawyers and tradesmen, who in revolutionary France sought to make a state grounded in abstract speculatists' theories of universal absolute rights instead of historical prescriptive rights, who revealed their lack of recognition of the historic importance of honor and the chivalric virtues and of feeling for national symbols in their treatment of Marie Antoinette, and who displayed an ignorance of government befitting their commercial egoism by disrupting a French state that was a growth of long centuries. They were for Burke sophistical mathematical innovators, and government was for him no problem in arithmetic. Of course he was as ready as any of his contemporaries to see the task of the legislator as that of balancing the clashing interests, usually economic, that make up the state. But at his most exalted moments, his view of the state is sheer mysticism. "Each contract of each particular state is but a clause in the great primeval contract of eternal society, linking the lower with the higher natures, connecting the visible and invisible world, according to a fixed compact sanctioned by the inviolable oath which holds all physical and all moral natures, each in their appointed place."

Though this last statement sounds static, Burke's view of the state and of the nation (and the Romantic view generally) is organic. The state is to be understood genetically as a product of the combined wisdom of earlier generations, whose wisdom should receive veneration as a source of those historic decisions that prescribed the political arrangements of the present. In accord with the new anti-mechanical, essentially biological views of nature then arising, the state was looked on as a living organism, and the political and social whole was taken to possess a reality beyond the mere sum of its parts, to have a life and a significance of its own, a belief sharply opposed to the atomism increasingly current in liberal thought. Though such a view did not make Burkean conservatives unwilling for any change to occur, it did make them chary of any sweeping change—aware of the immense difficulty of changing what centuries had, often unconsciously, built.

Faith in the wisdom of ancestors and distrust of the legislating of constitutions could also take on a fully reactionary tinge as it did with de Maistre, appearing there also as part of the medieval revival, which is connected, it seems, with every aspect of Romanticism. But devotion to the age of faith did not have to be reactionary, not always a call for a revived papal and aristocratic rule. It could likewise inspire reformers' efforts to establish a new universal faith to give a unity like that of medieval Europe to a war-torn world. Even the aristocratic *localism* possessed elements that buttressed a reformist critique of the present, seeking to preserve or revive guild customs, local estates, to provincial differences; to re-establish ties of brotherhood among men in an increasingly cold and unfeeling world; to substitute for the cash nexus, which appeared the sole link among men in an egoistic, individualist laissez-faire world, some meaningful personal connections.

The idealization of the medieval manor had a similar twofold effect. Medieval peasants were supposed to have been happy, natural, uncitified, and uncultured, literally in contact with the earth (a supposedly most beneficial tie), protected by the religious devotion of religious houses, or the noblesse oblige of the seigneurs whose whole lives brought them into naturally hierarchial relations with their peasants, relations filled with warm personal loyalty, mutual dependence, and so on. The origins of the ideology of the old American South grew here. Yet recalling such aspects of the medieval past could also serve as a call to reform, as in the writings of Carlyle, Disraeli, in Tory democracy and Shaftesbury's efforts at factory reform, where social reform was conceived on the model of the Christian relationships of an idealized past as an alternative to the disastrous effect of the new urbanism and technology. Even the rural communitarian experiments of utopian socialists, and later anarchist thought, derived much from medievalist primitivism. From the view of the peasant community grew all those theories and doctrines that glorified the natural ties of rural folk, ties undistorted by written legislation, but reinforced by the customary deference to the wisdom of the elders enshrined in the practice of the group.[3]

We can find critical-reformist implications also in the new interest in times and places not medieval, such as the concern for Turkey and the Arab world. Here was more of mankind's variety —valuable in itself—here was much that was neither Jacobin nor industrial; here contrast offered an implicit critique along with the quite undeniable escapism of which Romanticism is so often accused. Considering how actively engaged in the attempt to deal with their own age the men of the Romantic era were, it seems carping to object to their interest, for instance, in the Mediterranean. It might be suggested that their thought is the source not only of our own historical orientation, but, for the present moment even more important, of our willingness to think anthropologically, to take other cultures on their own terms and to try to understand them. It seems a necessary first step was perhaps to overvalue them, to glorify them instead of ignoring them or ignorantly vilifying them.

The organic conception of the state, the emphasis upon the peasant community, and the appreciation of diverse cultures are linked in Romantic nationalist thought. Of course, just as it was possible to be a conservative without being a Romantic, so there were nationalists, usually of a liberal strain, who showed little Romanticism. Cavour is a striking example. A follower of Cobdenite laissez-faire economics and of English liberal politics, as well as a full-fledged Machiavellian in international affairs, he stands in sharp contrast to Mazzini and Mickiewicz, both of whom saw their nations in Romantic terms and advocated Romantic behavior on their behalf.

The Romantic idea of the nation recalls Burke's mystical view. Peoples, after Herder (1744–1803), were seen as the builders of states and nations. Peoples, like individuals, were considered to possess a natural right to express themselves, to express the genius of the historic community, most purely represented in the peasantry, the *Volk*. According to the German philosopher Hegel, the supreme expression of a people's character was just in its building a state to suit it—to fit its diverse and unique character.

---

[3] Cobbett's desire to revive the English yeomanry as the backbone of the nation and Herzen's glorification of the Russian commune are typical examples.

But the building was not taken to have been a conscious rational construction; the creativity of the folk was rather like the almost automatic creativity of some artists, and its expression could be seen in areas like folk art and common law. And just as the diversity of artistic products or of religions bespoke the plenitude of human creation, just so the variety of political forms bespoke, or should bespeak, the diversity of natural human groups. Here Savigny follows Herder: Herder praising the creativity of the folk; Savigny seeking to protect the product of the folk, its common and customary law, against those who desired a rationalization and codification of German law in the fashion of the Napoleonic codes. Codification, a Benthamite rage, was an instance of the lack of veneration for the past that seemed to Romanticists to mark all their opponents. Such a view as Savigny's was conservative; but these ideas had radical implications for nations without their own states. For these, revolutionary change seemed needed, for only their own state, the outgrowth of their own unique qualities, would allow the full expression of those qualities. So, too, for nations whose constitutions were unsuitable to their national genius. State arrangements or legal relationships might now be judged by a new standard, which combined the relativist implication that there were no universally appropriate political arrangements with the threatening possibility that a new, but hazy absolute—the right of the nation (which was subject to a wide variety of definitions)—would contribute to fanaticism and violence. This was quickly evidenced since the nation also was linked to the new Messianic thought of the era—as in Mickiewicz's view of Poland as the suffering savior of the nations and in the idea of a German national mission in the East.

There had been a Napoleonic version of Messianism as well. Bonaparte had served as a symbol to tie together the primitivism and the élitism of Romantic political thought in French nationalist ideology. The image of the Emperor as savior of the Revolution—forgetting his dynastic marriage and his new aristocracy—the Emperor as heroic leader and spokesman for the French peasant and sans-culottes (together making up the people) connected the Romantic idea of genius to the Romantic idea of the people, and permitted the development of a political ideology of democratic caesarism that was influential into the twentieth century.

Bonapartism is one example of the way in which Romantic politics combined a new élitism, either a new heroic caesarism or a medievalist glorification of aristocracy, with a primitivist democratic strain that glorified the natural virtues of peasants or *sansculottes*, both unsullied by aristocratic culture and learning. The version of medieval or traditional peasantry tended to be pacific. The tradition of the urban lower orders, which the Revolution enhanced, was quite otherwise. It added another view of the politics of the untutored, one of which Robespierre had been a spokesman; i.e., the tradition of direct action, unfettered by rational considerations or the traditional politics of compromise, the action of the primitive mass democracy following its heart—often enough to hang someone from a lamppost. From the Terror through the revolutions of 1848, there was excessive glorification of the virtuous violence of the unlettered. Europe's intellectuals became increasingly frightened of these masses after the June Days and the Paris Commune, and they found few advocates again, until the late nineteenth century. Yet from the time of Robespierre till mid-century, a doctrine justifying vigilante justice on the ground of the natural virtue of the masses was widespread.

Such a doctrine was quite obviously attractive to those who despairingly sought sudden massive change, as did many in the era after 1815. It was increasingly possible to be liberal—more likely radical—and still be Romantic, as were the believers in an uncorrupted Romantic democracy, such as Mazzini or even some proponents of socialism, in the period up to 1848. The Revolution of 1789 had proved the possibility (for all the quarrel about the desirability) of sweeping change. Romantic revolutionaries who sought to break with the past and to create a new order, associationist, ecumenical, socialist, liberal nationalist, or Bonapartist, were dominated quite as fully as conservatives by the past—by the thoroughgoing historicizing of European political thought, so evident in the new relativism and in the deep concern for the customary, the symbolic, and the traditional. For by 1848 the Revolution and the Empire had become historical and mythical in their turn, and exercised controlling influence on the left as much as did medievalism on the right.

The expanded historical consciousness, to which the frightful puzzle of the Revolution contributed as much as the medieval revival did, also helped to break up a certain parochialism that is revealed in the smug satisfaction of Condorcet or Comte about

European progress. Much seeming cosmopolitanism was cosmopolitan only for western Europe. The extension of Europeans'
ability to comprehend others—men of other times and places at
least in part for what they were "for their own sakes"—also extended their ability to deal with their own domestic social and
political problems, slums and revolutions, by increasing the
breadth of their understanding of the variety of ways in which
men can meet the problems of life.

History

The Gothic revival in art and architecture, the German Romanticists' historical view of their own work, and their dating of
the beginnings of the modern era—as against the classic—from
the end of the Roman Empire, were artistic influences conducive
to the historicizing of Europeans' thought. The new ways of looking at man in society were popularized by the greatest teacher of
history of them all, the novelist Sir Walter Scott. Through him
and his imitators, a great public came to think historically, to
value the past, its own and that of others, and to sentimentalize
and dramatize it as well; to feel ready to employ it in present
disputes and to convey present disputes back into the interpretation of the past. Scott was also a great spokesman for, and ex-
emplar of, the literary art of history, the effort to convey the
reader into the past by portraying its unique and characteristic
traits.

The Revolution itself contributed to the developing historical
sense by requiring that men explain its seemingly monstrous irrationality (or unintelligibility). Here was a massive event apparently seeking to abolish history, the past, the feudal heritage.
Conservatives turned to history to preserve its products; critics of
the *philosophes* found in the Terror the natural outgrowth of
tampering with that which had been produced by the wisdom of
the ages. Above all, simply to comprehend the violence, the "extremes" of the Revolution required new thought. Very few of the
best minds in Europe could be satisfied with conspiracy theories

such as the Abbé Barruel propounded. Similarly, theological ex-
planations (e.g., a punishment by God for human sinfulness)
failed to satisfy a generation that had listened to skeptical *philosophes*, much as it might admire and desire a religious revival.
Historical forms of explanation came to the fore, genetic thinking
and investigation of origins were used instead of universal principles to make events seem intelligible. The French, above all,
turned to history to make sense out of what had happened. Certainly, they had polemic purpose and sought to ground and
justify their own political positions, but out of their controversies,
as Michelet's work exemplifies, "the Revolution" came increasingly to be seen as an outgrowth of tendencies originating in the
distant past—be it with the sins of the French kings, the morality
of the bourgeois leaders of the medieval communes, or the suffering of French peasants. The Revolution was thereby increasingly
justified in Romantic terms by the longevity of the heritage it
expressed. It became an ever more purely French phenomenon
and hence an adjunct to developing French nationalism, irritable
in defeat.

The Revolution and Napoleon were almost equally disruptive
outside France and, especially in Germany, the events of the
period after 1790 did much to arouse historical thought, a good
deal of it of a defensive character. Although the origins of
popular nationalism as an anti-French phenomenon may have
been exaggerated, it is impossible to deny that nationalist theory,
historically biased from the outset, arose among men afraid that
their homelands were about to be buried under the revolutionary wave, either of victorious *sans-culotte* hordes or Napoleonic
armies, and that all things dear to them—their historic traditions
—were to be swept away in a rationalization of their institutions.
Often motivated by jealousy as well as fear of France, German
thinkers stressed the marks of national difference and gloried in
them. Herder in the eighteenth century had portrayed the evolution of the cultures of nations and peoples as the essential fact of
history. He turned attention as no one else did to the develop-
mental character of historical change and to the organic manner
in which such change occurred, finding in a world of organisms
the nation to be chief. International affairs came to be seen by the

early nineteenth century as a competition of living organisms, national states, national cultures, each defined by its unique language (the tracing of the histories of languages by the science of philology provided a major spur to nationalist thought), by its arts—especially folk art—and by its special institutions, which were felt to have arisen from the unique character of the people itself and from its historically determined life. No one could build institutions which could survive; institutions, like languages or nations must *grow*. Just as the essential character of the universe was seen as historical, so, too, was the essential character of a people. Nations took on personalities, acquired vocations, tasks, or missions analogous to the one God gave the Israelites, duties to perform (usually at someone else's expense). Nations were also seen as expressions of the infinite potentiality of human kind. Each had a spirit, or genius, in terms of which it created. Each state, each nation (not always the same), or each era was viewed as of importance in itself or as making some important contribution to the development of a people. Besides becoming a part of contemporary politics, the past was becoming historically and philosophically interesting.

History as the life of nations found its philosopher in Hegel, who most fully expressed much contemporary thought of a far less philosophic order. Whereas others, in the metaphors of common parlance, could glibly discuss the spirit of a people or the spirit of an age, Hegel converted all this generally meaningless verbiage into a system that comprehended all human history and the meaning of the cosmos. Hegel contended that development of human reason in nature and society occurred through the growth of nation-states that performed providential missions in history. Human history was thus incorporated into cosmic development and nationalist historical thought legitimated by philosophy.

The craft of historical writing itself was not a source of much innovative thought; it tended to follow the ideas of the artists, philosophers, and social theorists, to draw general conceptions from them where needed, to share in rather than promote the historicizing of European thought, except in one vital regard— the historical study of much that had hitherto been slighted. To be sure, most history remained political history. The full complexity of culture, which Voltaire had sought to apprehend, only slowly became a conscious object of many historians, perhaps not fully exemplified until the cultural history of Burckhardt after mid-century. But beginnings were made, especially in institutional history; new attention was being paid to the history of law. Historians explained existing traits and institutions by tracing them to origins and describing their development. Herder's writings supported and promoted both speculation and research into folk culture, and opened up much greater interest in the early history of European peoples and in the Middle Ages—the era in which the nations were born. The theories of Vico (1668-1744), revived by Michelet and others in this period, lent greater prestige to historical knowledge as against scientific knowledge and especially promoted the belief that in the folk poetry of past ages might be found a people's essential character—that myths and legends if properly interpreted constituted valid evidence of the being of past peoples. Here were arguments for the sympathetic study of what had been held to be irrational ages, ages of superstition, by scholars concerned for culture as well as those studying institutions.

The growth of such interests was a major novelty among historians of the Romantic era. Although the Enlightenment had produced great history and great historians, of whom the greatest were Gibbon and Voltaire, no one could attribute to them much sympathy for the ages of fanatic faith. The eighteenth century had ideas of progress and development, but its historical thought tended to emphasize the "great ages" at the expense of the "barren" ages between. Now the barren ages came to seem the ages wherein germinated all the subsequent diversity of human development.

There were other striking contrasts between the older and the newer historical writing. Gibbon wrote great literary history, but he never sought to enter into the thoughts and feelings of an era he studied in the way Carlyle or Michelet did, seeking to transport their readers as they themselves felt they had been transported to another time and place. Enlightenment historians and their sociological successors in the nineteenth century tended to look for universal truths (e.g., influence of the geographical environment) to explain social developments. Romantic historians were more likely to turn to the newly conceived national character, or the powerful role of individuals instead.

In the Romantic era historians absorbed beliefs and promoted ideas that emerged after 1850 as *historicism*. Hans Meyerhoff's

description of historicism makes clear its derivation from Romanticism:

> It is the historian's aim to portray the bewildering, unsytematic variety
> of historical forms—peoples, nations, cultures, customs, institutions,
> songs, myths, and thoughts—in their unique, living expressions and in
> the process of continuous growth and transformation. This aim is not
> unlike the artist's; at any rate, it differs from the systematic, con-
> ceptual approach of the philosopher. The abstract concepts employed
> in philosophy are not adequate for rendering the concrete realities of
> history. Such abstract concepts are static and catch the common prop-
> erties of things and people, not their specific differences. . . . Thus the
> special quality of history does not consist in the statement of general
> laws or principles, but in the grasp, so far as possible, of the infinite
> variety of particular historical forms immersed in the passage of time.
> The meaning of history does not lie hidden in some universal struc-
> ture, whether deterministic or teleological, but in the multiplicity of
> individual manifestations at different ages and in different cultures. All
> of them are unique and equally significant strands in the tapestry of
> history; all of them, in Ranke's famous phrase, are immediate to
> God! . . .
>
> The historian, not unlike the artist, must recreate a character, the
> sense of a meeting, the atmosphere on the eve of a battle, the spirit of
> the Renaissance . . . he must draw upon imagination and sympathy in
> order to bring back to life . . . past shadows of people and movements,
> conflicts and victories, landscapes and physical hardships, secret pas-
> sions and social forces, in their specific and unique characteristics. . . .

Old ways of using history persisted, just as did old ways of
writing it. But the traditional use of history as a storehouse of
examples took on a new importance because of the need for
models from which something like appropriate action for the
present might be selected, so novel did much of the present seem.
The revolutionaries of 1789 had ransacked antiquity especially
for models of republican virtue, rhetoric, and even forms of political behavior. Later, of course, Napoleon was seen as a Caesar,
and he modeled himself in some degree upon the Roman. Such
models made novelty more intelligible, living in it less chaotic, for
the models helped control novel actions and shaped responses to
them. The imitative character of subsequent revolutionary behavior has often been pointed out, till in 1848 Tocqueville belittled
French revolutionaries for imitating the revolutionaries of 1789 to
1793; others all over the Continent were similarly imitative, finding their rules for revolutions in Parisian uprisings. The early

despair of Europe's monarchs in 1848, their nearly universal submission, shows how they, too, were dominated by the example of the French Revolution.

We have already noted that history came to play an increasing role in political controversy. Nationalist thought bred nationalist historical writing, eagerly polemical for and against the Revolution and its works, eagerly promoting the patriotic virtues. Some authors relied on cherished moments of past greatness to provide comfort for those who were deprived in the present and to build the spirit that might generate restorative action. Poles could look back on the great medieval kingdom of the Jagiellons (and come to hope for the most outrageously irrational boundaries for the next century and a half); the Serbs recalled the heroic defeat at Kossovo, which became a national holiday. Where a national heritage of greatness did not clearly exist, it might be invented. Competing nationalisms relied upon the study of the past, promoted it, and gloried in it, but the development of national mythologies could and did exacerbate antagonisms in Europe ever after. National histories offered examples just as the Revolution did, and Germans such as Ernst Arndt and Friedrich von Schlegel drew upon the German past to breed a heroic patriotism. National heroes were glorified as models for youth to imitate— and imitate youth did. One hero, of course, whose attraction surpassed national boundaries was Napoleon.[4] A whole cult of Bonapartism, to which historians made a major contribution, kept alive the heroic ideal in the minds of a generation of young Romanticists, offering them a dominant model for their actions and their dreams.

---

[4] Hegel also contributed to the cult of the hero, for he saw heroic figures (as one might do in a Napoleonic age) as summing up, quite unconsciously, the needs of their historical moment and leading their peoples on to the next preordained step of human development, which their greater sensitivity allowed them to discern. Hegel himself did not attribute such crucial causative agency to leading personalities as he is sometimes thought to have done. He was more concerned for the trends and tendencies that expressed the direction of change amid the welter of particulars. To these trends many historians were attending, but some were glad to adopt the great man theory—most notoriously expressed in Carlyle's theory of history—which was so convenient a form of explanation and so congenial to a Messianic age.

Personal Ideals

Many of the ideas discussed in the foregoing sections implied values that could control behavior. Of coures, there was much merely fashionable parroting of ideas. But Romantic ideas did help generate and shape action: revolutionaries in 1848 have ever since been criticized for having fallen prey to impractical Romantic ideals.

Romantic ideals, the controlling values for personal behavior as distinct from political theory, were passionately individualistic from the days of Rousseau forward, intensely concerned with the lack of match between society and its conventions, in fact much of the history of civilization, and mankind's emotional needs. Romanticists urged that man needed to express creatively his individual potentiality. In a natural world so flourishingly diverse, human potentiality was felt surely to be possessed of an immense, infinite variety of possible expressions. The expression of self was seen as most perfectly fulfilled in the creative mastering of a hostile environment. In a Calvinistic tone Carlyle pictures the swimmer breasting the antagonistic flood; Danton, in Büchner's play *Danton's Death*, is pictured riding the world as if it were a horse held only by its mane; Baudelaire's praises of the triumphant artist, Delacroix—all these fit the Romantic hero image. One leading model for heroic behavior was Napoleon, for obvious reasons. Napoleon was believed to have mastered the old European order and the chaos generated by the Revolution. As late as mid-century we find Mickiewicz turning to Napoleon III hoping for a revival of Napoleonic ideals. From the start, among some of Europe's best and most widely respected minds, Napoleon stood first as the hero of his age. Stendhal was a Bonapartist, even though he later satirized Julien Sorel's Napoleon worship. Byron, Heine, and many others found Napoleon's fall the most moving historical event of their era.

Napoleon was a Hegelian world-historical figure. For many he fitted the widely felt need for a new Messiah. He served as a symbol of the Promethean shaper of destiny—his energy appealing to the impatient—and his military success exemplifying the transfer of the tradition of aristocratic courage to less noble hands. He was seen (despite all the conventionality of his later court) as the opponent of the common standards, common sense, and bourgeois philistinism, and as vastly superior to bourgeois factions and interests generally. He served the Romanticists' desire to shock; he was a man of common origin who had been able to overcome his social limitations without, according to the legend, losing his ties to the common folk. The Napoleonic legend could in this regard be fitted with primitivism of the sentimental sort. And Napoleon the rebel closely matched the already popular noble bandit, the Byronic Corsair, as well as the Faust figure, the insatiable hero who attains an aim yet is fated to fall, or who fails gloriously. Goethe profoundly admired Napoleon and thought he saw in him that demonic element that added for so many a touch of the supernatural or superhuman to the Napoleonic figure. Goethe's Faust and Byron's Faustian Manfred adopt a demonic stance, a rejection of traditional limits, of the very limits of the human condition itself, especially the limits of human knowledge. With the chronological conjunction of such figures with the Napoleonic legend, intellectuals had models that showed similar desires both for a nearly sacrilegious overthrow of an old society and for a nearly sacrilegious effort to extend knowledge.

Such ideas appealed most strongly to youth after 1815, who saw this world as one wherein their seniors had deprived them of the chance for glory and for heroism, of any transcending activity in fact, and had forced them into the mold of philistine egoism.

After Napoleon, the possibilities of heroism seemed dimmed— as de Musset so clearly said. And the efforts men made to impose themselves upon an inimical society—in art, in Carbonarist plots, in the rejection of traditional social codes or of traditional morality—such efforts seemed puny when compared with those of a Napoleon. Only Lord Byron, the genius whose flouting of conventions placed him at war with society, the wanderer who felt out of place wherever he might go (as he showed in his self-analysis in *Childe Harold*), the poet who died the hero's death—only Byron could achieve a stature sufficient to become an alternative personification of the ideals of post-Napoleonic Romantic youth.

The early deaths of so many leading Romanticists, Byron among them, may help to account for the premium Romanticism

placed upon youth, despite its veneration for the past and approval of the wisdom of the elders. Romantic youth, like Schleiermacher, gloried in youth. It set the conflict of generations in the
forefront of its attention, a conflict that seemed to develop from
the varying experiences of groups whose lives were demarcated by
revolutionary events. And the youth—especially those university
students in Vienna—who took part in the revolutions of 1848
showed the power of the creed of the creative potential of the
young, disdain for the old, the hope that youth could shape the
world. Their acts serve as a measure of how great their frustration
had been. The young had only a moment to achieve hopes that
transcended the possible and practicable; consequently, they
failed.

Through the period to 1848 there developed an increasingly
sharp opposition as the young began to adopt a demonic stance.
The young Romanticists after 1815 were often revolutionaries,
even if only in art, such as the young Frenchmen who fought for
the showing of Hugo's *Hernani* despite the disapproval of the tra-
ditionalist critics or the power of the Academy. There was much
soaring ambition, much insatiable desire for experience, for self-
expression, for the heroic stance (often supported with glowing
rhetoric), for Promethean persistence against adversity or tor-
ment, and simply for notoriety. There was desire to break the
chains of tradition, to achieve new forms of freedom and the
possibility of creating anew. The revolutionaries' idea of cleans-
ing the earth for a new creation is as Romantic as Scott's glorification of medieval politics.

Such ideals are the product of frustration. They also promote
it. The very thirst for genius and its cult led to a wide variety of
efforts made by men seeking to satisfy themselves that they had
genius. Since genius must be original, could not be imitative,
great efforts went toward novelty—in style, dress, or shocking
behavior. Many Romanticists believed the philistines were sure to
be shocked by genius, to reject it and make it fight its way to success (presumably among these same philistines); what shocked
them could be taken to be the product of genius. There was a
real—not imagined—difficulty here, involving the need for intellectual and artistic youth to find new means of support, to make
their way as careers opened much too slowly to talent. Much of
the distress and the sometimes maudlin self-pity of the Romantic

youth expressed this clash of ideals against the reality of an increasingly predominant bourgeois culture, their lingering self-
doubts and fears of failure, which contrasted so sharply with their
hopes and ambitions. Georges Sorel, one of the last proponents of
much that the Romantic generations valued, has scathingly said
of the pessimism of the early nineteenth century:

> At the beginning of the nineteenth century, there was such a con-
> cert of groaning that pessimism became odious. Poets, who were not,
> as a matter of fact, much to be pitied, professed to be victims of fate,
> of human wickedness, and still more of the stupidity of a world which
> had not been able to distract them; they eagerly assumed the attitudes
> of a Prometheus called upon to dethrone jealous gods, and with a pride
> equal to that of the fierce Nimrod of Victor Hugo (whose arrows,
> hurled at the sky, fell back stained with blood), they imagined that
> their verses inflicted deadly wounds on the established powers who
> dared to refuse to bow down before them. The prophets of the Jews
> never dreamed of so much destruction to avenge their Jehovah as these
> literary people dreamed of to satisfy their vanity.

Sorel is quite unkind, and the problems that generated the pessimism were very great and very novel, of a major social order.
The ways and means for coping with them had not been invented
—probably have not been invented yet. The ambitions of youth
were stirred by the careers the Revolution had made famous, by
young men becoming generals in their twenties. When the Revolution ceased to offer promise; its absence left a void. And the
enthusiasm and zest of youthful creativity was often stifled or
destroyed. Hence, many voiced their distress. It is perhaps more
remarkable that so many others voiced their hope, their intention
to change the world, and that so many actually did something
about it.

They were assisted in facing their problems by the fact that
they faced them together—as a self-conscious generation, for instance. Their individualism did not reject the possibility of marking strongly the qualities that set their group apart.

So we find coterie behavior—the linking together of the individualist lives in, for example, Paris's Latin Quarter, or the German
artists into a Romantic School. There was much here that resembled the pose of the Humanists as they set themselves to revitalize their society together. So the Romanticists tended to draw
together, in London or the Lake District, in Paris or Berlin, and
found support in their common rebellions and approval of their

efforts to create careers. There was mutual admiration—some but little merited—and much simply imitative behavior and faddishness, as will develop in any coterie. But, other than among the artists, diversity remained too great for us legitimately to speak of a single Romantic movement, and even in the arts there were great national differences.

Nor was the Romanticists' individualism sharply at odds with the desire to revive association against the heartless egoism of their society, the desire to provide their age with a needed spiritual regeneration. They wanted the chance for selfless and self-transcending action in pursuit of an ideal; the ideals they pursued were often, as we have seen, aimed to benefit the mass of mankind, or the oppressed "People," or their own national group. Given the political and historical ideas available to them, they were likely to see themselves, as Lamartine did, upon a stage or in world history, contributing to developments far greater than themselves. They were only beginning to build an ideology for masses of men just attaining literacy and often still far from it. Their chief knowledge of groups was very narrow, being limited to the historical recreation of past social contexts—such as the medieval communes—to descriptions of mobs and mass behavior during the Revolution, biased either by sentiment or fear, or to their own direct knowledge of their own limited social circles. But such considerations do not detract from the admirableness of the urge to heroic action, intended to produce social benefit and especially to establish ties between men of different social groups (as in the nationalist revivals where urban intellectuals believed themselves becoming at one with a tradition-bound peasantry). We cannot deny the possibility of self-deception or hypocrisy, nor the persistent élitism that appears in the works of the most self-conscious democrats, who ever see themselves as *leading* their brothers. Yet the efforts of Romanticists to transcend themselves and to find or give meaning to their lives in nationalistic, or in democratic, socialist, or even frankly reactionary, causes became a constant and vitally creative feature of the society of the post-Revolutionary era.

A few words should be added on the choice of documents in this volume. Those included will make clear how arbitrary are the categories employed in dividing this Introduction, as well as the readings themselves. The piece from de Maistre's book could equally well have appeared in the section on Religion as in the one on Politics, and Byron's comment upon Napoleon or Novalis' essay might appear in the Politics section. Lamartine's *History* could have fallen under Personal Ideals, and so on. It is my hope that the documents will be read with a consciousness that they contain far more than one idea, represent more than one aspect of the protean character of Romanticism, as well as with an eye to all they contain besides Romanticism.

A major limitation in the following selection is obvious. This is a book of documents, written statements. The "documents"—the evidences of Romanticism—should ideally include works of painting, sculpture, music, and probably theoretical statements of aesthetic theory from these fields. That those who pursued the nonverbal arts shared the views and often the style of life of artists who wrote is undeniable. Delacroix's *Journals*, the *Autobiography of Benjamin Robert Haydon*, Jacques Barzun's study of *Berlioz and the Romantic Century*, Beethoven's *Journals*—all support the contention that Romanticism was not limited to purveyors of words. How could it be when its advocates often doubted the adequacy of words to convey, comprehend, or interpret the reality of their experience? But musical scores and paintings are not best appreciated on the pages of a book; and it can be contended that, skilled as so many of these Romanticists were in the nonverbal arts, they were not necessarily equally skilled in expressing what they were doing in words. So I have relied most heavily upon experts with words. Yet a further omission is obvious, for even from the literary men I have selected little of their artistic work, partly, of course, because it is so readily available and should be read in full. What I have included from art works themselves appears in the final section, where pieces from Goethe's *Werther* and Byron's poems are offered as representative not so much of art forms as of ideals of life styles. Besides such models of behavior for imitation, this volume attempts to present Romanticists' abstract, theoretical conceptions of the nature of the reality and of man's place and role in it. My major selections from artists are statements of aesthetic theory—of the nature of the reality the artist confronts and of his capacity to represent it, or to create a further and more perfect reality. Implicit here, obviously, is philosophy, in something less than its most sophisticated form. And in that rather simple form I suggest the philosophy of Romanticism was understood and acted upon by most of those who adopted it or lived it. Hence a further mission. There may have been formal philosophers who were Romantic. It is possible to identify philosophies that seem closely congruent with the attitudes and ideas of Romanticism—much of Hegel, much of Schelling, much of Schopenhauer. Yet the fact remains that such men and their ideas operated in a relatively narrow world of formal academic discipline and that their ideas in the original form were, and are, comparatively inaccessible. It is in their common-currency form, as transported by interpreters or as general notions (e.g., Hegel's evolutionary views or his idea of the hero, Fichte's intense egoism, Schelling's pantheism), that they formed part of Romantic attitudes. One other limitation must be noted. The writers here include one Pole (Mickiewicz), one Italian (Mazzini); the rest are English, French, and German. Further figures from the smaller states would more truthfully and fully have revealed the extent to which the ideas and attitudes of Romanticism spread across Europe. But one can't include everything. So I have chosen pieces that seemed to me most fully and satisfactorily to represent both the range and interconnections among the ideas and attitudes I call Romanticism and some of the most influential pieces that shaped these general views.

Part I: *Aesthetics*

1. August Wilhelm von Schlegel:
Lectures on Dramatic Literature

August Wilhelm von Schlegel (1767-1845) was the elder of the brothers who led the German Romantic school. He was educated at Göt-
tingen, became a professor at the University of Jena in 1798; after 1818
he taught at Bonn. Along with his brother, Friedrich von Schlegel
(1772-1829), who was probably the more original of the two, A. W.
Schlegel founded (in 1798) the *Athenaeum*, the journal in which appeared many of the early works of the Romantic school and in which
August Wilhelm and Friedrich sketched out the aesthetic theory of
the new Romanticism while promoting the works of Novalis, Schleiermacher, Brentano, and Tieck. August Wilhelm's translations of Shakespeare were immensely influential in developing the tastes to which the
new school appealed and served to exemplify portions of the new
doctrines. A. W. von Schlegel's scholarly work included translation of
Calderón and the introduction of the study of Sanskrit into Germany.
Largely through his association with Mme. de Staël, the ideas of the
school were brought to the attention of Europe to the West.

The following selection from his lectures in literary history exemplifies the sorts of distinctions among literary genres that the
Schlegels came to propound. The place of Christianity is sharply de-
lineated, and it is also notable that both the historical and nationalistic
orientations of the new Romanticism are revealed very clearly.

The selection is from John Black's translation of *A Course of Lectures on Dramatic Art and Letters* (Philadelphia, 1833), pp. 1-10, 12-
13, 16-17.

Lecture 1

THE OBJECT which we propose to ourselves in these Lectures is to
investigate the principles of dramatic literature, and to consider
whatever is connected with the fable, composition, and representation, of theatrical productions. We have selected the drama in

preference to every other department of poetry. It will not be expected of us that we should enter scientifically into the first principles of theory. Poetry is in general closely connected with the other fine arts; and, in some degree, the eldest sister and guide of the rest. The necessity for the fine arts, and the pleasure derivable from them, originate in a principle of our nature, which it is the business of the philosopher to investigate and to classify. This object has given rise to many profound disquisitions, especially in Germany; and the name of *aesthetic* (perceptive) has, with no great degree of propriety, been conferred on this department of philosophy. Aesthetics, or the philosophical theory of beauty and art, is of the utmost importance in its connexion with other inquiries into the human mind; but, considered by itself, it is not of sufficient practical instruction; and it can only become so by its union with the history of the arts. We give the appellation of criticism to the intermediate province between general theory and experience or history. The comparing together and judging the existing productions of the human mind must supply us with a knowledge of the means which are requisite for the conception and execution of masterly works of art.

We will therefore endeavour to throw light on the history of the dramatic art by the torch of criticism. In the course of this attempt it will be necessary to adopt many a proposition, without proof, from general theory; but I hope that the manner in which this shall be done will not be considered as objectionable.

Before I proceed farther, I wish to say a few words respecting the spirit of my criticism, a study to which I have devoted a great part of my life. We see numbers of men, and even whole nations, so much fettered by the habits of their education and modes of living, that they cannot shake themselves free from them, even in the enjoyment of the fine arts. Nothing to them appears natural, proper, or beautiful, which is foreign to their language, their manners, or their social relations. In this exclusive mode of seeing and feeling, it is no doubt possible, by means of cultivation, to attain a great nicety of discrimination in the narrow circle within which they are limited and circumscribed. But no man can be a true critic or connoisseur who does not possess a universality of mind, who does not possess the flexibility, which, throwing aside all personal predilections and blind habits, enables him to transport himself into the peculiarities of other ages and nations, to feel them as it were from their proper central point; and, what ennobles human nature, to recognize and respect whatever is beautiful and grand under those external modifications which are necessary to their existence, and which sometimes even seem to disguise them. There is no monopoly of poetry for certain ages and nations; and consequently that despotism in taste, by which it is attempted to make those rules universal which were at first perhaps arbitrarily established, is a pretension which ought never to be allowed. Poetry, taken in its widest acceptation, as the power of creating what is beautiful, and representing it to the eye or the ear, is a universal gift of Heaven, which is even shared to a certain extent by those whom we call barbarians and savages. Internal excellence is alone decisive, and where this exists we must not allow ourselves to be repelled by external appearances. Everything must be traced up to the root of our existence: if it has sprung from thence, it must possess an undoubted worth; but if, without possessing a living germ, it is merely an external appendage, it can never thrive nor acquire a proper growth. Many productions which appear at first sight dazzling phenomena in the province of the fine arts, and which as a whole have been honoured with the appellation of works of a golden age, resemble the mimic gardens of children: impatient to witness the work of their hands they break off here and there branches and flowers, and plant them in the earth; everything at first assumes a noble appearance; the childish gardener struts proudly up and down among his elegant beds, till the rootless plants begin to droop, and hang down their withered leaves and flowers, and nothing soon remains but the bare twigs, while the dark forest, on which no art or care was ever bestowed, and which towered up towards heaven long before human remembrance, bears every blast unshaken, and fills the solitary beholder with religious awe.

Let us now think of applying the idea which we have been developing, of the universality of true criticism, to the history of poetry and the fine arts. We generally limit it (although there may be much which deserves to be known beyond this circle) as we limit what we call universal history to whatever has had a nearer or more remote influence on the present cultivation of Europe: consequently to the works of the Greeks and Romans, and of those of the modern European nations, who first and chiefly distinguished themselves in art and literature. It is well known that, three centuries and a half ago, the study of ancient literature, by the diffusion of the Grecian language (for the Latin was never extinct) received a new life: the classical authors were sought after with avidity, and made accessible by means of the press; and the monuments of ancient art were carefully dug up and preserved. All this excited the human mind in a powerful manner, and formed a decided epoch in the history of our cultivation; the fruits have extended to our times, and will extend to a period beyond the power of our calculation. But the study of the ancients was immediately carried to a most pernicious extent. The learned, who were chiefly in the possession of this knowledge, and who were incapable of distinguishing themselves by their own productions, yielded an unlimited deference to the ancients, and with great appearance of reason, as they are models in their kind. They maintained that nothing could be hoped for the human mind but in the imitation of the ancients; and they only esteemed in the works of the moderns whatever resembled, or seemed to bear a resemblance to, those of antiquity. Everything else was rejected by them as barbarous and unnatural. It was quite otherwise with the great poets and artists. However strong their enthusiasm for the ancients, and however determined their purpose of entering into competition with them, they were compelled by the characteristic peculiarity of their minds, to proceed in a track of their own, and to impress upon their productions the stamp of their own genius. Such was the case with Dante among the Italians, the father of modern poetry; he acknowledged Virgil for his instructer, but produced a work which, of all others, differs the most from the Æneid, and far excels it in our opinion, in strength, truth, depth, and comprehension. It was the same afterwards with Ariosto, who has most unaccountably been compared to Homer; for nothing can be more unlike. It was the same in the fine arts with Michael Angelo and Raphael, who were without doubt well acquainted with the antique. When we ground our judgment of modern painters merely on their resemblance of the ancients, we must necessarily be unjust towards them; and hence Winkelmann has undoubtedly been guilty of injustice to Raphael. As the poets for the most part acquiesced in the doctrines of the learned, we may observe a curious struggle in them between their natural inclination and their imagined duty. When they sacrificed to the latter they were praised by the learned; but by yielding to their own inclinations they became the favourites of the people. What preserves the heroic poems of a Tasso and a Camoëns to this day alive, in the hearts and on the lips of their countrymen, is by no means their imperfect resemblance to Virgil, or even to Homer, but in Tasso the tender feeling of chivalrous love and honour, and in Camoëns the glowing inspiration of patriotic heroism.

Those very ages, nations, and classes, that were least in want of a poetry of their own, were the most assiduous in their imitation of the ancients. Hence the dull scholastic exercises which could at most excite a cold admiration. But, in the fine arts, mere imitation is always fruitless; what we borrow from others must be again as it were born in us, to produce a poetical effect. Of what avail is all foreign imitation? Art cannot exist without nature, and man can give nothing to his fellow men but himself.

The genuine followers of the ancients, those who attempted to rival them, who from a similarity of disposition and cultivation proceeded in their track, and acted in their spirit, were at all times as few as their mechanical spiritless imitators were numerous. The great body of critics, seduced by external appearance, have been always but too indulgent even to these imitators. They held them up as correct modern classics, while those animated poets, who had become the favourites of their respective nations, and to whose sublimity it was impossible to be altogether blind, were at most but tolerated by them as rude and wild natural geniuses. But the unqualified separation of genius and taste which they assume is altogether untenable. Genius is the almost unconscious choice of the highest degree of excellence, and consequently it is taste in its greatest perfection.

In this state, nearly, matters continued till a period not far back, when several inquiring minds, chiefly Germans, endeavoured to clear up the misconception, and to hold the ancients in proper estimation, without being insensible to the merits of the moderns of a totally different description. The apparent contradiction did not intimidate them.—The groundwork of human nature is no doubt everywhere the same; but in all our investigations we may observe that there is no fundamental power throughout the whole range of nature so simple, but that it is capable of dividing and diverging into opposite directions. The whole play of living motion hinges on harmony and contrast. Why then should not this phenomenon be repeated in the history of man? This idea led, perhaps, to the discovery of the true key to the ancient and modern history of poetry and the fine arts. Those who adopted it gave to the peculiar spirit of *modern* art, as opposed to the *antique* or *classical*, the name of *romantic*. The appellation is certainly not unsuitable: the word is derived from *romance*, the name of the language of the people which was formed from the mixture of Latin and Teutonic, in the same manner as modern cultivation is the fruit of the union of the peculiarities of the northern nations with the fragments of antiquity. Hence the cultivation of the ancients was much more of a piece than ours.

The distinction which we have just stated can hardly fail to appear well founded, if it can be shown that the same contrast in the labours of the ancients and moderns runs symmetrically, I might almost say systematically, throughout every branch of art, as far as our knowledge of antiquity extends; that it is as evident in music and the plastic arts as in poetry. This proposition still remains to be demonstrated in its full extent, though we have many excellent observations on different parts of the subject.

Among the foreign authors who wrote before this school can be said to have been formed in Germany, we may mention Rousseau, who acknowledged the contrast in music, and demonstrated that rhythmus and melody constituted the prevailing principle of the ancients, and harmony that of the moderns. In his prejudices against harmony, however, we altogether differ from him. On the subject of the plastic arts an ingenious observation was made by Hemsterhuys, that the ancient painters were probably too much sculptors, and that the modern sculptors are too much painters. This is the exact point of difference; for I shall distinctly show, in the sequel, that the spirit of ancient art and poetry is *plastic*, and that of the moderns *picturesque*.

By an example taken from another art, that of architecture, I shall endeavour to illustrate what I mean by this contrast. In the middle ages there prevailed a style of architecture, which, in the last centuries especially, was carried to the utmost degree of perfection; and which, whether justly or unjustly, has been called Gothic architecture. When, on the general revival of classical antiquity, the imitation of Grecian architecture became prevalent, and but too frequently without a due regard to the difference of climate and manners and the destination of the structure, the zealots of this new taste passed a sweeping sentence of condemnation on the Gothic, which they reprobated as tasteless, gloomy, and barbarous. This was in some degree pardonable in the Italians, among whom a love for ancient architecture, from the remains of classical edifices which they inherited, and the similarity of their climate to that of the Greeks, might in some sort be said to be innate. But with us, inhabitants of the North, the first powerful impression on entering a Gothic cathedral is not so easily eradicated. We feel, on the contrary, a strong desire to investigate and to justify the source of this impression. A very slight attention will convince us, that the Gothic architecture not only displays an extraordinary degree of mechanical dexterity, but also an astonishing power of invention; and, on a closer examination, we become impressed with the strongest conviction of its profound character, and of its constituting a full and perfect system in itself, as well as the Grecian.

To the application!—The Pantheon is not more different from Westminster Abbey or the church of St. Stephen at Vienna, than the structure of a tragedy of Sophocles from a drama of Shakespeare. The comparison between these wonderful productions of poetry and architecture might be carried still farther. But does our admiration of the one compel us to depreciate the other? May we not admit that each is great and admirable in its kind, although the one is, and ought to be, different from the other? The experiment is worth attempting. We will quarrel with no man for his predilection either for the Grecian or the Gothic. The world is wide, and affords room for a great diversity of objects. Narrow and exclusive prepossessions will never constitute a genuine critic or connoisseur, who ought, on the contrary, to possess the power of elevating himself above all partial views, and of subduing all personal inclinations.

For the justification of our object, namely, the grand division which we lay down in the history of art, and according to which we conceive ourselves equally warranted in establishing the same division in dramatic literature, it might be sufficient merely to have stated this contrast between the ancient, or classical, and the romantic. But as there are exclusive admirers of the ancients, who never cease asserting that all deviation from them is merely the whim of recent critics, who express themselves on the subject in a language full of mystery, but cautiously avoid conveying their sentiments in a tanglible shape, I shall endeavor to explain the origin and spirit of the *romantic*, and then leave the world to judge if the use of the word, and of the idea which it is intended to convey, are sufficiently justified.

The formation of the Greeks was a natural education in its utmost perfection. Of a beautiful and noble race, endowed with susceptible senses and a clear understanding, placed beneath a mild heaven, they lived and bloomed in the full health of existence; and, under a singular coincidence of favourable circumstances, performed all of which our circumscribed nature is capable. The whole of their art and their poetry is expressive of the consciousness of this harmony of all their faculties. They have invented the poetry of gladness.

Their religion was the deification of the powers of nature and of the earthly life: but this worship, which, among other nations, clouded the imagination with images of horror, and filled the heart with unrelenting cruelty, assumed, among the Greeks, a mild, a grand, and a dignified form. Superstition, too often the tyrant of the human faculties, seemed to have here contributed to their freest development. It cherished the arts by which it was ornamented, and the idols became models of ideal beauty.

But however far the Greeks may have carried beauty, and even morality, we cannot allow any higher character to their formation than that of a refined and ennobled sensuality. Let it not be understood that I assert this to be true in every instance. The conjectures of a few philosophers, and the irradiations of poetical inspiration, constitute an exception. Man can never altogether turn aside his thoughts from infinity, and some obscure recollections will always remind him of his original home; but we are now speaking of the principal object towards which his endeavours are directed.

Religion is the root of human existence. Were it possible for man to renounce all religion, including that of which he is unconscious, and over which he has no control, he would become a mere surface without any internal substance. When this centre is disturbed, the whole system of the mental faculties must receive another direction.

And this is what has actually taken place in modern Europe through the introduction of Christianity. This sublime and beneficent religion has regenerated the ancient world from its state of exhaustion and debasement; it has become the guiding principle in the history of modern nations, and even at this day, when many suppose they have shaken off its authority, they will find themselves in all human affairs much more under its influence than they themselves are aware.

After Christianity, the character of Europe, since the commencement of the middle ages, has been chiefly influenced by the Germanic race of northern conquerors, who infused new life and vigour into a degenerated people. The stern nature of the north drives man back within himself; and what is withdrawn from the free development of the senses, must, in noble dispositions, be added to their earnestness of mind. Hence the honest cordiality with which Christianity was received by all the Teutonic tribes, in whom it penetrated more deeply, displayed more powerful effects, and became more interwoven with all human feelings, than in the case of any other people.

From a union of the rough but honest heroism of the northern conquerors and the sentiments of Christianity, chivalry had its origin, of which the object was, by holy and respected vows, to guard those who bore arms from every rude and ungenerous abuse of strength, into which it was so easy to deviate.

With the virtues of chivalry was associated a new and purer spirit of love, an inspired homage for genuine female worth, which was now revered as the pinnacle of humanity; and, enjoined by religion itself under the image of a virgin mother, infused into all hearts a sentiment of unalloyed goodness.

As Christianity was not, like the heathen worship, satisfied with certain external acts, but claimed a dominion over the whole inward man and the most hidden movements of the heart; the feeling of moral independence was in like manner preserved alive by the laws of honour, a worldly morality, as it were, which was often a variance with the religious, yet in so far resembled it, that it never calculated consequences, but consecrated unconditionally certain principles of action, as truths elevated beyond all the investigation of casuistical reasoning.

Chivalry, love, and honour, with religion itself, are the objects of the natural poetry which poured itself out in the middle ages with incredible fulness, and preceded the more artificial formation of the romantic character. This age had also its mythology, consisting of chivalrous tales and legends; but their wonders and their heroism were the very reverse of those of the ancient mythology.

Several inquirers, who, in other respects, entertain the same conception of the peculiarities of the moderns, and trace them to the same source that we do, have placed the essence of the northern poetry in melancholy; and to this when properly understood, we have nothing to object.

Among the Greeks human nature was in itself all-sufficient; they were conscious of no wants, and aspired at no higher perfection than that which they could actually attain by the exercise of their own faculties. We, however, are taught by superior wisdom that man, through a high offence, forfeited the place for which he was originally destined; and that the whole object of his earthly existence is to strive to regain that situation, which, if left to his own strength, he could never accomplish. The religion of the senses had only in view the possession of outward and perishable blessings; and immortality, in so far as it was believed, appeared in an obscure distance like a shadow, a faint dream of this bright and vivid futurity. The very reverse of all this is the case with the Christian: everything finite and mortal is lost in the contemplation of infinity; life has become a shadow and darkness, and the first dawning of our real existence opens in the world beyond the grave. Such a religion must waken the foreboding, which slumbers in every feeling heart, to the most thorough consciousness, that the happiness after which we strive we can never here attain; that no external object can ever entirely fill our souls; and that every mortal enjoyment is but a fleeting and momentary deception. When the soul, resting as it were under the willows of exile, breathes out its longing for its distant home, the prevailing character of its songs must be melancholy. Hence the poetry of the ancients was the poetry of enjoyment, and ours is that of desire: the former has its foundation in the scene which is present, while the latter hovers betwixt recollection and hope. Let me not be understood to affirm that everything flows in one strain of wailing and complaint, and that the voice of melancholy must always be loudly heard. As the austerity of tragedy was not incompatible with the joyous views of the Greeks, so the romantic poetry can assume every tone, even that of the most lively gladness; but still it will always, in some shape or other, bear traces of the source from which it originated. The feeling of the moderns is, upon the whole, more intense, their fancy more incorporeal, and their thoughts more contemplative. In nature, it is true, the boundaries of objects run more into one another, and things are not so distinctly separated as we must exhibit them for the sake of producing a distinct impression.

The Grecian idea of humanity consisted in a perfect concord and proportion between all the powers,—a natural harmony. The moderns again have arrived at the consciousness of the internal discord which renders such an idea impossible; and hence the endeavour of their poetry is to reconcile these two worlds between which we find ourselves divided, and to melt them indissolubly into one another. The impressions of the senses are consecrated, as it were, from their mysterious connexion with higher feelings; and the soul, on the other hand, embodies its forebodings, or nameless visions of infinity, in the phenomena of the senses.

In the Grecian art and poetry we find an original and unconscious unity of form and subject; in the modern, so far as it has remained true to its own spirit, we observe a keen struggle to unite the two, as being naturally in opposition to each other. The Grecian executed what it proposed in the utmost perfection; but the modern can only do justice to its endeavours after what is infinite by approximation; and, from a certain appearance of imperfection, is in greater danger of not being duly appreciated. . . .

Before, however, entering upon such a history as we have now described, it will be previously necessary to consider what is meant by *dramatic, theatrical, tragic* and *comic*.

What is dramatic? To many the answer will seem very easy: where various persons are introduced conversing together, and the poet does not speak in his own person. This is, however, merely the first external foundation of the form; it is dialogue. When the characters deliver thoughts and sentiments opposed to each other, but which operate no change, and which leave the minds of both in exactly the same state in which they were at the commencement; the conversation may indeed be deserving of attention, but can be productive of no dramatic interest. I shall make this clear by alluding to a more tranquil species of dialogue,

not adapted for the stage, the philosophic. When, in Plato, Socrates asks the conceited sophist Hippias, what is the meaning of
the beautiful, the latter is at once ready with a superficial answer,
but is afterwards compelled by the disguised attacks of Socrates
to give up his former definition, and to grope about him for other
ideas, till, ashamed at last and irritated at the superiority of the
sage who has convicted him of his ignorance, he is reduced to quit
the field; this dialogue is not merely philosophically instructive,
but arrests the attention like a little drama. And therefore this animation in the progress of the thoughts, the anxiety with which we
look to the result, in a word, the dramatic nature of the dialogues
of Plato has always been very justly celebrated.

From this we may conceive the great charm of dramatic
poetry. Action is the true enjoyment of life, nay, life itself. Mere
passive enjoyments may lull us into a state of obtuse satisfaction,
but even then, when possessed of internal activity, we cannot
avoid being soon wearied. The great bulk of mankind are merely
from their incapacity for uncommon exertions, confined within a
narrow circle of insignificant operations. Their days flow on in
succession according to the drowsy laws of custom, their life is
imperceptible in its progress, and the bursting torrent of the first
passions of youth soon settles into a stagnant marsh. From the
discontent which they feel with their situation they are compelled to have recourse to all sorts of diversions, which uniformly
consist in a species of occupation that may be renounced at pleasure, and though a struggle with difficulties, yet with difficulties
that are easily surmounted. But of all diversions the theatre is
undoubtedly the most entertaining. We see important actions
when we cannot act importantly ourselves. The highest object of
human activity is man, and in the drama we see men, from motives of friendship or hostility, measure their powers with each
other, influence each other as intellectual and moral beings by
their thoughts, sentiments, and passions, and decidedly determine
their reciprocal relations. The art of the poet is to separate from
the fable whatever does not essentially belong to it, whatever, in
the daily necessities of real life, and the petty occupations to
which they give rise, interrupts the progress of important actions,
and to concentrate within a narrow space a number of events
calculated to fill the minds of the hearers with attention and expectation. In this manner it affords us a renovated picture of life;
a compendium of whatever is animated and interesting in human
existence. . . .

If the German genius has not developed itself with the same fulness and ease in the dramatic branch as in other departments of literature, this deficiency arises perhaps from the peculiar character of the nation. The Germans are a speculative people, that is, a people who wish to become acquainted with the principle of whatever they are engaged in by reflection and meditation. On that very account they are not sufficiently practical; for if we wish to act with dexterity, vigour, and determination, we must some time or other believe that we have become masters of our subject, and not to be perpetually returning to demonstrate its theory; we must even have settled ourselves into a certain partiality of idea. In the invention and conduct of a drama the practical spirit must prevail: the dramatic poet is not allowed to dream that he is inspired, he must go the straightest way to his object; and the Germans are but too apt to lose sight of their object in the course of their way to it. Besides, in the drama the national features must be marked in the most prominent manner, and the national character of the Germans is modest and averse to everything like pretension; and the noble endeavour to become acquainted with, and to appropriate to ourselves whatever is excellent in others, is not seldom accompanied with the undervaluing our own worth. Hence our stage has often, in form and subject, been under more than a due degree of foreign influence. Our object is not, however, the mere passive repetition of the Grecian or French, the Spanish or English theatres; but we seek, as it appears to me, a form which contains whatever is truly poetical in all these theatres, with the exception of what is founded in local circumstances; in the subject, however, the German national features ought certainly to predominate.

2. Madame de Staël: *Germany*

Christened Anne Louise Germaine Necker, Mme. de Staël (1766–1817) was the daughter of Louis XVI's finance minister, a man who attained short-lived popularity as a reformer at the outbreak of the French Revolution. She had been brought up in the atmosphere of the Enlightenment salon established by her mother, and became a confirmed intellectual. She married the Swedish ambassador to Paris, though she proceeded to establish a reputation for conquests of Europe's leading intellectual figures including Benjamin Constant, A. W. von Schlegel, and Sismondi.

Before 1789 she was already actively engaged in political life, becoming and remaining a moderate constitutional monarchist. She succeeded in alienating the government of the Republic sufficiently to bring about her exile by 1795 (she had been out of France during the Terror). And though she returned briefly on occasion to France, she remained an exile through most of the period until 1815, for she was a bitter and outspoken opponent and critic of Napoleon, who banished her in 1803. Her *Germany*, a product of her travels in exile, was her attempt to introduce Frenchmen to elements of German thought and society of which she considered most of them ignorant. Her other writings on politics and literature reveal many of the same interests as does *Germany:* the interplay of institutions and intellectual products as forming and expressing national character.

Elements that especially interested her in German life and thought (and she attempted to survey in her book almost all their elements, from religion to philosophy, from art to manners) were those which contrasted with what she considered leading French national traits, such as clarity and rationality. The distinction reveals her indebtedness to her association with the Schlegels in Germany. Her book helped to counteract the brief classical revival that accompanied the Napoleonic era, and, once released from the censorship, helped to acquaint Frenchmen, as it did the English-speaking world, with the novelty of German idealism, of its new religious inclinations, and of its literature. The brief chapter presented here gives her definition of Romanticism and shows her manner of linking it to national character. In many ways Mme. de Staël remained a product of the Enlightenment, a firm believer in progress, but with a Rousseauist bent toward sentiment. She was not, therefore, a wholehearted enthusiast for the new literature.

The selection is taken from *Germany*, with notes and appendices by O. W. Wight, (New York, 1859) Vol. 1, pp. 198–204.

Chapter XI

OF CLASSICAL AND ROMANTIC POETRY

THE WORD *romantic* has been lately introduced in Germany to designate that kind of poetry which is derived from the songs of the Troubadours; that which owes its birth to the union of chivalry and Christianity. If we do not admit that the empire of literature has been divided between paganism and Christianity, the North and the South, antiquity and the middle ages, chivalry and the institutions of Greece and Rome, we shall never succeed in forming a philosophical judgment of ancient and of modern taste. We sometimes consider the word classic as synonymous with

perfection. I use it at present in a different acceptation, considering classic poetry as that of the ancients, and romantic, as that
which is generally connected with the traditions of chivalry. This
division is equally suitable to the two eras of the world,—that
which preceded, and that which followed the establishment of
Christianity.

In various German works, ancient poetry has also been compared to sculpture, and romantic to painting; in short, the progress of the human mind has been characterized in every manner,
passing from material religions to those which are spiritual, from
nature to the Deity.

The French nation, certainly the most cultivated of all that are
derived from Latin origin, inclines towards classic poetry imitated from the Greeks and Romans. The English, the most illustrious of the Germanic nations, is more attached to that which
owes its birth to chivalry and romance; and it prides itself on the
admirable compositions of this sort which it possesses. I will not,
in this place, examine which of these two kinds of poetry deserves
the preference; it is sufficient to show, that the diversities of taste
on this subject do not merely spring from accidental causes, but
are derived also from the primitive sources of imagination and
thought.

There is a kind of simplicity both in the epic poems and tragedies of the ancients; because at that time men were completely
the children of nature, and believed themselves controlled by
fate, as absolutely as nature herself is controlled by necessity.
Man, reflecting but little, always bore the action of his soul without; even conscience was represented by external objects, and the
torch of the Furies shook the horrors of remorse over the head of
the guilty. In ancient times, men attended to events alone, but
among the moderns, character is of greater importance; and that
uneasy reflection, which, like the vulture of Prometheus, often
internally devours us, would have been folly amid circumstances
and relations so clear and decided, as they existed in the civil and
social state of the ancients.

When the art of sculpture began in Greece, single statues alone
were formed; groups were composed at a later period. It might be
said with equal truth, that there were no groups in any art: objects were represented in succession, as in bas-reliefs, without
combination, without complication of any kind. Man personified

nature; nymphs inhabited the waters, hamadryads the forests; but nature, in turn, possessed herself of man; and, it might be said, he resembled the torrent, the thunderbolt, the volcano, so wholly did he act from involuntary impulse, and so insufficient was reflection in any respect, to alter the motives or the consequences of his actions. The ancients, thus to speak, possessed a corporeal soul, and its emotions were all strong, decided, and consistent; it is not the same with the human heart as developed by Christianity: the moderns have derived from Christian repentance a constant habit of self-reflection.

But in order to manifest this kind of internal existence, a great variety of outward facts and circumstances must display, under every form, the innumerable shades and gradations of that which is passing in the soul. If in our days the fine arts were confined to the simplicity of the ancients, we should never attain that primitive strength which distinguishes them, and we should lose those intimate and multiplied emotions of which our souls are susceptible. Simplicity in the arts would, among the moderns, easily degenerate into coldness and abstraction, while that of the ancients was full of life and animation. Honor and love, valor and pity, were the sentiments which distinguished the Christianity of chivalrous ages; and those dispositions of the soul could only be displayed by dangers, exploits, love, misfortunes—that romantic interest, in short, by which pictures are incessantly varied. The sources from which art derives its effect are then very different in classic poetry and in that of romance; in one it is fate which reigns, in the other it is Providence. Fate counts the sentiments of men as nothing; but Providence judges of actions according to those sentiments. Poetry must necessarily create a world of a very different nature, when its object is to paint the work of destiny, which is both blind and deaf, maintaining an endless contest with mankind; and when it attempts to describe that intelligent order, over which the Supreme Being continually presides,—that Being whom our hearts supplicate, and who mercifully answers their petitions!

The poetry of the pagan world was necessarily as simple and well defined as the objects of nature; while that of Christianity requires the various colors of the rainbow to preserve it from being lost in the clouds. The poetry of the ancients is more pure as an art; that of the moderns more readily calls forth our tears.

But our present object is not so much to decide between classic and romantic poetry, properly so called, as between the imitation of the one and the inspiration of the other. The literature of the ancients is, among the moderns, a transplanted literature; that of chivalry and romance is indigenous, and flourishes under the influence of our religion and our institutions. Writers, who are imitators of the ancients, have subjected themselves to the rules of strict taste alone; for, not being able to consult either their own nature or their own recollections, it is necessary for them to conform to those laws by which the *chefs-d'oeuvre* of the ancients may be adapted to our taste; though the circumstances both political and religious, which gave birth to these *chefs-d' oeuvre* are all entirely changed. But the poetry written in imitation of the ancients, however perfect in its kind, is seldom popular, because, in our days, it has no connection whatever with our national feelings.

The French being the most classical of all modern poetry, is of all others least calculated to become familiar among the lower orders of the people. The stanzas of Tasso are sung by the gondoliers of Venice; the Spaniards and Portugese, of all ranks, know by heart the verses of Calderon and Camoëns. Shakespeare is as much admired by the populace in England as by those of a higher class. The poems of Goethe and Bürger are set to music, and repeated from the banks of the Rhine to the shores of the Baltic. Our French poets are admired wherever there are cultivated minds, either in our own nation, or in the rest of Europe; but they are quite unknown to the common people, and even to the class of citizens in our towns, because the arts, in France, are not, as elsewhere, natives of the very country in which their beauties are displayed.

Some French critics have asserted that German literature is still in its infancy. This opinion is entirely false; men who are best skilled in the knowledge of languages and the works of the ancients, are certainly not ignorant of the defects and advantages attached to the species of literature which they either adopt or reject; but their character, their habits, and their modes of reasoning, have led them to prefer that which is founded on the recollection of chivalry, on the wonders of the middle ages, to that which has for its basis the mythology of the Greeks. Romantic literature is alone capable of further improvement, because, being rooted in our own soil, that alone can continue to grow and acquire fresh life: it expresses our religion; it recalls our history; its origin is ancient, although not of classical antiquity.

Classic poetry, before it comes home to us, must pass through our recollections of paganism: that of the Germans is the Christian era of the fine arts; it employs our personal impressions to excite strong and vivid emotions; the genius by which it is inspired addresses itself immediately to our hearts, and seems to call forth the spirit of our own lives, of all phantoms at once the most powerful and the most terrible.

3. Heinrich Heine: *The Romantic School*

After a generation had passed since Mme. de Staël's *Germany*, Heinrich Heine (1797–1856), a German poet in exile in Paris, concluded that Frenchmen needed again to be acquainted, now more accurately, with the character of his native land. So he wrote *The Romantic School* (1836) and *Religion and Philosophy in Germany*, which reveal so well his mixed feelings about his Germany and its intellectual currents. He was born in the Rhineland while it was under French rule; in that part of Germany the Napoleonic Code was in force, and things French were much admired. He attended the University of Bonn, where A. W. von Schlegel was teaching, and came to know the promoter of the Romantic school first-hand. His early life was unsettled; he depended upon his uncle, a banker, for income while he turned his talents to poetry. He left Germany for Paris in 1831. Three years later he was implicated (without much foundation) in the Young Germany movement and formally exiled from his native land.

Heine was a monarchist who supported revolutions and approved Saint-Simonism, a proponent of emancipation for the Jewish people (he was never sure that he had been right to convert to Protestantism) and for all other oppressed people, and yet he was a German patriot whose love for his homeland was mystic and sentimental. He was a poet and critic and litterateur, not a major theorist; yet he could appraise the art and thought of his native land with a critical eye. His treatment of the German Romantic school is not kind, and perhaps a trifle unfair from one who was himself so taken with the myths and legends of the Middle Ages. Yet he could not accept the Christian rejection of life, which he saw as the chief trait of the first Romanticists, and so he urged instead a kind of pantheistic worship of life, an acceptance of the flesh. Heine the poet is one of Germany's great Romantic lyricists; Heine the critic is a follower by a generation of the Romantic school, and by no means one of them. One of the areas in which his views are most strikingly different is in social and political affairs, where his anticipation of a revolutionary regeneration soon to come is that of the pre-1848 era, not of the Restoration.

The following selection is from *The Works of Heinrich Heine*, translated from the German by Charles Godfrey Leland (New York and London, 1906), Vol. V, pp. 238–242, 249–252, 260–275. Reprinted by permission of E. P. Dutton & Co. Inc., in the United States and of William Heinemann, Ltd., in the British Commonwealth.

WHILE I announce these pages as a continuation of Madame de Staël's *De l'Allemagne*, I must, while praising the knowledge which can be gathered from that book, still advise great caution in consulting it, and stamp it as the work of a coterie. Madame de Staël, of glorious memory, has here, in the form of a book, opened a *Salon* in which she received German writers and gave them opportunity to become known to the civilised world of France; but in all the babble of many and most varied voices which resound from this book, on always hears most distinctly the fine treble of August Wilhelm von Schlegel. Where she is all herself, wherever this woman, so gifted with feeling, expresses herself freely, with all her flaming heart and all the fireworks of her sky-rockets of wit, and sparkling extravagancies, there the book is good and admirable.

But as soon as she obeys the influences of others, whenever she pays homage to some school the spirit of which is to her strange and incomprehensible, or as soon as the laudation of this school calls for Ultramontane tendencies directly contradictory to her Protestant clear-headedness, then the book becomes pitiable and unpleasant. Add to this that besides her unconscious party-spirit, she exercises a very conscious one, because by praising the spiritual life and idealism in Germany she means blame of the realism of France and the material splendour of the Empire. Her book *De l'Allemagne* is in this respect like the *Germania* of Tacitus, who, perhaps, by his eulogy of the Germans meant indirect satire of his Roman fellow-countrymen.

When I before spoke of a school to which Madame de Staël was devoted, and whose tendency she aided, I meant that which is called the Romantic. It will be made clear in this work that this was very different in Germany from what is known by the same name in France, and that its tendency was quite other than that of the French Romanticists.

But what was the Romantic school in Germany?
It was nothing else but the reawakening of the poetry of the
Middle Age, as it had shown itself in its songs, images, and architecture, in art and in life. But this poetry had risen from Christianity; it was a passion-flower which had sprung from the blood
of Christ. I do not know whether the melancholy passion-flower of
Germany is known by that name in France, and whether popular
legend attributes to it the same mystical origin. It is a strange
unpleasantly coloured blossom, in whose calyx we see set forth
the implements which were used in the crucifixion of Christ, such
as the hammer, pincers, and nails—a flower which is not so much
ugly as ghostly, whose sight even awakes in our soul a shuddering
pleasure, like the convulsively agreeable sensations which come
from pain itself. From this view the flower was indeed the fittest
symbol for Christianity itself, whose most thrilling chain was in
the luxury of pain.

Though in France only Roman Catholicism is understood by
the word Christianity, I must specially preface that I only speak
of the latter. I speak of that religion in whose first dogmas there is
a damnation of all flesh, and which not only allows the spirit
power over the flesh, but will also kill this to glorify the spirit. I
speak of that religion by whose unnatural requisitions sin and
hypocrisy really came into the world, in this that by the condemnation of the flesh the most innocent sensual pleasures became
sins, and because the impossibility of becoming altogether spiritual naturally created hypocrisy. I speak of that religion which by
teaching the doctrine of the casting away of all earthly goods,
and of dog-like abject humility and angelic patience, became the
most approved support of despotism. Men have found out the real
life and meaning (*Wesen*) of this religion, and do not now content themselves with promises of supping in Paradise; they know
that matter has also its merits, and is not all the devil's, and they
now defend the delights of this world, this beautiful garden of
God, our inalienable inheritance. And therefore, because we have
grasped so entirely all the consequences of that absolute spiritualism, we may believe that the Christian Catholic view of the world
has reached its end. Every age is a sphinx, which casts itself into
the abyss when man has guessed its riddle. . . .

There is in all these poems of the Middle Age a marked character which distinguishes them from those of Greece and Rome. We
characterise this difference by calling the first Romantic and the

other Classic. Yet these appellations are only uncertain rubrics, and have led hitherto to the most discouraging, wearisome entanglements, which become worse since we call antique poetry, instead of classic, Plastic. Here was the cause of much misunderstanding; for justly, all poets should work their material plastically, be it Christian or heathen; they should set it forth in clear outlines; in short, plastic form should be the main thing in modern Romantic art, quite as much as in the ancient. And are not the figures in the *Divina Commedia* of Dante or in the pictures of Raphael as plastic as those in Virgil? The difference lies in this, that the plastic forms in ancient art are absolutely identical with the subject or the idea which the artist would set forth, as, for example, that the wanderings of Ulysses mean nothing else but the journeyings of a man named Odysseus, who was son of Laertes and husband of Penelope; and further, that the Bacchus which we see in the Louvre is nothing else than the graceful, winsome son of Semele, with audacious melancholy in his eyes and sacred voluptuousness on his soft and arching lips. It is all otherwise in Romantic art, in which the wild wanderings of a knight have ever an esoteric meaning, symbolising perhaps the erring course of life. The dragon whom he overcomes is sin; the almond which from afar casts comforting perfume to the traveller is the Trinity, God the Father, God the Son, and God the Holy Ghost, which are three in one, as shell, fibre, and kernel make one nut. When Homer describes the armour of a hero, it is a good piece of work, worth so or so many oxen; but when a monk of the Middle Age describes in his poems the garments of the Mother of God, one may be sure that by this garb he means as many virtues, and a peculiar meaning lies hidden under this holy covering of the immaculate virginity of Maria, who, as her son is the almond-kernel, is naturally sung as the almond-flower. That is the character of the mediæval poetry which we call Romantic.

Classic art had only to represent the finite or determined, and its forms could be one and the same with the idea of the artist. Romantic art had to set forth, or rather signify, the infinite and purely spiritual, and it took refuge in a system of traditional, or rather of parabolistic symbols, as Christ himself had sought to render clear his spiritualistic ideas by all kinds of beautiful parables. Hence the mystical, problematic, marvellous, and transcendental in the art-work of the Middle Age, in which fantasy makes her most desperate efforts to depict the purely spiritual by means of sensible images, and invents colossal follies, piling Pelion on Ossa and Parcival on Titurel to attain to heaven.

Among other races where poetry attempted to display the infinite, and where monstrous fancies appeared, as, for instance, among the Scandinavians and Indians, we find poems which, being romantic, are also called such. . . .

Literary history is the great *Morgue* where every one seeks his dead, those whom he loves or to whom he is related. When I see there, among so many dead of little interest, a Lessing or a Herder, with their noble manly countenances, my heart throbs; I cannot pass them by without hastily kissing their dead lips.

Yet if Lessing did so much to destroy the imitating of French second-hand Greekdom, he still, by calling attention to the true works of art of Greek antiquity, gave an impulse to a new kind of ridiculous imitations. By his battling with religious superstition he advanced the sober search for clearer views which spread widely in Berlin, and had in the late blessed Nicolai[1] its chief organ, and in the General German Library its arsenal. The most deplorable mediocrity began to show itself more repulsively than ever, and flatness and insipidity blew themselves up like the frog in the fable.

It is a great mistake to suppose that Goethe, who had already come before the world, was generally known then in the true sense. His *Götz von Berlichingen* and his *Werther* were received with enthusiasm; but so too were the works of common bunglers, and Goethe had but a small niche in the temple of literature. As I have said, *Götz* and *Werther* had a spirited reception, but more on account of the subject-matter than of their artistic merits, which very few appreciated in these master-works. *Götz* was a dramatised romance of chivalry, and such writings were then the rage. In *Werther* the world saw the reproduction of a true story, that of young Jerusalem, who shot himself dead for love, and thereby, in those dead-calm days, made a great noise. People read with tears his touching letters; some shrewdly observed that the manner in which Werther had been banished from aristocratic society had increased his weariness of life. The discussion of suicide caused the book to be still more discussed; it occurred to

[1] Christoph Friedrich Nicolai (1733–1811), German bookseller and publicist. An opponent of authority in religion; in later life a hostile critic of the new literary tendencies deriving from Herder, Goethe, and Schiller. (Ed.)

several fools on this occasion to shoot themselves, and the book owing to its subject, went off like a shot. The novels of August Lafontaine were just as much read, and as this author wrote incessantly, he was more famous than Wolfgang Goethe. Wieland was the great poet then, with whom perhaps might be classed the ode-maker, Ramler of Berlin. Wieland was honoured idolatrously, far more at that time than Goethe. Iffland ruled the theatre with his dreary bourgeois dramas, and Kotzebue with his flat and frivolously witty jests.

It was in opposition to this literature that there sprung up in Germany, at the end of the last century, a school which we call the Romantic, and of which Messrs. August Wilhelm and Friedrich Schlegel have presented themselves as managing agents. Jena, where these and many other souls in like accord found themselves "off and on," was the centre from which the new æsthetic doctrine spread. I say doctrine, for this school began with judgments of the art works of the past and giving recipes for art works of the future, and in both directions the Schlegel school rendered great service to æsthetic criticism. By judging of such works of art as already existed, either their faults and failures were indicated, or their merits and beauties brought to light. In controversy and in thus indicating artistic shortcomings, the Messrs. Schlegel were entirely imitators of old Lessing; they obtained possession of his great battle-blade, but the arm of August William Schlegel was too tenderly weak, and the eyes of his brother Friedrich too mystically clouded for the former to strike so strongly and the latter so keenly and accurately as Lessing. True, in descriptive criticism, where the beauties of a work of art are to be set forth—where it came to a delicate feeling out of its characteristics, and bringing them home to our intelligence—then, compared to the Schlegels, old Lessing was nowhere. But what shall I say as to their recipes for preparing works of art? There we find in the Messrs. Schlegel a weakness which we think may also be detected in Lessing; for he is as weak in affirming as he is strong in denying. He rarely succeeds in laying down a fundamental principle, still more seldom a correct one. He wants the firm basis of a philosophy or of a philosophical system. And this is still more sadly the case with the brothers Schlegel.

Much is fabled as to the influence of Fichtean Idealism and Schelling's philosophy of Nature on the Romantic school, which is even declared to have sprung from it. But I see here at the most only the influence of certain fragments of thoughts from Fichte and Schelling, but not at all that of a philosophy; and this may be explained on the simple ground that Fichte's philosophy had lost its hold, and Fichte himself had made it lose its interest by a mingling of tenets and ideas from Schelling; and because, on the other hand, Schelling had never set forth a philosophy, but only a vague philosophising, an unsteady vacillating improvisation of poetical philosophemes. It may be that it was from the Fichtean Idealism—that deeply ironical system, where the I is opposed to the not-I and annihilates it—that the Romantic school took the doctrine of irony which the late Solger especially developed, and which the Schlegels at first regarded as the soul of art, but which they subsequently found to be fruitless, and exchanged for the more positive axioms of the Theory of Identity of Schelling. Schelling, who then taught in Jena, had indeed a great personal influence on the Romantic school: he is, what is not generally known in France, also a bit of a poet; and it is said that he was in doubt whether he should not deliver all his philosophical doctrines in a poetic or even metrical form. This doubt characterises the man.

But if the Messrs. Schlegel could not lay down any definite system for the great works which they prescribed to the poets of their school, they made up the defect by recommending the best productions of the past as patterns, and by making them accessible to their scholars. These were chiefly the works of the Christian-Catholic school of the Middle Age. The translation of Shakespeare, who stands on the border of this art, and smiles with Protestant clearness into our modern time, was intended for controversial purposes, which it would require too much space to explain here; and this translation was undertaken by August Wilhelm von Schlegel at a time before people had quite enthused themselves back into the Middle Age. Later, when this came to pass, Calderon was translated and exalted far above Shakespeare, because it was found that in him the piety of the Middle Age was most clearly and purely impressed, and that in its two leading motives, chivalry and monachism. The pious comedies of the Castilian priestly poet, whose flowers of fable are sprinkled with holy water and ecclesiastically incensed, were imitated with all their holy *grandeza*, all their sacerdotal luxury, all their consecrated conceits and craziness, and we saw flourishing in Germany those chequered-faithed, insanely profound poems in which

hearts were mystically enamoured, as in the *Andacht zum Kreutz*
—"Adoration of the Cross"—or beat in honour of the Virgin
Mary, as in *Der Standhafte Prinz*—"The Constant Prince"—and
Zacharias Werner carried matters in this direction as far as they
could well go without being shut up by the proper authority in
a madhouse.

"Our poetry," said the brothers Schlegel, "is old; our Muse is an
old wife with a distaff; our Cupid is not a blonde boy, but a
shrunk and shrivelled dwarf with grey hair; our feelings are
faded, our imagination is dry; we must re-freshen ourselves, we
must seek again the filled-up fountains of naïve, simple poesy
of the Middle Age, and then there will sparkle up again for us the
waters of youth." It was not necessary to speak thus twice to a
dried-up, arid people, especially to those poor souls with thirsty
throats who dwelt in the Prussian sands, who longed to become
youthful and blooming, and they rushed to the wondrous springs,
and swilled, swallowed, and swigged with immoderate desire.
But it happened to them as it did to the old lady's-maid of whom
this tale is told. She had observed that her mistress had a magic
elixir which restored youth, and one day when her dame had
departed, she took the vial of the elixir from her toilette table, but
instead of sipping a few drops, she took such a tremendous pull,
that owing to the greatly concentrated marvellous strength of the
rejuvenating reviver, she became not merely young, but a very
little child. And so indeed it happened to our admirable Tieck, one
of the best poets of the school, that he became almost a babe, and
bloomed into that babbling simplicity which Madame de Staël
had so much trouble to admire. She herself admits that it seemed
very singular to her when a character came forth in a drama
making his debut with the words, "I am the bold Bonifacius, and
I come to let you know," *et cætera*.

Ludwig Tieck had in his novel *Steinbald's Wanderungen*—
"The Travels of Steinbald"—and in "The Outpourings of the Heart
by an art-loving Monk," by a certain Wackenroder, which he
published, commended to artists the naïve rude beginnings of art
as models. The pious and childlike feeling which appears even in
their unskilfulness was advised for imitation. Of Raphael they
would not hear a word, and indeed cared little for Perugino, his
teacher, who was, however, far more prized, and in whom they
discovered remains of those excellences whose entire perfection
they so piously admired in the immortal master-works of Fra

Giovanno Angelico da Fiesole. To form a conception of the taste
of the art-enthusiasts of those times, one should go to the Louvre,
where the best pictures which were so absolutely admired are to
be seen. To get an idea of the mob of poets who imitated the
bards of the Middle Age in all possible metres, he should visit the
madhouse of Charenton.

And yet I think that those pictures in the first hall of the
Louvre are far too graceful to give an idea of the taste of those
days in art in Germany. One should think of these old Italian
pictures as translated into old German; for they regarded the
works of the old German painters as far more simple and childlike, therefore more worthy of imitation, then the old Italian. It
was declared that the Germans with their *Gemüth* (a word for
which there is no equivalent in French) could feel Christianity
more deeply than other nations; and Friedrich Schlegel and his
friend Joseph Görres rooted and rummaged in all the old towns on
the Rhine for the remains of old German pictures and carvings,
which were adored with blind faith as holy relics.

I have compared the German Parnassus of those days with
Charenton, but I believe it is too little said. A French lunacy is
far behind a German one, for in this latter madness, as Polonius
said, there is method; and that German lunacy was carried out
with a pedantry surpassing all belief, with a terrible conscientious
scrupulousness, with a thoroughness of which a superficial French
madman cannot even form an idea.

The political condition of Germany was then peculiarly favourable to a Christian Old-German movement. "Poverty teaches
prayer," says the proverb, and truly poverty or dire need was
never greater in Germany, and therefore the people were specially inclined to prayer, piety, and Christianity. There is no race
more devoted to its princes than ours; and what grieved them
more than the mournful condition to which their country had
been reduced by war and foreign rule was the melancholy sight
of their conquered rulers creeping to the feet of Napoleon. The
whole nation were like those true-hearted old servants whom we
pity in plays, the retainers in great families, who feel the humilia-
tions which their masters suffer more than the masters themselves; who weep their bitterest tears in secret when the family
plate must be sold, and even apply their own poor savings that
noble wax-tapers, and not plain tallow-candles, may appear on

the gentlefolk's table. The universal unrest and depression found relief in religion, and there sprung up a pietistic yielding to the will of God, from whom alone help was hoped for. And indeed none other save God could help against Napoleon. There could be no more reliance on earthly armies, and eyes must be raised in hope only to Heaven.

And so we could also have borne peacefully enough with Napoleon. But our princes, while they hoped that God would free them from him, also indulged the thought that the united forces of their people might also be of great assistance, and they sought with this intention to awaken a common feeling among the Germans; and even the most eminent personages now spoke of German nationality, of a common German Fatherland, of the union of the Christian-German races, and of the unity of Germany. We were ordered to become patriots, and patriots we became; for we do everything which our princes command.

But one should not here understand by patriotism quite the same feeling which the word implies in France. The patriotism of the Frenchman consists in this, that his heart is thereby warmed; by this warmth it expands, spreads, and no longer embraces his nearest emotions, but all France and all the realm of civilisation. The patriotism of the German, however, is shown by his heart becoming narrower and shrinking up and drawing in like leather in a frost; by hating everything foreign, and being no longer European or cosmopolite, but only a closely-cramped *Deutscher*. So we saw the ideal churl and clownishness reduced to system by Jahn,[2] the beginning of a shabby, clumsy, unwashed opposition to the sentiment which is the very highest and holiest which Germany ever brought forth, namely, that humanity, that universal fraternisation of mankind, that cosmopolitanism to which our great minds, Lessing, Herder, Schiller, Goethe, and Jean Paul, were ever devoted.

What happened soon after in Germany is too well known to you all. When God, the snow, and the Cossacks had destroyed the better portion of Napoleon's forces, we Germans received the all-superior command to free ourselves from foreign yoke, and we flamed up in manly rage at the slavery too long endured, and we

[2] Friedrich Ludwig Jahn (1778–1852) German nationalist who promoted gymnastic training originally to develop soldiers for the Napoleonic wars.

inspired ourselves with the good tunes and bad verses of Körner's songs, and we conquered our freedom; for we do everything which our princes command.

During a time when men were arming for such a strife, a school most unfriendly to all that was French, and which exalted with enthusiasm everything which was German in life, art, and letters, naturally found vigorous support. The Romantic school then went hand in hand with the efforts of our Governments and the secret societies, and August Wilhelm Schlegel conspired against Racine with the same object as that with which Minister Stein conspired against Napoleon. The school swam with the stream of the time, which was a stream running back to its source. When at last German patriotism and German nationality thoroughly triumphed, there triumphed too as decidedly with it the popular German-Christian Romantic school, and the "New German Religious-Patriotic Art." Napoleon, the great classic—even as classic as Alexander and Cæsar—fell, and Messrs. August Wilhelm and Friedrich Schlegel, who were quite as romantic as Tom Thumb and Puss-in-Boots, arose—rose as victors.

But here too came the reaction which follows on the heels of every excess. As spiritualistic Christendom was a reaction against the brutal rule of Imperial Roman materialism; as the renewed love for joyous Greek art and learning was the same against the Christian spiritualism, deteriorated to imbecile asceticism; as the awakening of mediæval romance was a counter-action against the prosaic imitation of old classic art; so we now see also a recoil against the restoration of that Catholic-feudal thought, and that knighthood and priesthood which had been preached in form and language under the greatest contrarieties.

When these highly-praised models, the art-masters of the Middle Age, were so extolled and exalted, their excellence was explained by the fact that those men believed in the subjects which they set forth, and that they in their artless simplicity could do more than the later artists without faith, who had advanced so much further in *technique* or practical execution, and that this faith had wrought miracles in them. And, in faith, how could one otherwise explain the glories of a Fra Angelica da Fiesole or the poem of Brother Ottfried? Therefore, the artists who were in earnest, and would fain reproduce the divine distortions of those marvellous pictures and the holy awkwardness of those marvellous poems, and, in short, the ineffable mysticism of all the old works, made up their minds to repair to the same Hippocrene where the old masters had imbibed their miraculous inspiration. They pilgrimed to Rome, where the Viceregent of Christ could revive and strengthen consumptive German art with the milk of his she-ass; they went to the bosom of the only beatifying Roman Catholic Apostolic Church. No formal transition was needed for many hangers-on of the Romantic school; they were—as for example—Görres and Clemens Brentano, born Catholics, and they only renounced the free-thinking views which they had formed. But others were born and brought up as Protestants —for instance, Friedrich Schlegel, Ludwig Tieck, Novalis, Werrer, Schütz, Carové, and Adam Müller, and their conversion required a public confirmation. Here I have only mentioned writers—the number of painters who abjured in shoals the evangelical faith, and with it reason and common-sense, was much greater.

When the world saw how these young people stood in a queue pressing for tickets of admission to the Roman Catholic Church, and crowded again into the old prison-house of the soul, from which their fathers had with such might and pain delivered themselves, it shook its head, in Germany, very significantly. But when it was found that a propaganda of priests and gentlemen who had conspired against the religion and political freedom of Europe had a hand in the game, and that it was really Jesuitism which was enticing German youth to ruin with the soft melodies of romance, as did the rat-catcher the children of Hameln, great displeasure and flaming rage burst up among the friends of intellectual freedom and of Protestantism. . . .

4. William Wordsworth: Preface to *Lyrical Ballads*

William Wordsworth (1770–1850) was early left by the deaths of his
parents in the care of uncles. He was educated at Cambridge. In 1791
he visited France, and was stirred to great enthusiasm for the Revolution, embracing a Rousseauistic belief in the virtues of "the people."
But the wars of the Revolution and England's participation in them, as
well as the "excesses" of the Terror, cooled his enthusiasm as it had
that of so many of his generation, until he had clearly become a conservative in his writings after about 1804. Many young admirers regarded his conversion to the established powers as fully evident when
he took the post of stamp distributor. His emotional ties were to the
countryside of the Lake District, where he spent so much of his life.
As an old man, in 1843, on the death of Southey, he became Poet
Laureate.

    Lyrical Ballads, first published in 1798, was a product of collabora-
tion with Coleridge ("The Rime of the Ancient Mariner" appeared in
it). The Preface was first added to the second edition (1800); it was
expanded in 1802 and subjected to minor revisions for subsequent editions. In the Preface Wordsworth expresses most of his key conceptions regarding the novelty of his own work, and it is for this reason
often seen as demarcating the old aesthetics of the eighteenth century
from what was to follow. The beneficent presence of nature and its
uplifting effect upon those who live most closely to it (a kind of
reverence for nature that influenced a whole generation as the nineteenth century opened), the admirable and natural spontaneous quality
of peasant expression and feeling—all this anti-urbanism and primitivism was not very new, but in a major æsthetic pronouncement it
surely was. There was much else, too, that was far from novel: the
associationist psychology, for instance, and traces of utilitarianism. But
the glorification of the poet's genius and of his superior sensitivity, of
poetry over science, the setting aside of rules of traditional poetic
diction, and the view of poetry as "the spontaneous overflow of powerful feelings," bespeaking a trust in the natural, the emotional, and the
original—all this was far nearer to revolutionary thought. Especially
striking too is Wordsworth's concern over the relation of the artist to
his readers, what might be called the role of the poet as moralizer.

    The text that follows is from the version of the Preface which ap-
peared in 1845, and is taken from *The Complete Poetical Works of
William Wordsworth* (Houghton Mifflin & Company, Boston, 1911),
Vol. X, pp. 4–11, 17–24.

SEVERAL OF my Friends are anxious for the success of these Poems,
from a belief that, if the views with which they were composed

were indeed realised, a class of Poetry would be produced, well adapted to interest mankind permanently, and not unimportant in the quality and in the multiplicity of its moral relations: and on this account they have advised me to prefix a systematic defence of the theory upon which the Poems were written. But I was unwilling to undertake the task, knowing that on this occasion the Reader would look coldly upon my arguments, since I might be suspected of having been principally influenced by the selfish and foolish hope of *reasoning* him into an approbation of these particular Poems: and I was still more unwilling to undertake the task, because adequately to display the opinions, and fully to enforce the arguments, would require a space wholly disproportionate to a preface. For, to treat the subject with the clearness and coherence of which it is susceptible, it would be necessary to give a full account of the present state of the public taste in this country, and to determine how far this taste is healthy or depraved; which, again, could not be determined without pointing out in what manner language and the human mind act and re-act on each other, and without retracing the revolutions, not of literature alone, but likewise of society itself. I have therefore altogether declined to enter regularly upon this defence; yet I am sensible that there would be something like impropriety in abruptly obtruding upon the Public, without a few words of introduction, Poems so materially different from those upon which general approbation is at present bestowed.

It is supposed that by the act of writing in verse an Author makes a formal engagement that he will gratify certain known habits of association; that he not only thus apprises the Reader that certain classes of ideas and expressions will be found in his book, but that others will be carefully excluded. This exponent or symbol held forth by metrical language must in different areas of literature have excited very different expectations: for example, in the age of Catullus, Terence, and Lucretius, and that of Statius or Claudian; and in our own country, in the age of Shakespeare and Beaumont and Fletcher, and that of Donne and Cowley, or Dryden, or Pope. I will not take upon me to determine the exact import of the promise which, by the act of writing in verse, an Author in the present day makes to his reader; but it will undoubtedly appear to many persons that I have not fulfilled the terms of an engagement thus voluntarily contracted. They who have been accustomed to the gaudiness and inane phraseology of many modern writers, if they persist in reading this book to its conclusion, will, no doubt, frequently have to struggle with feelings of strangeness and awkwardness: they will look round for poetry, and will be induced to inquire by what species of courtesy these attempts can be permitted to assume that title. I hope, therefore, the reader will not censure me for attempting to state what I have proposed to myself to perform; and also (as far as the limits of a preface will permit) to explain some of the chief reasons which have determined me in the choice of my purpose: that at least he may be spared any unpleasant feeling of disappointment, and that I myself may be protected from one of the most dishonourable accusations which can be brought against an Author; namely, that of an indolence which prevents him from endeavouring to ascertain what is his duty, or, when his duty is ascertained, prevents him from performing it.

The principal object, then, proposed in these Poems, was to choose incidents and situations from common life, and to relate or describe them throughout, as far as was possible, in a selection of language really used by men, and, at the same time, to throw over them a certain colouring of imagination, whereby ordinary things should be presented to the mind in an unusual aspect; and further, and above all, to make these incidents and situations interesting by tracing in them, truly though not ostentatiously, the primary laws of our nature: chiefly, as far as regards the manner in which we associate ideas in a state of excitement. Humble and rustic life was generally chosen, because in that condition the essential passions of the heart find a better soil in which they can attain their maturity, are less under restraint, and speak a plainer and more emphatic language; because in that condition of life our elementary feelings co-exist in a state of greater simplicity, and, consequently, may be more accurately contemplated, and more forcibly communicated; because the manners of rural life germinate from those elementary feelings, and, from the necessary character of rural occupations, are more easily comprehended, and are more durable; and, lastly, because in that condition the passions of men are incorporated with the beautiful and permanent forms of nature. The language, too, of these men has been adopted (purified indeed from what appear to be its real defects, from all lasting and rational causes of dislike or disgust), because such men hourly communicate with the best objects from which the best part of language is originally derived; and because, from their rank in society and the sameness and narrow circle of their intercourse, being less under the influence of social vanity, they convey their feelings and notions in simple and unelaborated expressions. Accordingly, such a language, arising out of repeated experience and regular feelings, is a more permanent, and a far more philosophical language, than that which is frequently substituted for it by Poets, who think that they are conferring honour upon themselves and their art in proportion as they separate themselves from the sympathies of men, and indulge in arbitrary and capricious habits of expression, in order to furnish food for fickle tastes and fickle appetites of their own creation.[1]

I cannot, however, be insensible to the present outcry against the triviality and meanness, both of thought and language, which some of my contemporaries have occasionally introduced into their metrical compositions; and I acknowledge that this defect, where it exists, is more dishonourable to the Writer's own character than false refinement or arbitrary innovation, though I should contend at the same time that it is far less pernicious in the sum of its consequences. From such verses the Poems in these volumes will be found distinguished at least by one mark of difference, that each of them has a worthy *purpose*. Not that I always began to write with a distinct purpose formally conceived, but habits of meditation have, I trust, so prompted and regulated my feelings, that my descriptions of such objects as strongly excite those feelings will be found to carry along with them a *purpose*. If this opinion be erroneous, I can have little right to the name of a Poet. For all good poetry is the spontaneous overflow of powerful feelings: and though this be true, Poems to which any value can be attached were never produced on any variety of subjects but by a man who, being possessed of more than usual organic sensibility, had also thought long and deeply. For our continued influxes of feeling are modified and directed by our thoughts, which are indeed the representatives of all our past feelings; and as, by contemplating the relation of these general representatives to each other, we discover what is really important to men, so, by

---

[1] It is worth while here to observe that the affecting parts of Chaucer are almost always expressed in language pure and universally intelligible even to this day.

the repetition and continuance of this act, our feelings will be connected with important subjects, till at length, if we be originally possessed of much sensibility, such habits of mind will be produced that, by obeying blindly and mechanically the impulses of those habits, we shall describe objects, and utter sentiments, of such a nature, and in such connection with each other, that the understanding of the Reader must necessarily be in some degree enlightened, and his affection strengthened and purified.

It has been said that each of these Poems has a purpose. Another circumstance must be mentioned which distinguishes these Poems from the popular Poetry of the day; it is this, that the feeling therein developed gives importance to the action and situation, and not the action and situation to the feeling.

A sense of false modesty shall not prevent me from asserting that the Reader's attention is pointed to this mark of distinction, far less for the sake of these particular Poems than from the general importance of the subject. The subject is indeed important! For the human mind is capable of being excited without the application of gross and violent stimulants; and he must have a very faint perception of its beauty and dignity who does not know this, and who does not further know, that one being is elevated above another in proportion as he possesses this capability. It has therefore appeared to me, that to endeavour to produce or enlarge this capability is one of the best services in which, at any period, a Writer can be engaged; but this service, excellent at all times, is especially so at the present day. For a multitude of causes, unknown to former times, are now acting with a combined force to blunt the discriminating powers of the mind, and, unfitting it for all voluntary exertion, to reduce it to a state of almost savage torpor. The most effective of these causes are the great national events which are daily taking place, and the increasing accumulation of men in cities, where the uniformity of their occupations produces a craving for extraordinary incident which the rapid communication of intelligence hourly gratifies. To this tendency of life and manners the literature and theatrical exhibitions of the country have conformed themselves. The invaluable works of our elder writers, I had almost said the works of Shakespeare and Milton, are driven into neglect by frantic novels, sickly and stupid German Tragedies, and deluges of idle and extravagant stories in verse.—When I think upon this degrading thirst after outrageous stimulation, I am almost ashamed to have spoken of the feeble endeavour made in these volumes to counteract it; and, reflecting upon the magnitude of the general evil, I should be oppressed with no dishonourable melancholy, had I not a deep impression of certain inherent and indestructible qualities of the human mind, and likewise of certain powers in the great and permanent objects that act upon it, which are equally inherent and indestructible; and were there not added to this impression a belief that the time is approaching when the evil will be systematically opposed by men of greater powers, and with far more distinguished success. . . .

Taking up the subject, then, upon general grounds, let me ask, what is meant by the word Poet? What is a Poet? To whom does he address himself? And what language is to be expected from him?—He is a man speaking to men: a man, it is true, endowed with more lively sensibility, more enthusiasm and tenderness, who has a greater knowledge of human nature, and a more comprehensive soul, than are supposed to be common among mankind; a man pleased with his own passions, and volitions, and who rejoices more than other men in the spirit of life that is in him; delighting to contemplate similar volitions and passions as manifested in the goings-on of the Universe, and habitually impelled to create them where he does not find them. To these qualities he has added a disposition to be affected more than any other men by absent things as if they were present; an ability of conjuring up in himself passions, which are indeed far from being the same as those produced by real events, yet (especially in those parts of the general sympathy which are pleasing and delightful) do more nearly resemble the passions produced by real events than anything which, from the motions of their own minds merely, other men are accustomed to feel in themselves:—whence, and from practice, he has acquired a greater readiness and power in expressing what he thinks and feels, and especially those thoughts and feelings which, by his own choice, or from the structure of his own mind, arise in him without the immediate external excitement.

But whatever portion of this faculty we may suppose even the greatest Poet to possess, there cannot be a doubt that the language which it will suggest to him must often, in liveliness and truth, fall short of that which is uttered by men in real life under the actual pressure of those passions, certain shadows of which the Poet thus produces, or feels to be produced, in himself.

However exalted a notion we would wish to cherish of the character of a Poet, it is obvious that, while he describes and imitates passions, his employment is in some degree mechanical compared with the freedom and power of real and substantial action and suffering. So that it will be the wish of the Poet to bring his feelings near to those of the persons whose feelings he describes, nay, for short spaces of time, perhaps, to let himself slip into an entire delusion, and even confound and identify his own feelings with theirs; modifying only the language which is thus suggested to him by a consideration that he describes for a particular purpose, that of giving pleasure. Here, then, he will apply the principle of selection which has been already insisted upon. He will depend upon this for removing what would otherwise be painful or disgusting in the passion; he will feel that there is no necessity to trick out or to elevate nature: and the more industriously he applies this principle the deeper will be his faith that no words, which *his* fancy or imagination can suggest, will be to be compared with those which are the emanations of reality and truth.

But it may be said by those who do not object to the general spirit of these remarks, that, as it is impossible for the Poet to produce upon all occasions language as exquisitely fitted for the passion as that which the real passion itself suggests, it is proper that he should consider himself as in the situation of a translator, who does not scruple to substitute excellences of another kind for those which are unattainable by him; and endeavours occasionally to surpass his original, in order to make some amends for the general inferiority to which he feels he must submit. But this would be to encourage idleness and unmanly despair. Further, it is the language of men who speak of what they do not understand; who talk of Poetry, as of a matter of amusement and idle pleasure; who will converse with us as gravely about a *taste* for Poetry, as they express it, as if it were a thing as indifferent as a taste for rope-dancing, or Frontiniac or Sherry. Aristotle, I have been told, has said, that Poetry is the most philosophic of all writing: it is so: its object is truth, not individual and local, but general and operative; not standing upon external testimony, but carried alive into the heart by passion; truth which is its own testimony, which gives competence and confidence to the tribunal to which it appeals, and receives them from the same tribunal. Poetry is the image of man and nature. The obstacles which stand in the way of the fidelity of the Biographer and Historian, and of their consequent utility, are incalculably greater than those which are to be encountered by the Poet who comprehends the dignity of his art. The Poet writes under one restriction only, namely, the necessity of giving immediate pleasure to a human Being possessed of that information which may be expected from him, not as a lawyer, a physician, a mariner, an astronomer, or a natural philosopher, but as a Man. Except this one restriction, there is no object standing between the Poet and the image of things; between this, and the Biographer and Historian, there are a thousand.

Nor let this necessity of producing immediate pleasure be considered as a degradation of the Poet's art. It is far otherwise. It is an acknowledgment of the beauty of the universe, an acknowledgment the more sincere because not formal, but indirect; it is a task light and easy to him who looks at the world in the spirit of love: further, it is a homage paid to the native and naked dignity of man, to the grand elementary principle of pleasure, by which he knows, and feels, and lives, and moves. We have no sympathy but what is propagated by pleasure: I would not be misunderstood; but wherever we sympathise with pain, it will be found that the sympathy is produced and carried on by subtle combinations with pleasure. We have no knowledge, that is, no general principles drawn from the contemplation of particular facts, but what has been built up by pleasure, and exists in us by pleasure alone. The Man of science, the Chemist and Mathematician, whatever difficulties and disgusts they may have had to struggle with, know and feel this. However painful may be the objects with which the Anatomist's knowledge is connected, he feels that his knowledge is pleasure; and where he has no pleasure he has no knowledge. What then does the Poet? He considers man and the objects that surround him as acting and reacting upon each other, so as to produce an infinite complexity of pain and pleasure; he considers man in his own nature and in his ordinary life as contemplating this with a certain quantity of immediate knowledge, with certain convictions, intuitions, and deductions, which from habit acquire the quality of intuitions; he considers him as looking upon this complex scene of ideas and sensations, and

finding everywhere objects that immediately excite in him sympathies, which from the necessities of his nature, are accompanied
by an overbalance of enjoyment.

   To this knowledge which all men carry about with them, and
to these sympathies in which, without any other discipline than
that of our daily life, we are fitted to take delight, the Poet principally directs his attention. He considers man and nature as essentially adapted to each other, and the mind of man as naturally the
mirror of the fairest and most interesting properties of nature.
And thus the Poet, prompted by this feeling of pleasure, which
accompanies him through the whole course of his studies, con-
verses with general nature, with affections akin to those which,
through labour and length of time, the Man of science has raised
up in himself, by conversing with those particular parts of nature
which are the objects of his studies. The knowledge both of the
Poet and the Man of science is pleasure; but the knowledge of the
one cleaves to us as a necessary part of our existence, our natural
and unalienable inheritance; the other is a personal and individual acquisition, slow to come to us, and by no habitual and direct
sympathy connecting us with our fellow-beings. The Man of science seeks truth as a remote and unknown benefactor; he cherishes and loves it in his solitude: the Poet, singing a song in which
all human beings join with him, rejoices in the presence of truth
as our visible friend and hourly companion. Poetry is the breath
and finer spirit of all knowledge; it is the impassioned expression
which is in the countenance of all Science. Emphatically may it
be said of the Poet, as Shakespeare hath said of man, "that he
looks before and after." He is the rock of defence for human
nature; an upholder and preserver, carrying everywhere with him
relationship and love. In spite of difference of soil and climate, of
language and manners, of laws and customs: in spite of things
silently gone out of mind, and things violently destroyed; the Poet
binds together by passion and knowledge the vast empire of
human society, as it is spread over the whole earth and over all
time. The objects of the Poet's thoughts are everywhere; though
the eyes and senses of man are, it is true, his favourite guides, yet
he will follow wheresoever he can find an atmosphere of sensation
in which to move his wings. Poetry is the first and last of all
knowledge—it is as immortal as the heart of man. If the labours
of Men of science should ever create any material revolution,

direct or indirect, in our condition, and in the impressions which we habitually receive, the Poet will sleep then no more than at present; he will be ready to follow the steps of the Man of science, not only in those general indirect effects, but he will be at his side, carrying sensation into the midst of the objects of the science itself. The remotest discoveries of the Chemist, the Botanist, or Mineralogist, will be as proper objects of the Poet's art as any upon which it can be employed, if the time should ever come when these things shall be familiar to us, and the relations under which they are contemplated by the followers of these respective sciences shall be manifestly and palpably material to us as enjoying and suffering beings. If the time should ever come when what is now called science, thus familiarised to men, shall be ready to put on, as it were, a form of flesh and blood, the Poet will lend his divine spirit to aid the transfiguration, and will welcome the Being thus produced as a dear and genuine inmate of the household of man.—It is not, then, to be supposed that any one, who holds that sublime notion of Poetry which I have attempted to convey, will break in upon the sanctity and truth of his pictures by transitory and accidental ornaments, and endeavour to excite admiration of himself by arts, the necessity of which must manifestly depend upon the assumed meanness of his subject. . . .

5. Percy Bysshe Shelley: "A Defence of Poetry"

Percy Bysshe Shelley (1792–1822) was the son of a member of Parliament and heir to a baronetcy. He attended Eton and then Oxford, from which he was expelled for publishing a pamphlet called *The Necessity of Atheism*. He began to publish his poetry in 1813, but it was only after he had left his first wife in favor of Mary Wollstonecraft Godwin—whom he later married—that his major poetical works appeared. In 1819, the Shelleys went to Italy, where he died in 1822 in a boating accident.

Shelley was from the first an opponent of authority—as his Oxford experience shows—and he believed profoundly in the natural goodness of man. He remained an ardent reformer throughout his life, coming more and more to adopt the view that poets might change the world (as he suggests in "A Defence of Poetry," much of which is presented below). Justice, freedom, and love were major themes in his poetry, which he used to express much of the social and political spirit that was the hallmark of youthful Romanticism.

His views in the "Defence" (which was written in 1821, but was first published posthumously in 1840 in *Essays, Letters from Abroad, Translations and Fragments*), his major theoretical statement on the arts, are more unequivocally Romantic than Wordsworth's views. Shelley gives the argument an historical setting. He uses a Coleridgean idea of the creative imagination. The artist is more exalted than he is by Wordsworth, his expression of his immediate unstudied, or natural, responses is more highly praised, while the moral value of his work is again strongly emphasized, especially in view of the social evils of Shelley's day.

The text is from *Shelley's Literary and Philosophic Criticism*, (London, 1909), pp. 120–126, 129–132, 137–139, 140–141, 148–156, 159.

ACCORDING TO one mode of regarding those two classes of mental action, which are called reason and imagination, the former may be considered as mind contemplating the relations borne by one thought to another, however produced; and the latter, as mind acting upon those thoughts so as to colour them with its own light, and composing from them, as from elements, other thoughts, each containing within itself the principle of its own integrity. The one is τὸ ποιεῖν, or the principle of synthesis, and has for its objects those forms which are common to universal nature and existence itself; the other is the τὸ λογίζειν, or principle of analysis, and its action regards the relations of things, simply as relations; considering thoughts, not in their integral unity, but as the algebraical representations which conduct to certain general results. Reason is the enumeration of quantities already known; imagination is the perception of the value of those quantities, both separately and as a whole. Reason respects the differences, and imagination the similitudes of things. Reason is to the imagination as the instrument to the agent, as the body to the spirit, as the shadow to the substance.

Poetry, in a general sense, may be defined to be "the expression of the imagination": and poety is connate with the origin of man. Man is an instrument over which a series of external and internal impressions are driven, like the alternations of an ever-changing wind over an Aeolian lyre, which move it by their motion to ever-changing melody. But there is a principle within the human

being, and perhaps within all sentient beings, which acts otherwise than in the lyre, and produces not melody alone, but harmony, by an internal adjustment of the sounds or motions thus
excited to the impressions which excite them. It is as if the lyre
could accommodate its chords to the motions of that which
strikes them, in a determined proportion of sound; even as the
musician can accommodate his voice to the sound of the lyre. A
child at play by itself will express its delight by its voice and
motions; and every inflexion of tone and every gesture will bear
exact relation to a corresponding antitype in the pleasurable impressions which awakened it; it will be the reflected image of
that impression; and as the lyre trembles and sounds after the
wind has died away, so the child seeks, by prolonging in its voice
and motions the duration of the effect, to prolong also a consciousness of the cause. In relation to the objects which delight a
child, these expressions are, what poetry is to higher objects. The
savage (for the savage is to ages what the child is to years)
expresses the emotions produced in him by surrounding objects in
a similar manner; and language and gesture, together with plastic
or pictorial imitation, become the image of the combined effect of
those objects, and of his apprehension of them. Man in society,
with all his passions and his pleasures, next becomes the object of
the passions and pleasures of man; an additional class of emotions
produces an augmented treasure of expressions; and language,
gesture, and the imitative arts, become at once the representation
and the medium, the pencil and the picture, the chisel and the
statue, the chord and the harmony. The social sympathies, or
those laws from which, as from its elements, society results, begin
to develop themselves from the moment that two human beings
coexist; the future is contained within the present, as the plant
within the seed; and equality, diversity, unity, contrast, mutual
dependence, become the principles alone capable of affording the
motives according to which the will of a social being is deter-
mind to action, inasmuch as he is social; and constitute pleasure
in sensation, virtue in sentiment, beauty in art, truth in reasoning,
and love in the intercourse of kind. Hence men, even in the infancy of society, observe a certain order in their words and actions, distinct from that of the objects and the impressions represented by them, all expression being subject to the laws of that

from which it proceeds. But let us dismiss those more general considerations which might involve an inquiry into the principles of society itself, and restrict our view to the manner in which the imagination is expressed upon its forms.

In the youth of the world, men dance and sing and imitate natural objects, observing in these actions, as in all others, a certain rhythm or order. And, although all men observe a similar, they observe not the same order, in the motions of the dance, in the melody of the song, in the combinations of language, in the series of their imitations of natural objects. For there is a certain order or rhythm belonging to each of these classes of mimetic representation, from which the hearer and the spectator receive an intenser and purer pleasure than from any other: the sense of an approximation to this order has been called taste by modern writers. Every man in the infancy of art observes an order which approximates more or less closely to that from which this highest delight results: but the diversity is not sufficiently marked, as that its gradations should be sensible, except in those instances where the predominance of this faculty of approximation to the beautiful (for so we may be permitted to name the relation between this highest pleasure and its cause) is very great. Those in whom it exists in excess are poets, in the most universal sense of the word; and the pleasure resulting from the manner in which they express the influence of society or nature upon their own minds, communicates itself to others, and gathers a sort of reduplication from that community. Their language is vitally metaphorical; that is, it marks the before unapprehended relations of things and perpetuates their apprehension, until the words which represent them become, through time, signs for portions or classes of thoughts instead of pictures of integral thoughts; and then if no new poets should arise to create afresh the associations which have been thus disorganized, language will be dead to all the nobler purposes of human intercourse. These similitudes or relations are finely said by Lord Bacon to be "the same footsteps of nature impressed upon the various subjects of the world";[1] and he considers the faculty which perceives them as the storehouse of axioms common to all knowledge. In the infancy of society every author is necessarily a poet, because language itself is

---

[1] *De Augment. Scient.*, cap. i, lib. iii.

poetry; and to be a poet is to apprehend the true and the beautiful, in a word, the good which exists in the relation, subsisting,
first between existence and perception, and secondly between
perception and expression. Every original language near to its
source is in itself the chaos of a cyclic poem: the copiousness of
lexicography and the distinctions of grammar are the works of a
later age, and are merely the catalogue and the form of the creations of poetry.

But poets, or those who imagine and express this indestructible
order, are not only the authors of language and of music, of the
dance, and architecture, and statuary, and painting; they are the
institutors of laws, and the founders of civil society, and the in-
ventors of the arts of life, and the teachers, who draw into a
certain propinquity with the beautiful and the true, that partial
apprehension of the agencies of the invisible world which is
called religion. Hence all original religions are allegorical, or
susceptible of allegory, and, like Janus, have a double face of
false and true. Poets, according to the circumstances of the age
and nation in which they appeared, were called, in the earlier
epochs of the world, legislators, or prophets: a poet essentially
comprises and unites both these characters. For he not only beholds intensely the present as it is, and discovers those laws according to which present things ought to be ordered, but he beholds the future in the present, and his thoughts are the germs of
the flower and the fruit of latest time. Not that I assert poets to be
prophets in the gross sense of the word, or that they can foretell
the form as surely as they foreknow the spirit of events: such is
the pretence of superstition, which would make poetry an
attribute of prophecy, rather than prophecy an attribute of
poetry. A poet participates in the eternal, the infinite, and the
one; as far as relates to his conceptions, time and place and number are not. The grammatical forms which express the moods of
time, and the difference of persons, and the distinction of place,
are convertible with respect to the highest poetry without injuring it as poetry; and the choruses of Aeschylus, and the book of
Job, and Dante's *Paradise*, would afford, more than any other
writings, examples of this fact, if the limits of this essay did not
forbid citation. The creations of sculpture, painting, and music,
are illustrations still more decisive.

Language, colour, form, and religious and civil habits of action, are all the instruments and materials of poetry; they may be called poetry by that figure of speech which considers the effect as a synonym of the cause. But poetry in a more restricted sense expresses those arrangements of language, and especially metrical language, which are created by that imperial faculty, whose throne is curtained within the invisible nature of man. And this springs from the nature itself of language, which is a more direct representation of the actions and passions of our internal being, and is susceptible of more various and delicate combinations, than colour, form, or motion, and is more plastic and obedient to the control of that faculty of which it is the creation. For language is arbitrarily produced by the imagination, and has relation to thoughts alone; but all other materials, instruments, and conditions of art, have relations among each other, which limit and interpose between conception and expression. The former is a mirror which reflects, the latter as a cloud which enfeebles, the light of which both are mediums of communication. Hence the fame of sculptors, painters, and musicians, although the intrinsic powers of the great masters of these arts may yield in no degree to that of those who have employed language as the hieroglyphic of their thoughts, has never equalled that of poets in the restricted sense of the term; as two performers of equal skill will produce unequal effects from a guitar and a harp. The fame of legislators and founders of religions, so long as their institutions last, alone seems to exceed that of poets in the restricted sense; but it can scarcely be a question, whether, if we deduct the celebrity which their flattery of the gross opinions of the vulgar usually conciliates, together with that which belonged to them in their higher character of poets, any excess will remain. . . .

Poetry is ever accompanied with pleasure: all spirits on which it falls open themselves to receive the wisdom which is mingled with its delight. In the infancy of the world, neither poets themselves nor their auditors are fully aware of the excellence of poetry: for it acts in a divine and unapprehended manner, beyond and above consciousness; and it is reserved for future generations to contemplate and measure the mighty cause and effect in all the strength and splendour of their union. Even in modern times, no living poet ever arrived at the fullness of his fame; the jury which sits in judgment upon a poet, belonging as he does to all time, must be composed of his peers: it must be impanelled by Time from the selectest of the wise of many generations. A poet is a nightingale, who sits in darkness and sings to cheer its own solitude with sweet sounds; his auditors are as men entranced by the melody of an unseen musician, who feel that they are moved and softened, yet know not whence or why. The poems of Homer and his contemporaries were the delight of infant Greece; they were the elements of that social system which is the column upon which all succeeding civilization has reposed. Homer embodied the ideal perfection of his age in human character; nor can we doubt that those who read his verses were awakened to an ambition of becoming like to Achilles, Hector, and Ulysses: the truth and beauty of friendship, patriotism, and persevering devotion to an object, were unveiled to the depths in these immortal creations: the sentiments of the auditors must have been refined and enlarged by a sympathy with such great and lovely impersonations, until from admiring they imitated, and from imitation they identified themselves with the objects of their admiration. Nor let it be objected, that these characters are remote from moral perfection, and that they can by no means be considered as edifying patterns for general imitation. Every epoch, under names more or less specious, has deified its peculiar errors; Revenge is the naked idol of the worship of a semi-barbarous age; and Self-deceit is the veiled image of unknown evil, before which luxury and satiety lie prostrate. But a poet considers the vices of his contemporaries as a temporary dress in which his creations must be arrayed, and which cover without concealing the eternal proportions of their beauty. An epic or dramatic personage is understood to wear them around his soul, as he may the ancient armour or the modern uniform around his body; whilst it is easy to conceive a dress more graceful than either. The beauty of the internal nature cannot be so far concealed by its accidental vesture, but that the spirit of its form shall communicate itself to the very disguise, and indicate the shape it hides from the manner in which it is worn. A majestic form and graceful motions will express themselves through the most barbarous and tasteless costume. Few poets of the highest class have chosen to exhibit the beauty of their conceptions in its naked truth and splendour; and it is doubtful whether the alloy of costume, habit, &c., be not necessary to temper this planetary music for mortal ears.

The whole objection, however, of the immorality of poetry
rests upon a misconception of the manner in which poetry acts to
produce the moral improvement of man. Ethical science arranges
the elements which poetry has created, and propounds schemes
and proposes examples of civil and domestic life: nor is it for
want of admirable doctrines that men hate, and despise, and censure, and deceive, and subjugate one another. But poetry acts in
another and diviner manner. It awakens and enlarges the mind
itself by rendering it the receptable of a thousand unapprehended
combinations of thought. Poetry lifts the veil from the hidden
beauty of the world, and makes familiar objects be as if they were
not familiar; it reproduces all that it represents, and the impersonations clothed in its Elysian light stand thenceforward in the
minds of those who have once contemplated them, as memorials
of that gentle and exalted content which extends itself over all
thoughts and actions with which it coexists. The great secret of
morals is love; or a going out of our own nature, and an identification of ourselves with the beautiful which exists in thought, action, or person, not our own. A man, to be greatly good, must
imagine intensely and comprehensively; he must put himself in
the place of another and of many others; the pains and pleasures
of his species must become his own. The great instrument of
moral good is the imagination; and poetry administers to the
effect by acting upon the cause. Poetry enlarges the circumference of the imagination by replenishing it with thoughts of ever
new delight, which have the power of attracting and assimilating
to their own nature all other thoughts, and which form new intervals and interstices whose void for ever craves fresh food. Poetry
strengthens the faculty which is the organ of the moral nature of
man, in the same manner as exercise strengthens a limb. A poet
therefore will do ill to embody his own conceptions of right and
wrong, which are usually those of his place and time, in his poetical creations, which participate in neither. By this assumption of
the inferior office of interpreting the effect, in which perhaps after
all he might acquit himself but imperfectly, he would resign a
glory in a participation in the cause. There was little danger that
Homer, or any of the eternal poets, should have so far misunderstood themselves as to have abdicated this throne of their widest
dominion. Those in whom the poetical faculty, though great, is
less intense, as Euripides, Lucan, Tasso, Spenser, have frequently

affected a moral aim, and the effect of their poetry is diminished in exact proportion to the degree in which they compel us to advert to this purpose. . . .

The drama being that form under which a greater number of modes of expression of poetry are susceptible of being combined than any other, the connexion of poetry and social good is more observable in the drama than in whatever other form. And it is indisputable that the highest perfection of human society has ever corresponded with the highest dramatic excellence; and that the corruption or the extinction of the drama in a nation where it has once flourished, is a mark of a corruption of manners, and an extinction of the energies which sustain the soul of social life. But, as Machiavelli says of political institutions, that life may be preserved and renewed, if men should arise capable of bringing back the drama to its principles. And this is true with respect to poetry in its most extended sense: all language, institution and form, require not only to be produced but to be sustained: the office and character of a poet participates in the divine nature as regards providence, no less than as regards creation.

Civil war, the spoils of Asia, and the fatal predominance first of the Macedonian, and then of the Roman arms, were so many symbols of the extinction or suspension of the creative faculty in Greece. The bucolic writers, who found patronage under the lettered tyrants of Sicily and Egypt, were the latest representatives of its most glorious reign. Their poetry is intensely melodious; like the odour of the tuberose, it overcomes and sickens the spirit with excess of sweetness; whilst the poetry of the preceding age was as a meadow-gale of June, which mingles the fragrance of all the flowers of the field, and adds a quickening and harmonizing spirit of its own, which endows the sense with a power of sustaining its extreme delight. The bucolic and erotic delicacy in written poetry is correlative with that softness in statuary, music, and the kindred arts, and even in manners and institutions, which distinguished the epoch to which I now refer. Nor is it the poetical faculty itself, or any misapplication of it, to which this want of harmony is to be imputed. An equal sensibility to the influence of the senses and the affections is to be found in the writings of Homer and Sophocles: the former, especially, has clothed sensual and pathetic images with irresistible attractions. Their superiority over these succeeding writers consists in the presence of those thoughts which belong to the inner faculties of our nature, not in the absence of those which are connected with the external: their incomparable perfection consists in a harmony of the union of all. It is not what the erotic poets have, but what they have not, in which their imperfection consists. It is not inasmuch as they were poets, but inasmuch as they were not poets, that they can be considered with any plausibility as connected with the corruption of their age. Had that corruption availed so as to extinguish in them the sensibility to pleasure, passion, and natural scenery, which is imputed to them as an imperfection, the last triumph of evil would have been achieved. For the end of social corruption is to destroy all sensibility to pleasure; and, therefore, it is corruption. It begins at the imagination and the intellect as at the core, and distributes itself thence as a paralysing venom, through the affections into the very appetites, until all become a torpid mass in which hardly sense survives. At the approach of such a period, poetry ever addresses itself to those faculties which are the last to be destroyed and its voice is heard, like the footsteps of Astraea,[2] departing from the world. Poetry ever communicates all the pleasure which men are capable of receiving: it is ever still the light of life; the source of whatever of beautiful or generous or true can have place in an evil time. It will readily be confessed that those among the luxurious citizens of Syracuse and Alexandria, who were delighted with the poems of Theocritus, were less cold, cruel, and sensual than the remnant of their tribe. But corruption must utterly have destroyed the fabric of human society before poetry can ever cease. The sacred links of that chain have never been entirely disjoined, which descending through the minds of many men is attached to those great minds, whence as from a magnet the invisible effluence is sent forth, which at once connects, animates, and sustains the life of all. It is the faculty which contains within itself the seeds at once of its own and of social renovation. And let us not circumscribe the effects of the bucolic and erotic poetry within the limits of the sensibility of those to whom it was addressed. They may have perceived the beauty of those immortal compositions, simply as fragments and isolated portions: those who are more finely organized, or born in a happier

---

[2] Daughter of Zeus and Themis, a star maiden who lived on earth during the Golden Age; at its end she was placed among the stars. (Ed.)

age, may recognize them as episodes to that great poem, which all poets, like the co-operating thoughts of one great mind, have built up since the beginning of the world. . . .

The true poetry of Rome lived in its institutions; for whatever of beautiful, true, and majestic, they contained, could have sprung only from the faculty which creates the order in which they consist. The life of Camillus, the death of Regulus; the expectation of the senators, in their godlike state, of the victorious Gauls: the refusal of the republic to make peace with Hannibal, after the battle of Cannae, were not the consequences of a refined calculation of the probable personal advantage to result from such a rhythm and order in the shows of life, to those who were at once the poets and the actors of these immortal dramas. The imagination beholding the beauty of this order, created it out of itself according to its own idea; the consequence was empire, and the reward everliving fame. These things are not the less poetry. . . . They are the episodes of that cyclic poem written by Time upon the memories of men. The Past, like an inspired rhapsodist, fills the theatre of everlasting generations with their harmony.

At length the ancient system of religion and manners had fulfilled the circle of its revolutions. And the world would have fallen into utter anarchy and darkenss, but that there were found poets among the authors of the Christian and chivalric systems of manners and religion, who created forms of opinion and action never before conceived; which, copied into the imaginations of men, become as generals to the bewildered armies of their thoughts. It is foreign to the present purpose to touch upon the evil produced by these systems: except that we protest, on the ground of the principles already established, that no portion of it can be attributed to the poetry they contain. . . .

But let us not be betrayed from a defence into a critical history of poetry and its influence on society. Be it enough to have pointed out the effects of poets, in the large and true sense of the word, upon their own and all succeeding times.

But poets have been challenged to resign the civic crown to reasoners and mechanists, on another plea. It is admitted that the exercise of the imagination is most delightful, but it is alleged that that of reason is more useful. Let us examine as the grounds of this distinction, what is here meant by utility. Pleasure or good, in a general sense, is that which the consciousness of a sensitive and intelligent being seeks, and in which, when found, it acquiesces. There are two kinds of pleasure, one durable, universal and permanent; the other transitory and particular. Utility may either express the means of producing the former or the latter. In the former sense, whatever strengthens and purifies the affections, enlarges the imagination, and adds spirit to sense, is useful. But a narrower meaning may be assigned to the word utility, confining it to express that which banishes the importunity of the wants of our animal nature, the surrounding men with security of life, the dispersing the grosser delusions of superstition, and the conciliating such a degree of mutual forbearance among men as may consist with the motives of personal advantage.

Undoubtedly the promoters of utility, in this limited sense, have their appointed office in society. They follow the footsteps of poets, and copy the sketches of their creations into the book of common life. They make space, and give time. Their exertions are of the highest value, so long as they confine their administration of the concerns of the inferior powers of our nature within the limits due to the superior ones. But whilst the sceptic destroys gross superstitions, let him spare to deface, as some of the French writers have defaced, the eternal truths charactered upon the imaginations of men. Whilst the mechanist abridges, and the political economist combines labour, let them beware that their speculations, for want of correspondence with those first principles which belong to the imagination, do not tend, as they have in modern England, to exasperate at once the extremes of luxury and want. They have exemplified the saying, "To him that hath, more shall be given; and from him that hath not, the little that he hath shall be taken away." The rich have become richer, and the poor have become poorer; and the vessel of the state is driven between the Scylla and Charybdis of anarchy and despotism. Such are the effects which must ever flow from an unmitigated exercise of the calculating faculty.

It is difficult to define pleasure in its highest sense; the definition involving a number of apparent paradoxes. For, from an inexplicable defect of harmony in the constitution of human nature, the pain of the inferior is frequently connected with the pleasures of the superior portions of our being. Sorrow, terror, anguish, despair itself, are often the chosen expressions of an approximation of the highest good. Our sympathy in tragic fiction depends on this principle; tragedy delights by affording a shadow of the pleasure which exists in pain. This is the source also of the melancholy which is inseparable from the sweetest melody. The pleasure that is in sorrow is sweeter than the pleasure of pleasure itself. And hence the saying, "It is better to go to the house of mourning, than to the house of mirth." Not that this highest species of pleasure is necessarily linked with pain. The delight of love and friendship, the ecstasy of the admiration of nature, the joy of the perception and still more of the creation of poetry, is often wholly unalloyed.

The production and assurance of pleasure in this highest sense is true utility. Those who produce and preserve this pleasure are poets or poetical philosophers.

The exertions of Locke, Hume, Gibbon, Voltaire, Rousseau,[3] and their disciples, in favour of oppressed and deluded humanity, are entitled to the gratitude of mankind. Yet it is easy to calculate the degree of moral and intellectual improvement which the world would have exhibited, had they never lived. A little more nonsense would have been talked for a century or two; and perhaps a few more men, women, and children, burnt as heretics. We might not at this moment have been congratulating each other on the abolition of the Inquisition in Spain. But it exceeds all imagination to conceive what would have been the moral condition of the world if neither Dante, Petrarch, Boccaccio, Chaucer, Shakespeare, Calderon, Lord Bacon, nor Milton, had ever existed; if Raphael and Michael Angelo had never been born; if the Hebrew poetry had never been translated; if a revival of the study of Greek literature had never taken place; if no monuments of ancient sculpture had been handed down to us; and if the poetry of the religion of the ancient world had been extinguished together with its belief. The human mind could never, except by the intervention of these excitements, have been awakened to the invention of the grosser sciences, and that application of analytical reasoning to the aberrations of society, which it is now attempted to exalt over the direct expression of the inventive and creative faculty itself.

We have more moral, political and historical wisdom, than we

[3] Although Rousseau has been thus classed, he was essentially a poet. The others, even Voltaire, were mere reasoners.

know how to reduce into practice; we have more scientific and economical knowledge than can be accommodated to the just distribution of the produce which it multiplies. The poetry in these systems of thought, is concealed by the accumulation of facts and calculating processes. There is no want of knowledge respecting what is wisest and best in morals, government, and political economy, or at least, what is wiser and better than what men now practise and endure. But we let *"I dare not* wait upon *I would,* like the poor cat in the adage."* We want the creative faculty to imagine that which we know; we want the generous impulse to act that which we imagine; we want the poetry of life: our calculations have outrun conception; we have eaten more than we can digest. The cultivation of those sciences which have enlarged the limits of the empire of man over the external world, has, for want of the poetical faculty, proportionally circumscribed those of the internal world; and man, having enslaved the elements, remains himself a slave. To what but a cultivation of the mechanical arts in a degree disproportioned to the presence of the creative faculty, which is the basis of all knowledge, is to be attributed the abuse of all invention for abridging and combining labour, to the exasperation of the inequality of mankind? From what other cause has it arisen that the discoveries which should have lightened, have added a weight to the curse imposed on Adam? Poetry, and the principle of Self, of which money is the visible incarnation, are the God and Mammon of the world.

The functions of the poetical faculty are two-fold; by one it creates new materials of knowledge and power and pleasure; by the other it engenders in the mind a desire to reproduce and arrange them according to a certain rhythm and order which may be called the beautiful and the good. The cultivation of poetry is never more to be desired than at periods when, from an excess of the selfish and calculating principle, the accumulation of the materials of external life exceed the quantity of the power of assimilating them to the internal laws of human nature. The body has then become too unwieldy for that which animates it.

Poetry is indeed something divine. It is at once the centre and circumference of knowledge; it is that which comprehends all science, and that to which all science must be referred. It is at the same time the root and blossom of all other systems of thought; it is that from which all spring, and that which adorns all; and that which, if blighted, denies the fruit and the seed, and withholds from the barren world the nourishment and the succession of the scions of the tree of life. It is the perfect and consummate surface and bloom of all things; it is as the odour and the colour of the rose to the texture of the elements which compose it, as the form and splendour of unfaded beauty to the secrets of anatomy and corruption. What were virtue, love, patriotism, friendship—what were the scenery of this beautiful universe which we inhabit; what were our consolations on this side of the grave—and what were our aspirations beyond it, if poetry did not ascend to bring light and fire from those eternal regions where the owl-winged faculty of calculation dare not ever soar? Poetry is not like reasoning, a power to be exerted according to the determination of the will. A man cannot say, "I will compose poetry." The greatest poet even cannot say it; for the mind in creation is as a fading coal, which some invisible influence, like an inconstant wind, awakens to transitory brightness; this power arises from within, like the colour of a flower which fades and changes as it is developed, and the conscious portions of our natures are unprophetic either of its approach or its departure. Could this influence be durable in its original purity and force, it is impossible to predict the greatness of the results; but when composition begins, inspiration is already on the decline, and the most glorious poetry that has ever been communicated to the world is probably a feeble shadow of the original conceptions of the poet. I appeal to the greatest poets of the present day, whether it is not an error to assert that the finest passages of poetry are produced by labour and study. The toil and the delay recommended by critics, can be justly interpreted to mean no more than a careful observation of the inspired moments, and an artificial connexion of the spaces between their suggestions by the intertexture of conventional expressions; a necessity only imposed by the limitedness of the poetical faculty itself; for Milton conceived the *Paradise Lost* as a whole before he executed it in portions. We have his own authority also for the muse having "dictated" to him the "unpremeditated song." And let this be an answer to those who would allege the fifty-six various readings of the first line of the *Orlando Furioso*. Compositions so produced are to poetry what mosaic is to painting. This instinct and intuition of the poetical faculty is still more observable in the plastic and pictorial arts; a great statue or picture grows under the power of the artist as a child in the mother's womb; and the very mind which directs the hands in formation is incapable of accounting to itself for the origin, the gradations, or the media of the process.

Poetry is the record of the best and happiest moments of the happiest and best minds. We are aware of evanescent visitations of thought and feeling sometimes associated with place or person, sometimes regarding our own mind alone, and always arising unforeseen and departing unbidden, but elevating and delightful beyond all expression: so that even in the desire and regret they leave, there cannot but be pleasure, participating as it does in the nature of its object. It is as it were the interpenetration of a diviner nature through our own; but its footsteps are like those of a wind over the sea, which the coming calm erases, and whose traces remain only, as on the wrinkled sand which paves it. These and corresponding conditions of being are experienced principally by those of the most delicate sensibility and the most enlarged imagination; and the state of mind produced by them is at war with every base desire. The enthusiasm of virtue, love, patriotism, and friendship, is essentially linked with such emotions; and whilst they last, self appears as what it is, an atom to a universe. Poets are not only subject to these experiences as spirits of the most refined organization, but they can colour all that they combine with the evanescent hues of this ethereal world; a word, a trait in the representation of a scene or a passion, will touch the enchanted chord, and reanimate, in those who have ever experienced these emotions, the sleeping, the cold, the buried image of the past. Poetry thus makes immortal all that is best and most beautiful in the world; it arrests the vanishing apparitions which haunt the interlunations of life, and veiling them, or in language or in form, sends them forth among mankind, bearing sweet news of kindred joy to those with whom their sisters abide—abide, because there is no portal of expression from the caverns of the spirit which they inhabit into the universe of things. Poetry redeems from decay the visitations of the divinity in man.

Poetry turns all things to loveliness; it exalts the beauty of that which is most beautiful, and it adds beauty to that which is most deformed; it marries exultation and horror, grief and pleasure, eternity and change; it subdues to union under its light yoke, all irreconcilable things. It transmutes all that it touches, and every form moving within the radiance of its presence is changed by wondrous sympathy to an incarnation of the spirit which it breathes: its secret alchemy turns to potable gold the poisonous waters which flow from death through life; it strips the veil of familiarity from the world, and lays bare the naked and sleeping beauty, which is the spirit of its forms.

All things exist as they are perceived; at least in relation to the percipient. "The mind is its own place, and of itself can make a heaven of hell, a hell of heaven." But poetry defeats the curse which binds us to be subjected to the accident of surrounding impressions. And whether it spreads its own figured curtain, or withdraws life's dark veil from before the scene of things, it equally creates for us a being within our being. It makes us the inhabitants of a world to which the familiar world is a chaos. It reproduces the common universe of which we are portions and percipients, and it purges from our inward sight the film of familiarity which obscures from us the wonder of our being. It compels us to feel that which we perceive, and to imagine that which we know. It creates anew the universe, after it has been annihilated in our minds by the recurrence of impressions blunted by reiteration. . . .

Poets are the hierophants of an unapprehended inspiration; the mirrors of the gigantic shadows which futurity casts upon the present; the words which express what they understand not; the trumpets which sing to battle, and feel not what they inspire; the influence which is moved not, but moves. Poets are the unacknowledged legislators of the world.

6. John Keats: Letter to Benjamin Bailey

The inclusion of a single letter by John Keats (1795–1821) does much less than justice to one of Romanticism's most attractive, most influential, and most paradigmatic figures. This young genius, who died young bravely, gave himself wholly to his art with an intensity and depth of feeling seldom matched. And in his letters, which reveal an immensely attractive personality, he gave expression to views of art and life that, whether original or derivative, were felt deeply and lived fully. Few have so entirely adopted the Romantic dedication to art as a means of knowing and shaping reality, and to feeling as the test of reality, or shown such sensitivity to the beauties of the natural world.

After his parents' death, Keats was apprenticed to a surgeon, and in 1816 was licensed as an apothecary. But by then he had begun his poetic career, and thereafter devoted himself to literature. The reviews of his early work were destructive, and he began to obtain recognition only as he neared his death. A voyage to Italy in 1820 was necessitated by the advanced stages of tuberculosis. He died in Rome in February, 1821.

The text is from *The Letters of John Keats*, 1814-1821, Volume I, edited by Hyder Edward Rollins, Harvard University Press, Cambridge, Mass., pp. 182–187. Copyright © 1958, by the President and Fellows of Harvard College, reprinted by permission of the publishers.

Address: Mr. B. Bailey/Magdalen Hall/Oxford—
Postmarks: LEATHERHEAD; O 22 NO 22 1817
MY DEAR BAILEY,

I will get over the first part of this (*un*said) [1] Letter as soon as possible for it relates to the affair of poor Crips—To a Man of your nature, such a Letter as Haydon's must have been extremely cutting—What occasions the greater part of the World's Quarrels? simply this, two Minds meet and do not understand each other time enough to p[r]aevent any shock or surprise at the conduct of either party—As soon as I had known Haydon three days I had got enough of his character not to have been surp[r]-ised at such a Letter as he has hurt you with. Nor when I knew it was it a principle with me to drop his acquaintance although with you it would have been an imperious feeling. I wish you knew all that I think about Genius and the Heart—and yet I think you are thoroughly acquainted with my innermost breast in that respect or you could not have known me even thus long and still hold me worthy to be your dear friend. In passing however I must say of one thing that has pressed upon me lately and encreased my Humility and capability of submission and that is this truth—Men of Genius are great as certain ethereal Chemicals operating on the Mass of neutral intellect—by [but] they have not any individuality, any determined Character. I would call the top and head of those who have a proper self Men of Power—

But I am running my head into a Subject which I am certain I

[1] A pun on the legal use of "said": " 'This said letter' . . . would be Haydon's to Bailey: 'this *un*said letter' " the present one.

could not do justice to under five years s[t]udy and 3 vols octavo
—and moreover long to be talking about the Imagination—so my
dear Bailey do not think of this unpleasant affair if possible—do
not—I defy any ha[r]m to come of it—I defy—I'll shall write to
Crips this Week and reque[s]t him to tell me all his goings on
from time to time by Letter wherever I may be—it will all go on
well—so dont because you have suddenly discover'd a Coldness
in Haydon suffer yourself to be teased. Do not my dear fellow. O
I wish I was as certain of the end of all your troubles as that of
your momentary start about the authenticity of the Imagination.
I am certain of nothing but of the holiness of the Heart's affections and the truth of Imagination—What the imagination seizes
as Beauty must be truth—whether it existed before or not—for I
have the same Idea of all our Passions as of Love they are all in
their sublime, creative of essential Beauty—In a Word, you may
know my favorite Speculation by my first Book and the little song
I sent in my last—which is a representation from the fancy of the
probable mode of operating in these Matters—The Imagination
may be compared to Adam's dream—he awoke and found it
truth. I am the more zealous in this affair, because I have never
yet been able to perceive how any thing can be known for truth
by consequitive reasoning—and yet it must be—Can it be that
even the greatest Philosopher ever (when) arrived at his goal
without putting aside numerous objections—However it may be,
O for a Life of Sensations rather than of Thoughts! It is "a Vision
in the form of Youth" a Shadow of reality to come—and this
consideration has further conv[i]nced me for it has come as auxil-
iary to another favorite Speculation of mine, that we shall enjoy
ourselves here after by having what we called happiness on Earth
repeated in a finer tone and so repeated—And yet such a fate can
only befall those who delight in sensation rather than hunger as
you do after Truth—Adam's dream will do here and seems to be a
conviction that Imagination and its empyreal reflection is the
same as human Life and its spiritual repetition. But as I was
saying—the simple imaginative Mind may have its rewards in the
repeti[ti]on of its own silent Working coming continually on the
spirit with a fine suddenness—to compare great things with small
—have you never by being surprised with an old Melody—in a
delicious place—by a delicious voice, fe[l]t over again your very
speculations and surmises at the time it first operated on your

soul—do you not remember forming to yourself the singer's face more beautiful that [than] it was possible and yet with the elevation of the Moment you did not think so—even then you were mounted on the Wings of Imagination so high—that the Prototype must be here after—that delicious face you will see—What a time! I am continually running away from the subject—sure this cannot be exactly the case with a complex Mind—one that is imaginative and at the same time careful of its fruits—who would exist partly on sensation partly on thought—to whom it is necessary that years should bring the philosophic Mind—such an one I consider your's and therefore it is

drink

necessary to your eternal Happiness that you not only (have) this old Wine of Heaven which I shall call the redigestion of our most ethereal Musings on Earth; but also increase in knowledge and know all things. I am glad to hear you are in a fair Way for Easter—you will soon get through your unpleasant reading and then!—but the world is full of troubles and I have not much reason to think myself pesterd with many—I think Jane or Marianne has a better opinion of me than I deserve—for really and truly I do not think my Brothers illness connected with mine—you know more of the real Cause than they do—nor have I any chance of being rack'd as you have been—you perhaps at one time thought there was such a thing as Worldly Happiness to be arrived at, at certain periods of time marked out—you have of necessity from your disposition been thus led away—I scarcely remember counting upon any Happiness—I look not for it if it be not in the present hour—nothing startles me beyond the Moment. The setting sun will always set me to rights—or if a Sparrow come before my Window I take part in its existince and pick about the Gravel. The first thing that strikes me on hea[r]ing a Misfortune having befalled another is this. "Well it cannot be helped.—he will have the pleasure of trying the resourses of his spirit, and I beg now my dear Bailey that hereafter should you observe any thing cold in me not to but [put] it to the account of heartlessness but abstraction—for I assure you I sometimes feel not the influence of a Passion or Affection during a whole week—and so long this sometimes continues I begin to suspect myself and the genuiness of my feelings at other times—thinking them a

few barren Tragedy-tears—My Brother Tom is much improved—
he is going to Devonshire—whither I shall follow him—at present I am just arrived at Dorking to change the Scene—change
the Air and give me a spur to wind up my Poem, of which there
are wanting 500 Lines. I should have been here a day sooner but
the Reynoldses persuaded me to spop [stop] in Town to meet
your friend Christie—There were Rice and Martin—we talked
about Ghosts—I will have some talk with Taylor and let you
know—when please God I come down a[t] Christmas—I will
find that Examiner if possible. My best regards to Gleig—My
Brothers to you and Mrs. Bentley

Your affectionate friend
John Keats—

I want to say much more to you—a few hints will set me going
Direct Burford Bridge near dorking

7. Victor Hugo: Preface to *Cromwell*

Victor Marie Hugo (1802–1885), was a chief spokesman for the
artistic rebellion that was French Romanticism. The production of his
play *Hernani* (1830) became the moment of battle for young artists
and authors (Berlioz, Delacroix, and Gautier supported him) against
political censorship and conservative classical criticism; whatever the
qualities of the play, it helped break the hold of classical theory and
the impress of Racine and Corneille on the French stage. Not at all
incidentally, it heralded a blurring of the distinctions that had long set
off the popular melodrama as an entertainment of the lower classes
from the high tragedy aimed at cultured audiences.

Hugo's Preface to *Cromwell* (1827) typifies its author, revealing his
self-dramatization, his flowing rhetoric, the lack of cohesiveness in his
theoretical pronouncements. Appearing just three years before *Hernani*, it purported to serve as a manifesto of a new drama. It contained
much, however, that was old: the attachment to verse, the view of the
artist as mirror, etc. But it was effectively combative. It ably appropriated the styles of argument already typical of Romanticism, such as a
foundation in history (even if the history had to be invented), and
marked as its chief traits of modernity the assimilation of a Christian
view of life into art, a plea for local color and characteristic historical
data, and praise for the irregularity of Shakespeare's genius. Others

went further, Stendhal, for instance, but few achieved such notoriety as Hugo.

Although Hugo was the son of a Napoleonic general, his Bonapartism did not survive into the Second Empire. He had been a representative in the Assembly of the Second Republic, which was overthrown by the *coup d'état* of December 1851. He went into exile, returning only with the establishment of the Third Republic in 1871. His republican politics were impassioned and histrionic, but intensely felt.

He was one of the nineteenth century's most prolific authors, a writer of immensely popular poetry in his time, and of novels—the most memorable of which are *The Hunchback of Notre Dame* and *Les Misérables*. The first showed the immense influence of Scott and of the medieval revival, the second the concern for social problems that came to dominate the novels of mid-century.

The Preface to *Cromwell* is too long to appear uncut. Chiefly, I have omitted exemplary details and a rather long discussion of the advantages of verse drama, without, I trust, disrupting the argument or distorting the tone and intent.

The text is reprinted from *The Dramatic Works of Victor Hugo*, translated by George Burnham Ives, published by Little, Brown & Company (New York, 1909), Vol. III, pp. 3, 5–8, 11–12, 17–18, 21–31, 33–35, 40–41, 47–48, 50–51.

THE DRAMA contained in the following pages has nothing to commend it to the attention or the good will of the public. It has not, to attract the interest of political disputants, the advantage of the veto of the official censorship, nor even, to win for it at the outset the literary sympathy of men of taste, the honour of having been formally rejected by an infallible reading committee. . . .

Not without some hesitation, moreover, did the author determine to burden his drama with a preface. . . .

This said, let us pass on.

Let us set out from a fact. The same type of civilization, or to use a more exact, although more extended expression, the same society, has not always inhabited the earth. The human race as a whole has grown, has developed, has matured, like one of ourselves. It was once a child, it was once a man: we are now looking on at its impressive old age. Before the epoch which modern society has dubbed "ancient," there was another epoch which the ancients called "fabulous," but which it would be more accurate to call "primitive." Now, as poetry is always superposed upon society, we propose to try to demonstrate, from the form of its society, what the character of the poetry must have been in those three great ages of the world—primitive times, ancient times, modern times.

In primitive times, when man awakes in a world that is newly created, poetry awakes with him. In the face of the marvellous things that dazzle and intoxicate him, his first speech is a hymn simply. He is still so close to God that all his meditations are ecstatic, all his dreams are visions. His bosom swells, he sings as he breathes. His lyre has but three strings—God, the soul, creation; but this threefold mystery envelops everything, this threefold idea embraces everything. The earth is still almost deserted. There are families, but no nations; patriarchs, but no kings. Each race exists at its own pleasure; no property, no laws, no contentions, no wars. Everything belongs to each and to all. Society is a community. Man is restrained in nought. He leads that nomadic pastoral life with which all civilizations begin, and which is so well adapted to solitary contemplation, to fanciful reverie. He follows every suggestion, he goes hither and thither, at random. His thought, like his life, resembles a cloud that changes its shape and its direction according to the wind that drives it. Such is the first man, such is the first poet. He is young, he is cynical. Prayer is his sole religion, the ode is his only form of poetry. . . .

By slow degrees, however, this youth of the world passes away. All the spheres progress; the family becomes a tribe, the tribe becomes a nation. Each of these groups of men camps about a common centre, and kingdoms appear. The social instinct succeeds the nomadic instinct. The camp gives place to the city, the tent to the palace, the ark to the temple. The chiefs of these nascent states are still shepherds, it is true, but shepherds of nations; the pastoral staff has already assumed the shape of a sceptre. Everything tends to become stationary and fixed. Religion takes on a definite shape; prayer is governed by rites; dogma sets bounds to worship. Thus the priest and king share the paternity of the people; thus theocratic society succeeds the patriarchal community.

Meanwhile the nations are beginning to be packed too closely on the earth's surface. They annoy and jostle one another; hence the clash of empires—war. They overflow upon another; hence, the migrations of nations—voyages. Poetry reflects these momentous events; from ideas it proceeds to things. It sings of ages, of nations, of empires. It becomes epic, it gives birth to Homer. . . .

But it is in the ancient tragedy, above all, that the epic breaks out at every turn. It mounts the Greek stage without losing aught, so to speak, of its immeasurable, gigantic proportions. Its characters are still heroes, demi-gods, gods; its themes are visions, oracles, fatality; its scenes are battles, funeral rites, catalogues. That which the rhapsodists formerly sang, the actors declaim—that is the whole difference. . . .

But the age of the epic draws near its end. Like the society that it represents, this form of poetry wears itself out revolving upon itself. Rome reproduces Greece, Virgil copies Homer, and, as if to make a becoming end, epic poetry expires in the last parturition.

It was time. Another era is about to begin, for the world and for poetry.

A spiritual religion, supplanting the material and external paganism, makes its way to the heart of the ancient society, kills it, and deposits, in that corpse of a decrepit civilization, the germ of modern civilization. This religion is complete, because it is true; between its dogma and its cult, it embraces a deep-rooted moral. And first of all, as a fundamental truth, it teaches man that he has two lives to live, one ephemeral, the other immortal; one on earth, the other in heaven. It shows him that he, like his destiny, is twofold; that there is in him an animal and an intellect, a body and a soul; in a word, that he is the point of intersection, the common link of the two chains of beings which embrace all creation—of the chain of material beings and the chain of incorporeal beings; the first starting from the rock to arrive at man, the second starting from man to end at God. . . .

Behold, then, a new religion, a new society; upon this twofold foundation there must inevitably spring up a new poetry. Previously—we beg pardon for setting forth a result which the reader has probably already foreseen from what has been said above—previously, following therein the course pursued by the ancient polytheism and philosophy, the purely epic muse of the ancients had studied nature in only a single aspect, casting aside without pity almost everything in art which, in the world subjected to its imitation, had not relation to a certain type of beauty. A type which was magnificent at first, but, as always happens with everything systematic, became in later times false, trivial and conventional. Christianity leads poetry to the truth. Like it, the modern muse will see things in a higher and broader light. It will realize that everything in creation is not humanly *beautiful*, that the ugly exists beside the beautiful, the unshapely beside the graceful, the grotesque on the reverse of the sublime, evil with good, darkness with light. It will ask itself if the narrow and relative sense of the artist should prevail over the infinite, absolute sense of the Creator; if it is for man to correct God; if a mutilated nature will be the more beautiful for the mutilation, if art has the right to duplicate, so to speak, man, life, creation; if things will progress better when their muscles and their vigour have been taken from them; if, in short, to be incomplete is the best way to be harmonious. Then it is that, with its eyes fixed upon events that are both laughable and redoubtable, poetry will take a great step, a decisive step, a step which, like the upheaval of an earthquake, will change the whole face of the intellectual world. It will set about doing as nature does, mingling in its creations—but without confounding them—darkness and light, the grotesque and the sublime; in other words, the body and the soul, the beast and the intellect; for the starting-point of religion is always the starting-point of poetry. All things are connected.

Thus, then, we see a principle unknown to the ancients, a new type, introduced in poetry; and as an additional element in anything modifies the whole of the thing, a new form of the art is developed. This type is the grotesque; its new form is comedy.

And we beg leave to dwell upon this point; for we have now indicated the significant feature, the fundamental difference which, in our opinion, separates modern from ancient art, the present form from the defunct form; or, to use less definite but more popular terms, *romantic* literature from *classical* literature.

"At last!" exclaim the people who for some time past *have seen what we were coming at,* "at last we have you—you are caught in the act. So then you put forward the ugly at a type for imitation, you make the *grotesque* an element of art. But the graces; but good taste! Don't you know that art should correct nature? that we must *ennoble* art? that we must *select?* Did the ancients ever exhibit the ugly or the grotesque? Did they ever mingle comedy and tragedy? The example of the ancients, gentlemen! And Aristotle, too; and Boileau; and La Harpe. Upon my word!"

These arguments are sound, doubtless, and, above all, of extraordinary novelty. But it is not our place to reply to them. We are constructing no system here—God protect us from systems!

We are stating a fact. We are a historian, not a critic. Whether the fact is agreeable or not matters little; it is a fact. Let us resume, therefore, and try to prove that it is of the fruitful union of the grotesque and the sublime types that modern genius is born—so complex, so diverse in its forms, so inexhaustible in its creations; and therein directly opposed to the uniform simplicity of the genius of the ancients; let us show that that is the point from which we must set out to establish the real and radical difference between the two forms of literature. . . .

It would be mere surplusage to dwell . . . upon the influence of the grotesque in the third civilization. Everything tends to show its close creative alliance with the beautiful in the so-called "romantic" period. Even among the simplest popular legends there are none which do not somewhere, with an admirable instinct, solve this mystery of modern art. Antiquity could not have produced *Beauty and the Beast.*

It is true that at the period at which we have arrived the predominance of the grotesque over the sublime in literature is clearly indicated. But it is a spasm of reaction, an eager thirst for novelty, which is but temporary; it is an initial wave which gradually recedes. The type of the beautiful will soon resume its rights and its role, which is not to exclude the other principle, but to prevail over it. It is time that the grotesque should be content with a corner of the picture in Murillo's royal frescoes, in the sacred pages of Veronese; content to be introduced in two marvellous *Last Judgments,* in which art will take a just pride, in the scene of fascination and horror with which Michelangelo will embellish the Vatican; in those awe-inspiring representations of the fall of man which Rubens will throw upon the arches of the Cathedral of Antwerp. The time has come when the balance between the two principles is to be established. A man, a poet-king, *poeta soverano,* as Dante calls Homer, is about to adjust everything. The two rival genii combine their flames, and thence issues Shakespeare.

We have now reached the poetic culmination of modern times. Shakespeare is the drama; and the drama, which with the same breath moulds the grotesque and the sublime, the terrible and the absurd, tragedy and comedy—the drama is the distinguishing characteristic of the third epoch of poetry, of the literature of the present day. . . .

The poetry born of Christianity, the poetry of our time, is, therefore, the drama; the real results from the wholly natural combination of two types, the sublime and the grotesque, which meet in the drama, as they meet in life and in creation. For true poetry, complete poetry, consists in the harmony of contraries. Hence, it is time to say aloud—and it is here above all that exceptions prove the rule—that everything that exists in nature exsists in art.

On taking one's stand at this point of view, to pass judgment on our petty conventional rules, to disentangle all those trivial problems which the critics of the last two centuries have laboriously built up about the art, one is struck by the promptitude with which the question of the modern stage is made clear and distinct. The drama has but to take a step to break all the spider's webs with which the militia of Lilliput have attempted to fetter its sleep.

And so, let addle-pated pedants (one does not exclude the other) claim that the deformed, the ugly, the grotesque should never be imitated in art; one replies that the grotesque is comedy, and that comedy apparently makes a part of art. Tartuffe is not handsome, Pourceaugnac is not noble, but Pourceaugnac and Tartuffe are admirable flashes of art.

If, driven back from this entrenchment to their second line of custom-houses, they renew their prohibition of the grotesque coupled with the sublime, of comedy melted into tragedy, we prove to them that, in the poetry of Christian nations, the first of these two types represents the human beast, the second the soul. These two stalks of art, if we prevent their branches from mingling, if we persistently separate them, will produce by way of fruit, on the one hand abstract vices and absurdities, on the other, abstract crime, heroism and virtue. The two types, thus isolated and left to themselves, will go each its own way, leaving the real between them, at the left hand of one, at the right hand of the other. Whence it follows that after all these abstractions there will remain something to represent—man; after these tragedies and comedies, something to create—the drama.

In the drama, as it may be conceived at least, if not executed, all things are connected and follow one another as in real life. The body plays its part no less than the mind; and men and events, set in motion by this twofold agent, pass across the stage, burlesque and terrible in turn, and sometimes both at once. Thus the judge will say: "Off with his head and let us go to dinner!" Thus the Roman Senate will deliberate over Domitian's turbot. Thus Socrates, drinking the hemlock and discoursing on the immortal soul and the only God, will interrupt himself to suggest that a cock be sacrificed at Æsculapius. Thus Elizabeth will swear and talk Latin. Thus Richelieu will submit to Joseph the Capuchin, and Louis XI to his barber, Maitre Olivier le Diable. Thus Cromwell will say: "I have Parliament in my bag and the King in my pocket"; or, with the hand that signed the death sentence of Charles the First, smear with ink the face of a regicide who smilingly returns the compliment. Thus Caesar, in his triumphal car, will be afraid of overturning. For men of genius, however great they be, have always within them a touch of the beast which mocks at their intelligence. Therein they are akin to mankind in general, for therein they are dramatic. "It is but a step from the sublime to the ridiculous," said Napoleon, when he was convinced that he was mere man; and that outburst of a soul on fire illumines art and history at once; that cry of anguish is the résumé of the drama and of life. . . .

We see how quickly the arbitrary distinction between the species of poetry vanishes before common sense and taste. No less easily one might demolish the alleged rule of the two unities. We say *two* and not *three* unities, because unity of plot or of *ensemble*, the only true and well-founded one, was long ago removed from the sphere of discussion.

Distinguished contemporaries, foreigners and Frenchmen, have already attacked, both in theory and in practice, that fundamental law of the pseudo-Aristotelian code. Indeed, the combat was not likely to be a long one. At the first blow it cracked, so worm-eaten was that timber of the old scholastic hovel!

The strange thing is that the slaves of routine pretend to rest their rule of the two unities on probability, whereas reality is the very thing that destroys it. Indeed, what could be more improbable and absurd than this porch or peristyle or ante-chamber— vulgar places where our tragedies are obliging enough to develop themselves; whither conspirators come, no one knows whence, to declaim against the tyrant and the tyrant to declaim against the conspirators. . . .

Where did anyone ever see a porch or peristyle of that sort? What could be more opposed—we will not say to the truth, for the scholastics hold it very cheap, but to probability? The result is that everything that is too characteristic, too intimate, too local, to happen in the ante-chamber or on the street-corner—that is to say, the whole drama—takes place in the wings. We see on the stage only the elbows of the plot, so to speak; its hands are somewhere else. Instead of scenes we have narrative; instead of tableaux, descriptions. Solemn-faced characters, placed, as in the old chorus, between the drama and ourselves, tell us what is going on in the temple, in the palace, on the public square, until we are tempted many a time to call out to them: "Indeed! then take us there! It must be very entertaining—a fine sight!" To which they would reply no doubt: "It is quite possible that it might entertain or interest you, but that isn't the question; we are the guardians of the dignity of the French Melpomene." And there you are!

"But," someone will say, "this rule that you discard is borrowed from the Greek drama." Wherein, pray, do the Greek stage and drama resemble our stage and drama? Moreover, we have already shown that the vast extent of the ancient stage enabled it to include a whole locality, so that the poet could, according to the exigencies of the plot, transport it at his pleasure from one part of the stage to another, which is practically equivalent to a change of stage-setting. Curious contradiction! the Greek theatre, restricted as it was to a national and religious object, was much more free than ours, whose only object is the enjoyment, and, if you please, the instruction, of the spectator. The reason is that the one obeys only the laws that are suited to it, while the other takes upon itself conditions of existence which are absolutely foreign to its essence. One is artistic, the other artificial.

People are beginning to understand in our day that exact localization is one of the first elements of reality. The speaking or acting characters are not the only ones who engrave on the minds of the spectators a faithful representation of the facts. The place where this or that catastrophe took place becomes a terrible and inseparable witness thereof; and the absence of silent characters of this sort would make the greatest scenes of history incomplete in the drama. Would the poet dare to murder Rizzio elsewhere than in Mary Stuart's chamber? to stab Henri IV elsewhere than in Rue de la Ferronerie, all blocked with drays and carriages? to burn Jeanne d'Arc elsewhere than in the Vieux-Marché? to despatch the Duc de Guise elsewhere than in that chateau of Blois where his ambition aroused a popular assemblage to frenzy?

to behead Charles I and Louis XVI elsewhere than in those ill-omened localities whence Whitehall or the Tuileries may be seen, as if their scaffolds were appurtenances of their palaces?

Unity of time rests on no firmer foundation than unity of place. A plot forcibly confined within twenty-four hours is as absurd as one confined within a peristyle. Every plot has its proper duration as well as its appropriate place. Think of administering the same dose of time to all events! of applying the same measure to everything! You would laugh at a cobbler who should attempt to put the same shoe on every foot. To cross unity of time and unity of place like the bars of a cage, and pedantically to introduce therein, in the name of Aristotle, all the deeds, all the nations, all the figures which Providence sets before us in such vast numbers in real life,—to proceed thus is to mutilate men and things, to cause history to make wry faces. Let us say, rather, that everything will die in the operation, and so the dogmatic mutilaters reach their ordinary result: what was alive in the chronicles is dead in tragedy. That is why the cage of the unities often contains only a skeleton. . . .

"But," the customs-officers of thought will cry, "great geniuses have submitted to these rules which you spurn!" Unfortunately, yes. But what would those admirable men have done if they had been left to themselves? At all events they did not accept your chains without a struggle. You should have seen how Pierre Corneille, worried and harassed at his first step in the art on account of his marvellous work, *Le Cid*, struggled under Mairet, Claveret, d'Aubignac and Scudéri! How he denounced to posterity the violent attacks of those men, who, he says, made themselves "all white with Aristotle!" You should read how they said to him—and we quote from books of the time: "Young man, you must learn before you teach; and unless one is a Scaliger or a Heinsius that is intolerable!" Thereupon Corneille rebels and asks if their purpose is to force him "much below Claveret." Here Scudéri waxes indignant at such a display of pride, and reminds the "thrice great author of *Le Cid* of the modest words in which Tasso, the greatest man of his age, began his apology for the finest of his works against the bitterest and most unjust censure perhaps that will ever be pronounced. M. Corneille," he adds, "shows in his replies that he is as far removed from that author's moderation as from his merit." The young man *so justly and gently reproved* dares to protest; thereupon Scudéri returns to the charge; he calls to his assistance the Eminent Academy: "Pronounce, O my Judges, a decree worthy of your eminence, which will give all Europe to know that *Le Cid* is not the *chef-d'œuvre* of the greatest man in France, but the least judicious performance of M. Corneille himself. You are bound to do it, both for your own private renown; and for that of our people in general, who are concerned in this matter; inasmuch as foreigners who may see this precious masterpiece—they who have possessed a Tasso or a Guarini—might think that our greatest masters were no more than apprentices."

These few instructive lines contain the everlasting tactics of envious routine against growing talent—tactics which are still followed in our own day, and which, for example, added such a curious page to the youthful essays of Lord Byron. Scudéri give us its quintessence. In like manner the earlier works of a man of genius are always preferred to the newer ones, in order to prove that he is going down instead of up—*Mélite* and *La Galérie de Palais* placed above *Le Cid*. And the names of the dead are always thrown at the heads of the living—Corneille stoned with Tasso and Guarini (Guarini!), as, later, Racine will be stoned with Corneille, Voltaire with Racine, and as to-day, everyone who shows signs of rising is stoned with Corneille, Racine and Voltaire. These tactics, as will be seen, are well-worn; but they must be effective as they are still in use. . . .

But still the same refrain is repeated, and will be, no doubt, for a long while to come: "Follow the rules! Copy the models! It was the rules that shaped the models." One moment! In that case there are two sorts of models, those which are made according to the rules, and, prior to them, those according to which the rules are made. Now, in which of these two categories should genius seek a place for itself? Although it is always disagreeable to come in contact with pedants, is it not a thousand times better to give them lessons than to receive lessons from them? And then—copy! Is the reflection equal to the light? Is the satellite which travels unceasingly in the same circle equal to the central creative planet? With all his poetry Virgil is no more than the moon of Homer.

And whom are we to copy, I pray to know? The ancients? We have just shown that their stage has nothing in common with ours. . . .

Whom shall we copy, then? The moderns? What! Copy copies! God forbid!

"But," someone else will object, "according to your conception of the art, you seem to look for none but great poets, to count always upon genius." Art certainly does not count upon mediocrity. It prescribes no rules for it, it knows nothing of it; in fact, mediocrity has no existence so far as art is concerned; art supplies wings, not crutches. Alas! D'Aubignac followed rules, Campistron copied models. What does it matter to Art? It does not build its palaces for ants. It lets them make their ant-hill, without taking the trouble to find out whether they have built their burlesque imitation of its palace upon its foundation.

The critics of the scholastic school place their poets in a strange position. On the one hand they cry incessantly: "Copy the models!" On the other hand they have a habit of declaring that "the models are inimitable"! Now, if their craftsman, by dint of hard work, succeeds in forcing through this dangerous defile some colourless tracing of the masters, these ungrateful wretches, after examining the new *refaccimiento,* exclaim sometimes: "This doesn't resemble anything!" and sometimes: "This resembles everything!" And by virtue of a logic made for the occasion each of these formulae is a criticism.

Let us then speak boldly. The time for it has come, and it would be strange if, in this age, liberty, like the light, should penetrate everywhere except to the one place where freedom is most natural—the domain of thought. Let us take the hammer to theories and poetic systems. Let us throw down the old plastering that conceals the facade of art. There are neither rules nor models; or, rather, there are no other rules than the general laws of nature, which soar above the whole field of art, and the special rules which result from the conditions appropriate to the subject of each composition. The former are of the essence, eternal, and do not change; the latter are variable, external, and are used but once. The former are the framework that supports the house; the latter the scaffolding which is used in building it, and which is made anew for each building. In a word, the former are the flesh and bones, the latter the clothing, of the drama. But these rules are not written in the treatises on poetry. Richelet has no idea of their existence. Genius, which divines rather than learns, devises for each work the general rules from the general plan of things, the special rules from the separate *ensemble* of the subject treated; not after the manner of the chemist, who lights the fire under his furnace, heats his crucible, analyzes and destroys; but after the manner of the bee, which flies on its golden wings, lights on each flower and extracts its honey, leaving it as brilliant and fragrant as before.

The poet—let us insist on this point—should take counsel therefore only of nature, truth, and inspiration which is itself both truth and nature. . . .

But nature! Nature and truth!—And here, in order to prove that, far from demolishing art, the new ideas aim only to reconstruct is more firmly and on a better foundation, let us try to point out the impassable limit which in our opinion, separates reality according to art from reality according to nature. It is careless to confuse them as some ill-informed partisans of *romanticism* do. Truth in art cannot possibly be, as several writers have claimed, *absolute* reality. Art cannot produce the thing itself. Let us imagine, for example, one of those unreflecting promoters of absolute nature, of nature viewed apart from art, at the performance of the romantic play, say *Le Cid*. "What's that?" he will ask at the first word. "The Cid speaks in verse? It isn't *natural* to speak in verse." —"How would you have him speak, pray?"—"In prose." Very good. A moment later, "How's this?" he will continue if he is consistent; "the Cid is speaking French!"—"Well?"—"Nature demands that he speak his own language; he can't speak anything but Spanish."

We shall fail entirely to understand, but again—very good. You imagine that this is all? By no means: before the tenth sentence in Castillian, he is certain to rise and ask if the Cid who is speaking is the real Cid, in flesh and blood. By what right does the actor, whose name is Pierre or Jacques take the name of the Cid? That is *false*. There is no reason why he should not go on to demand that the sun should be substituted for the footlights, *real* trees and *real* houses for those deceitful wings. For, once started on that road, logic has you by the collar, and you cannot stop.

We must admit, therefore, or confess ourselves ridiculous, that the domains of art and of nature are entirely distinct. Nature and art are two things—were it not so, one or the other would not exist. Art, in addition to its idealistic side, has a terrestrial, material side. Let it do what it will, it is shut in between grammar and prosody, between Vaugeles and Richelet. For its most capricious creations, it has formulae, methods of execution, a complete apparatus to set in motion. For genius there are delicate instruments, for mediocrity, tools.

It seems to us that someone has already said that the drama is a mirror wherein nature is reflected. But if it be an ordinary mirror, a smooth and polished surface, it will give only a dull image of objects, with no relief—faithful, but colourless; everyone knows that colour and light are lost in a simple reflection. The drama, therefore, must be a concentrating mirror, which, instead of weakening, concentrates and condenses the coloured rays, which makes of a mere gleam a light, and of a light a flame. Then only is the drama acknowledged by art.

The stage is an optical point. Everything that exists in the world—in history, in life, in man—should be and can be reflected therein, but under the magic wand of art. Art turns the leaves of the ages, of nature, studies chronicles, strives to reproduce actual facts (especially in respect to manners and peculiarities, which are much less exposed to doubt and contradiction than are concrete facts), restores what the chroniclers have lopped off, harmonises what they have collected, divines and supplies their omissions, fills their gaps with imaginary scenes which have the colour of the time, groups what they have left scattered about, sets in motion anew the threads of Providence which work the human marionettes, clothes the whole with a form at once poetical and natural, and imparts to it that vitality of truth and brilliancy which gives birth to illusion, that prestige of reality which arouses the enthusiasm of the spectator, and of the poet first of all, for the poet is sincere. Thus the aim of art is almost divine; to bring to life again if it is writing history, to create if it is writing poetry.

It is a grand and beautiful sight to see this broad development of a drama wherein art powerfully seconds nature; of a drama wherein the plot moves on to the conclusion with a firm and unembarrassed step, without diffuseness and without undue compression; of a drama, in short, wherein the poet abundantly fulfills the multifold object of art, which is to open to the spectator a double prospect, to illuminate at the same time the interior and the exterior of mankind: the exterior by their speech and their acts, the interior, by asides and monologues; to bring together, in a word, in the same picture, the drama of life and the drama of conscience.

It will readily be imagined that, for a work of this kind, if the poet must choose (and he must), he should choose, not the *beautiful*, but the *characteristic*. Not that it is advisable to "make local colour," as they say to-day; that is, to add as an afterthought a few discordant touches here and there to a work that is at best utterly conventional and false. The local colour should not be on the surface of the drama, but in its substance, in the very heart of the work, whence it spreads of itself, naturally, evenly, and, so to speak, into every corner of the drama, as the sap ascends from the root to the tree's topmost leaf. The drama should be thoroughly impregnated with this colour of the time, which should be, in some sort, in the air, so that one detects it only on entering the theater, and that on going forth one finds one's self in a different period and atmosphere. It requires some study, some labour, to attain this end; so much the better. It is well that the avenues of art should be obstructed by those brambles from which everybody recoils except those of powerful will. Besides, it is this very study, fostered by an ardent inspiration, which will ensure the drama against a vice that kills it—the *commonplace*. To be commonplace is the failing of short-sighted, short-breathed poets. In this tableau of the stage, each figure must be held down to its most prominent, most individual, most precisely defined characteristic. Even the vulgar and the trivial should have an accent of their own. Like God, the true poet is present in every part of his work at once. Genius resembles the die which stamps the king's effigy on copper and golden coins alike.

We do not hesitate—and this will demonstrate once more to honest men how far we are from seeking to discredit the art—we do not hesitate to consider verse as one of the means best adapted to protect the drama from the scourge we have just mentioned, as one of the most powerful dams against the irruption of the commonplace, which, like democracy, is always flowing between full banks in men's minds. . . .

However, whether the drama should be written in prose is only a secondary question. The rank of a work is certain to be fixed, not according to its form, but according to its intrinsic value. In questions of this sort, there is only one solution. There is but one weight that can turn the scale in the balance of art—that is genius.

Meanwhile, the first, the indispensable merit of a dramatic writer, whether he write in prose or verse, is correctness. Not a mere superficial correctness, the merit or defect of the descriptive school, which makes Lhomond and Restaut the two wings of its Pegasus; but that intimate, deep-rooted, deliberate correctness, which is permeated with the genius of language, which has sounded its roots and searched its etymology; always unfettered, because it is sure of its footing, and always more in harmony with the logic of the language. Our Lady Grammar leads the one in leading-strings; the other holds grammar in leash. It can venture anything, can create or invent its style; it has a right to do so. For, whatever certain men may have said who did not think what they were saying, and among whom we must place, notably, him who writes these lines, the French tongue is not *fixed* and never will be. A language does not become fixed. The human intellect is always on the march, or, if you prefer, in movement, and languages with it. Things are made so. When the body changes how could the coat not change? The French of the nineteenth century can no more be the French of the eighteenth, than that is the French of the seventeenth, or than the French of the seventeenth is that of the sixteenth. Montaigne's language is not Rabelais's, Pascal's is not Montaigne's, Montesquieu's is not Pascal's. Each of the four languages, taken by itself, is admirable because it is original. Every age has its own ideas; it must have also words adapted to those ideas. Languages are like the sea, they move to and fro incessantly. At certain times they leave one shore of the world of thought and overflow another. All that their waves thus abandon dries up and vanishes. It is in this wise that ideas vanish, that words disappear. It is the same with human tongues as with everything. What can be done? It is the decree of fate. In vain, therefore, should we seek to petrify the mobile physiognomy of our idiom in a fixed form. In vain do our literary Joshuas cry out to the language to stand still; languages and the sun do not stand still. The day when they become *fixed*, they are dead.—That is why the French of a certain contemporary school is a dead language. . . .

It is evident that, in its present proportions, this drama could not be given at one of our theatrical performances. It is too long. The reader will perhaps comprehend, none the less, that every part of it was written for the stage. It was on approaching his subject to study it that the author recognized, or thought that he recognized, the impossibility of procuring the performance of a faithful reproduction of it on our stage, in the exceptional position it now occupies, between the academic Charybdis and the administrative Scylla, between the literary juries and the political censorship. He was required to choose: either the wheedling, tricky, false tragedy, which may be acted, or the audaciously true drama, which is prohibited. The first was not worth the trouble of writing, so he preferred to attempt the second. That is why, hopeless of ever being put on the stage, he abandoned himself, freely and submissively, to the whims of composition, to the pleasure of painting with a freer hand, to the developments which his subject demanded, and which, even if they keep his drama off the stage, have at all events the advantage of making it almost complete from the historical standpoint. However, the reading committees are an obstacle of the second class only. If it should happen that the dramatic censorship, realizing how far this harmless, conscientious and accurate picture of Cromwell and his time is removed from our own age, should sanction its production on the stage, in that case, but only in that case, the author might perhaps extract from this drama a play which would venture to show itself on the boards, and would be hissed. . . .

There is to-day the old literary régime as well as the old political régime. The last century still weighs upon the present one at almost every point. It is notaby oppressive in the matter of criticism. For instance, you find living men who repeat to you this definition of taste let fall by Voltaire: "Taste in poetry is no different from what it is in women's clothes." Taste, then, is coquetry. Remarkable words, which depict marvellously the painted, *moucheté*, powdered poetry of the eighteenth century—that literature in paniers, pompons and falbalas. They give an admirable résumé of an age with which the loftiest geniuses could not come in contact without becoming petty, in one respect of another; of an age when Montesquieu was able and apt to produce *Le Temple de Gnide*, Voltaire *Le Temple du Goût*, Jean-Jacques [Rousseau] *Le Devin du Village*.

Taste is the common sense of genius. This is what will soon be demonstrated by another school of criticism, powerful, outspoken, well-formed,—a school of the century which is beginning to put forth vigorous shoots under the dead and withered branches of the old school. This youthful criticism, as serious as the other is frivolous, as learned as the other is ignorant, has already established organs that are listened to, and one is sometimes surprised to find, even in the least important sheets, excellent articles emanating from it. Joining hands with all that is fearless and superior in letters, it will deliver us from two scourges: tottering *classicism*, and false *romanticism*, which has the presumption to show itself at the feet of the true. For modern genius already has its shadow, its copy, its parasite, its *classic*, which forms itself upon it, smears itself with its colours, assumes its livery, picks up its crumbs, and *like the sorcerer's pupil*, puts in play, with words retained by the memory, elements of theatrical action of which it has not the secret. Thus it does idiotic things which its master many a time has much difficulty in making good. But the thing that must be destroyed first of all is the old false taste. Present-day literature must be cleansed of its rust. In vain does the rust eat into it and tarnish it. It is addressing a young, stern, vigorous generation, which does not understand it. The train of the eighteenth century is still dragging in the nineteenth; but we, we young men who have seen Bonaparte, are not the ones who will carry it.

8. Charles Baudelaire: "The Salon of 1846"

Charles Baudelaire (1821–1867) is one of the latest figures included in this volume. His work is transitional. His poetry, as in *Les Fleurs du mal*, is usually classed with that of the Symbolists. Yet his adulation of Delacroix, France's greatest Romantic painter, and the real critical insight with which he brought the qualities of Delacroix and others of that generation to public attention make him also a spokesman for Romantic painting. He was a great art critic, stressing the immense importance of original creative genius and urging a view of imagination that echoes Coleridge's concept. For Baudelaire, the artist took rank as a profound truthteller—as he does for Shelley—but of a truth far different from the philosopher's. As a critic, he sought to share some of the artist's effort to counteract the materialism of the age, a task to be performed by fulfilling his duty toward art, not toward philosophy, politics, or society.

Baudelaire also served as France's main popularizer of the works and ideas of Poe, in what was one of the great international ifluences of its kind.

He was troubled throughout his life by poverty and illness. His work reveals his profound sensitivity, his distaste for nature's senselessness, his pessimism and his horror of life. There is also an attraction to the horrible, and an inclination to taste and test all illicit and extreme sensual possibilities, to shock, to rebel.

The brief selection that follows is from his art criticism, "The Salon of 1846," from *The Mirror of Art*, translated and edited by Jonathan Mayne (Doubleday Anchor Books, Doubleday & Co., Inc., Garden City, N.Y., 1956), pp. 43–45, reprinted by permission of the publishers.

What Is Romanticism?

FEW PEOPLE today will want to give a real and positive meaning to this word; and yet will they dare assert that a whole generation would agree to join a battle lasting several years for the sake of a flag which was not also a symbol?

If you think back to the disturbances of those recent times, you will see that if few romantics have survived, it is because few of them discovered romanticism, though all of them sought it sincerely and honestly.

Some applied themselves only to the choice of subjects; but they had not the temperament for their subjects. Others, still believing in a Catholic society, sought to reflect Catholicism in their works. But to call oneself a romantic and to look systematically at the past is to contradict oneself. Some blasphemed the Greeks and the Romans in the name of romanticism: but you can only make Romans and Greeks into romantics if you are one yourself. Many others have been misled by the idea of truth in art, and local colour. Realism had already existed for a long time when that great battle took place, and besides, to compose a tragedy or a picture to the requirements of M. Raoul Rochette is to expose yourself to a flat contradiction from the first comer if he is more learned than M. Raoul Rochette.[1]

Romanticism is precisely situated neither in choice of subjects nor in exact truth, but in a mode of feeling.

[1] A well-known archaeologist (1789–1854), who held several important positions, and published many books on his subject.

They looked for it outside themselves, but it was only to be found within.

For me, Romanticism is the most recent, the latest expression of the beautiful.

There are as many kinds of beauty as there are habitual ways of seeking happiness.

This is clearly explained by the philosophy of progress; thus, as there have been as many ideals as there have been ways in which the peoples of the earth have understood ethics, love, religion, etc., so romanticism will not consist in a perfect execution, but in a conception analogous to the ethical disposition of the age.

It is because some have located it in a perfection of technique that we have had the *rococo* of romanticism, without question the most intolerable of all forms.

Thus it is necessary, first and foremost, to get to know those aspects of nature and those human situations which the artists of the past have disdained or have not known.

To say the word Romanticism is to say modern art—that is, intimacy, spirituality, colour, aspiration towards the infinite, expressed by every means available to the arts.

Thence it follows that there is an obvious contradiction between romanticism and the works of its principal adherents.

Does it surprise you that colour should play such a very important part in modern art? Romanticism is a child of the North, and the North is all for colour; dreams and fairy-tales are born of the mist. England—that home of fanatical colourists, Flanders and half of France are all plunged in fog; Venice herself lies steeped in her lagoons. As for the painters of Spain, they are painters of contrast rather than colourists.

The South, in return, is all for nature; for there nature is so beautiful and bright that nothing is left for man to desire, and he can find nothing more beautiful to invent than what he sees. There art belongs to the open air; but several hundred leagues to the north you will find the deep dreams of the studio and the gaze of the fancy lost in horizons of grey.

The South is as brutal and positive as a sculptor even in his most delicate compositions; the North, suffering and restless, seeks comfort with the imagination, and if it turns to sculpture, it will more often be picturesque than classical.

Raphael, for all his purity, is but an earthly spirit ceaselessly investigating the solid; but that scoundrel Rembrandt is a sturdy idealist who makes us dream and guess at what lies beyond. The first composes creatures in a pristine and virginal state—Adam and Eve; but the second shakes his rags before our eyes and tells us of human sufferings.

And yet Rembrandt is not a pure colourist, but a harmonizer. How novel then would be the effect, and how matchless his romanticism, if a powerful colourist could realize our dearest dreams and feelings for us in a colour appropriate to their subjects!

But before passing on to an examination of the man who up to the present is the most worthy representative of romanticism, I should like to give you a series of reflections on colour, which will not be without use for the complete understanding of this little book.

Part II: *Religion*

---

9. Novalis: "Christendom or Europe"

Friedrich Philipp von Hardenberg (1772–1801) was another of the young artists of the Romantic era who died at a tragically early age as a result of consumption. He was of noble Saxon descent. He studied under tutors before undertaking legal studies at Jena, Leipzig, and Wittenberg. In 1794, having completed his legal preparation, he began to work at a minor government post and later served in the administration of the salt mines of the Elector of Saxony. For his literary career, he adopted the pen name "Novalis," which was derived from the medieval name of some family connections.

Most of his writing was done after 1797, when he became a part of the Romantic circle that formed around the Schlegel brothers at Jena, a group that included Schleiermacher and Tieck. Novalis's verse and prose express and exemplify much of the theory of the Romantic school just as it was being formulated, a formulation in which he took part. He glorified the heart and the feelings and the poetic spirit as necessary to balance the cold, scientific rationality of the Enlightenment, and he worked freely in the world of myth.

His "Christendom or Europe" is mythical to a degree, though its tone is predominantly that of mere exposition until the final description of the coming age of faith. The portrayal of the spiritual unity of the Middle Ages is an expression of the growing glorification of the age of faith and papal dominion, well before historical scholarship cast cold water on that image (the scholarship itself grew largely out of the revived interest Novalis exemplifies). The need for a new faith and the description of the symptoms that demand it will be seen echoed in such diverse places as the work of the Saint-Simonians and of Mickiewicz.

The selection is from *The Political Thought of the German Romantics*, edited by H. S. Reiss (New York, 1955), pp. 126–141, reprinted by permission of the publishers, Barnes & Noble, Inc., in New York and Basil Blackwell, in Great Britain.

THOSE WERE fine, magnificent times when Europe was a Christian
country, when one Christendom inhabited this civilized continent
and one great common interest linked the most distant provinces of this vast spiritual empire.—Dispensing with great secular
possessions, *one* sovereign governed and united the great political
forces.—Immediately under him was an enormous guild, open to
all, which carried out his commands and eagerly strove to con-
solidate his beneficent power. Every member of this society was
everywhere honoured; and if the common people sought from him
comfort or help, protection or advice, gladly and generously ten-
dering to his various needs, by way of recompense, he in his turn
gained protection, respect, and audience from his superiors. They
were the elect, armed with miraculous powers and treated as
children of heaven, whose presence and affection dispensed manifold blessings. Their proclamations inspired childlike faith. Mankind could serenly go about its daily business on earth, for these
holy men safeguarded the future, forgave every sin and obliter-
ated and transfigured all life's discolorations. They were the experienced pilots on the vast uncharted seas in whose care mankind could disparage all storms and count on safely reaching and
landing on the shores of its true home. The wildest and most
insatiable desires had to yield to the reverence and obedience
commanded by their words. Peace emanated from them.—They
preached nothing but love of our holy and beautiful lady of
Christendom, who, endowed with divine power, was ready to
rescue every believer from the most terrible dangers. They told of
saintly men, long dead, who had resisted earthly temptations
through their attachment and fidelity to the blessed mother and
her sweet, celestial child, and who had thus attained divine
honour and were now beneficent protectors of their living brethren, willing helpers in need, intercessors for human frailties and
the powerful friends of mankind before the throne of heaven.
With what serenity did men leave beautiful congregations in
churches full of mystery, adorned with stirring pictures, filled
with sweet fragrance and enriched by sacred exalting music.
There the consecrated relics of former godfearing persons were
gratefully preserved in precious containers.—And the divine
goodness and omnipotence, the beneficent might of these blessed

pious beings were revealed in these relics through glorious miracles and signs. In the same way, lovers keep a lock of hair or the
letters of their dead sweethearts and sustain their sweet ardour
with such objects till death reunites them. Everything that had
belonged to these beloved persons was collected with ardent care,
and to obtain or even only to touch so consoling a relic was
accounted the greatest good fortune. Now and then divine grace
seemed to have visited some strange image or tomb in particular,
to which men flocked from all parts with beautiful offerings and
departed having received heaven's gifts of inner peace and bodily
health in return. This mighty peace-loving society assiduously
sought to let all men share this beautiful faith, and sent its members into all continents of the world to proclaim everywhere the
gospel of life and to make the kingdom of heaven the only kingdom in this world. The wise sovereign of the Church rightly opposed any presumptuous development of human capacities at the
expense of religious sense as also any untimely and dangerous
discoveries in the sphere of knowledge. Thus he forbade bold
thinkers to assert publicly that the earth is merely an insignificant
planet, for he knew well that men in losing their respect for their
residence and their earthly home would also lose respect for their
celestial home and for their race. They would prefer limited knowledge to infinite faith and come to despise all that is great and awe-
inspiring, regarding it merely as the dead effect of scientific law.
All the wise and respected men of Europe assembled at his court.
All treasures flowed thither, destroyed Jerusalem was avenged
and Rome itself became Jerusalem, the sacred seat of divine rule
on earth. Princes submitted their disputes to the father of Christendom, willingly laid their crowns and their magnificence at his
feet, and indeed considered it an augmentation of their glory to
spend as members of this high guild the evening of their lives in
divine meditation within the solitary walls of monasteries. How
beneficent this government was, how appropriate this institution
to man's inner nature is shown by the powerful aspirations of all
other human forces, the harmonious development of all abilities,
the immense height reached by individuals in all spheres of the
sciences of life and of the arts, and by the trade in spiritual and
physical goods which flourished everywhere in Europe and as far
as the most distant Indies.

Such were the main features of this truly Catholic and Christian age. But mankind was not yet mature or educated enough for this splendid kingdom. It was a first love that died under the pressure of commercial life, a love whose memory was ousted by egotistical cares and whose bond was afterwards denounced as a deceit and an illusion and condemned in the light of later experiences; and then destroyed for ever by a large section of Europeans. This great inner schism accompanied as it was by destructive wars was a remarkable sign of what culture can do to spiritual awareness, or at least of the temporary harmfulness of culture at a certain level. That eternal awareness cannot be destroyed, but it can be dimmed, paralyzed and displaced by other senses. In an old community spiritual inclinations and pride of race diminish and men grow accustomed to applying all their thoughts and endeavours solely to the means of achieving comfort; their needs and the arts of satisfying them become more complicated; avaricious man needs so much time to acquaint himself with these arts and to acquire skill in their exercise, that no time remains for quiet recollection, for attentive contemplation of the inner world. In cases of conflict present interest seems to mean more to him; so the beautiful flowers of his youth, faith and love, wilt and give way to the cruder fruits of knowledge and possession. In late autumn people look back on spring as on a childish dream and hope naïvely that the filled granaries will last for ever. Some degree of solitude seems necessary for the development of higher insight, and if the world is too much with us we must suffocate many a seed of spiritual growth and drive away the gods who flee the restless tumult of social distractions and the negotiation of petty affairs. Besides, we are dealing with times and periods which surely must be cyclic, an alternation of opposite tendencies? Is it not their very nature to be impermanent, to wax and to wane, and is not also a resurrection, a rejuvenation in new and vital form certainly to be expected of them with complete certainty. Progressive, ever-increasing evolutions on an ever-increasing scale are the stuff of history.

What has not so far reached perfection will do so in a future attempt or in one later still; nothing that history has seized upon is ephemeral; it re-emerges renewed in ever richer forms from countless metamorphoses. Having appeared once in full power and glory, Christianity ruled until the time of the next world inspiration as a ruin, as the mere letter of the law, in ever-increasing impotence and mockery. An infinite inertia lay heavy on the guild of a clergy grown too secure. They stagnated in authority and comfort, while the laity snatched from them the torch of experience and learning and far outstripped them on the path of education. Forgetting their real office to be the first among men in spirit, insight and education, they let unworthy inclinations prevail over them; and the baseness and meanness of their outlook was the more repugnant in being associated with the priestly vestment and vocation. Thus respect and confidence, the pillars of this as of every empire, crumbled away, undermining the guild and silently destroying the real power of Rome long before the actual revolution. Only expedient, i.e. temporary measures preserved the corpse of the constitution from too speedy a dissolution; in particular, the abolition of the right of priests to marry. A measure, which if analogously applied to the similar class of soldiers could give this class a terrible coherence and prolong its life considerably. What was more natural than that a fiery agitator should finally preach open rebellion against the despotic letter of the former constitution, and all the more successfully for being himself a member of the guild.

The insurgents rightly called themselves Protestants, for they were solemnly protesting against the presumptuousness of a seemingly tyrannous and illegitimate power to rule over conscience. For the time being they reassumed their right to investigate, determine and choose their religion, a right which had been tacitly surrendered to an authority now considered to have lapsed. They also established a number of sound principles, introduced a number of praiseworthy measures and abolished a number of pernicious articles; but they forgot the inevitable consequences of their actions; separating the inseparable, they divided the indivisible Church and unforgivably divorced themselves from the general body of Christianity, through and in which alone genuine and lasting rebirth was possible. A state of religious anarchy must be no more than temporary, for the basic need to dedicate a number of men solely to this high vocation and to make them independent of secular power in this respect remains present and valid.

The setting up of consistories and the retention of a kind of clergy did not answer this need and was no satisfactory substitute. Unfortunately heads of states had intervened in this schism, and many of them used these disputes to secure and extend their power and revenue as territorial princes. Glad to be rid of papal influence, they took the new consistories under their own wing and were passionately concerned to prevent any complete reunion of the Protestant churches. With this irreligious enclosure of religion within the state boundaries, the ground was thus prepared for a gradual undermining of religious cosmopolitanism that deprived religion of its great political influence as peacemaker, its specific function as the uniting, individualizing principle, as Christendom. Religious peace was concluded according to completely mistaken and anti-religious principles. The continuation of so-called Protestantism involved the sheer self-contradiction of perpetrating revolutionary government.

Protestantism, however, is not based solely on the pure concept of protest, for Luther treated Christianity generally in a cavalier fashion; failing to recognize its true spirit, he introduced another law and another religion, namely the sacred universal authority of the Bible, with the unfortunate result of bringing a wholly alien science—philology—into religious matters. Its corrupting influence becomes unmistakable from that time onward. As if obscurely aware of this error, a large section of Protestants raised Luther himself to the rank of an evangelist and canonized his translation.

A choice fatal to the religious sense had been made, since nothing destroys its sensitivity so much as the letter of the law. Previously the letter could never have been so harmful, for the Catholic faith was so comprehensive, flexible and rich in content. The Bible had been made esoteric and the councils and the supreme pontiff still wielded their sacred power; but now with the destruction of these antidotes and the absolute vulgarization of the Bible the latter's meagre content and the crude, abstract schematization of religion became all the more obviously oppressive and made free animation, penetration and revelation on the part of the Holy Ghost infinitely more difficult.

The history of Protestantism, therefore, records no more splendid manifestations of the Supernatural; at the outset it was briefly illumined by a fire from heaven, but the source of holy inspiration was soon seen to run dry. Secular power began to rule, the artistic sense suffers in sympathy with religion; and only rarely does a pure, eternal spark of life emerge and a small community come into being. This spark is extinguished, and the community is split up again and borne away by the stream, as happened with Zinzendorf, Jacob Boehme, and several others. The moderate thinkers retain the upper hand and the age approaches a complete atony of the higher organs, a period of practical unbelief. With the Reformation Christendom was lost, and from that time onward it no longer existed. Catholics and Protestants or Calvinists stood further apart from one another than they did from Mohammedans and Pagans. The remaining Catholic states continued to stagnate, imperceptibly reacting to the harmful influence of the neighbouring Protestant states. Modern Politics originated first during this period, and individual powerful states sought to occupy the vacant universal seat of authority, of which the royal throne was now a symbol.

Most princes considered it degrading to concern themselves with an enfeebled clergy. They felt for the first time the full measure of their power on earth, they saw the heavenly might inactive against the abuse of its representatives on earth, and gradually sought to throw off the burdensome Roman yoke and to make themselves independent on earth, without bringing this to the attention of their still zealously papist subjects. Their uneasy consciences were calmed by clever pastors who lost nothing by the fact that their spiritual children took upon themselves the right of disposing of the Church's wealth.

It was fortunate for tradition that a new order now arose and became active. The dying spirit of the hierarchy seemed to have imparted to it the remnants of its genius, rearming the old order with new strength, and with wonderful insight and perseverance espousing the cause of the Papal realm and its more powerful regeneration. No such society had previously been found in the history of the world. The ancient Roman senate itself had not designed plans for the conquest of the world with greater security of success. Never before had a greater idea been executed with such profound judgement. This society will always be a model for all societies which feel an organic yearning for infinite expansion and eternal duration—but it will also demonstrate that the unguarded moment alone foils even the most clever enterprises and that the natural growth of a whole race irresistibly suppresses the artificial growth of one of its parts. All individual things have in themselves their own measure of capability, only the capacity of the race is immeasurable. All plans must fail if they do not take into consideration the talents of the race in their entirety. This society becomes even more remarkable as mother of those societies which we term secret, a still immature, but certainly important seed of historical growth. The new Lutheranism, not Protestantism, could certainly not have found a more dangerous rival. The whole spell of the Catholic faith became still more powerful in its hand, the treasures of the sciences flowed back into its cell. They sought to regain a hundredfold what had been lost in Europe, in other parts of the world, in the most distant west and east, and furthermore to assume the Apostolic dignity and vocation and maintain its rights. They, too, did not fall behind in striving for popularity, for they knew only too well how much Luther owed to his demagogic arts, to his study of the common people. Everywhere they founded schools, infiltrated the confessionals, mounted the lecturing desks and kept the printing presses busy; they became poets and sages, ministers and martyrs; in their tremendous extension from America via Europe to China they maintained a unique balance of action and doctrine. From their schools they selected and recruited their order. They preached with destructive zeal against the Lutherans and sought to make it the most urgent duty of Catholic Christendom to exterminate these heretics as the devil's own companions in the most cruel manner. The Catholic states and especially the papal chair owed it solely to them that they long survived the Reformation. Who knows how ancient the world would still be, if weak superiors, jealousy of princes and of other ecclesiastic orders, court intrigues and unusual circumstances had not interrupted their bold course and almost destroyed with them this last protective defence of the Catholic constitution. Now this formidable order lies dormant in a miserable condition at the frontiers of Europe; perhaps under another name it will one day spread thence with new force over its old home, like the people that protect it.

The Reformation had been a sign of the age. It was important for the whole of Europe, though it had been broken out publicly only in a free Germany. The best minds of all the nations had secretly reached maturity and in the delusive feeling of their vocation rebelled all the more boldly against out-dated compulsion. The scholar is instinctively the enemy of the clergy according to the old constitution; if they are divided the learned and clerical classes must wage wars of extermination against each other; for they are fighting for the same position. This division became increasingly prominent, and the nearer the history of Europe approached the age of triumphant learning, the more science and faith came into decisive opposition and the more ground did the scholars win. Faith was held responsible for the general stagnation, and it was hoped that an all-penetrating knowledge would bring it to an end. Everywhere religious life suffered from the manifold persecutions of its own previous nature and temporal personality. The result of the modern mode of thought was called philosophy and included everything which was antagonistic to the old order, especially attacks on religion. What started as a personal hatred against the Catholic faith gradually changed into a hatred against the Bible, against the Christian faith and finally against religion itself. Further religious hatred extended very naturally and consequently to all objects of enthusiasm, and denounced imagination and feeling, morality and the love of art, the future and the past as heretical, and gave man the highest place in the order of natural beings. Out of the infinite creative music of the universe it made a uniform rattling of a gigantic mill, which, driven by the current of chance in which it floated, is supposed to be a mill-in-itself, without builder and miller and thus truly a genuine *perpetuum mobile*, a mill grinding itself.

One enthusiasm was generously left to the miserable human race and as a touchstone of the highest education was made indispensable to everyone thus concerned—namely, the enthusiasm for this grand and magnificent philosophy and more especially for its priests and mystagogues. France was so fortunate as to become the source and seat of this new faith, which was pieced together from mere knowledge. However ill-reputed poetry was in this new church, there were, nevertheless, a few poets among them who, for the sake of effect, still used the old ornamentation and the old light, but in doing so ran the danger of kindling the new world system with the old fire. Wiser members, however, knew how to pour cold water on the listeners who had already been inspired. The members were unceasingly occupied with purging poetry from nature, from the soil, from human souls and from the sciences, exterminating all traces of the sacred, polluting the memory of exalting events and men by means of their sarcasm, and robbing the world of all its motley ornamentation. Light became their favourite subject on account of its mathematical obedience and freedom of movement. They were more interested in the refraction of its rays than in the play of its colours, and thus they named after it their great enterprise, enlightenment. In Germany this enterprise was carried on more thoroughly; the educational system was reformed, attempts were made to give the old religion a more modern, rational and universal sense by carefully divesting it of everything wonderful and mysterious; all learning was put to the one use of cutting any refuge in history, by seeking to ennoble history as a domestic and civil portrait of morals and families. God was made an idle spectator of this great moving pageant in which the scholars performed. He became, in the end, the servant and admirer of poets and players. They took pleasure in enlightening the common people and in training them to this cultured enthusiasm. Thus arose a new European guild of philanthropists and men of enlightenment. It is a pity that nature remained so wonderful and incomprehensible, so poetical and infinite, defying all attempts to modernize it. If anywhere there arose an ancient superstition about a higher world or something similar, alarm was immediately sounded on all sides and, if possible, the dangerous spark was suppressed by philosophy and wit; nevertheless, tolerance was the watchword of the educated, and especially in France it was synonymous with philosophy. This history of modern scepticism is the key to all the monstrous phenomena of the modern age, and only in this century and especially in its latter half has it begun to grow to an immense size and variety. A second reformation more far-reaching and more characteristic was unavoidable, inevitably affecting first that country which was most modernized and which had lain longest in an asthenic state as a result of lack of freedom. The supernatural fire would long since have found release and foiled the clever plans of enlightenment, had they not been supported by the pressure and influence of secular power. But at the very moment when a dispute arose among scholars and governments, among the enemies of religion and their whole confederacy, religion had to step forward again as a third principal intermediary; every one of its friends must now recognize and proclaim its appearance, even if he has not previously been sufficiently attentive. No historically-minded person can doubt that the age of resurrection has arrived, and that precisely the events which appeared to be directed against its renaissance and which threatened to complete its decline, have become the most favourable signs of its regeneration. True anarchy begets religion and from the destruction of everything positive it raises its glorious head as the maker of a new world. As if by his own power, man ascends unfettered towards heaven, the higher faculties sever themselves from the common uniform mixture, from the complete dissolution of all human talents and forces, and become apparent as the original kernel of earthly formation. The spirit of God hovers over the waters, and a celestial island becomes visible for the first time over the receding wave as the dwelling-place of new men, as the region of the flux of eternal life.

Let the genuine observer regard the new revolutionary times calmly and impartially. Does not the revolutionary appear to him like Sisyphus? Now he has attained the summit of his equilibrium and the mighty burden rolls down on the other side. It will never remain on high unless an attraction towards heaven keeps it balanced at the summit. All your pillars are too weak, if your state retains its attraction towards the earth. But, in linking it to the heights of heaven by a nobler aspiration and by relating it to the universe, you will find in it a never-tiring spring and your endeavours will be richly rewarded. I refer you to history; search in its instructive continuity for similar moments and learn to use the magic wand of analogy.

Shall the revolution remain the French Revolution, as the Reformation was the Lutheran reformation? Shall Protestantism once more be established contrary to nature as a revolutionary government? Is the letter without the spirit merely to replace another letter without the spirit? Do you look for the seed of destruction in the old institution and in the old spirit? and do you think you know a better institution, a better spirit? Oh, that the spirit of spirits might inspire you, or that you might abandon this foolish endeavour to mould and direct history and mankind! Is Religion not independent, peculiar to itself, infinitely lovable and prophetic? To study it, and learn from it, to follow in its footsteps, to keep pace with it, faithfully following its promises and hints—has occurred to no one.

In France much has been done for religion by depriving it of its civic rights and leaving merely the right to live in the domestic community, not in *form*, but in all its countless individual forms. Like a strange and insignificant orphan, it must first win again universal love before it is once more publicly worshipped again and is combined with worldly things to give friendly counsel and to inspire the mind. The attempt of that great iron mask which, under the name of Robespierre, sought in religion the centre and power of the republic remains historically remarkable; equally remarkable is the coldness of feeling with which theophilanthropy, that mysticism of modern enlightenment, has been received; remarkable, too, are the new conquests of the Jesuits, and also the fact that modern political conditions have brought us nearer to the East.

For the remaining European countries, with the exception of Germany, one can merely prophesy peace, a new and higher religious life will pulsate, absorbing all other secular interests. In Germany, however, the traces of a new world can be pointed to with complete certainty. Germany goes its slow but sure way in advance of other European countries. While they are occupied with war, speculation and the party-spirit, the German educates himself with great zeal to become a member of a higher epoch of culture, and this advance must in the course of time give him a marked superiority over the others. A fermenting interest in the arts and sciences can be perceived. New, fresh sources are being tapped, and an immense spiritual development is about to take place. The sciences were never in better hands and never aroused greater expectations; the various aspects of objects are traced, everything is turned over, investigated and criticized. No stone is left unturned; the writers become increasingly characteristic and powerful, every ancient monument of history, every art, every science is regenerated with sympathetic interest and embraced with a new love. Everywhere there is to be found unparalleled versatility. A wonderful profundity, a brilliant polish, extensive knowledge is evident everywhere, and often these attributes are boldly paired. A powerful presentiment of creative wilfulness and boundlessness, of infinite variety and sacred singularity and of the unlimited capacity of the inner humanity appears to have become active everywhere. Awakened from the matutinal dream of helpless childhood, a part of the race exercises its newly-found strength on the vipers which encircle its cradle and try to deprive it of the use of its limbs. All these things are merely intimations, unconnected and crude, but they betray to the historical sense a universal individuality, a new history and a new mankind; the sweetest embrace of a young church taken unawares and of a loving God, and simultaneously the ardent conception of a new Messias in its thousand aspects. Who does not feel hope with a sweet shame? The newborn child will be the image of its father, it will be a new golden age with dark infinite eyes, a prophetic age which will perform miracles and heal wounds, which will comfort and kindle eternal life—a great age of reconciliation, a saviour who, like a true genius, will be at home among men, believed but not seen, and visible to the faithful in countless forms. He will be consumed as bread and wine, embraced as a loved one, he will be breathed in as air, and heard as word and song, and like death he will be received by the soul of the departing body with heavenly joy and sublime sufferings.

Now we stand high enough to smile back upon those past ages we have mentioned above and to recognize in those strange follies remarkable crystallizations of historical matter. We would like to press the hands of those scholars and philosophers in gratitude; for that illusion had to be shattered and the scientific view of things validated for the benefit of later generations. In a more charming and colourful guise, poetry like an ornate India stands in face of the cold and lifeless Spitzbergen of armchair reason. In order that India might be so warm and magnificent in the centre of our planet, a cold, rigid sea, lifeless cliffs, mist instead of the starry sky and a long night had to render both poles inhospitable. The anchorites in the deserts of reason were oppressed by the significance of mechanism; the delight of first insight overpowered them, the old order avenged itself on them; with wonderful self-denial they sacrificed the most sacred and beautiful things in the world to this first self-awareness. They were the first to recognize and proclaim again by deed the sanctity of nature, the infinite quality of art, the necessity of knowledge, the respect for the secular and the omnipresence of the truly historical by the deed putting an end to the higher, more universal reign of phantoms which was more dreadful than they themselves believed.

Only by a more accurate knowledge of religion will it be possible to judge better those fearful products of religious sleep, those dreams and deliria of the sacred organ, and only then to assess properly the importance of that gift. Phantoms rule where there are no gods. The period of transition from Greek mythology to Christianity is the origin and the explanation of the European phantoms. Come then, you philanthropists and encyclopaedists, into the peace-making lodge and receive the brotherly kiss, take off the grey veil and look with young love at the magnificence of nature, of history and of mankind. I will lead you to a brother who shall speak to you so that your hearts will open and you will resuscitate the presentiment so dear to you, and embrace it again, recognizing what you had dimly comprehended but which, with your awkward earthly reason, you were unable fully to grasp.

This brother is the pulse of the modern age; those who have felt no longer doubt his advent but step proudly forward from the throng into the new group of disciples of his epoch. He has made a new veil for the saints, which fitting close to them betrays their heavenly stature and yet covers them more chastely than before. As the spirit is for the body, so is the veil for the virgin her indispensable organ, of which the folds are the letters of her sweet annunciation; the infinite play of the folds is a music of numbers, for language is too wooden and too bold for the virgin, and her lips open only for song. To me it means the solemn call to a new original assembly, the mighty beat of wings of a passing angelic herald. They are the first pains of labour, let everyone prepare himself for birth.

Physics has reached its furthest limit, and we can now more easily survey the guild of scholars. In recent times the poverty of the external sciences has become ever more apparent through our growing familiarity. Nature began to look more barren, and accustomed to the splendour of our discoveries we saw more clearly that it was merely a borrowed light and that, using the known tools and methods, we would not find and construct that which is fundamental, or that for which we were searching. Every scholar had to admit to himself that one science is nothing without the other; thus arose scientific attempts at mystification; the strange being of philosophy as a purely described scientific element became now a symmetrical basic norm of the sciences. Others brought the concrete sciences into new relationships with one another, furthering a lively traffic between them, and seeking to clarify their natural historical classification. Thus it continues, and it can easily be gauged how favourable must be this intercourse with the external and internal world, with the higher education of reason, with the knowledge of the former and the stimulation and culture of the latter, and how, under these circumstances, the storm must pass and there must re-emerge living astronomy and the old heaven together with the yearning for it.

Now we turn to the political spectacle of our time. The ancient and the new worlds are in a state of struggle, the imperfection and terrible phenomena bear witness to the imperfections and destitution of previous institutions.

How would it be if here too, as in the sciences, a closer and more varied connection and contact of the European states were first and foremost the historical aims of war, if Europe were now to be rescued from her previous slumber, if Europe wanted to awaken again, if a state of all the states, a political theory of science were to confront us! Should then the hierarchy, that symmetrical and basic norm of the state, be the principle of the community of states as it is the intellectual view of the body politic? It is impossible for secular forces to find their own equilibrium, a third element which is both secular and supernatural can alone fulfil this task. No peace can be concluded among the disputing powers, for all peace is merely an illusion and an armistice; and from the point of view of the cabinets and of common conviction no union is conceivable. Both elements have great and necessary claims and must put them forward since they are impelled by the spirit of the world and of mankind. Both are ineradicable powers of the human soul; on the one hand, veneration of the ancient world, loyalty to the historical constitution, love of the patriarchal monuments and the ancient and glorious state family, and joy in obedience; on the other hand, the delightful feeling of freedom, the unqualified expectation of vast domains, pleasure in what is new and young, informal contact with all fellow citizens, pride in man's universality, joy in personal rights and in the property of the whole, and strong civic sense. Neither should hope to destroy the other, all conquests mean nothing, for the innermost capital of every kingdom does not lie behind walls of earth and cannot be taken by storm.

Who knows whether there has been enough of war, but it will never cease unless the palm-branch is grasped, which a spiritual power alone can offer. Blood will continue to stream over Europe till the nations become aware of their terrible madness which drives them round in circles, and till, moved and calmed by sacred music, they approach former altars in motley throngs to undertake works of peace and celebrate with hot tears a great banquet of love as a festival of peace on the smoking battlefields. Only religion can reawaken Europe, make the people secure, and instal Christendom with a new magnificence in its old office of peacemaker in the world, visible to the whole world.

Do nations possess all the attributes of man except that sacred organ—his heart? Do they not, as men do, become friends at the coffins of their beloved ones and do they not forget all hostility when divine mercy speaks to them when they are united by one misfortune, one lament, one feeling which fills their eyes with tears? Are they not stirred by infinite power of sacrifice and surrender, and do they not long to be friends and allies? Where is now that ancient, blessed belief in the government of God on earth which alone can bring salvation? Where is that divine trust of men in one another, that sweet devotion in the outpourings inspired by God, that all-embracing spirit of Christendom?

Christianity has three forms. One is the productive element of religion which inspires joy in all religion. The second acts as an intermediary in the form of the belief in the capacity of all earthly things to be the bread and wine of Eternal Life. The third is the belief in Christ, in the Virgin and the Saints. Choose whichever you like, choose all three, and you will thereby become Christians and members of one single, eternal, ineffably happy community.

The ancient Catholic faith, the last of these forms, was applied Christianity come to life. Its omnipresence in life, its love for art, its profound humanity, the inviolability of its marriages, its philanthropic communicativeness, its delight in poverty, obedience and loyalty, and contain the basic features of its constitution and make it unmistakable as the true religion.

It has been purified by the river of time and in undivided union with the two other forms of Christianity will eternally bless the earth.

Its accidental form has been almost entirely destroyed, the old papacy lies in its grave, and Rome has become a ruin for the second time. Shall not Protestantism finally cease to exist and give way to a new, more lasting Church? The other continents are waiting for Europe's reconciliation and resurrection before they join and become fellow-citizens of the kingdom of heaven. Shall there not soon again exist in Europe a multitude with truly sacred minds, shall not all those who have religious kinship be filled with yearning to see heaven on earth? And shall they not assemble eagerly to chant sacred songs?

Christendom must again become alive and effective, and form for itself a visible Church without consideration to national frontiers, a Church which, eager to become the mediator between the old and new world, receives into its bosom all souls thirsting for a spiritual life.

It must once more pour out the ancient cornucopia of blessing over the nations. Christendom will arise from the sacred heart of a venerable European Council, and the business of religious awakening will be performed according to an all-embracing Divine plan. No one will then be able to protest further against Christian and secular compulsion, for the essence of the Church will be true freedom, and all necessary reforms will be carried out under its guidance as peaceful and formal processes of the state. When? How soon? This we must not ask. Have patience; it will and must come, this sacred age of eternal peace, when the new Jerusalem is the capital of the world; and until that time, be serene and brave amidst the dangers of this present age, companions of my faith, proclaim the divine gospel by word and deed, and remain faithful until death to the true, infinite belief.

10. Friedrich Schleiermacher: *Speeches on Religion to Its Cultured Despisers*

Friedrich Schleiermacher (1768–1834) was one of the central figures in the German Romantic school. He had been brought up in the Pietist Moravian faith, and, after serving as tutor in a noble family, he went to Berlin in 1796 as chaplain of the Charity Hospital. There, he joined the circle that was so significantly to influence his career. Friedrich von Schlegel and Ludwig Tieck urged him to put his views on religion in writing—selections from the result, his first major work, *Speeches on Religion to its Cultured Despisers* (1799), follow. Schleiermacher went on to become a teacher of theology at Halle, where he had earlier studied, and in 1810 he became a member of the theological faculty at the new University of Berlin, while serving as preacher at a Berlin church. As he grew older he revised the *Speeches*, clarifying what had been rather vague conceptions, expressing more fully the views of a mature theologian, rather than those of a young, enthusiastic controversialist.

Most important among Schleiermacher's imagined audience in these speeches were the Enlightenment proponents of a rational religion of nature (natural religion), and it was against them especially that the author propounded his view of religion, not as a form of discursive knowledge, but as feeling. He rejects the importance of dogma, and adopts a relativism that cherishes the diversity of faiths the scholarship of the age was so assiduously studying. The *Speeches* do not prove; rather they evoke or urge or suggest, because their author saw his subject as transcending traditional forms of rational argument. There is here much that seems pantheist, much that stresses the immense importance of private individual feelings, and much, too, that is openly German nationalist. It has seemed justifiable here as nowhere else in this volume to link together selected segments from the whole book partly because Schleirmacher *is* verbose, but also because the volume suggests, as I believe no other single volume does, almost all the chief themes of Romanticism. Rudolph Otto has written: ". . . the work is a monument of the young Romantic school. Stemming directly from this circle and its atmosphere, it is a veritable manifesto of the Romantics in its views of nature and history; its struggle against rationalist culture and the Philistinism of rationalism in the state, church, school and society; its leaning toward fantasy, melancholy, presentiment, mysticism . . . its championship of the individual, and in its preference for the strange and the curious as over against 'universal reason.' "

The selections are from John Oman's translation, 1893, appearing in the Harper Torchbook edition of 1958, pp. 8–11, 36, 39–40, 51–55, 124–128, 226–227, 252–253.

PERMIT ME to speak of myself. You know that what is spoken at the instigation of piety cannot be pride, for piety is always full of humility. Piety was the mother's womb, in whose sacred darkness my young life was nourished and was prepared for a world still sealed for it. In it my spirit breathed ere it had yet found its own place in knowledge and experience. It helped me as I began to sift the faith of my fathers and to cleanse thought and feeling from the rubbish of antiquity. When the God and the immortality of my childhood vanished from my doubting eyes it remained to me. Without design of mine it guided me into active life. It showed me how, with my endowments and defects, I should keep myself holy in an undivided existence, and through it alone I have learnt friendship and love. In respect of other human excellences, before your judgment-seat, ye wise and understanding of the people, I know it is small proof of possession to be able to speak of their value. They can be known from description, from observation of others, or, as all virtues are known, from the ancient and general traditions of their nature. But religion is of such a sort and is so rare, that whoever utters anything of it, must necessarily have had it, for nowhere could he have heard it. Of all that I praise, all that I feel to be the true work of religion, you would find little even in the sacred books. To the man who has not himself experienced it, it would only be an annoyance and a folly.

Finally, if I am thus impelled to speak of religion and to deliver my testimony, to whom should I turn if not to the sons of Germany? Where else is an audience for my speech? It is not blind predilection for my native soil or for my fellows in government and language, that makes me speak thus, but the deep conviction that you alone are capable, as well as worthy, of having awakened in you the sense for holy and divine things. Those proud Islanders whom many unduly honour, know no watchword but *gain* and *enjoyment*. Their zeal for knowledge is only a sham fight, their worldly wisdom a false jewel, skilfully and deceptively composed, and their sacred freedom itself too often and too easily serves self-interest. They are never in earnest with anything that goes beyond palpable utility. All knowledge they have robbed of life and use only as dead wood to make masts and helms for the life's voyage in pursuit of gain. Similarly they know nothing of religion, save that all preach devotion to ancient usages and defend its institutions, regarding them as a protection wisely cherished by the constitution against the natural enemy of the state.

For other reasons I turn from the French. On them, one who honours religion can hardly endure to look, for in every act and almost in every word, they tread its holiest ordinances under foot. The barbarous indifference of the millions of the people, and the witty frivolity with which individual brilliant spirits behold the sublimest fact of history that is not only taking place before their eyes, but has them all in its grasp, and determines every movement of their lives, witnesses clearly enough how little they are capable of a holy awe or a true adoration. What does religion more abhor than the unbridled arrogance with which the rulers of the people bid defiance to the eternal laws of the world? What does it inculcate more strongly than that discreet and lowly moderation of which aught, even the slightest feeling, does not seem to be suggested to them? What is more sacred to it than that lofty Nemesis, of whose most terrible dealings in the intoxication of infatuation they have no understanding? Where varied punishments that formerly only needed to light on single families to fill whole peoples with awe before the heavenly Being and to dedicate to eternal Fate the works of the poets for centuries, are a thousandfold renewed in vain, how ludicrously would a single lonely voice resound unheard and unnoticed.

Only in my native land is that happy clime which refuses no fruit entirely. There you find, though it be only scattered, all that adorns humanity. Somewhere, in individuals at least, all that grows attains its most beautiful form. Neither wise moderation, nor quiet contemplation is wanting; there, therefore, religion must find a refuge from the coarse barbarism and the cold worldly mind of the age. . . .

It is true that religion is essentially contemplative. You would never call anyone pious who went about in impervious stupidity, whose sense is not open for the life of the world. But this contemplation is not turned, as your knowledge of nature is, to the existence of a finite thing, combined with and opposed to another finite thing. It has not even, like your knowledge of God—if for once I might use an old expression—to do with the nature of the first cause, in itself and in its relation to every other cause and operation. The contemplation of the pious is the immediate consciousness of the universal existence of all finite things, in and through the Infinite, and of all temporal things in and through the Eternal. Religion is to seek this and find it in all that lives and moves, in all growth and change, in all doing and suffering. It is to have life and to know life in immediate feeling, only as such an existence in the Infinite and Eternal. Where this is found religion is satisfied, where it hides itself there is for her unrest and anguish, extremity and death. Wherefore it is a life in the infinite nature of the Whole, in the One and in the All, in God, having and possessing all things in God, and God in all. Yet religion is not knowledge and science, either of the world or of God. Without being knowledge, it recognizes knowledge and science. In

itself it is an affection, a revelation of the Infinite in the finite,
God being seen in it and it in God. . . .

Wherefore, you will find every truly learned man devout and
pious. Where you see science without religion, be sure it is trans-
ferred, learned up from another. It is sickly, if indeed it is not that
empty appearance which serves necessity and is no knowledge at
all. And what else do you take this deduction and weaving together of ideas to be, which neither live nor correspond to any
living thing? Or in ethics, what else is this wretched uniformity
that thinks it can grasp the highest human life in a single dead
formula? The former arises because there is no fundamental feeling of that living nature which everywhere presents variety and
individuality, and the latter because the sense fails to give infinity
to the finite by determining its nature and boundaries only from
the Infinite. Hence the dominion of the mere notion; hence the
mechanical erections of your systems instead of an organic structure; hence the vain juggling with analytical formulas, in which,
whether categorical or hypothetical, life will not be fettered. Science is not your calling, if you despise religion and fear to surrender yourself to reverence and aspiration for the primordial.
Either science must become as low as your life, or it must be
separated and stand alone, a division that precludes success. If
man is not one with the Eternal in the unity of intuition and
feeling which is immediate, he remains, in the unity of consciousness which is derived, for ever apart. . . .

Music is one great whole; it is a special, a self-contained revelation of the world. Yet the music of each people is a whole by
itself, which again is divided into different characteristic forms,
till we come to the genius and style of the individual. Each actual
instance of this inner revelation in the individual contains all
these unities. Yet while nothing is possible for a musician, except
in and through the unity of the music of his people, and the unity
of music generally, he presents it in the charm of sound with all
the pleasure and joyousness of boundless caprice, according as his
life stirs in him, and the world influences him. In the same way,
despite the necessary elements in its structure, religion is, in its
individual manifestations whereby it displays itself immediately
in life, from nothing farther removed than from all semblance of
compulsion or limitation. In life, the necessary element is taken

up, taken up into freedom. Each emotion appears as the free self-determination of this very disposition, and mirrors one passing moment of the world.

It would be impious to demand here something held in constraint, something limited and determined from without. If anything of this kind lies in your conception of system then you must set it quite aside. A system of perceptions and feelings you may yourselves see to be somewhat marvellous. Suppose now you feel something. Is there not at the same time an accompanying feeling or thought—make your own choice—that you would have to feel in accordance with this feeling, and not otherwise were but this or that object, which does not now move you, to be present? But for this immediate association your feeling would be at an end, and a cold calculating and refining would take its place. Wherefore it is plainly an error to assert that it belongs to religion, to be conscious of the connection of its separate manifestations, not only to have it within, and to develop it from within, but to see it described and to comprehend it from without, and it is presumption to consider that, without it, piety is poverty-stricken. The truly pious are not disturbed in the simplicity of their way, for they give little heed to all the so-called religious systems that have been erected in consequence of this view.

Poor enough they are too, far inferior to the theories about music, defective though they be. Among those systematizers there is less than anywhere, a devout watching and listening to discover in their own hearts what they are to describe. They would rather reckon with symbols, and complete a designation which is about as accidental as the designation of the stars. It is purely arbitrary and never sufficient, for something new that should be included, is always being discovered, and a system, anything permanent and secure, anything corresponding to nature, and not the result of caprice and tradition, is not to be found in it. The designation, let the forms of religion be ever so inward and self-dependent, must be from without. Thousands might be moved religiously in the same way, and yet each, led, not so much by disposition, as by external circumstances, might designate his feeling by different symbols. Furthermore, those systematizers are less anxious to present the details of religion than to subordinate them one to the other, and to deduce them from a higher. Nothing is of less importance to religion, for it knows nothing of deducing and connecting. There is no single fact in it that can be called original and chief. Its facts are one and all immediate. Without dependence on any other, each exists for itself. True, a special type of religion is constituted by one definite kind and manner of feeling, but it is mere perversion to call it a principle, and to treat it as if the rest could be deduced from it. This distinct form of a religion is found, in the same way, in every single element of religion. Each expression of feeling bears on it immediately this peculiar impress. It cannot show itself without it, nor be comprehended without it. Everything is to be found immediately and not proved from something else. Generals, which include particulars, combination and connection belong to another sphere, if they rest on reality, or they are merely a work of phantasy and caprice. Every man may have his own regulation and his own rubrics. What is essential can neither gain nor lose thereby. Consequently, the man who truly knows the nature of his religion, will give a very subordinate place to all apparent connection of details, and will not sacrifice the smallest for the sake of it.

By taking the opposite course, the marvellous thought has arisen of a universality of one religion, of one single form which is true, and in respect of which all others are false. Were it not that misunderstanding must be guarded against, I would say that it is only by such deducing and connecting that such a comparison as true and false, which is not peculiarly appropriate to religion, has ever been reached. It only applies where we have to do with ideas. Elsewhere the negative laws of your logic are not in place. All is immediately true in religion, for except immediately how could anything arise? But that only is immediate which has not yet passed through the stage of idea, but has grown up purely in the feeling. All that is religious is good, for it is only religious as it expresses a common higher life. But the whole circumference of religion is infinite, and is not to be comprehended under one form, but only under the sum total of all forms. It is infinite, not merely because any single religious organization has a limited horizon, and, not being able to embrace all, cannot believe that there is nothing beyond; but more particularly, because everyone is a person by himself, and is only to be moved in his own way, so that for everyone the elements of religion have most characteristic differences. Religion is infinite, not only because something new is ever being produced in time, by the endless relations both active and passive between different minds and the same limited matter; not only because the capacity for religion is never perfected, but is ever being developed anew, is ever being more beautifully reproduced, is ever entering deeper into the nature of man; but religion is infinite on all sides. As the knowledge of its eternal truth and infallibility accompanies knowledge, the consciousness of this infinity accompanies religion. It is the very feeling of religion, and must therefore accompany everyone that really has religion. He must be conscious that his religion is only part of the whole; that about the same circumstances there may be views and sentiments quite different from his, yet just as pious; and that there may be perceptions and feelings belonging to other modifications of religion, for which the sense may entirely fail him.

You see how immediately this beautiful modesty, this friendly, attractive forbearance springs from the nature of religion. How unjustly, therefore, do you reproach religion with loving persecution, with being malignant, with overturning society, and making blood flow like water. Blame those who corrupt religion, who flood it with an army of formulas and definitions, and seek to cast it into the fetters of a so-called system. What is it in religion about which men have quarrelled and made parties and kindled wars? About definitions, the practical sometimes, the theoretical always, both of which belong elsewhere. Philosophy, indeed, seeks to bring those who would know to a common knowledge. Yet even philosophy leaves room for variety, and the more readily the better it understands itself. But religion does not, even once, desire to bring those who believe and feel to one belief and one feeling. Its endeavour is to open in those who are not yet capable of religious emotions, the sense for the unity of the original source of life. But just because each seer is a new priest, a new mediator, a new organ, he flees with repugnance the bald uniformity which would again destroy this divine abundance. . . .

Man is born with the religious capacity as with every other. If only his sense for the profoundest depths of his own nature is not crushed out, if only all fellowship between himself and the Primal Source is not quite shut off, religion would, after its own fashion, infallibly be developed. But in our time, alas! that is exactly what, in very large measure, does happen. With pain I see daily how the rage for calculating and explaining suppresses the sense. I see how all things unite to bind man to the finite, and to a very small portion of the finite, that the infinite may as far as possible vanish from his eyes.

Who hinders the prosperity of religion? Not you, not the doubters and scoffers. Even though you were all of one mind to have no religion, you would not disturb Nature in her purpose of producing piety from the depths of the soul, for your influence could only later find prepared soil. Nor, as is supposed, do the immoral most hinder the prosperity of religion, for it is quite a different power to which their endeavours are opposed. But the discreet and practical men of to-day are, in the present state of the world, the foes of religion, and their great preponderance is the cause why it plays such a poor and insignificant role, for from tender childhood they maltreat man, crushing out his higher aspirations. . . .

In proportion as man must busy himself in a narrow way with a single object, to rescue the universality of the sense an impulse awakes in everyone to allow the dominating activity and all its kindred to rest, and to open all organs to the influence of all impressions. By a secret and most helpful sympathy this impulse is strongest when the general life reveals itself most clearly in our own breasts and in the surrounding world. But to yield to this impulse in comfortable inactivity cannot be permitted, for, from the middle-class standpoint, it would be laziness and idling. In everything there must be design and aim; somewhat has always to be performed, and if the spirit can no more serve, the body must be exercised. Work and play, but no quiet, submissive contemplation!

But most of all, men are to be taught to analyze and explain. By this explaining they are completely cheated of their sense, for, as it is conducted, it is absolutely opposed to any perceptive sense. *Sense* of its own accord seeks objects for itself, it advances to meet them and it offers to embrace them. It communicates something to them which distinguishes them as its possession, its work.

It will find and be found. But this *explaining* knows nothing of this living acquisition, of this illuminating truth, of the true spirit of discovery in childlike intuition. But from first to last, objects are to be transcribed accurately in thought as something simply given. They are, God be thanked, for all men ever the same, and who knows how long already they have been docketed in good order with all their qualities defined. Take them, then, only as life brings them, and understand that and nothing more. But to seek for yourselves and to wish to have living intercourse with things is eccentric and high-flown. It is a vain endeavour, availing nothing in human life, where things are only to be seen and handled as they have already presented themselves.

Fruitful in human life this endeavour is not, except that, without it, an active life, resting on true inward culture, is not to be found. The sense strives to comprehend the undivided impress of something whole; it will perceive what each thing is and how it is; it will know everything in its peculiar character. But that is not what they mean by understanding. What and how are too remote for them, around whence and to what end, they eternally circle. They seek to grasp nothing in and for itself, but only in special aspects, and therefore, not as a whole, but only piecemeal. To inquire or thoroughly examine whether the object they would understand is a whole, would lead them too far. Were this their desire, they could hardly escape so utterly without religion.

But all must be used for some excellent purpose, wherefore they dissever and anatomize. This is how they deal with what exists chiefly for the highest satisfaction of the sense, with what, in their despite, is a whole in itself, I mean with all that is art in nature and in the works of man. Before it can operate they annihilate it by explaining it in detail. Having first by decomposition robbed it of its character as art, they would teach and impress this or that lesson from the fragments.

You must grant that this is the practice of our people of understanding, and you must confess that a superabundance of sense is necessary if anything is to escape this hostile treatment. On that account alone the number must be small who are capable of such a contemplation of any object as might awake in them religion . . .

The charge that everyone who allows himself to be embraced in a positive religion, can only be an imitator of those who have given it currency and cannot develop himself individually, is baseless. This judgment no more applies here, than it would to the state or to society. It seems to us morbid or quixotic for any one to maintain that he has no room in any existing institution, and that he must exclude himself from society. We are convinced that every healthy person will, in common with many, have a great national character. Just because he is rooted in it and influenced by it, he can develop his individuality with the greatest precision and beauty. Similarly, in religion only morbid aberration so cuts off a man from a life in fellowship with those among whom nature has placed him, that he belongs to no great whole. Somewhere, on a great scale, everyone will find exhibited or will himself exhibit what for him is the middle-point of religion. To every such common sphere we ascribe a boundless activity that goes into detail, in virtue of which all individual characteristics issue from its bosom. Thus understood, the church is with right called the common mother of us all.

To take the nearest example, think of Christianity as a definite individual form of the highest order. First there is in our time the well known outward division, so definite and pronounced. Under each section there is then a mass of different views and schools. Each exhibits a characteristic development, and has a founder and adherents, yet the last and most personal development of religiousness remains for each individual, and so much is it one with his nature that no one can fully acquire it but himself. And the more a man, by his whole nature, has a claim to belong to you, ye cultured, the more religion must reach this stage in him, for his higher feeling, gradually developing and uniting with other educated capacities, must be a characteristic product. . . .

In all ways the Deity is to be contemplated and worshipped. Varied types of religion are possible, both in proximity and in combination, and if it is necessary that every type be actualized at one time or another, it is to be desired that, at all times, there should be a dim sense of many religions. The great moments must be few in which all things agree to ensure to one among them a wide-extended and enduring life, in which the same view is developed unanimously and irresistibly in a great body, and many persons are deeply affected by the same impression of the divine. Yet what may not be looked for from a time that is so manifestly the border land between two different orders of things? If only the intense crisis were past, such a moment might arrive. Even now a prophetic soul, such as the fiery spirits of our time have, turning its thoughts to creative genius, might perhaps indicate the point that is to be for the future generations the centre for their fellowship with the Deity. But however it be, and however long such a moment may still linger, new developments of religion, whether under Christianity or alongside of it, must come and that soon, even though for a long time they are only discernible in isolated and fleeting manifestations. Out of nothing a new creation always comes forth, and in all living men in whom the intellectual life has power and fulness, religion is almost nothing. From some one of the countless occasions it will be developed in many and take new shape in new ground. Were but the time of caution and timidity past! Religion hates loneliness, and in youth especially, which for all things is the time of love, it wastes away in a consuming longing. When it is developed in you, when you are conscious of the first traces of its life, enter at once into the one indivisible fellowship of the saints, which embraces all religions and in which alone any can prosper. Do you think that because the saints are scattered and far apart, you must speak to unsanctified ears? You ask what language is secret enough—is it speech, writing, deed, or quiet copying of the Spirit? All ways, I answer, and you see that I have not shunned the loudest. In them all sacred things remain secret and hidden from the profane. They may gnaw at the shell as they are able, but to worship the God that is in you, do not refuse us.

11. François de Chateaubriand:
The Genius of Christianity

François-René de Chateaubriand (1768–1848) was the Frenchman most influential in the romanticizing of Catholicism. His *Génie du Christianisme* (published in 1802), from which selected chapters appear below, made his literary reputation, which had begun with the publication of *Atala* in 1801, a story of love and Christian faith among American Indians, and was much furthered by the novelette *René* (included in the *Génie*) a portrayal of the soul-searching and heart-rending efforts of a sensitive youth to find himself and his place in an inimical world. *René* recalled Goethe's *Werther* and the Rousseau of the *Confessions*, and was to find reflection in Musset's *Confession* and in Byronism.

Chateaubriand visited America in 1791, fought for the counterrevolution, and lived as an émigré in exile in London. After the *Génie* was published, Napoleon sent him as ambassador to Rome; he later served the Restoration Monarchy as foreign minister, supporting with French arms the restoration of Ferdinand VII in Spain in 1823. Under the July Monarchy he reigned as the leading figure in French Romantic letters.

Chateaubriand's Christianity is a faith distinguished for its beauty; his faith is quite untheological, frankly irrational, a matter primarily of feeling. Nature, as God's handiwork, constituted a source, rather than a proof of religion. In this, his views closely resemble the Protestant Schleiermacher's.

The selections are from Charles I. White's translation (Baltimore, 1857), pp. 170–174, 296–298, 384–387, 473–478.

Two Views of Nature

WHAT WE have said respecting animals and plants leads us to a more general view of the scenes of nature. Those wonders which, separately considered, so loudly proclaimed the providence of God, will now speak to us of the same truth in their collective capacity.

We shall place before the reader two views of nature; one an ocean scene, the other a land picture; one sketched in the middle of the Atlantic, the other in the forests of the New World. Thus, no one can say that the imposing grandeur of this scenery has been derived from the works of man.

The vessel in which we embarked for America having passed the bearing of any land, space was soon enclosed only by the twofold azure of the sea and of the sky. The color of the waters resembled that of liquid glass. A great swell was visible from the west, though the wind blew from the east, while immense undulations extended from the north to the south, opening in their valleys long vistas through the deserts of the deep. The fleeting scenes changed with every minute. Sometimes a multitude of verdant hillocks appeared to us like a series of graves in some vast cemetery. Sometimes the curling summits of the waves resembled white flocks scattered over a heath. Now space seemed circumscribed for want of an object of comparison; but if a billow reared its mountain crest, if a wave curved like a distant shore, or a squadron of sea-dogs moved along the horizon, the vastness of space again suddenly opened before us. We were most powerfully impressed with an idea of magnitude, when a light fog, creeping along the surface of the deep, semed to increase immensity itself.

Oh! how sublime, how awful, at such times, is the aspect of the ocean! Into what reveries does it plunge you, whether imagination transports you to the seas of the north, into the midst of frosts and tempests, or wafts you to southern islands, blessed with happiness and peace!

We often rose at midnight and sat down upon deck, where we found only the officer of the watch and a few sailors silently smoking their pipes. No noise was heard, save the dashing of the prow through the billows, while sparks of fire ran with a white foam along the sides of the vessel. God of Christians! it is on the waters of the abyss and on the vast expanse of the heavens that thou hast particularly engraven the characters of thy omnipotence! Millions of stars sparkling in the azure of the celestial dome—the moon in the midst of the firmament—a sea unbounded by any shore—infinitude in the skies and on the waves—proclaim with most impressive effect the power of thy arm! Never did thy greatness strike me with profounder awe than in those nights, when, suspended between the stars and the ocean, I beheld immensity over my head and immensity beneath my feet!

I am nothing; I am only a simple, solitary wanderer, and often have I heard men of science disputing on the subject of a Supreme Being, without understanding them; but I have invariably remarked, that it is in the prospect of the sublime scenes of nature that this unknown Being manifests himself to the human heart. One evening, after we had reached the beautiful waters that bathe the shores of Virginia, there was a profound calm, and every sail was furled. I was engaged below, when I heard the bell that summoned the crew to prayers. I hastened to mingle my supplications with those of my travelling companions. The officers of the ship were on the quarter-deck with the passengers, while the chaplain, with a book in his hand, was stationed at a little distance before them; the seamen were scattered at random over the poop; we were all standing, our faces toward the prow of the vessel, which was turned to the west.

The solar orb, about to sink beneath the waves, was seen through the rigging, in the midst of boundless space; and, from the motion of the stern, it appeared as if it changed its horizon every moment. A few clouds wandered confusedly in the east, where the moon was slowly rising. The rest of the sky was serene; and toward the north, a water-spout, forming a glorious triangle with the luminaries of day and night, and glistening with all the colors of the prism, rose from the sea, like a column of crystal supporting the vault of heaven.

He had been well deserving of pity who would not have recognised in this prospect the beauty of God. When my companions, doffing their tarpaulin hats, entoned with hoarse voice their simple hymn to Our Lady of Good Help, the patroness of the seas, the tears flowed from my eyes in spite of myself. How affecting was the prayer of those men, who, from a frail plank in the midst of the ocean, contemplated the sun setting behind the waves! How the appeal of the poor sailor to the Mother of Sorrows went to the heart! The consciousness of our insignificance in the presence of the Infinite,—our hymns, resounding to a distance over the silent waves,—the night approaching with its dangers,—our vessel, itself a wonder among so many wonders,—a religious crew, penetrated with admiration and with awe,—a venerable priest in prayer,—the Almighty bending over the abyss, with one hand staying the sun in the west, with the other raising the moon in the east, and lending, through all immensity, an attentive ear to the feeble voice of his creatures,—all this constituted a scene which no power of art can represent, and which it is scarcely possible for the heart of man to feel.

Let us now pass to the terrestrial scene.

I had wandered one evening in the woods, at some distance from the cataract of Niagara, when soon the last glimmering of daylight disappeared, and I enjoyed, in all its loneliness, the beauteous prospect of night amid the deserts of the New World.

An hour after sunset, the moon appeared above the trees in the opposite part of the heavens. A balmy breeze, which the queen of night had brought with her from the east, seemed to precede her in the forests, like her perfumed breath. The lonely luminary slowly ascended in the firmament, now peacefully pursuing her azure course, and now reposing on groups of clouds which resembled the summits of lofty, snow-covered mountains. These clouds, by the contraction and expansion of their vapory forms, rolled themselves into transparent zones of white satin, scattering in airy masses of foam, or forming in the heavens brilliant beds of down so lovely to the eye that you would have imagined you felt their softness and elasticity.

The scenery on the earth was not less enchanting: the soft and bluish beams of the moon darted through the intervals between the trees, and threw streams of light into the midst of the most profound darkness. The river that glided at my feet was now lost in the wood, and now reappeared, glistening with the constellations of night, which were reflected on its bosom. In a vast plain beyond this stream, the radiance of the moon reposed quietly on the verdure. Birch-trees, scattered here and there in the savanna, and agitated by the breeze, formed shadowy islands which floated on a motionless sea of light. Near me, all was silence and repose, save the fall of some leaf, the transient rustling of a sudden breath of wind, or the hooting of the owl; but at a distance was heard, at intervals, the solemn roar of the Falls of Niagara, which, in the stillness of the night, was prolonged from desert to desert, and died away among the solitary forests.

The grandeur, the astonishing solemnity of this scene, cannot be expressed in language; nor can the most delightful nights of Europe afford any idea of it. In vain does imagination attempt to soar in our cultivated fields; it everywhere meets with the habitations of men: but in those wild regions the mind loves to penetrate into an ocean of forests, to hover round the abysses of cataracts, to meditate on the banks of lakes and rivers, and, as it were, to find itself alone with God.

Of the Unsettled State of the Passions

WE HAVE yet to treat of a state of the soul which, as we think, has not been accurately described; we mean that which precedes the development of the strong passions, when all the faculties, fresh, active, and entire, but confined in the breast, act only upon themselves, without object and without end. The more nations advance in civilization, the more this unsettled state of the passions predominates; for then the many examples we have before us, and the multitude of books we possess, give us knowledge without experience; we are undeceived before we have enjoyed; there still remain desires, but no illusions. Our imagination is rich, abundant, and full of wonders; but our existence is poor, insipid, and destitute of charms. With a full heart, we dwell in an empty world, and scarcely have we advanced a few steps when we have nothing more to learn.

It is inconceivable what a shade this state of the soul throws over life; the heart turns a hundred different ways to employ the energies which it feels to be useless to it. The ancients knew but little of this secret inquietude, this irritation of the stifled passions fermenting all together; political affairs, the sports of the Gymnasium and the Campus Martius, the business of the forum and of the popular assemblies, engaged all their time, and left no room or this tedium of the heart.

On the other hand, they were not disposed to exaggerations, to hopes and fears without object, to versatility in ideas and sentiments, and to perpetual inconstancy, which is but a continual disgust,—dispositions which we acquire in the familiar society of the fair sex. Women, independently of the direct passion which they excite among all modern nations, also possess an influence over the other sentiments. They have in their nature a certain ease which they communicate to ours; they render the marks of the masculine character less distinct; and our passions, softened by the mixture of theirs, assume, at one and the same time, something uncertain and delicate.

Finally, the Greeks and Romans, looking scarcely any farther than the present life, and having no conception of pleasures more perfect than those which this world affords, were not disposed, like us, by the character of their religion, to meditation and desire. Formed for the relief of our afflictions and our wants, the Christian religion incessantly exhibits to our view the twofold picture of terrestrial griefs and heavenly joys, and thus creates in the heart a source of present evils and distant hopes, whence spring inexhaustible abstractions and meditations. The Christian always looks upon himself as no more than a pilgrim travelling here below through a vale of tears and finding no repose till he reaches the tomb. The world is not the object of his affections, for he knows that the days of man are few, and that this object would speedily escape from his grasp.

The persecutions which the first believers underwent had the effect of strengthening in them this disgust of the things of this life. The invasion of the barbarians raised this feeling to the highest pitch, and the human mind received from it an impression of melancholy, and, perhaps, even a slight tincture of misanthropy, which has never been thoroughly removed. On all sides arose convents; hither retired the unfortunate, smarting under the disappointments of the world, or souls who chose rather to remain

strangers to certain sentiments of life than to run the risk of finding themselves cruelly deceived. But, nowadays, when these ardent souls have no monastery to enter, or have not the virtue that
would lead them to one, they feel like strangers among men.
Disgusted with the age, alarmed by religion, they remain in the
world without mingling in its pursuits; and then we behold that
culpable sadness which springs up in the midst of the passions,
when these passions, without object, burn themselves out in a
solitary heart.

GOTHIC CHURCHES

EVERY THING *ought to be in its proper place.* This is a truth
become trite by repetition; but without its due observance there
can be nothing perfect. The Greeks would not have been better
pleased with an Egyptian temple at Athens than the Egyptians
with a Greek temple at Memphis. These two monuments, by
changing places, would have lost their principal beauty; that is to
say, their relations with the institutions and habits of the people.
This reflection is equally applicable to the ancient monuments of
Christianity. It is even curious to remark how readily the poets
and novelists of this infidel age, by a natural return toward the
manners of our ancestors, introduce dungeons, spectres, castles,
and Gothic churches, into their fictions,—so great is the charm of
recollections associated with religion and the history of our country. Nations do not throw aside their ancient customs as people
do their old clothes. Some part of them may be discarded; but
there will remain a portion, which with the new manners will
form a very strange mixture.

In vain would you build Grecian temples, ever so elegant and
well-lighted, for the purpose of assembling the *good people* of St.
Louis and Queen Blanche, and making them adore a *metaphysi-
cal God;* they would still regret those *Notre Dames* of Rheims
and Paris,—those venerable cathedrals, overgrown with moss, full
of generations of the dead and the ashes of their forefathers; they
would still regret the tombs of those heroes, the Montmorencys,
on which they loved to kneel during mass; to say nothing of the
sacred fonts to which they were carried at their birth. The reason
is that all these things are essentially interwoven with their manners; that a monument is not venerable, unless a long history of
the past be, as it were, inscribed beneath its vaulted canopy, black

with age. For this reason, also, there is nothing marvellous in a temple whose erection we have witnessed, whose echoes and whose domes were formed before our eyes. God is the eternal law; his origin, and whatever relates to his worship, ought to be enveloped in the night of time.

You could not enter a Gothic church without feeling a kind of awe and a vague sentiment of the Divinity. You were all at once carried back to those times when a fraternity of cenobites, after having meditated in the woods of their monasteries, met to prostrate themselves before the altar and to chant the praises of the Lord, amid the tranquillity and the silence of night. Ancient France seemed to revive altogether; you beheld all those singular costumes, all that nation so different from what it is at present; you were reminded of its revolutions, its productions, and its arts. The more remote were these times the more magical they appeared, the more they inspired ideas which always end with a reflection on the nothingness of man and the rapidity of life.

The Gothic style, notwithstanding its barbarous proportions, possesses a beauty peculiar to itself.[1]

The forests were the first temples of the Divinity, and in them men acquired the first idea of architecture. This art must, therefore, have varied according to climates. The Greeks turned the elegant Corinthian column, with its capital of foliage, after the model of the palm-tree. The enormous pillars of the ancient Egyptian style represent the massive sycamore, the oriental fig, the banana, and most of the gigantic trees of Africa and Asia.

The forests of Gaul were, in their turn, introduced into the temples of our ancestors, and those celebrated woods of oaks thus maintained their sacred character. Those ceilings sculptured into foliage of different kinds, those buttresses which prop the walls and terminate abruptly like the broken trunks of trees, the coolness of the vaults, the darkness of the sanctuary, the dim twilight of the aisles, the secret passages, the low doorways,—in a word, every thing in a Gothic church reminds you of the labyrinths of a wood; every thing excites a feeling of religious awe, of mystery, and of the Divinity.

---

[1] Gothic architecture, as well as the sculpture in the same style, is supposed to have been derived from the Arabs. Its affinity to the monuments of Egypt would rather lead us to imagine that it was transmitted to us by the first Christians of the East; but we are more inclined to refer to its origin to nature.

The two lofty towers erected at the entrance of the edifice overtop the elms and yew-trees of the churchyard, and produce the most picturesque effect on the azure of heaven. Sometimes their twin heads are illumined by the first rays of dawn; at others they appear crowned with a capital of clouds or magnified in a foggy atmosphere. The birds themselves seem to make a mistake in regard to them, and to take them for the trees of the forest; they hover over their summits, and perch upon their pinnacles. But, lo! confused noises suddenly issue from the top of these towers and scare away the affrighted birds. The Christian architect, not content with building forests, has been desirous to retain their murmurs; and, by means of the organ and of bells, he has attached to the Gothic temple the very winds and thunders that roar in the recesses of the woods. Past ages, conjured up by these religious sounds, raise their venerable voices from the bosom of the stones, and are heard in every corner of the vast cathedral. The sanctuary re-echoes like the cavern of the ancient Sibyl; loud-tongued bells swing over your head, while the vaults of death under your feet are profoundly silent.

Moral Harmonies

Popular Devotions

We now take leave of the physical harmonies of religious monuments and the scenes of nature, and enter upon the moral harmonies of Christianity. The first to be considered are *those popular devotions* which consist in certain opinions and practices of the multitude which are neither enjoined nor absolutely prohibited by the Church. They are, in fact, but harmonies of religion and of nature. When the common people fancy that they hear the voices of the dead in the winds, when they talk of nocturnal apparitions, when they undertake pilgrimages to obtain relief from their afflictions, it is evident that these opinions are only affecting relations between certain scenes of nature, certain sacred doctrines, and the sorrows of our hearts. Hence it follows that the more of these popular devotions a religion embraces, the more poetical it must be; since poetry is founded on the emotions of the soul and the accidents of nature rendered mysterious by the intervention of religious ideas.

We should indeed be deserving of pity, if, subjecting every

thing to the rules of reason, we rigorously condemned these notions which assist the common people to endure the woes of life
and teach them a morality which the best laws will never give. It
is good, and it is something beautiful at the same time, that all
our actions should be full of God, and that we should be incessantly surrounded by his miracles.

The vulgar are wiser than philosophers. Every fountain, every
cross beside a road, every sigh of the wind at night, brings with it
a prodigy. For him who possesses faith, nature is a continual
wonder. Is he afflicted? he looks at his little picture or medal, and
finds relief. Is he anxious once more to behold a relative, a friend?
he makes a vow, seizes the pilgrim's staff, climbs the Alps or the
Pyrenees, visits Our Lady of Loretto, or St. James in Galicia; on
his knees he implores the saint to restore to him a son, (a poor
sailor, wandering, perhaps, on the high seas) to prolong the life
of a parent or of a virtuous wife. His heart is lightened. He sets
out on his return to his cottage: laden with shells, he makes the
hamlets resound with his joy, and celebrates, in simple strains,
the beneficence of the blessed Virgin, the mother of God. Everybody wishes to have something belonging to the pilgrim. How
many ailments have been cured merely by a blessed ribbon! The
pilgrim at length reaches home, and the first person that greets
him on his arrival is his wife after a happy delivery, a son returned home, or a father restored to health.

Happy, thrice happy they who possess faith! They cannot
smile, without thinking that they will rejoice in the eternal smiles
of Heaven; they cannot weep, without thinking that the time of
their sorrowing will soon be over. Their tears are not lost: religion
collects them in her urn, and presents them to the Most High.

The steps of the true believer are never solitary; a good angel
watches by his side, counsels him in his dreams, and protects him
from the evil spirit. This heavenly friend is so devoted to his
interests that he consents for his sake to be an exile upon earth.

Did there exist among the ancients any thing more admirable
than the many customs that prevailed among our religious forefathers? If they discovered the body of a murdered man in a
forest, they erected a cross on the spot in token of pity. This cross
demanded of the Samaritan a tear for the unfortunate traveller,
and of the inhabitant of the faithful city a prayer for his brother.
And then, this traveller was, perhaps, a poor stranger, who had
fallen at a great distance from his native land, like that illustrious

Unknown sacrificed by the hands of men far away from his celestial country! What an intercourse between us and God! What prodigious elevation was thus given to human nature! How astonishing that we should thus discover a resemblance between our fleeting days and the eternal duration of the Sovereign of the universe!

We shall say nothing of those jubilees which, substituted for secular games, plunge all Christendom into the bath of repentance, purify the conscience, and offer a religious amnesty to repenting sinners. Neither shall we relate how, in public calamities, both high and low walked barefoot from church to church, to endeavor to avert the wrath of God. The pastor headed the solemn procession with a cord about his neck, the humble victim devoted for the welfare of his flock. The fear of these evils was not encouraged among the people by an ebony crucifix, a bit of blessed laurel, or an image of the patron saint. How often has the Christian knelt before these religious symbols to ask of God that assistance which could not be obtained from man!

Who has not heard of our Lady of the Woods, who inhabits the aged thorn or the mossy cavity of a spring, and is so celebrated in the hamlet for her miracles? Many a matron will tell you, that after having invoked the good Mary of the Woods she suffered less from the pains of childbirth. The maiden who had lost her lover would often fancy in the moonlight that she saw the spirit of her young betrothed in this solitary spot, or heard his voice in the low murmur of the stream. The doves that drink from these waters have always the power of generation, and the flowers that grow on their borders never cease to bloom. It was fitting that the tutelar saint of the forest should accomplish effects as tender in their nature as the moss amid which she dwells, and as charming as the fountain that veils her from human sight.

It is particularly in the great events of life that religious customs impart their consolations to the unfortunate. We once were spectators of a shipwreck. The mariners, on reaching the shore, stripped off all their clothes, with the exception of their wet trousers and shirts. They had made a vow to the Virgin during the storm. They repaired in procession to a little chapel dedicated to St. Thomas, preceded by the captain, and followed by the people, who joined them in singing the *Ave Maris Stella*. The priest said the mass appointed for the shipwrecked, and the sailors hung their garments, dripping with sea-water, as votive offerings, against the walls of the chapel. Philosophy may fill her pages with high-sounding words, but we question whether the unfortunate ever go to hang up their garments in her temple.

Death, so poetical because of its bordering upon things immortal, so mysterious on account of its silence, could not but have a thousand ways of announcing itself to the vulgar. Sometimes its token was heard in the ringing of a distant bell; at others, the person whose dissolution drew nigh heard three knocks upon the floor of his chamber. A nun of St. Benedict, on the point of quitting the world, found a crown of white thorn at the entrance of her cell. Did a mother lose her son abroad, her dreams immediately apprised her of this misfortune. Those who withhold their belief in presentiments will never know the secret channels by which two hearts, bound by the ties of love, hold mutual intercourse from one end of the world to the other. Frequently would some cherished departed one appear to a friend on earth, soliciting prayers for the rescue of his soul from the purgatorial flame, and its admission to the company of the elect. Thus did religion accord to friendship some share in the sublime prerogative which belongs only to God, of imparting eternal happiness.

Opinions of a different kind, but still of a religious character, inspired feelings of humanity; and such is their simplicity that they embarrass the writer. To destroy the nest of a swallow, to kill a robin redbreast, a wren, a cricket—the attendant on the rural hearth, a dog grown old in the service of a family, was a deed which never failed, it was said, to be followed by some visitation. From an admirable respect for age, it was thought that persons advanced in years were of propitious influence in a house, and that an old servant brought good luck to his master. Here we meet with some traces of the affecting worship of the *Lares*, and are reminded of the daughter of Laban carrying her household gods along with her.

The vulgar were persuaded that no person could commit a wicked action without being haunted all the rest of his life by frightful apparitions. Antiquity, wiser than we, would have forborne to destroy these useful accordances of religion, of conscience, and of morality. Neither would it have rejected another opinion, according to which it was deemed certain that every man possessing ill-gotten wealth had entered into a covenant with the spirit of darkness and made over his soul to hell.

Finally, wind, rain, sunshine, the seasons, agriculture, birth, infancy, marriage, old age, death, had all their respective saints and images, and never were people so surrounded with friendly divinities as were the Christian people.

It is not the question now to enter into a rigid examination of these opinions. So far from laying any injunctions on the subject, religion served, on the contrary, to prevent the abuse of them, and to check their extravagancies. The only question is whether their aim be moral, whether they have a stronger tendency than the laws themselves to keep the multitude in the paths of virtue. What sensible man has any doubt of this? By your incessant declamations against superstition, you will at length open a door for every species of crime. A circumstance that cannot fail to surprise the sophists is, that, amid all the evils which they will have occasioned, they will not even enjoy the satisfaction of seeing the common man more incredulous. If he shakes off the influence of religion, he will supply its place with monstrous opinions. He will be seized with a terror the more strange as he will be ignorant of its object: he will shudder in a churchyard, where he has set up the inscription, *Death is an eternal sleep;* and, while affecting to despise the Divine power, he will go to consult the gipsy, and, trembling, seek his destinies in the motley figures of a card.

The marvellous, a future state, and hope, are required by man, because he feels himself formed to survive this terrestrial existence. *Conjuration, sorcery,* are with the vulgar but the instinct of religion, and one of the most striking proofs of the necessity of a public worship. He who believes nothing is not far from believing every thing; you have conjurors when you cease to have prophets, enchantments when you renounce religious ceremonies, and you open the dens of sorcerers when you shut up the temples of the Lord.

12. Félicité de Lamennais: *Words of a Believer*

Félicité Robert de Lamennais (1782–1854) was in his youth a thoroughly reactionary opponent of the French Revolution. His central concern in religion was with the problem of authority. In 1808, in a study of the state of the French Church, he was urging the need for a religious revival and for the enhancement of the social importance of the clergy. In 1811 he began teaching mathematics at a Church college, and was ordained a priest in 1816. His four-volume *Essai sur L'Indifférence en Matière de Religion* appeared between 1817 and 1823. He argued for an approach to religion other than the rationalist (as had Schleiermacher and Chateaubriand) and placed new emphasis upon the apologetic value of the common consent of mankind—which he felt was expressed by the papacy. Against skepticism and tolerance he offered ultramontane Catholicism, a position that settled ill with the Gallican majority of the French clergy. Lamennais and such followers as Montalembert and Lacordaire moved increasingly toward favoring the separation of Church and State, offering in their journal, *L'Avenir*, the surprising combination of political liberalism and ultramontanism. The combination was opposed in Rome as well as in France. Lamennais suspended the journal, and his views were condemned in the papal Encyclical *Mirari vos*. Deserted by the papacy, he turned for authority again to the common consent of mankind, preaching more radical democracy in *Words of a Believer* (1834), which ended his connection with the Catholic Church. In the Assembly of the Second Republic to which he was elected after the Revolution of 1848, he sat on the extreme left. By then he had come to propound a faith in the future of Humanity.

His impassioned style was important in his establishing himself as he did, first as a major influence upon conservative Catholic thought in the restoration, then as a source of the new liberal Catholicism, and finally as a spokesman for a democratic faith that took on all the coloration of religion. His *Words of a Believer* was very widely read, and made its author's reputation among the French lower classes.

The chapters that follow are from the 1834 American edition published by Charles de Behr, pp. 24–32, 39–45, 49–51, 63–70, 91–98, 112–115, 124–127.

IV.

YE ARE sons of the same father, and the same mother hath nourished you; wherefore then love ye not one another as brethren? Wherefore treat ye one another rather as enemies?

He who loveth not his brother is cursed seven times, and he who maketh himself the enemy of his brother is cursed seventy times seven.

It is for this, that kings, and princes, and all those whom the world calls great have been cursed: they have not loved their brethren, and they have treated them as enemies.

Love ye one another, and fear not the great, nor princes, nor kings.

They are strong against you only because ye are not united, and because that ye love not one another as brethren.

Say not "he is of one nation, and I of another people," for all nations have had on earth the same father, who is Adam, and have in heaven the same father, who is God.

If one member be smitten, the whole body suffereth. Ye are all the same body: nor can one of you be oppressed, without all being oppressed.

If a wolf throw himself into the flock, he devoureth not all at once: he seizeth one of the flock and eateth it. Afterward, his hunger having returned, he seizeth another and devoureth it, and thus it is even to the last, for his hunger returneth always.

Be not ye like unto the sheep, who, when the wolf hath taken away one from among them, are affrighted for a moment, and then return to their pasture. For, they think, "perhaps, he will content himself with his first or second prey, and wherefore should I disquiet myself concerning those which he hath devoured? What are his doings to me? He hath but left more food for me."

Verily, I say unto you: those who thus think within themselves, are destined to become food for the beast who liveth upon flesh and blood.

V.

WHEN THOU seest a man conducted to prison or to execution, be not hasty to say: "this is a wicked man who hath committed some crime against society:"—

For perhaps he is a good man, willing to be of service to his fellow-men, and on this account he is punished by their oppressors.

When thou seest a people loaded with chains, and delivered to the executioner, be not hasty to say: "this is a turbulent people, whose pleasure is to trouble the peace of the world:"—

For perhaps those people are martyrs who die for the safety of the human family.

Eighteen centuries ago, in a city of the East, the chief priests and the kings of that day, nailed to a cross, after having beaten with rods, one whom they called seditious, and a blasphemer.

But, on the day of his death, there was great terror in Hell, and great joy in Heaven:

For the blood of that Just One hath saved the world.

VI.

WHEREFORE IS it that the animals find their nourishment, each one seeking that which is appropriate to his own species? It is because, among them, none stealeth that which belongeth to another, and because, each one is content with that which satisfieth his necessities.

If, in the hive, one bee should say, all the honey which is here is mine; and moreover should dispose, as she thought proper, of the fruits of the common labour, what would become of the other bees?

The earth is a great hive, and men are as the bees.

Each bee hath a right to the portion of honey necessary for her subsistence, and if, among men, some lack necessaries, it is because justice and charity have vanished from among them.

Justice is life, and charity is yet another life, still sweeter and more abundant.

There have gone out false prophets, who have persuaded some men, that all others were born for them; and what these have believed, others also have credited on the word of false prophets.

When this word of falsehood prevailed, angels wept in heaven; for they foresaw, that much of violence, much of crime, and much of evil were about to cover the earth.

Men, equal among themselves, are born for God alone; and whosoever speaketh contrary to this, speaketh blasphemy.

Let him who would be the greatest among you, be your servant; and let him who would be the first among you be the servant of all.

The law of God is a law of love; and love raiseth not itself above others, but sacrificeth itself for others.

He who sayeth in his heart:—I am not like other men, but other men are given to me, that I may command them, and dispose of them and theirs according to my caprice:—such an one is the child of the Devil.

And Satan is the king of this world, for he is the king of all those who think and act thus; and those who think and act thus, are by his counsels, made the masters of the world.

But their empire shall last only for a time, and the end of that time is at hand.

A great battle shall be fought; and the angel of justice and the angel of love shall fight on the side of those who have armed themselves to re-establish among men the reign of justice and the reign of love.

And many shall die in that battle, and their name shall remain upon earth, like a ray of the glory of God.

Therefore, ye sufferers, take courage, strengthen your hearts; for to-morrow cometh the day of trial, the day when each one shall, with joy, lay down his life for his brethren; and the day which followeth, shall be the day of deliverance.

VIII.

IN THE beginning, it was not necessary that man should work to live, the earth, of herself, supplied all his necessities.

But man did that which was evil: and as he had revolted against God, the earth revolted against him.

Then it happened unto him, as it happeneth to the child who hath rebelled against his father; the father withdraweth from him his love, and abandoneth him to himself; and the servants of the house refuse to serve him, and he wandereth hither and thither seeking a wretched subsistence, and eating the bread which he hath earned by the sweat of his brow.

Since that time, God hath condemned all men to labour, and all have their labour, whether it be of body or of mind; and those who say, "I will not work," are the most miserable.

For as the worms devour the dead, so vices devour them; and if there be not vices, there is at least heaviness of heart.

And when God willed that man should work, he concealed a treasure in his toil, because he is a Father, and the love of a Father dieth not.

And as to him who maketh good use of this treasure and wasteth it not in his folly, there cometh a time of repose to him, and then is he as men were in the beginning.

And God also gave the precept:—help ye one another, for ye have among you the strongest and the weakest, the infirm and the vigorous; and yet all must live.

And if ye do thus, all shall live; for I will recompense the pity which ye have shewn to your brethren, and I will make your labour productive.

And that which God hath promised is always fulfilled, and

never hath it been seen, that he who aideth his brethren, hath wanted bread.

But there was in the former times a wicked man, and cursed of Heaven. And this man was strong, and hated labour; insomuch that he said to himself: "what shall I do?—if I work not I shall die, and labour is insupportable to me."

Then there entered into his heart a thought of hell, and he went forth in the night, and seized some of his brethren while they slept, and loaded then with chains.

For, said he, I will force them with rods, and the scourge, to labour for me, and I will eat of the fruit of their toil.

And he did that which he had thought; and others, seeing it, did likewise, and there were no more brethren; there were masters and slaves.

That day was a day of sorrow over the whole earth.

A long time after, there arose another man, more wicked than the first, and more accursed of Heaven.

Seeing that men were every where multiplied, and that their multitude was innumerable, he said unto himself:

I am able enough, it may be, to chain some and force them to labour for me; but it would be necessary to feed them and this would diminish my gain. Let us do better: let them work for nothing! They will die indeed, but as their number is great, I shall amass wealth before they are much diminished, and there will always remain enough of them.

Now all that multitude lived on that which they received in exchange for their labour.

Having thus communed with himself, he addressed himself to some among them and said unto them: "Ye work during six hours, and for your labour there is given unto you a piece of money; work during twelve hours, and you may gain two pieces of money; and ye may live better, ye, and your wives, and your little ones."

And they believed him.

Afterwards he said to them: ye work no more than half of the days in the year: work all the days of the year and your gain will be doubled.

And, again they believed him.

But after that, it came to pass, that the quantity of work having become greater than a half, without the demand for work becoming greater, the half of those who before lived by their labour, no longer found persons to employ them.

Then that wicked man, whom they had believed, said unto them, I will give work to you all, upon condition, that you will work for the same length of time, and that I shall not pay you more than the half of that which I now pay you: for I would willingly do you a service, but I am not willing to ruin myself.

And as they were sore pressed with hunger, they, and their wives, and their little ones, they accepted the terms of this wicked man, and they blessed him; for, said they, he giveth unto us life.

And continuing to deceive them after this manner, that wicked man increased their labour more and more, and diminished more and more their hire.

And they died for want of necessaries, and others pressed forward to take their places, for a poverty so great had come upon that land, that whole families sold themselves for a morsel of bread.

And that wicked man who lied to his brethren, amassed more wealth than the wicked man who had chained them.

The name of the last is TYRANT; to the other, Hell alone can furnish a name.

X.

WHEN THE whole earth groaned in expectation of deliverance, a voice was lifted up in Judea, the voice of Him who came to suffer, and to die for his brethren, of Him who was called in scorn, the son of the carpenter.

But that son of the carpenter, poor and forsaken of the world, said, "Come unto me all ye that travail and are heavy laden, and I will refresh you."

And from that day even unto this, not one of those who have believed on him, hath abode in misery without consolation.

To cure the evils which afflict men, he preached to all, that justice which is the beginning of love, and that love which is the consummation of justice.

But justice commands respect for the rights of others, and sometimes love is willing to surrender even her own, for the sake of peace, or of some other good.

What would the world become, if right should cease to reign, if each one had not security as to his person, and could not enjoy, without fear, that which belongs to him?

Better were it to live in the forests' depths, than in a society thus delivered up to robbery.

That which you take to-day, another will take from you to-morrow. Men will be more miserable than the birds of the air, which the other birds rob not of their food, or their nest.

Who is he that is poor? It is he who hath as yet no property.

What wisheth he? To cease to be poor, that is to say, to acquire some property.

But he who robs, he who plunders, what doeth he, but abolish, as much as in him lieth, this very right of property.

To plunder, to snatch away, is therefore, to attack the poor, as well as the rich; it is to overturn the foundation of all society among men.

And thus, he who possesses nothing, never can possess any thing, because others possess it already; since these last alone, can give him something in exchange for his work.

Order is the benefit, the interest of all.

Drink not of the cup of crime, for at the bottom of it, there is bitter distress, and anguish, and death.

XIII.

It was a night of darkness. A starless sky hung heavily over the earth, like a covering of black marble over a tomb.

And nothing broke the stillness of that night, but a strange noise, as of the light rustling of wings, which at times is heard over the country, and the city.

And then the darkness thickened, and every one felt his soul shrink within him, and a shudder ran through his veins.

And in a hall hung with black, and lighted by the dull red glimmer of a single lamp, seven men, clothed in purple, with crowns upon their heads, were sitting upon seven seats of iron.

And in the middle of the hall, was raised a throne composed of bones, and at the foot of the throne, in place of a footstool, there was a crucifix overturned; and before the throne, a table of ebony, and upon the table a vessel filled with blood, red and foaming, and a human skull.

And these seven men, with crowns, seemed pensive and sad;

and from the depths of their sunken sockets, their eyes, from time to time, shot forth sparks of livid fire.

And one of them, raising himself, approached the throne with tottering step, and placed his foot upon the crucifix.

At that moment, his limbs trembled, and he seemed about to faint. The rest looked on him, motionless; they made not the slightest movement, but an indescribable expression passed over their features, and an unearthly smile contracted their lips.

And he who had seemed about to faint stretched forth his hand, and seized the vessel filled with blood, and poured it out into the skull and drank of it.

And the draught seemed to strengthen him.

And raising his head, this cry came forth from his breast, like the sound of the dull death rattle.

Cursed be Christ, who hath restored liberty to the earth! And the other six crowned men raised themselves together, and together sent forth the same cry:

"Cursed be Christ, who hath restored liberty to the earth!"

After which, sitting down again upon their seats of iron, the first said:

My brethren, what shall we do to stifle liberty? For our reign is finished if hers commences. Our cause is the same; let each one, therefore, propose that which shall seem good unto him.

Hearken then! This is my counsel. Before Christ came, who was able to stand before us? It is his religion which hath ruined us. Let us abolish the religion of Christ.

And they all answered, it is true; let us abolish the religion of Christ.

And the second advanced toward the throne, took the human skull, poured the blood into it, drank it, and spake as follows:

It is not religion alone which should be abolished, but learning and thought also: for learning will discover that which it is not for our interest the world should know: and thought is always ready to contend against force.

And all answered, it is true; let us abolish learning and thought.

And, after having done as the first two had done, a third spake:

When we shall have again plunged men into their stupidity, by taking from them religion, and learning, and thought, we shall have done much, but there will still remain something more for us to do.

The brute possesseth instinct, and dangerous sympathies. It is necessary that one nation should not hear the cry of another people, lest if the one should murmur and rise, the other may be tempted to imitate. Let, then, no murmuring from without penetrate our kingdoms.

And all answered, it is true; let no murmuring from without penetrate our kingdoms.

And a fourth said:—We have our interest, and the people have theirs opposed to ours; if they unite to defend that interest against us, how shall we resist them?

Divide and conquer. Let us make in every province, in every town, in every hamlet, an interest opposed to that of other hamlets, of other towns, and of other provinces.

In this way, all will hate each other, and they will not think of uniting against us.

And all answered, it is true; divide and conquer, concord would ruin us.

And a fifth, having twice filled with blood, and twice emptied the skull, said:

I approve of all these measures, they are good but insufficient. Make men brutes, it is well; but frighten the brutes, strike terror into them by an inexorable justice, and the severest punishments, if ye would not, sooner or later, be devoured by them. The executioner is the prime-minister of a good prince.

And all answered: It is true. The executioner is the prime-minister of a good prince.

And a sixth said, I acknowledge the advantage of prompt, terrible, and inevitable punishments. Still there are heroic and desperate spirits who brave punishment.

Would you govern men easily, make them effeminate by voluptuousness. Virtue will avail us nothing, she nourisheth strength; rather let us exhaust them by corruption.

And all answered, it is true; let us exhaust strength, and energy, and courage by corruption.

Then the seventh, having like the others, drunk from the human skull, spake after this manner, his feet on the crucifix.

Down with Christ! there is a war of extermination, eternal war betwixt him and us.

But how shall we detach the people from him? It is a vain endeavour. What then shall be done? Hearken unto me.—it is necessary to gain the priests of Christ with riches, with honours, and with power.

And they will command the people in the name of Christ, to be subject to us in all that we may do, all that we may order.

And the people will believe them, and obey them for conscience' sake, and our power will be firmer than before.

And all answered, it is true: let us gain the priests of Christ.

And suddenly, the lamp which lighted the hall went out, and the seven men vanished in the darkness.

And it was said to a righteous man who, at that moment, watched and prayed before the cross: My day approacheth, adore and fear nothing.

XIX.

YE HAVE but one father, who is God; and one master, who is Christ.

When, therefore, it shall be said of those who possess great power upon the earth: "Behold, your masters," believe it not. If they are righteous, they are your servants; if they are not righteous, they are your tyrants.

All men are born equal; no man upon entering the world, brings with him the right to command.

I have seen in his cradle a wailing and drivelling infant, and around him stood old men watching, who called him, "my Lord," and kneeling worshipped him. And I perceived there all the misery of man.

It is sin which hath made princes: because, instead of loving and helping one another like brethren, men began to harm one another.

Then they chose from among them one or more whom they believed to be the most righteous, to protect the good against the wicked; and that the weak might live in peace.

And the power which they exercised was a legitimate power, for it was the power of God, who willeth that justice should reign, and the power of the people which hath elected them.

And therefore each one is bound in conscience to obey them.

But there were soon found those who wished to reign of themselves, as if their nature was more elevated than that of their brethren.

And the power of these last is not legitimate, for it is the power of Satan, and their dominion is the dominion of pride and of covetousness.

And therefore when nothing but more of evil is to be dreaded from this, every man may, and sometimes ought, in conscience to resist them.

In the scales of eternal justice our will weigheth more than the will of kings; for it is the people who make kings, and kings are made for the people; not the people for kings.

Our heavenly Father hath not made the limbs of his children to be fettered with irons, nor their souls to be murdered by slavery.

He hath united them in families, and all families are sisters; he hath united them in nations, and all nations are sisters; and whosoever separateth family from family, and nation from nation, putteth asunder what God hath joined together; he doeth the work of Satan.

And that which uniteth family to family, and nation to nation, is primarily the law of God, the law of justice, and the law of love; and afterward the law of liberty, which is also the law of God.

For without liberty, what union would exist among men? They would be joined as the horse is joined to his rider, as the lash of the master to the back of the slave.

If, therefore, some man cometh and sayeth: Ye are mine; answer, No, we belong to God, who is our Father, and to Christ, who is our only Master.

XX.

BE YE not deceived with vain words. Many shall seek to persuade you, that ye are truly free, because they shall have written upon a leaf of paper the word *liberty*, and shall have posted it up on every highway.

Liberty is no placard which one reads at the corners of the streets. She is a living power which a man feels within himself and round about him; the guardian genius of the domestic hearth, the protector of social rights, and the first of these rights.

The oppressor who covereth himself with her name, is the worst of all oppressors. He joineth hypocrisy to tyranny, and profanation to injustice; for the name of liberty is holy.

Beware then of those who cry, Liberty, Liberty, and yet who destroy her by their works.

Is it ye who have chosen those who govern you, who command you to do this, and not to do that, who tax your property, your industry, and your labour? And if it be not ye, how are ye free?

Can ye dispose of your children as ye think fit, trust to whom ye please the care of instructing them, and forming their manners? And if ye have not this power, how are ye free?

The birds of heaven, and even the insects, meet together jointly to do that which none of them could do alone. Have ye the privilege of meeting together jointly to consult of your interests, to defend your rights, to obtain some solace for your evils? And if ye cannot do this, how then are ye free?

Can ye travel from place to place, no man hindering you; can ye use the fruits of the earth and the products of your labour? place your finger in the water of the sea and cause one drop of it to fall in the poor earthen vessel, where your food is preparing, without exposing yourselves to the payment of a penalty, or without being dragged to prison? And if ye have not these privileges, how are ye free?

Can ye, when ye lie down at night, say that no man shall come during your sleep to search the secret places of your mansion, to snatch you from the bosom of your family, and cast you in the depths of a dungeon, because timid power is afraid you will defy it? And if ye have not these privileges, how then are ye free?

Liberty shall shine upon you, when by the force of courage and perseverance ye shall be emancipated from all these bonds.

Liberty shall shine upon you, when ye shall exclaim from the depths of your hearts, We will be free; when to become free, ye shall be ready to sacrifice every thing, to suffer every thing.

Liberty shall shine upon you, when at the foot of the cross upon which Christ died for you, ye shall have sworn to die for one another.

XXIV.

EVERY THING which cometh into the world hath a harbinger which precedeth it.

When the sun is about to rise, the horizon is coloured with a thousand streaks of light, and the east appeareth on fire.

When the tempest comes, a loud roaring is heard upon the banks and the waves are furiously agitated.

The innumerable and varied thoughts which cross and mingle in the horizon of the spiritual world are the signs which announce the rise of the sun of intelligence.

The confused murmur, and the internal agitation of the people, are to me the precursors of the tempest which shall soon pass over the trembling nations.

Be ye therefore ready, for the time is at hand.

And in that day there shall be great terror, and such cries as have not been heard since the days of the flood.

Kings shall be hurled from their thrones; they shall strive with both hands to hold fast their crowns, carried away by the winds, and they themselves shall be swept away with them.

The rich and the mighty shall come out naked from their palaces, for fear of being buried in their ruins.

They shall be seen wandering in the streets, begging of him that passeth by, a rag to cover their nakedness, a crust of bread to appease their hunger; and I know not that they shall obtain it.

And there shall be some men seized with a thirst for blood, who shall worship Death and shall strive to cause him to be worshipped.

And Death shall stretch forth his skeleton hand as if to bless them, and that benediction shall fall upon their hearts, and they shall cease to beat forever.

And the wise men shall be troubled in their learning, for it shall appear to them as a little dim speck, when the sun of intelligence shall arise.

And as he mounts on high, his warmth shall melt the clouds heaped up by the tempest; and they shall be but a light vapour which the gentle wind shall drive toward the West.

The heaven hath never before been so serene, nor the earth so green and so fertile.

And in place of the feeble twilight, which we now call day, a light, living and pure, shall shine from on high, like the reflection of the face of God.

And men shall look upon that light and they shall say: We knew neither ourselves nor others, we knew not that which belongeth unto man. Now we know all things.

And every man shall then love his brother, and rejoice to serve him: and there shall be neither small nor great, for love shall equalize all; and all families shall be as one family, and all nations as one nation.

This is the interpretation of the mystic letters which the blinded Jews fastened to the cross of Christ.

XXVII.

WHO WAS it that pressed around Christ to be taught by his words? The people.

Who was it that followed him into the mountains and the desert places to hear his precepts? The people.

Who desired to make him a king? The people.

Who spread their garments and cast branches before him, crying, Hosanna, as he entered Jerusalem? The people.

Who was it that reviled him for healing the sick on the sabbath-day? The scribes and the pharisees.

Who insidiously questioned him and laid snares to take him? The scribes and the pharisees.

Who said of him: he hath a devil? Who called him a gluttonous man and a wine-bibber? The scribes and the pharisees.

Who treated him as a seditious fellow and blasphemer? Who leagued together to put him to death? Who crucified him upon Calvary between two thieves?

The scribes and pharisees, the teachers of the law, king Herod and his courtiers, the Roman governor, and the chief priests.

Their hypocritical cunning deceived even the people. They urged them to demand the death of him who had fed them in the desert with seven loaves, who restored health to the sick, sight to the blind, hearing to the deaf, and the use of their limbs to the palsied.

But Jesus perceiving that they had seduced the people, as the serpent seduced the woman, prayed his Father, saying: Father, forgive them, for they know not what they do.

Nevertheless, after eighteen centuries, the Father hath not yet forgiven them, and they drag their punishment over the whole earth, and over the whole earth they are beneath the slaves.

The mercy of Christ excludes no man. He hath come into the world to save not some men, but all men. He hath shed for each of us a drop of blood.

But the small, the weak, the humble, the poor, all those who suffered, he loved them with a love of preference.

His heart did beat with the hearts of the people, and the hearts of the people beat with his heart.

And it is through the love of Christ that a sick people revives, and an oppressed people receives the power of emancipating themselves.

Woe unto those who forsake him, who deny him! their misery is incurable, their bondage eternal.

13. The Saint-Simonians:
The Doctrine of Saint-Simon:
An Exposition, First Year, 1828-1829

The Saint-Simonians were followers of Claude Henri Saint–Simon (1760–1825), the gifted and eccentric reformer whom they took as their prophet of a new faith. Saint-Simon had fought in the American Revolution and revealed his ties to the Enlightment by urging the production of a new Encyclopedia. His desire was first for the integration of the sciences, then for government by scientists. It was not until after the Napoleonic era that he wrote *The New Christianity* (1825), the culmination of a series of intellectual changes that produced along the way a new version of history. The new doctrine comprehended or anticipated much of the new tendency to turn to history and to historical forms of understanding that was developing in Germany. It looked toward an era of technocratic control, under which the world would be run by an élite of the able, for the good of the many, all obeying a gospel of work. His doctrine attracted disciples, especially Barthélemy Prosper Enfantin (1796–1864) and Saint-Amand Bazard (1791–1832). These were the leading figures who built the cult after the master's death, although such others as August Comte, Augustin Thierry, and the Perière brothers were also followers. The members of the cult dressed as monks and awaited the arrival of a female Messiah. Despite such oddities, the group produced a number of the leading business figures of the Second Empire.

Bazard gave most of the lectures in 1828–1829 that outlined the doctrine of the new faith. I have selected the lecture on religion because it so clearly reflects what I see as the dominant motive of such a group: the rejection of the egoism of the present and a call for a religiously motivated associationist spirit. This attitude clearly carried over to such later thinkers as Mazzini. All the Saint-Simonians's social doctrine is imbedded in their master's philosophy of history, wherein critical stages supervene upon organic eras. Their present they saw as the last stage of a critical era, which, since the Reformation, had destroyed the unity of thought, feeling, and action that had characterized the Middle Ages. And just as Christian faith had directed moral action and had provided the bases for philosophy and science and the framework for social and political institutions, so now again (as so many religious reformers were to argue in the era after 1789) was to be the time for a new faith to give form, shape, and direction to men's actions, to bind together science and philosophy, and provide moral unity. The selection is reprinted with the permission of Georg G. Iggers from *The Doctrine of Saint-Simon: An Exposition, First Year, 1828–1829*, for which he provided translation, notes, and Introduction (Boston, 1958), pp. 201–213.

Thirteenth Session (*June* 17, 1829)

INTRODUCTION TO THE RELIGIOUS QUESTION

Gentlemen:

In presenting to you most of the principal ideas of Saint-Simon, we have tried particularly to make you understand that society is to be organized according to a general idea and ceaselessly to be guided in its entirety and in its details according to this idea.

In our last sessions, we spoke of the means of social direction, and above all of education, the first and most powerful of all. We said that education was destined, on the one hand, to put individual wills in harmony with the general goal, to make them concur sympathetically towards this goal and, on the other hand, to distribute among the members of society the special knowledge needed to carry out the various types of work and fulfill the various functions of society at the particular stages of civilization.

We have also spoken of another great means of social direction, namely legislation, which in organic epochs is at once penal and remunerative. We have shown that when deprived, like all social facts during critical periods, of the moral sanction which alone can give it a positive value, legislation is reduced to a negative role, namely the purely material and entirely brutal repression of vicious and retrograde abnormalities.

We have said that all these ideas have remained incomplete, since we were unable to present them to you in their entirety as long as we have not raised you to a sufficiently elevated point of view to evaluate their full importance. We could not yet approach the tremendous problem which comprises all the others and whose solution gives all human facts a new meaning.

We may be asked why it was not our first task to pose and answer this great problem which we claim to be indispensable to the understanding of all the others.

This delay was intentional. Considering the moral disposition of our age, we thought that we should first of all develop the ideas of our master to the point where the necessity of examining this problem would be understood by everyone. This procedure is necessary to draw adequate attention to the problem under discussion, the terms of which are such as to arouse the strongest antipathy.

This problem can be expressed thus: Has mankind a religious future? And if so, can religion be reduced to a conception or to purely individual contemplation? Should one not conceive of it as inward thought, isolated from the totality of the sentiments and from each person's system of ideas, without any influence on his social action and political life? Or shall the religion of the future not appear as the expression, as the outburst of the collective thought of mankind, as the synthesis of all its conceptions, of all its modes of being? Should it not take its place in the political order and dominate it entirely? These, gentlemen, are the important questions which we must examine. This is the vast field which we shall enter; for the moment, we do not claim to explore it to its fullest extent but shall at least survey its principal directions.

Doubtless, courage was needed by the men who first dared to trouble mankind in its religious beliefs when all, princes and subjects, artists and scientists, warriors and industrialists, unanimously recognized the existence of one God, of one providential order.

Times have changed greatly.

We certainly do not claim to be heroes for introducing the foundations of a new religion to you. In this indulgent, or rather indifferent, century, all opinions, as we know, can appear without danger, especially when they seem not to go beyond the narrow confines of a philosophic school. But we also know that we are speaking to men who consider themselves superior because they are unbelievers, and who smile scornfully at all religious ideas, which they relegate to the dark ages, to what they call the barbarism of the Middle Ages, and to the childhood of mankind. We do not fear to brave this smile. Voltairian sarcasm and the arrogant scorn of modern materialism can dispel from some men's hearts the vague sentimentality common today. They can frighten away and confound that type of individual religiosity which in vain seeks forms to express itself, but they are powerless to destroy deep conviction.

Yes, gentlemen, we have come here to expose ourselves to this sarcasm and scorn. For following Saint-Simon and in his name, we come to proclaim that mankind has a religious future; that the religion of the future will be greater and more powerful than all those in the past; that it will, like those which preceded it, be the synthesis of all conceptions of mankind and, moreover, of all modes of being. Not only will it dominate the political order, but the political order will be totally a religious institution; for nothing will be conceived of outside of God or will develop outside of His law. Let us add finally that this religion will embrace the entire world because the law of God is universal.

These are the propositions at which the school of Saint-Simon has arrived concerning the great problem occupying us at this moment. We have such confidence, or rather such deep faith, in the truth of these propositions that we do not believe that we are taking any risk by acknowledging that if their falsity were successfully demonstrated, the structure we have erected would be overthrown.

We repeat that we are far from exhausting such a vast subject in one session. Keeping in mind the prejudices prevalent in an age when religious questions are considered to have been judged once and for all, we are at this moment concerned only with combatting this preconceived disfavor and with destroying the arguments presented against even hearing an examination of these vital questions.

Religion, we are told from all sides, is a fruit of the childhood of societies, a product of the times when imagination was their only torch. Why should one concern oneself with it today? The advances of science and its astonishing discoveries have emancipated the human mind in this respect and should preserve it from ever again falling prey to the illusions of earlier times. Science has undermined the very foundations of religion. It has reduced the priests to their true roles of dupes and impostors. It has demonstrated that their teachings were mere illusions if not lies.

Gentlemen, what does the magic word "science" mean to those who use it with such assurance and arrogance? Science! But which one? Astronomy, physics, chemistry, geology, or physiology? We acquainted ourselves thoroughly with the sciences to learn what they taught, but certainly became neither pagan nor Catholic. This confused agglomeration of bits of isolated knowledge, however, without link or unity, furnished us no proof, no argument of any value against the two great foundations of the entire religious structure: God and a providential plan.

True, the European societies have become irreligious. This, at least, is the general character which they present at their peaks today. But it isn't science, or rather, to use the anarchic language of our epoch, "the sciences" that have brought about this passing phenomenon. It is the philosophic ideas of the last three centuries whose origin and character we must presently determine. The scholars have doubtless ardently participated in the destruction of the religious ideas. But it was not as scholars and in consequence of their previous works in this connection that they were led to direct their research toward giving an irreligious interpretation to the facts which they observed. They did so in the capacity of fervent disciples of the critical philosophy. And with little reflection, indeed, it will be seen that nothing less than the philosophic faith that inspired them was necessary for them to find (in their systems on spontaneous generation, for example) an unchallengeable demonstration against the existence of God; for them to find above all, as they claim, a proof of disorder in the existence of facts which they could not classify and whose functions they could not explain—which discovery should only have proved to them their own ignorance. It is not from their positive works that the scholars have drawn their irreligious faith, as they seem to believe, but from a hypothesis, the critical hypothesis which in one form or another has implicitly or explicitly proclaimed that no love, no intelligence, and no force governs the world; that all is left to chance; that man, the incidental product of some general fermentation, has no destiny in the chaos in which he lives, a chaos which doubtless will some day blindly annihilate him as it has blindly created him.

No, gentlemen, the sciences have not brought about the irreligion which we witness. And if one reflects about the nature of the sciences, he will see that the tribute paid by the scientists to this critical hypothesis is the result of a manifest violation of their mission, of the mission which they have assigned themselves with just pride. And, indeed, what do they propose? What do they claim? What is their goal? To co-ordinate the phenomena according to the laws governing the universe; to relate all isolated laws as far as possible to one single law.

But, gentlemen, mark the entire significance of the word "law." Consider the disposition which leads all scientists to link all phenomena, a disposition without which science would be impossible. Indeed, to be able to study the world, the scientist above all must believe that a certain order presides over it, that his environment is not an immense chaos, that his predictions will not be deceived by a secret and unfathomable fatalism. Yes, gentlemen, this is the faith indispensable to the scholar. He must adopt as his first hypothesis that all is interlinked in the universe if he wants to draw any conclusion whatsoever from his observations.

Yet even if through this inevitable hypothesis the scientists were not unwittingly bearing witness of the existence of a providence, their authority in religious matters could at least be challenged by means of the method which they claim to be using exclusively, and to which they attach the positive character of their works. What do they really claim? To be limiting themselves to observing phenomena, to classifying them impartially, passively, according to the order in which they occur, without worrying about their cause and their end in relation to man and his destiny. It is, therefore, evident that in the present state of scientific claims any investigation by scientists in the field of religion can only be a digression from and a formal contradiction to the rules which they have laid down for themselves and in which they glory.

Take the religious standpoint, but one more elevated and broader than any mankind has yet attained. As long as science preserves its atheistic character, which is considered essential to it, science will not give expression to man's faculty to know successively and progressively the laws by which God governs the world: in brief, the providential plan. None of the discoveries upon which atheism, when threatened, relies will be able to escape the formula: "This is how God manifests himself."

No, gentlemen, it is not the destiny of science, as many seem to believe, to be the eternal enemy of religion and constantly to restrict religion's realm in order some day entirely to dispossess it. On the contrary, science is called upon to extend and constantly to strengthen the realm of religion, since each of science's advances is to give man a broader view of God and of His plans for mankind. And have not the illustrious leaders of science felt so, even those men in whose footsteps the scientists of our day glory to follow? Behold Newton, raising himself to the idea of gravitation and humbly bowing before God whose will he has just discovered. Hear Kepler render thanks unto God in a hymn full of enthusiasm for having revealed to him the simplicity and grandeur of the plan upon which He has founded the universal mechanism. Listen how Leibniz, according to de Maistre's pronouncement the greatest man in science, declares that if he attaches any value to science, it is above all in order to have the right to speak of God. You will then recognize that the higher science rises, the more it approaches religion, and that finally scientific inspiration in its highest state of exaltation becomes one with religious inspiration.

We have said, gentlemen, that one must go back to the critical philosophy to explain the atheistic deviations of science. Let us attempt to explain the origin of this philosophy, of this moral state of societies, which is not a new phenomenon in this world.

In our first sessions we showed at various points that mankind successively passed through organic and critical epochs. In the organic epoch, mankind moved with regularity, under the sway of a common belief, toward an ardently desired goal. During the critical epoch, all forces were engaged in destroying the principles and institutions which had guided the preceding society.

We said at that point, without developing the idea further, that the critical epochs had always been irreligious. It is easy to explain this, their dominant characteristic.

The work of destruction until now has been a special task provoked by the present general feeling of uneasiness and has been undertaken without a plan for reorganization, at least without an idea which could serve to this end. When the time of the critical epochs or the epochs of destruction arrives, new realities arise. Society experiences new needs which cannot be admitted or understood by the overly narrow and now inflexible framework of the established belief and of the political institution based upon it. However, these new realities, these demands of the future, seek to come to light and to assume their rightful place. At first they unsuccessfully batter the old order, but by their repeated shocks they end in shattering and overthrowing it. Society then presents the picture of embittered war, of complete anarchy, where sentiments of the hate alone seem to be able to develop. Frightened by the confusion which they observe, no longer able to perceive the order to be established, experiencing nothing but repugnance for the order which has just perished and in which they see only a long, oppressive deception, men of thought soon arrive at the conclusion that the world has been abandoned to disorder, and that it is the plaything of chance and of blind fatalism. When all the hopes which had first animated the struggle vanish after some futile attempts to create a new harmony, man delights in contemplating all the facts which seem to give evidence of disorder. If he looks at the past of mankind, if he studies history, he does so to tell of murders and betrayals, to assign base and shabby causes to events and treacherous intentions to deeds, and to combine his examples in a way leaving no hope for the future. And when he looks at the world which surrounds him, he at once wants to deprive it of life, to treat it as an inorganic entity, as a being without morality, that is, without destiny. But soon he does not even perceive an ingenious mechanism. He sees everywhere a picture of disorder without providence, and he reflects about all that surrounds this society which repels and hurts him. And just as history appears to him as merely a series of bloody revolutions, nature appears to him as the sphere of tempests and storms, of volcanoes and floods. Everywhere he sees disorder, and it seems to him that Mirabeau or Byron alone speak the language of genius.

But, gentlemen, when man has arrived at this moral state, the necessary consequence of the critical epochs, God withdraws from his heart: for God and order are two identical conceptions to him. But as soon as God ceases to dwell in the heart of man, all morality disappears too, for there is morality only for him who conceives of a destiny which can be conceived only in God.

This sad picture which presents itself to our eyes is not occurring for the first time. The period which separates polytheism from Christianity offers a similar one. Is this not a reason for hoping that the exhausted beliefs of Catholicism will soon give place to new ones?

We have just said that the necessary consequence of organic [sic] epochs has been the loosening, or rather the breaking, of all moral links. We need to explain what we mean.

We have shown previously that critical epochs can be divided into two distinct periods: one forms the beginning of those epochs during which society, united by a fervent faith in the doctrines of destruction, acts in concert to overthrow the former religious and social institution; the other comprises the interval separating destruction from reconstruction during which men, disgusted with the past and the uncertainties of the future, are no longer united by any faith or common enterprises. What we have said concerning the absence of morality in critical periods refers only to the second of the two periods which they include, but not at all to the first, or to the men who figure in it and who, through some sort of inconsistency, preach hatred through love; call for destruction while believing to be building; provoke disorder because they desire order; and establish slavery on the altar they erect to liberty. Gentlemen, let us admire these men. Let us pity them merely for having been given the terrible mission which they have fulfilled with devotion and love for mankind. Let us pity them, for they were born to love and their entire life was dedicated to hate. But let us not forget that the pity with which they inspire us should be a lesson to us; that it should increase our desires and confirm our hopes in a better future—in a future in which the men who are capable of love will ceaselessly be able to apply their love.

No, gentlemen, the men who have delivered mankind from the beliefs and institutions which arrested its progress after having aided it could not be without morality. From the height upon which the doctrine of Saint-Simon places you, look down on the careers of those who just accomplished for the last time that terrible task, and you will see that they merely put the finishing strokes on the work begun by Christianity and through their acts bore witness to their faith in the divine word which eighteen hundred years ago proclaimed the day of human brotherhood to the slaves.

We have just shown that the sciences cannot offer a single valid argument against religious ideas; that those arguments supposedly found in the sciences were in obvious contradiction to the nature and purpose of the sciences and to the ideas which served as the foundation of science; that one must attribute the atheism of the scientists of our day to the influence of critical philosophy alone and to the antipathies aroused by it against Catholicism and not to their specialized works, as has usually been done. But, of course, it is not enough to have refuted the testimony brought against religion in the name of science. Indeed, whatever may be the source of atheism, one can at least confront us with it as a fact and ask us if this fact has been produced in vain and if it is not rather imposing in view of the number and above all the authority of the men who testify to the impossibility of a new religious future.

We know, gentlemen, that to the superior men of our time, deep faith is only blind fanaticism, and religious beliefs are nothing but absurd superstitions. But we also know that at the same time when this change in outlook was taking place in modern societies, egoism became dominant. The noblest feelings are daily denounced as prejudices. We know that despite the work of philanthropic political economists (*philanthropes économistes*), the immense majority of the human species sees in the minority merely idle exploiters, not protectors and leaders who sustain and guide them. And because we know all this, we do not despair for the religious future of mankind, for we believe not only in the return but also in the progress of the general sympathies of devotion and of association.

Doubtless, Christian ideas have lost their force, and we shall not seek to hide this fact by showing the temples still filled with the faithful today. But, gentlemen, you have not forgotten that when Jesus appeared on earth, faith in paganism had also been shattered in the world. The first families of Rome were already refusing to let their daughters fill the functions of vestals, formerly always reserved for the highest nobility, which had guarded this privilege jealously. In order that the priesthood could maintain itself yet for a while, an edict of Augustus was required which opened the order to the daughters of the emancipated.

Among us, too, the social superiors have left the ranks of the clergy which formerly had attracted all the men of great ability. The disciples of Voltaire have laughed at the priests. Did not Cicero ridicule the augurers? We have skeptics and epicureans, but those of Rome were as good as ours. We flee from the Church to run to the theater, and we thereby act like the Romans when they fled to the circus.

But perhaps you will say that we, at least, have no magicians, no sorcerers, no soothsayers; that the credulity of the people is less great today; that the people would reject beliefs which the barbarians would have accepted.

But first of all, it is not a question of the future of beliefs which captivated the peoples of eighteen hundred years ago, nor of keeping the external forms which these beliefs took. Moreover, we must call attention to the fact that it is not right to make us seem more unbelieving than we are, for we have deep faith. You say that we have neither sorcerers nor magicians, and you conclude that we are not believing. This is a false conclusion. It proves only that sorcery and magic are too crude means to deceive the men of our day; that our charlatanism is more elevated, our juggling more refined and subtle. Nor are examples lacking here. We could show you enough stages, pulpits, and rostrums surrounded by an openmouthed and often duped public. By command we could mention the hotheaded convictions which often make an egoistic bourgeois seem like a devoted citizen. Mankind never lacks faith. One will no more have to ask whether man has the inclination to believe than whether he will some day renounce love. Rather, it is merely a question of knowing on which men and ideas he will bestow his confidence and for what guarantees he will ask before abandoning himself to them.

You may be certain, gentlemen, that we are as believing as the Romans. We should be ashamed of our credulity if it delivered us defenselessly to egoism, but let us thank God for this precious gift if it makes us confidently embrace the inspirations of devotion.

Our incredulity is not an obstacle to the appearance of new religious ideas. It is rather in our credulity that these ideas find an obstacle.

After having refuted this opinion, we should not hide that there is another, almost opposite opinion which merits examination and which we had to neglect while we rejected the first.

Thus, we shall be told that we paint the present period falsely in antireligious colors, and that society includes many men highly endowed with true piety. And we shall be confronted with the example, which we have just quoted, of the church doors being besieged by masses of faithful.

To the first part of the objection, we reply first of all that the importance we attach to what merits the name of a religious system prevents us from attributing any significance to the more or less mystic contemplations which, at mankind's expense, absorb some individuals with beliefs of their own who through the process of abstraction seem to have forgotten that they are not alone in the world. Moreover, if one intends to speak of the men who are still connected with formulated, public beliefs, with the various sects of Catholicism and Protestantism, we shall point out that Gallican and Jansenist Catholics, Ultramontanes and Jesuits, Lutheran or Calvinist Protestants, Socinians, Episcopalians, Presbyterians, Independents, Quakers, Methodists, and others have as rallying points only dogmas which, despite the significance which they seem to attach to them, are so insignificant in their own eyes that the difference existing between these dogmas, differences completely separating them in their religious practices, introduce no distinctions in their individual or political conduct. They are in agreement not only among themselves but also with the atheists on the things which interest mankind most. Their so-called religious beliefs tend rather to separate them from society than to bind them to it. And finally, if these beliefs are considered only from a practical, which means from a moral and political standpoint, they constitute veritable atheism; for their religious opinions, having so to say only a purely speculative meaning, are almost foreign to society and separate the believers from society rather than uniting them with it. They contain the seed of atheism instead of being the expression of a truly religious sentiment.

But we shall call your attention to the second part of the objection we have just raised. Yes, gentlemen, the temples are still full. Without stopping to take into consideration those who are believers because it is the thing to do or from idleness or calculation: does this fact not prove the ineffectiveness of the critics who claim that they have been able to destroy the most irresistible need of man? Haven't they used all forces at man's disposal to arrive at this goal? Haven't they closed the churches? Haven't they substituted the entire library of the eighteenth century for the holy writings? Gentlemen, if the temples of polytheism had been closed a century before the coming of Jesus, the Greeks and Romans would have returned to fetishism rather than to have lived without religious beliefs and worship. And, similarly, the peoples of our day would return to polytheism if the word of Christ would no longer be preached to them. We do not hesitate to say with you that what is not atheism today is ignorance and superstition. But if we want to heal mankind of this wound, if we want it to abandon the beliefs and practices which we consider unworthy of it, if we want it to leave the Church of the Middle Ages, we must open the Church of the future. Let us stand ready, as de Maistre has said, for a tremendous event in the divine order toward which, as all must notice, we are marching at an accelerated speed. Let us say with him that there is no longer religion on earth and that mankind cannot remain in this state. But more fortunate than de Maistre, we shall no longer wait for the man of genius whom he prophesies and who, according to him, shall soon reveal to the world the natural affinity of religion and science. Saint-Simon has appeared.

Part III: *Politics*

14. Edmund Burke: *An Appeal from the New to the Old Whigs*

Edmund Burke (1729–1797) was born in Dublin, and after attending Trinity College there, proceeded to London to study law. Yet his early pursuits were largely literary (his *Inquiry into the Origin of our Ideas on the Sublime and the Beautiful* was a major statement of aesthetic theory), and he became editor of the *Annual Register* at thirty. Six years later he entered the House of Commons and became secretary to the Marquis of Rockingham, leader of the Whig Party. In Parliament he served the Whig cause with eloquent writings and speeches against George III's efforts to establish personal control, and in support of the American colonies, Roman Catholic emancipation, and abolition of the slave trade.

Burke was the great opponent of the French Revolution. His *Reflections on the Revolution in France* (1790) conclusively established the conservative position and laid the basis for theoretical opposition to the Revolution in an organic theory of society and in the feelings of patriotism and veneration long before the "excesses" that marked the Terror turned many early supporters and the undecided against the course events were taking in France. He held a middle position, attacking despotism on the one hand and foolish radical reformers on the other, maintaining the validity of the settlement in England of 1688–1689—the great Whig triumph. In this, he remained one of the founders of modern liberalism, as well as of conservatism. The following selection from his *An Appeal from the New to the Old Whigs* (1791), in which he sought to justify his stand on the Revolution to the pro-French Whigs, shows his veneration of the seventeenth-century settlement. From Edmund Burke, *An Appeal from the New to the Old Whigs*, edited by John M. Robson (Indianapolis, Ind., 1962), pp. 132–138. Copyright © 1962, by The Bobbs-Merrill Company, Inc., reprinted by permission of the Liberal Arts Press Division.

Virtues of the British Constitution
and the Value of Adherence to It

THE THEORY contained in his book [i.e., Burke's *Reflections*] is not to furnish principles for making a new constitution, but for illustrating the principles of a constitution already made. It is a theory drawn from the *fact* of our government. They who oppose it are bound to show that his theory militates with that fact; otherwise, their quarrel is not with his book, but with the constitution of their country. The whole scheme of our mixed constitution is to prevent any one of its principles from being carried as far as, taken by itself and theoretically, it would go. Allow that to be the true policy of the British system, then most of the faults with which that system stands charged will appear to be, not imperfections into which it has inadvertently fallen, but excellencies which it has studiously sought. To avoid the perfections of extreme, all its several parts are so constituted as not alone to answer their own several ends, but also each to limit and control the others; insomuch that, take which of the principles you please, you will find its operation checked and stopped at a certain point. The whole movement stands still rather than that any part should proceed beyond its boundary. From thence it results that in the British constitution there is a perpetual treaty and compromise going on, sometimes openly, sometimes with less observation. To him who contemplates the British constitution, as to him who contemplates the subordinate material world, it will always be a matter of his most curious investigation to discover the secret of this mutual limitation. . . .

They who have acted, as in France they have done, upon a scheme wholly different, and who aim at the abstract and unlimited perfection of power in the popular part, can be of no service to us in any of our political arrangements. They who in their headlong career have overpassed the goal can furnish no example to those who aim to go no further. The temerity of such speculators is no more an example than the timidity of others. The one sort scorns the right; the other fears it; both miss it. But those who by violence go beyond the barrier are without question the most mischievous, because, to go beyond it, they overturn and destroy it. To say they have spirit is to say nothing in their praise. The untempered spirit of madness, blindness, immorality, and impiety deserves no commendation. He that sets his house on fire because his fingers are frostbitten can never be a fit instructor in the method of providing our habitations with a cheerful and salutary warmth. We want no foreign examples to rekindle in us the flame of liberty. The example of our own ancestors is abundantly sufficient to maintain the spirit of freedom in its full vigor, and to qualify it in all its exertions. The example of a wise, moral, well-natured, and well-tempered spirit of freedom is that alone which can be useful to us, or in the least degree reputable or safe. Our fabric is so constituted, one part of it bears so much on the other, the parts are so made for one another, and for nothing else, that to introduce any foreign matter into it is to destroy it. . . .

This British constitution has not been struck out at a heat by a set of presumptuous men, like the Assembly of pettifoggers run mad in Paris.

> 'Tis not the hasty product of a day,
> But the well-ripened fruit of wise delay.

It is the result of the thoughts of many minds in many ages. It is no simple, no superficial thing, nor to be estimated by superficial understandings. An ignorant man, who is not fool enough to meddle with his clock, is, however, sufficiently confident to think he can safely take to pieces and put together, at his pleasure, a moral machine of another guise, importance, and complexity, composed of far other wheels and springs and balances and counteracting and cooperating powers. Men little think how immorally they act in rashly meddling with what they do not understand. Their delusive good intention is no sort of excuse for their presumption. They who truly mean well must be fearful of acting ill. The British constitution may have its advantages pointed out to wise and reflecting minds, but it is of too high an order of excellence to be adapted to those which are common. It takes in too many views, it makes too many combinations, to be so much as comprehended by shallow and superficial understandings. Profound thinkers will know it in its reason and spirit. The less inquiring will recognize it in their feelings and their experience. They will thank God they have a standard which, in the most essential point of this great concern, will put them on a par with the most wise and knowing.

If we do not take to our aid the foregone studies of men reputed intelligent and learned, we shall be always beginners. But men must learn somewhere, and the new teachers mean no more than what they effect, as far as they succeed—that is, to deprive men of the benefit of the collected wisdom of mankind and to make them blind disciples of their own particular presumption. Talk to these deluded creatures (all the disciples and most of the masters) who are taught to think themselves so newly fitted up and furnished, and you will find nothing in their houses but the refuse of *Knaves' Acre*—nothing but the rotten stuff, worn out in the service of delusion and sedition in all ages, and which, being newly furbished up, patched, and varnished, serves well enough for those who, being unacquainted with the conflict which has always been maintained between the sense and the nonsense of mankind, know nothing of the former existence and the ancient refutation of the same follies. It is near two thousand years since it has been observed that these devices of ambition, avarice, and turbulence were antiquated. They are, indeed, the most ancient of all commonplaces—commonplaces sometimes of good and necessary causes; more frequently of the worst, but which decide upon neither. . . .

Rational and experienced men tolerably well know, and have always known, how to distinguish between true and false liberty and between the genuine adherence and the false pretense to what is true. But none, except those who are profoundly studied, can comprehend the elaborate contrivance of a fabric fitted to unite private and public liberty with public force, with order, with peace, with justice, and, above all, with the institutions formed for bestowing permanence and stability, through ages, upon this invaluable whole.

Place, for instance, before your eyes such a man as Montesquieu. Think of a genius not born in every country or every time: a man gifted by Nature with a penetrating, aquiline eye, with a judgment prepared with the most extensive erudition, with a Herculean robustness of mind, and nerves not to be broken with labor—a man who could spend twenty years in one pursuit. Think of a man like the universal patriarch in Milton (who had drawn up before him in his prophetic vision the whole series of the generations which were to issue from his loins): a man capable of placing in review, after having brought together from the East, the West, the North, and the South, from the coarseness of the rudest barbarism to the most refined and subtle civilization, all the schemes of government which had ever prevailed amongst mankind, weighing, measuring, collating, and comparing them all, joining fact with theory, and calling into council, upon all this infinite assemblage of things, all the speculations which have fatigued the understandings of profound reasoners in all times. Let us then consider that all these were but so many preparatory steps to qualify a man, and such a man, tinctured with no national prejudice, with no domestic affection, to admire and to hold out to the admiration of mankind the constitution of England. And shall we Englishmen revoke to such a suit? Shall we, when so much more than he has produced remains still to be understood and admired, instead of keeping ourselves in the schools of real science, choose for our teachers men incapable of being taught—whose only claim to know is that they have never doubted—from whom we can learn nothing but their own indocility—who would teach us to scorn what in the silence of our hearts we ought to adore?

Different from them are all the great critics. They have taught us one essential rule. I think the excellent and philosophic artist, a true judge, as well as a perfect follower of Nature, Sir Joshua Reynolds, has somewhere applied it, or something like it, in his own profession. It is this: that, if ever we should find ourselves disposed not to admire those writers or artists (Livy and Virgil, for instance, Raphael or Michelangelo) whom all the learned had admired, not to follow our own fancies, but to study them, until we know how and what we ought to admire, and if we cannot arrive at this combination of admiration with knowledge, rather to believe that we are dull than that the rest of the world has been imposed on. It is as good a rule, at least, with regard to this admired constitution. We ought to understand it according to our measure, and to venerate where we are not able presently to comprehend.

Such admirers were our fathers, to whom we owe this splendid inheritance. Let us improve it with zeal, but with fear. Let us follow our ancestors, men not without a rational, though without an exclusive confidence in themselves—who, by respecting the reason of others, who, by looking backward as well as forward, by the modesty as well as by the energy of their minds, went on insensibly drawing this constitution nearer and nearer to its perfection by never departing from its fundamental principles nor introducing any amendment which had not a subsisting root in the laws, constitution, and usages of the kingdom. Let those who have the trust of political or of natural authority ever keep watch against the desperate enterprises of innovation; let even their benevolence be fortified and armed. They have before their eyes the example of a monarch insulted, degraded, confined, deposed; his family dispersed, scattered, imprisoned; his wife insulted to his face, like the vilest of the sex, by the vilest of all populace, himself three times dragged by these wretches in an infamous triumph; his children torn from him, in violation of the first right of Nature, and given into the tuition of the most desperate and impious of the leaders of desperate and impious clubs; his revenues dilapidated and plundered; his magistrates murdered; his clergy proscribed, persecuted, famished; his nobility degraded in their rank, undone in their fortunes, fugitives in their persons; his armies corrupted and ruined; his whole people impoverished, disunited, dissolved; whilst through the bars of his prison, and amidst the bayonets of his keepers, he hears the tumult of two conflicting factions, equally wicked and abandoned, who agree in principles, in dispositions, and in objects, but who tear each other to pieces about the most effectual means of obtaining their common end: the one contending to preserve for a while his name, and his person, the more easily to destroy the royal authority— the other clamoring to cut off the name, the person, and the monarchy together, by one sacrilegious execution. All this accumulation of calamity, the greatest that ever fell upon one man, has fallen upon his head, because he had left his virtues unguarded by caution— because he was not taught that, where power is concerned, he who will confer benefits must take security against ingratitude.

I have stated the calamities which have fallen upon a great prince and nation, because they were not alarmed at the approach of danger, and because, what commonly happens to men surprised, they lost all resource when they were caught in it. When I speak of danger, I certainly mean to address myself to those who consider the prevalence of the new Whig doctrines as an evil.

The Whigs of this day have before them, in this Appeal, their constitutional ancestors; they have the doctors of the modern school. They will choose for themselves. The author of the *Reflections* has chosen for himself. If a new order is coming on, and all the political opinions must pass away as dreams, which our ancestors have worshipped as revelations, I say for him that he would rather be the last (as certainly he is the least) of that race of men than the first and greatest of those who have coined to themselves Whig principles from a French die unknown to the impress of our fathers in the constitution.

15. Joseph de Maistre: *Essay on the Generative Principle of Political Constitutions*

Joseph de Maistre (1753–1821) was the outstanding spokesman for Catholic conservatism of the ultramontane variety in the Revolutionary era. He was from Savoy, then part of the Kingdom of Sardinia. When French troops took Savoy, he fled to Switzerland. In 1802 he was named the Sardinian representative to St. Petersburg, where he wrote the work from which the selection below is taken. He returned to Savoy in 1817 and became a minister of state, in charge of judicial matters.

He is clearly a disciple of Burke, especially in his organic view of the state, his denial of the possibility of efforts at political creation, his distaste for written constitutions, and his awareness of the force of myths. Yet, he is quite independent in his heavy theological emphasis, in his stress upon international Catholicism and the sovereignty of the pope, rather than upon the national churches, and he serves as a theorist for the alliance the Revolution created among the Continental nobility, their kings, and the institutional Church—an alliance that dominated post-Napoleonic Continental politics. He strongly emphasized the power of man's sinful passions, to the point of glorifying the executioner as the bastion of society, and he saw history as providential, the Revolution as God's punishment of France, and existing social organizations as ordained by God.

There follows the 1814 Preface to his *Essay on the Generative Principle of Political Constitutions* (1808–1809), from the translation published in Boston in 1847, pp. vii-xxii.

Preface

POLITICAL SCIENCE, which is, perhaps, the most thorny of all sciences, by reason of the difficulty perpetually arising, of discerning what is stable or changeable in its elements, presents a very strange phenomenon, well calculated to make every wise man, called to the administration of states, to tremble; it is this, that whatever good sense perceives, at first view, in this science, as an evident truth, is almost always found, when experience has spoken, not only false, but pernicious.

To begin at the foundation. If we had never heard governments spoken of, and men were called upon to deliberate, for example, on hereditary or elective monarchy, we should justly regard one who should decide for the former, as a madman: the arguments against it appear so naturally to reason, that it is useless to repeat them. History, however, which is experimental politics, demonstrates, that an hereditary monarchy is the government which is the most stable, the happiest, and most natural to man; and an elective monarchy, on the contrary, is the worst form of government known.

With respect to population, commerce, prohibitive laws, and a thousand other important subjects, the most plausible theory is almost always found to be contradicted and annulled by experience. Let us cite a few examples.

What method must be adopted to render a state powerful? "It is necessary, first of all, to favour population by every possible means." On the contrary, every law, tending directly to favour population, without regard to other considerations, is bad. It is even necessary, to endeavour to establish in the state a certain moral power, tending to diminish the number of marriages, and to render them less hasty. The proportion of births over deaths, as ascertained by tables, only proves, ordinarily, the number of the wretched. Etc., etc. French economists had sketched the demonstration of these truths: the excellent work of Malthus has completed it.

How shall scarcity and famine be prevented? "Nothing is more simple. It is necessary to prohibit the exportation of grains." On the contrary, a premium must be allowed to those who export them. The example and authority of England has constrained us to swallow this paradox.

How shall exchange be maintained in favour of a particular country? "It is unquestionably necessary to prevent the specie from going out of it, and consequently to see to it, by severe prohibitory laws, that the state buys no more than it sells." On the contrary, these means have never been employed without lowering the exchange, or, what amounts to the same thing, without augmenting the indebtedness of the nation; and never can the opposite course be taken without raising it, that is to say, without making it evident that the credit of the nation over its neighbors is increased. Etc., etc.

But the observation we are now considering recurs most frequently in that which is most substantial and fundamental in politics; I mean in the very constitution of empires. It is said that the German philosophers have invented the word *Metapolitics* to be to *Politics*, what *Metaphysics* is to *Physics*. This new term appears to be very happily invented to express the *Metaphysics of Politics*, for there is such a thing; and this science deserves the profound attention of observers.

An anonymous writer [de Maistre himself—Ed.] who has been much occupied with speculations of this nature, and who has endeavored to fathom the hidden foundations of the social edifice, believed himself to be in the right when, nearly twenty years ago, he advanced, as so many incontestable axioms, the following propositions, diametrically opposed to the theories of that time.

1. No constitution results from deliberation; the rights of the people are never written, or never except as simple declarations of pre-existing rights not written, of which nothing more can be said, than that they exist because they exist.

2. Human action in such cases if so far circumscribed, that the men who act are only circumstances.

3. The rights of the *people*, properly so called, proceed almost always from the concessions of sovereigns, and then it is possible to trace them historically; but the rights of the sovereign and of the aristocracy have neither date nor known authors.

4. These concessions themselves have always been preceded by a state of things which rendered them necessary, and which did not depend upon the sovereign.

5. Although written laws are only the declarations of pre-existing rights, yet it does not follow that all these rights can be written.

6. The more is written, the weaker the constitution.

7. No nation can give liberty to itself, if it has it not.

8. Lawgivers, strictly speaking, are extraordinary men, belonging perhaps only to the ancient world and to the youth of nations.

9. These lawgivers even, notwithstanding their wonderful power, have only collected the pre-existing elements, and have always acted in the name of the Divinity.

10. Liberty, in a sense, is the gift of kings; for all nations were constituted free by kings.

11. There never has existed a free nation which had not, in its natural constitution, germs of liberty as old as itself; and no nation has ever successfully attempted to develop, by its fundamental written laws, other rights than those which existed in its natural constitution.

12. No assembly of men can give existence to a nation. An attempt of this kind ought even to be ranked among the most memorable acts of folly.

It does not appear that, since the year 1796, the date of the first edition of the work we quote, there has anything passed in the world to induce the author to abandon his theory. We believe on the contrary, that it may be useful at this moment to develop the theory fully, and to trace it to its ultimate results; the most important of which is, doubtless, the one that is found announced in these terms, in the tenth chapter of the same work, viz.:

Man cannot create a sovereign. At the utmost, he may be the instrument in dethroning the sovereign, and delivering his kingdom to another sovereign already royal. . . . Moreover there never has existed a royal family to whom a plebian origin could be assigned. If such a phenomenon should appear, it would create an era in the world.

With respect to this proposition we may reflect, that the *divine judgment* has just now sanctioned it in a manner sufficiently solemn. But who knows whether the ignorant levity of our age will not seriously say, if he had willed it, he would still be in his place! just as is now repeated after two centuries; if Richard Cromwell has possessed the genius of his father, he would have fixed the protectorate in his family; which is precisely the same as to say, if this family had not ceased to reign, it would reign still.

It is written BY ME KINGS REIGN. This is not a phrase of the church, a metaphor of the preacher; it is a literal truth, simple and palpable. It is a law of the political world. God *makes* kings in the literal sense. He prepares royal races; maturing them under a cloud which conceals their origin. They appear at length *crowned with glory and honour;* they take their places; and this is the most certain sign of their legitimacy.

The truth is, that they arise as it were of themselves, without violence on the one part, and without marked deliberation on the other: it is a species of magnificent tranquillity, not easy to express. *Legitimate usurpation* would seem to me to be the most appropriate expression (if not too bold) to characterize these kinds of origins, which time hastens to consecrate.

Let no one, then, permit himself to be dazzled by the most splendid human appearances. Who has ever concentrated in himself more of them than the extraordinary personage whose fall still resounds throughout Europe? Has there ever been a sovereignty outwardly so well fortified, a greater consolidation of means, a man more powerful, more active, more formidable? For a long time we saw him trample under foot twenty nations silent and frozen with dread; and his power at length had struck certain roots which might have led even *hope to despair*. Yet he is fallen, and so low, that Pity while contemplating him, draws back for fear of being *touched* by him. We may observe, moreover, in passing, that for a reason *somewhat* different, it has become equally difficult to speak of this man, and of his august rival who has rid the world of him. The one escapes insult, and the other praise. But to return.

In a work known only to a few persons at St. Petersburgh, the author wrote in the year 1810, "If, when two parties encounter each other in a revolution, on one side precious victims are seen to fall, we may rest assured that this party will triumph at last, notwithstanding all appearances to the contrary."

The truth of this assertion has also just been verified in a manner the most striking, and the least expected. The moral order has its laws as well as the physical, and the investigation of these laws is altogether worthy of occupying the meditations of a true philosopher. After an entire age of criminal trifling, it is high time to recall to mind what we are, and to trace all knowledge back to its source. It is this that has induced the author of this little work to permit it to escape from the timid portfolio which has retained it for five years. He permits the date of it to stand, and gives it to the world, word for word, just as it was written at that time. Friendship has called forth this publication, which perhaps is so much the worse for the author; for this good dame is, on certain occasions, as blind as her brother. Be this as it may, the mind which has dictated the work enjoys a privilege well understood; he may doubtless be mistaken sometimes on indifferent points; he may exaggerate, or speak too confidently; he may, in fine, offend against language or taste; and in this case, so much the better for the evil disposed, *if perchance there be any such;* but there will always be left to him the well founded hope of not displeasing any one, since he loves all the world; and, moreover, he will enjoy the perfect assurance of interesting a numerous and very estimable class of men, without the possibility of injuring a single person!—a *confidence* altogether tranquilizing.

16. Friedrich von Savigny: *Of the Vocation of our Age for Legislation and Jurisprudence*

Friedrich Karl von Savigny (1779–1861) is the most famous figure in the German historical school of legal theory. The work from which the following selection is taken is his pamphlet *Of the Vocation of Our Age for Legislation and Jurisprudence* (1814), which is a polemic against the efforts to introduce into Germany a uniform code of law like the Napoleonic Code (which had been imposed in some German territories by the victorious French armies).

Savigny held the chair of law at the University of Berlin from 1810 to 1842. His reputation was made as a legal scholar and historian of law (his study of Roman law, *Right of Possession,* was published in 1803). He anticipated the later interest among historians—e.g., Sir Henry Maine in England—in the study of the development of institutions. The selections that follow show Savigny's adoption of the organic view of society, and his preference for the natural customary product of the people themselves, his nationalism, and the strong historical inclination of his thought.

Savigny was Minister of Justice in Prussia from 1842 to 1848.

The selection here is from Abraham Hayward's translation (London, 1831) of *Of the Vocation of our Age for Legislation and Jurisprudence,* pp. 17–30, 58–60, 130–139.

IN MANY countries of Germany, a want, of an adventitious nature, has now raised the question as to the best mode of dealing with the law; and thus a question, which our governments were for a long time enabled to leave unagitated, has grown into a general subject of deliberation amongst statesmen and jurists. But a more honourable motive than the mere want, has contributed to bring about this public deliberation,—the feeling that Germany, on her deliverance from oppression, is imperatively called upon by every living energy, to shew herself not unworthy of the times. It is no mark of presumption therefore, but right and proper, for every man, who has a heart for his vocation, and a clear conception of it, publicly to communicate his views; and jurists should, least of all, be behindhand in this respect. For it is precisely in the law that the difference between the present time and the past is remarkable. Much perversion, in particular instances, may undoubtedly still occur upon the subject, from misconception or bad intention; but we are once again at liberty to ask, what is proper and expedient? The subject may again be viewed without reference to external considerations: rulers may again act according to conviction, and place their honour in the general weal. No one can say as much of the time that is past. When the code broke into Germany, and ate in, further and further, like a cancer, there was no mention of its intrinsic merits, scarcely here and there in empty phrases; extraneous motives, wholly foreign to the proper value of the code, determined every thing,—a state of things flagitious in itself, independently of the consideration that the object in view was the most pernicious of all objects. Until now, therefore, it was fruitless to speak upon the subject. Those who, during this period, did speak upon it, were partly advocates of the bad cause from interested motives; partly, with inconceivable simplicity, stultified by it; most of them merely assisted in the undertaking, as practical men, without adopting an opinion of their own; some few voices, well meriting attention, were raised, rebuking and warning; others, making signs and indicating, but none with any hope of success. That once again a diversity of opinions may exist; that once again the decision can be a subject of dispute, is one of the blessings which God has vouchsafed to us; for only from this diversity can a living and firm unity proceed,—the unity of conviction, for which our nature compels us to struggle in all matters of mind.

But there are two modes of carrying on a controversy; one hostile, and one amicable. We adopt the first when we find the motive and object to be bad; the latter, when we are investigating the means to objects of general good. The former would be applicable, even now when there is no longer any question of the code, should any one maintain that this is the proper time for each particular state of Germany to isolate itself, that the law is a fit instrument for the purpose, and that every government should provide a separate code for itself, in order to remove, even from the law, every thing that might revive a recollection of the common national tie. This view is any thing but imaginary; on the contrary, many a government notoriously inclines to it; but a certain apprehension prevents it from being publicly avowed at present, and I doubt whether it has ever been advanced in any work on the law. Wholly different is it with the plans, which, up to the present time, have been proposed with regard to this law; for with them, even where we do not agree, the amicable mode is possible; and this leads, if not to the unanimity of the disputants, at least to a better understanding on the whole.

Of two opinions as to the establishment of the law, with which I am acquainted, the one inclines to the restoration of the old system, the other to the adoption of a general code for all the states of Germany. To illustrate this second opinion, some observations are necessary here; as it must be considered in a two-fold historical connection.

In the first place, it is connected with many plans and experiments of the kind since the middle of the eighteenth century. During this period the whole of Europe was actuated by a blind rage for improvement. All sense and feeling of the greatness by which other times were characterized, as also of the natural development of communities and institutions, all, consequently, that is wholesome and profitable in history, was lost; its place was supplied by the most extravagant anticipations of the present age, which was believed to be destined to be nothing less than to the being a picture of absolute perfection. This impulse manifested itself in all directions; what it has effected in religion and government, is known; and it is also evident how everywhere, by a natural reaction, it could not fail to pave the way for a new and more lively love for what is permanent. The law was likewise affected by it. Men longed for new codes, which, by their completeness, should insure a mechanically precise administration of justice; insomuch that the judge, freed from the exercise of private opinion, should be confined to the mere literal application: and at the same time, they were to be divested of all historical associations, and, in pure abstraction, be equally adapted to all nations and all times. It would be very erroneous to ascribe this impulse, and these applications of it, to any false teachers in particular; it was, with some highly honourable exceptions, the opinion of nations. It was, therefore, not in the power of the governments to ward off all the effects; and, in fact, the mere tempering and controlling of it might often be looked upon as highly meritorious, and as a proof of internal vigour. On comparing the present time with the past, we may be allowed to congratulate ourselves. An historical spirit has been every where awakened, and leaves no room for the shallow self-sufficiency above alluded to. And although young writers often adopt a similar tone, it is no longer the prevailing one. Even in the above-mentioned plans of codes, this pleasing comparison is partially confirmed. Free from those extravagant pretensions, they are directed to a fixed practical object, and the reasonings, also, on which they are founded, are good. The lapse of this period, however, secures to us the great advantage of being able to take counsel by their experience. Those theories have successively given rise to codes for three great countries. These, and, in part, their effects, are before us, and it would be unpardonable to despise the lesson which, in the way of encouragement or warning, they are capable of affording us. In the second place, those plans are connected with a general theory of the origin of all positive law, which was always prevalent with the great majority of German jurists. According to this theory, all law, in its concrete form, is founded upon the express enactments of the supreme power. Jurisprudence has only the contents of the enactments for its object. Accordingly, legislation itself, and jurisprudence as well, are of a wholly accidental and fluctuating nature; and it is very possible that the law of to-morrow may not at all resemble the law of to-day. A complete code is, consequently, of primary importance, and it is only in case of its defectiveness that we can ever be exposed to the lamentable necessity of making shift with customary law as an uncertain kind of supplement. This theory is of much greater antiquity than the theory above-mentioned; both have come into hostile collision on many points, but have far oftener agreed very well. The conviction that there is a practical law of nature or reason, an ideal legislation for all times and all circumstances, which we have only to discover to

bring positive law to permanent perfection, often served to reconcile them. Whether there be any real foundation for this theory of
the origin of positive law, will be seen in the next chapter.

WE first inquire of history, how law has actually developed itself
amongst nations of the nobler races; the question—What may be
good, or necessary, or, on the contrary, censurable herein,—will
be not at all prejudiced by this method of proceeding.

In the earliest times to which authentic history extends, the law
will be found to have already attained a fixed character, peculiar
to the people, like their language, manners and constitution. Nay,
these phenomena have no separate existence, they are but the
particular faculties and tendencies of an individual people, in-
separably united in nature, and only wearing the semblance of
distinct attributes to our view. That which binds them into one
whole is the common conviction of the people, the kindred consciousness of an inward necessity, excluding all notion of an accidental and arbitrary origin.

How these peculiar attributes of nations, by which they are
first individualized, originated—this is a question which cannot
be answered historically. Of late, the prevalent opinion has been
that all lived at first a sort of animal life, advancing gradually to a
more passable state, until at length the height on which they now
stand, was attained. We may leave this theory alone, and confine
ourselves to the mere matter of fact of that first authentic condition of the law. We shall endeavour to exhibit certain general
traits of this period, in which the law, as well as the language,
exists in the consciousness of the people.

This youth of nations is poor in ideas, but enjoys a clear perception of its relations and circumstances, and feels and brings
the whole of them into play; whilst we, in our artificial complicated existence, are overwhelmed by our own riches, instead of
enjoying and controlling them. This plain natural state is particularly observable in the law; and as, in the case of an individual, his
family relations and patrimonial property may possess an additional value in his eyes from the effect of association,—so on the
same principle, it is possible for the rules of the law itself to be
amongst the objects of popular faith. But these moral faculties
require some bodily existence to fix them. Such, for language, is
its constant uninterrupted use; such, for the constitution, are

palpable and public powers,—but what supplies its place with regard to the law? In our times it is supplied by rules, communicated by writing and word of mouth. This mode of fixation, however, presupposes a high degree of abstraction, and is, therefore, not practicable in the early time alluded to. On the contrary, we then find symbolical acts universally employed where rights and duties were to be created or extinguished: it is their palpableness which externally retains law in a fixed form; and their solemnity and weight correspond with the importance of the legal relations themselves, which have been already mentioned as peculiar to this period. In the general use of such formal acts, the Germanic races agree with the ancient Italic, except that, amongst these last, the forms themselves appear more fixed and regular, which perhaps arose from their city constitutions. These formal acts may be considered as the true grammar of law in this period; and it is important to observe that the principal business of the early Roman jurists consisted in the preservation and accurate application of them. We, in latter times, have often made light of them as the creation of barbarism and superstition, and have prided ourselves on not having them, without considering that we, too, are at every step beset with legal forms, to which, in fact, only the principal advantages of the old forms are wanting,—namely, their palpableness, and the popular prejudice in their favour, whilst ours are felt by all as something arbitrary, and therefore burdensome. In such partial views of early times we resemble the travellers, who remark, with great astonishment, that in France the little children, nay, even the common people, speak French with perfect fluency.

But this organic connection of law with the being and character of the people, is also manifested in the progress of the times; and here, again, it may be compared with language. For law, as for language, there is no moment of absolute cessation; it is subject to the same movement and development as every other popular tendency; and this very development remains under the same law of inward necessity, as in its earliest stages. Law grows with the growth, and strengthens with the strength of the people, and finally dies away as the nation loses its nationality. But this inward progressive tendency, even in highly cultivated times, throws a great difficulty in the way of discussion. It has been maintained above, that the common consciousness of the people is the peculiar seat of law. This, for example, in the Roman law, is easily conceivable of its essential parts, such as the general definition of marriage, of property, &c.&c., but with regard to the endless detail, of which we have only a remnant in the Pandects,[1] every one must regard it as impossible.

This difficulty leads us to a new view of the development of law. With the progress of civilization, national tendencies become more and more distinct, and what otherwise would have remained common, becomes appropriated to particular classes; the jurists now become more and more a distinct class of the kind; law perfects its language, takes a scientific direction, and, as formerly it existed in the consciousness of the community, it now devolves upon the jurists, who thus, in this department, represent the community. Law is henceforth more artificial and complex, since it has a twofold life; first, as part of the aggregate existence of the community, which it does not cease to be; and, secondly, as a distinct branch of knowledge in the hands of the jurists. All the latter phenomena are explicable by the co-operation of those two principles of existence; and it may now be understood, how even the whole of that immense detail might arise from organic causes, without any exertion of arbitrary will or intention. For the sake of brevity, we call, technically speaking, the connection of law with the general existence of the people—the political element; and the distinct scientific existence of law—the technical element.

At different times, therefore, amongst the same people, law will be natural law (in a different sense from our law of nature), or learned law, as the one or the other principle prevails, between which a precise line of demarcation is obviously impossible. Under a republican constitution, the political principle will be able to preserve an immediate influence longer than in monarchical states; and under the Roman republic in particular, many causes co-operated to keep this influence alive, even during the progress of civilization. But in all times, and under all constitutions, this influence continues to shew itself in particular applications, as where the same constantly-recurring necessity makes a general consciousness of the people at large possible. Thus, in most cities, a separate law for menial servants and house-renting

---

[1] Compilation of extracts from the writings of Roman jurists, prepared in 533; the chief repository of Roman law. (Ed.)

will grow up and continue to exist, equally independent of positive rules and scientific jurisprudence: such laws are the individual remains of the primitive legal formations. Before the great
overthrow of almost all institutions, which we have witnessed,
cases of this sort were of much more frequent occurrence in the
small German states than now, parts of the old Germanic institutions having frequently survived all revolutions whatever. The
sum, therefore, of this theory is, that all law is originally formed
in the manner, in which, in ordinary but not quite correct language, customary law is said to have been formed: i.e. that it is
first developed by custom and popular faith, next by jurisprudence,—everywhere, therefore, by internal silently-operating
powers, not by the arbitrary will of a law-giver. . .

The most important argument urged in favour of the uniformity of the law, is, that our love for our common country is
enhanced by it, but weakened by a multiplicity of particular
laws. If this supposition be well founded, every German of good
feeling will wish that Germany may have throughout the same
system of law. But this very supposition is now the subject of
discussion.

The well-being of every organic being, (consequently of
states,) depends on the maintenance of an equipoise between the
whole and its parts—on each having its due. For a citizen, a town,
a province to forget the state to which they belong, is a very
common phenomenon, and every one will regard this as an unnatural and morbid state of things. But for this very reason a
lively affection for the whole can only proceed from the thorough
participation in all particular relations; and he only who takes
good care of his own family, will be a truly good citizen. It is,
therefore, an error to suppose that the common weal would gain
new life by the annihilation of all individual relations. Were it
possible to generate a peculiar corporate spirit in every class,
every town, nay, every village, the common weal would gain
new strength from this heightened and multiplied individuality.
When, therefore, the influence of law on the love of counfry, is
the question, the particular laws of particular provinces and
states are not to be regarded as obstacles. In this point of view,
the law merits praise, in so far as it falls in, or is adapted to fall in,
with the feelings and consciousness of the people; blame, if, like

an uncongenial and arbitrary thing, it leaves the people without participation. That, however, will be oftener and more easily the case with the distinct systems of particular districts, although it certainly is not every municipal law that will be truly popular.

Indeed, for this political end, no state of law appears more favourable than that which was formerly general in Germany: great variety and individuality in particulars, but with the common law for the general foundation, constantly reminding all the Germanic nations of their indissoluble unity. The most pernicious, however, in this point of view, is the light and capricious alteration of law; and even were uniformity and fitness attainable by change, the advantage would not be worth naming in comparison with the political disadvantage just alluded to. That which is thus constructed by men's hands before our eyes, will always hold a very different place in popular estimation from that which has not so plain and palpable an origin; and when we, in our praiseworthy zeal, inveigh against this decision as a blind prejudice, we ought not to forget that all faith in, and feeling for, that which is not on a level with us, but more exalted than we, depends upon the same kind of spirit. This consideration might well lead us to doubt of the impropriety of the decision.

In considering the course to be pursued, we must distinguish between those countries in which common-law and provincial-law (only somewhat interrupted by the brief reign of the code) were in force up to the present time, from those which are already living under codes of domestic manufacture.

In the countries where the common-law prevails, as in all others, a good state of the law will depend on three things; first, sufficient authorities; secondly, a sufficient ministry of justice; lastly, good forms of procedure. I shall subsequently refer to these three points, as tests of the soundness of my plan.

With regard, in the first place, to the authorities, to which even the proposed code was to conform, the same mixed system of common-law and provincial-law, which formerly prevailed throughout the whole of Germany, ought, in my opinion, to be substituted for the code, or retained where the code was not in force: I hold these authorities to be sufficient, nay, excellent, provided jurisprudence does what it ought to do, and what can only be done by means of it. For if we consider our actual condition, we find ourselves in the midst of an immense mass of juridical notions and theories which have descended, and been multiplied, from generation to generation. At present, we do not possess and master this matter, but are controlled and mastered by it, whether we will or not. This is the ground of all the complaints of the present state of our law, which I admit to be well-founded: this, also, is the sole cause of the demand for codes. This matter encompasses and hems us in on all sides, often without our knowing it. People might think to annihilate it, by severing all historical associations, and beginning an entirely new life. But such an undertaking would be built on a delusion. For it is impossible to annihilate the impressions and modes of thought of the jurists now living,—impossible to change completely the nature of existing legal relations; and on this twofold impossibility rests the indissoluble organic connection of generations and ages; between which, development only, not absolute end and absolute beginning, is conceivable. In particular, the altering of single, nay of many, legal doctrines, is doing absolutely nothing towards this object; for, as before observed, the modes of thought, with the speculations and questions that may arise, will still be influenced by the pre-existing system, and the subserviency of the past to the present will manifest itself even where the present is purposely opposed to the past. There is consequently no mode of avoiding this overruling influence of the existing matter; it will be injurious to us so long as we ignorantly submit to it; but beneficial, if we oppose to it a vivid creative energy, obtain the mastery over it by a thorough grounding in history, and thus appropriate to ourselves the whole intellectual wealth of preceding generations. We have, therefore, no choice but either, as Bacon says, *sermocinari tamquam e vinculis*,[1] or to learn by the profound study of jurisprudence, how to use this historical matter freely as our instrument: there is no other alternative. Were we to adopt the last, the scientific principle, as the nobler part, might of itself gain on its own account: our present position, too, affords particular grounds for this opinion. First, the general turn for science, which is natural to the Germans, and whereby they have been enabled to take the lead of other nations in many things; secondly, much in our political

---

[1] May be translated: "Discuss as though in bonds." (Ed.)

circumstances. For this reason, the experience of other nations or times cannot be adduced in opposition; neither the state of the law in England, nor the state of the law in the time of our forefathers. As to our forefathers, Möser has explained in an excellent article, the difference between what he calls arbitrariness and what he calls wisdom; with the former, freedom and justice might consist, so long as juries formed of the peers of the parties adjudicated; we can never dispense with wisdom. As a substitute for it, the adherence to middling authorities deserves in this respect (bad as it may be in others) all estimation, and may serve as a means of protection against the ruinous alternation of arbitrariness and wisdom.

Only when by zealous study we shall have perfected our knowledge, and, more particularly, sharpened our historical and political sense, will a sound judgment on the matter that has come down to us be possible. Until then it might be more prudent to pause before considering the existing law as loose practice, impolitic exclusiveness, and mere juridical apathy: but, most especially, to hesitate upon the application of the dissecting knife to our present system. In applying it we might strike unawares upon sound flesh, and thus charge ourselves with the heaviest of all responsibilities to posterity. The historical spirit, too, is the only protection against a species of self-delusion, which is ever and anon reviving in particular men, as well as in whole nations and ages; namely, the holding that which is peculiar to ourselves to be common to human nature in general. Thus, in times past, by the omission of certain prominent pecularities, a natural law was formed out of the Institutes, which was looked upon as the immediate emanation of reason. There is no one who would not regard this proceeding with pity; and yet we meet with people daily, who hold their juridical notions and opinions to be the offspring of pure reason, for no earthly reason but because they are ignorant of their origin. When we lose sight of our individual connection with the great entirety of the world and its history, we necessarily see our thoughts in a false light of universality and originality. There is only the historical sense to protect us against this, to turn which upon ourselves is indeed the most difficult of applications.

One might be tempted to admit this historical grounding of the matter in which we are necessarily involved, to be necessary in our present position, but, at the same time, to consider it an evil, from its engrossing energies which might be directed to more useful ends. This would be a melancholy view, because the feeling of an inevitable evil would be excited by it; but we may console ourselves with the conviction that it is false. On the contrary, this necessity is to be deemed a great good in itself. In the history of all considerable nations we find a transition from circumscribed, but fresh and vigorous, individuality, to undefined universality. The law undergoes the same, and in it, likewise, the consciousness of nationality may, in the end, be lost. . . . That, at the same time, the peculiar advantage, by which the old law was characterised, is lost, is obvious. To talk of going back to this past time, were a vain and idle proposition; but it is a wholly different affair to keep its distinguishing excellencies fully in view, and thus guard our minds against the narrowing influence of the present,—which is certainly both practicable and salutary. History, even in the infancy of a people, is ever a noble instructress, but in ages such as ours she has yet another and holier duty to perform. For only through her can a lively connection with the primitive state of the people be kept up; and the loss of this connection must take away from every people the best part of its spiritual life. That, consequently, by which according to this theory, the common law and the provincial laws are to become truly useful and unobjectionable as authorities, is the strict historical method of jurisprudence. Its character does not consist, as some recent opponents have strangely maintained, in an exclusive admiration of the Roman law; nor in desiring the unqualified preservation of any one established system, to which, indeed, it is directly opposed. . . . On the contrary, its object is to trace every established system to its root, and thus discover an organic principle, whereby that which still has life, may be separated from that which is lifeless and only belongs to history. But the subject matter of jurisprudence, which is to be treated in this manner, is, with regard to the common law, threefold, from which three principal divisions of our jurisprudence are derived: Roman law, German law, and new modifications of the two. The Roman law (as already observed) besides its historical importance, has the advantage of being able, by reason of its high state of cultivation, to serve as a pattern and model for our scientific labours. This advantage is wanting to the Germanic law; but this law possesses another not inferior advantage. It is directly and popularly connected with us, and we are not to allow ourselves to be led astray by the circumstance that most of the primitive forms have, to all practical purposes, disappeared. For the national foundation of these forms, the turn of mind from which they emanated, outlives the forms themselves, and it is not to be decided beforehand, how much of the old Germanic institutions, political as well as legal, may be revived. Not indeed in letter, but in spirit; though it is only from the old letter that we learn to become acquainted with the original spirit. Lastly, the modification of the two primitive systems is not to be slighted. For during the long course, reaching to our time, which these primitive systems have run, much of a wholly different character has naturally established and developed itself; partly to meet the actual wants of the people as they arose, partly, in a more scientific manner, in the hands of the jurists. This last preponderates here, and the history of our jurisprudence from the middle ages downwards, forms its groundwork. One principal object of this third division of our science ought to be the gradual purification of the present system from that which has been produced through the mere ignorance and dullness of uncultivated times, without any real practical demand for it.

17. Walter Savage Landor: *Imaginary Conversations*

Walter Savage Landor (1775–1864) remained a political radical after Coleridge and Wordsworth had given up their early enthusiasm for the democratic phase of the French Revolution. He was a great traveler as well as a prolific author of verse and of prose, of which his *Imaginary Conversations* are probably the best-known works. They were published over a period of thirty years from 1824. Many are historical. The selection here, however, deals with an event of Landor's own time. It is a Romantic view of what many took to be a romantic act—the murder of Kotzebue (a popular conservative dramatist in the employ of the Russian government) by Karl Sandt, a probably unbalanced member of the *Burschenshaften*, the liberal and nationalist student movement that grew up just after the Napoleonic wars. The act itself served as a pretext for the Carlsbad Decrees of 1819, which brought the German universities under strict governmental control and disrupted the liberal movement.

Not only does this "Conversation" express the sentiments of liberal-nationalism, but it expresses its rhetoric as well, while revealing that its morality still bears comparison to the classical era's version of civic virtue.

The selection is from *The Works of Walter Savage Landor*, edited by T. Earle Welby, Methuen and Co., Ltd. (London, 1927), Vol. VIII, pp. 79–87. Reprinted by permission of the publishers.

VI. Sandt and Kotzebue

SANDT. GENERALLY men of letters in our days, contrary to the practice of antiquity, are little fond of admitting the young and unlearned into their studies or their society.

KOTZEBUE. They should rather those than others. The young *must* cease to be young, and the unlearned *may* cease to be unlearned. According to the letters you bring with you, sir, there is only youth against you. In the seclusion of a college life, you appear to have studied with much assiduity and advantage, and to have pursued no other courses than the paths of wisdom.

SANDT. Do you approve of the pursuit?

KOTZEBUE. Who does not?

SANDT. None, if you will consent that they direct the chase, bag the game, inebriate some of the sportsmen, and leave the rest behind in the slough. May I ask you another question?

KOTZEBUE. Certainly.

SANDT. Where lie the paths of wisdom? I did not expect, my dear sir, to throw you back upon your chair. I hope it was no rudeness to seek information from you?

KOTZEBUE. The paths of wisdom, young man, are those which lead us to truth and happiness.

SANDT. If they lead us away from fortune, from employments, from civil and political utility; if they cast us where the powerful persecute, where the rich trample us down, and where the poorer (at seeing it) despise us, rejecting our counsel and spurning our consolation; what valuable truth do they enable us to discover, or what rational happiness to expect? To say that wisdom leads to truth, is only to say that wisdom leads to wisdom; for such is truth. Nonsense is better than falsehood; and we come to that.

KOTZEBUE. How?

SANDT. No falsehood is more palpable than that wisdom leads to happiness; I mean in this world; in another we may well indeed believe that the words are constructed of very different materials. But here we are, standing on a barren molehill that crumbles and sinks under our tread; here we are, and show me from hence, Von Kotzebue, a discoverer who has not suffered for his discovery, whether it be of a world or of a truth, whether a Columbus or a Galileo. Let us come down lower. Show me a man who has detected the injustice of a law, the absurdity of a tenet, the malversation of a minister or the impiety of a priest, and who has not been stoned, or hanged, or burnt, or imprisoned, or exiled, or reduced to poverty. The chain of Prometheus is hanging yet upon his rock, and weaker limbs writhe daily in its rusty links. Who then, unless for others, would be a darer of wisdom? And yet, how full of it is even the inanimate world? We may gather it out of stones and straws. Much lies within the reach of all: little has been collected by the wisest of the wise. O slaves to passion! O minions to power! ye carry your own scourges about you; ye endure their tortures daily; yet ye crouch for more. Ye believe that God beholds you; ye know that he will punish you, even worse than ye punish yourselves; and still ye lick the dust where the Old Serpent went before you.

KOTZEBUE. I am afraid, sir, you have formed to yourself a romantic and strange idea both of happiness and of wisdom.

SANDT. I too am afraid it may be so. My idea of happiness is, the power of communicating peace, good-will, gentle affections, ease, comfort, independence, freedom, to all men capable of them.

KOTZEBUE. The idea is, truly, no humble one.

SANDT. A higher may descend more securely on a stronger mind. The power of communicating those blessings to the capable is enough for my aspirations. A stronger mind may exercise its faculties in the divine work of creating the capacity.

KOTZEBUE. Childish! childish! Men have cravings enow already; give them fresh capacities, and they will have fresh appetites. Let us be contented in the sphere wherein it is the will of Providence to place us; and let us render ourselves useful in it to the uttermost of our power, without idle aspirations after impracticable good.

SANDT. O sir! you lead me where I tremble to step; to the haunts of your intellect, to the recesses of your spirit. Alas! alas!

how small and how vacant is the central chamber of the lofty pyramid!

KOTZEBUE. Is this to me?

SANDT. To you, and many mightier. Reverting to your own words; could not you yourself have remained in the sphere you were placed in?

KOTZEBUE. What sphere? I have written dramas and novels and travels. I have been called to the Imperial Court of Russia.

SANDT. You sought celebrity: I blame not that. The thick air of multitudes may be good for some constitutions of mind, as the thinner of solitudes is for others. Some horses will not run without the clapping of hands; others fly out of the course rather than hear it. But let us come to the point. Imperial courts! What do they know of letters? What letters do they countenance, do they tolerate?

KOTZEBUE. Plays.

SANDT. Playthings.

KOTZEBUE. Travels.

SANDT. On their business. O ye paviours of the dreary road along which their cannon rolls for conquest! my blood throbs at every stroke of your rammers. When will ye lay them by?

KOTZEBUE. We are not such drudges.

SANDT. Germans! Germans! Must ye never have a rood on earth ye can call your own, in the vast inheritance of your fathers?

KOTZEBUE. Those who strive and labour, gain it, and many have rich possessions.

SANDT. None; not the highest.

KOTZEBUE. Perhaps you may think them insecure; but they are not lost yet, although the rapacity of France does indeed threaten to swallow them up. But her fraudulence is more to be apprehended than her force. The promise of liberty is more formidable than the threat of servitude. The wise know that she never will bring us freedom; the brave know that she never can bring us thraldom. She herself is alike impatient of both; in the dazzle of arms she mistakes the one for the other, and is never more agitated than in the midst of peace.

SANDT. The fools who went to war against her, did the only thing that could unite her; and every sword they drew was a conductor of that lightning which fell upon their heads. But we must now look at our homes. Where there is no strict union, there is no perfect love; and where no perfect love, there is no true helper. Are you satisfied, sir, at the celebrity and the distinctions you have obtained?

KOTZEBUE. My celebrity and distinctions, if I must speak of them, quite satisfy me. Neither in youth nor in advancing age, neither in difficult nor in easy circumstances, have I ventured to proclaim myself the tutor or the guardian of mankind.

SANDT. I understand the reproof, and receive it humbly and gratefully. You did well in writing the dramas, and the novels, and the travels; but, pardon my question, who called you to the courts of princes in strange countries?

KOTZEBU. They themselves.

SANDT. They have no more right to take you away from your country, than to eradicate a forest, or to subvert a church in it. You belong to the land that bore you, and were not at liberty (if right and liberty are one, and unless they are, they are good for nothing), you were not at liberty, I repeat it, to enter into the service of an alien.

KOTZEBUE. No magistrate, higher or lower, forbade me. Fine notions of freedom are these!

SANDT. A man is always a minor in regard to his fatherland; and the servants of his fatherland are wrong and criminal if they whisper in his ear that he may go away, that he may work in another country, that he may ask to be fed in it, and that he may wait there until orders and tasks are given for his hands to execute. Being a German, you voluntarily placed yourself in a position where you might eventually be coerced to act against Germans.

KOTZEBUE. I would not.

SANDT. Perhaps you think so.

KOTZEBUE. Sir, I know my duty.

SANDT. We all do; yet duties are transgressed, and daily. Where the will is weak in accepting, it is weaker in resisting. Already have you left the ranks of your fellow-citizens; already have you taken the enlisting-money and marched away.

KOTZEBUE. Phrases! metaphors! and let me tell you, M. Sandt, not very polite ones. You have hitherto seen little of the world, and you speak rather the language of books than of men.

SANDT. What! are books written by some creatures of less intellect than ours? I fancied them to convey the language and reasonings of men. I was wrong, and you are right, Von Kotzebue! They are, in general, the productions of such as have neither the constancy of courage nor the continuity of sense, to act up to what they know to be right, or to maintain it, even in words, to the end of their lives. You are aware that I am speaking now of political ethics. This is the worst I can think of the matter; and bad enough is this.

KOTZEBUE. You misunderstand me. Our conduct must fall in with our circumstances. We may be patriotic, yet not puritanical in our patriotism; not harsh, nor intolerant, nor contracted. The philosophical mind should consider the whole world as its habitation, and not look so minutely into it as to see the lines that divide nations and governments; much less should it act the part of a busy shrew, and take pleasure in giving loose to the tongue, at finding things a little out of place.

SANDT. We will leave the shrew where we find her: she certainly is better with the comedian than with the philosopher. But this indistinctness in the moral and political line begets indifference. He who does not keep his own country more closely in view than any other, soon mixes land with sea, and sea with air, and loses sight of everything, at last, for which he was placed in contact with his fellow men. Let us unite, if possible, with the nearest: let usages and familiarities bind us: this being once accomplished, let us confederate for security and peace with all the people round, particularly with people of the same language, laws, and religion. We pour out wine to those about us, wishing the same fellowship and conviviality to others: but to enlarge the circle would disturb and deaden its harmony. We irrigate the ground in our gardens: the public road may require the water equally: yet we give it rather to our borders; and first to those that lie against the house! God himself did not fill the world at once with happy creatures: he enlivened one small portion of it with them, and began with single affections, as well as pure and unmixed. We must have an object and an aim, or our strength, if any strength belongs to us, will be useless.

KOTZEBUE. There is much good sense in these remarks: but I am not at all times at leisure and in readiness to receive instruction. I am old enough to have laid down my own plans of life; and I trust I am by no means deficient in the relations I bear to society.

SANDT. Lovest thou thy children? Oh! my heart bleeds! But the birds can fly; and the nest requires no warmth from the parent, no cover against the rain and the wind.

KOTZEBUE. This is wildness: this is agony. Your face is laden

with large drops; some of them tears, some not. Be more rational
and calm, my dear young man! and less enthusiastic.

SANDT. They who will not let us be rational, make us enthusiastic by force. Do you love your children? I ask you again. If you
do, you must love them more than another man's. Only they who
are indifferent to all, profess a parity.

KOTZEBUE. Sir! indeed your conversation very much surprises
me.

SANDT. I see it does: you stare, and would look proud. Emperors and kings, and all but maniacs, would lose that faculty
with me. I could speedily bring them to a just sense of their
nothingness, unless their ears were calked and pitched, although I
am no Savonarola. He too died sadly!

KOTZEBUE. Amid so much confidence of power, and such an
assumption of authority, your voice is gentle, almost plaintive.

SANDT. It should be plaintive. Oh, could it but be persuasive!

KOTZEBUE. Why take this deep interest in me? I do not merit
nor require it. Surely anyone would think we had been acquainted with each other for many years.

SANDT. What! should I have asked you such a question as the
last, after long knowing you?

KOTZEBUE. (*aside*). This resembles insanity.

SANDT. The insane have quick ears, sir, and sometimes quick
apprehensions.

KOTZEBUE. I really beg your pardon.

SANDT. I ought not then to have heard you, and beg yours. My
madness could release many from a worse; from a madness which
hurts them grievously; a madness which has been and will be
hereditary: mine, again and again I repeat it, would burst
asunder the strong swathes that fasten them to pillar and post.
Sir! sir! if I entertained not the remains of respect for you, in your
domestic state, I should never have held with you this conversation. Germany is Germany: she ought to have nothing political in
common with what is not Germany. Her freedom and security
now demand that she celebrate the communion of the faithful.
Our country is the only one in all the explored regions on earth
that never has been conquered. Arabia and Russia boast it falsely;
France falsely; Rome falsely. A fragment of the empire of Darius
fell and crushed her: Valentinian was the footstool of Sapor, and
Rome was buried in Byzantium. Boys must not learn this, and

men will not. Britain, the wealthiest and most powerful of nations, and, after our own, the most literate and humane, received
from us colonies and laws. Alas! those laws, which she retains as
her fairest heritage, we value not: we surrender them to gangs of
robbers, who fortify themselves within walled cities, and enter
into leagues against us. When they quarrel, they push us upon
one another's sword, and command us to thank God for the vic-
tories that enslave us. These are the glories we celebrate; these
are the festivals we hold, on the burial-mounds of our ancestors.
Blessed are those who lie under them! blessed are also those who
remember what they are, and call upon their names in the holiness of love.

KOTZEBUE. Moderate the transport that inflames and consumes
you. There is no dishonour in a nation being conquered by a
stronger.

SANDT. There may be great dishonour in letting it be the
stronger; great, for instance, in our disunion.

KOTZEBUE. We have only been conquered by the French in our
turn.

SANDT. No, sir, no: we have not been, in turn or out. Our puny
princes were disarmed by promises and lies: they accepted paper
crowns from the very thief who was sweeping into his hat their
forks and spoons. A cunning traitor snared incautious ones,
plucked them, devoured them, and slept upon their feathers.

KOTZEBUE. I would rather turn back with you to the ancient
glories of our country than fix my attention on the sorrowful
scenes more near to us. We may be justly proud of our literary
men, who unite the suffrage of every capital, to the exclusion of
almost all their own.

SANDT. Many Germans well deserve this honour, others are
manger-fed and hirelings.

KOTZEBUE. The English and the Greeks are the only nations that
rival us in poetry, or in any works of imagination.

SANDT. While on this high ground we pretend to a rivalship
with England and Greece, can we reflect without a sinking of the
heart on our inferiority in political and civil dignity? Why are we
lower than they? Our mothers are like their mothers; our children
are like their children; our limbs are as strong, our capacities are
as enlarged; our desire of improvement in the arts and sciences is
neither less vivid and generous, nor less temperate and well-di-

rected. The Greeks were under disadvantages which never bore in any degree on us; yet they rose through them vigorously and erectly. They were Asiatic in what ought to be the finer part of the affections; their women were veiled and secluded, never visited the captive, never released the slave, never sat by the sick in the hospital, never heard the child's lesson repeated in the school. Ours are more tender, compassionate, and charitable, than poets have feigned of the past, or prophets have announced of the future; and, nursed at their breasts and educated at their feet, blush we not at our degeneracy? The most indifferent stranger feels a pleasure at finding, in the worst-written history of Spain, her various kingdoms ultimately mingled, although the character of the governors, and perhaps of the governed, is congenial to few. What delight then must overflow on Europe, from seeing the mother of her noblest nation rear again her venerable head, and bless all her children for the first time united!

KOTZEBUE. I am bound to oppose such a project.

SANDT. Say not so: in God's name, say not so.

KOTZEBUE. In such confederacy I see nothing but conspiracy and rebellion, and I am bound, I tell you again, sir, to defeat it, if possible.

SANDT. Bound! I must then release you.

KOTZEBUE. How should you, young gentleman, release me?

SANDT. May no pain follow the cutting of the knot. But think again! think better: spare me!

KOTZEBUE. I will not betray you.

SANDT. That would serve nobody: yet, if in your opinion betraying me could benefit you or your family, deem it no harm; so much greater has been done by you in abandoning the cause of Germany. Here is your paper; here is your ink.

KOTZEBUE. Do you imagine me an informer?

SANDT. From maxims and conduct such as yours, spring up the brood, the necessity, and the occupation of them. There would be none, if good men thought it a part of goodness to be as active and vigilant as the bad. I must go, sir! Return to yourself in time! How it pains me to think of losing you! Be my friend!

KOTZEBUE. I would be.

SANDT. Be a German!

KOTZEBUE. I am.

SANDT. (*having gone out*). Prejurer and profaner! Yet his heart is kindly. I must grieve for him! Away with tenderness! I disrobe him of the privilege to pity me or to praise me, as he would have done had I lived of old. Better men shall do more. God calls them; me too he calls; I will enter the door again. May the greater sacrifice bring the people together, and hold them evermore in peace and concord. The lesser victim follows willingly. (*Enters again*)

Turn! die! (*Strikes*)

Alas! alas! no man ever fell alone. How many innocent always perish with the guilty, and writhe longer!

Unhappy children! I shall weep for you elsewhere. Some days are left me. In a very few the whole of this little world will lie between us. I have sanctified in you the memory of your father. Genius but reveals dishonour; commiseration covers it.

18. Giuseppe Mazzini: *Letter to Lamennais*

Giuseppe Mazzini (1805–1872) was one of Europe's first professional revolutionaries and Italy's most famous and probably most influential nationalist. Because of his youthful involvement in his native Genoa with the underground Carbonarist group, which sought to revive some of the unity and freedom Italians had enjoyed during the Napoleonic régime, he was imprisoned in 1831. Exiled, he spent most of the next two decades in Switzerland, where he sought to promote the cause of national liberation and unity for Italy by exporting illegal publications and by subversive correspondence. To this end he founded the Young Italy movement in 1831.

The document that follows is Mazzini's letter to Lamennais, and it brings to the fore two central aspects of Mazzini's view of the religious situation. He, like so many of his contemporaries, believed that Europe was ripe for a new faith, and his expectations came increasingly to resemble those of the Saint-Simonians. Their conclusions derived in part from a conviction of the historicity of beliefs, that the aptness of beliefs for one era debarred them from contributing successfully to the needs of other times. Since the old Catholic faith that united Christendom in the Middle Ages had become outdated in a world torn by egoism, what was needed was a new faith. Mazzini admired Lamennais's effort to democratize Catholicism; but his own critique of Catholicism included the demand for the deposition of the pope from temporal authority—to Mazzini, the Papal States were the most resistant of those petty political divisions that perpetuated the régime of tutelage for the Italian people.

Mazzini's nationalism was not exclusive; he helped to promote other young nationalist groups, and envisaged—as Herder had before him—the peaceful coexistence of liberated nationalities. Yet, there is in his thought an authoritarian element, chiefly moral and religious—a kind of theocratic assurance that the faith he promoted is undeniably the right one. In practice, however, when Mazzini returned to Italy to direct the short-lived Roman Republic until its downfall in 1849, he demonstrated that his actual political tendencies were libertarian and humanitarian, though assuredly anticlerical.

After the defeat of the Roman Republic, Mazzini once again went into exile, spending most of his time thus until his death in England. He continued to advocate national revolution, and his followers played a large part in the Risorgimento of 1859 and 1860. Garibaldi, of course, his fellow triumvir at Rome in 1849, perpetuated the Mazzinian strand in the final confrontation with Cavour and the Piedmontese. Though a national democratic Italian republic did not emerge for nearly a century and although the monarchy triumphed instead, it is fair to accord to Mazzini the triumph of having provided the myths, the rhetoric, and, for many, the faith that permeated the heroic elements of the Risorgimento.

Mazzini also contributed to the development of the vocation of revolutionary; like Blanqui and Bakunin among his contemporaries, and Lenin in particular later, he converted subversive activity into the pursuit of a high moral aim, with its own austere ethic and fraternity of exile.

The selection is from *Life and Writings of Joseph Mazzini* (London 1890), Vol. III, pp. 40–49.

12th October 1834

Sir—I received your letter of the 14th September. I shall preserve it as a precious relic; as one of those records which comfort and retemper the soul in those nameless hours which sometimes bow us down with all the weight of a painful past and present, and whisper doubts of the future. I send you a number of *Young Italy*. In it you will find the germs of our ideas and belief, though without their full development; but we conceived that, as our object was to change the very basis and point of departure of the revolutionary spirit in Italy, it was more important to insist upon general principles than to run the risk of losing ourselves or going astray among the multitude of secondary questions.

We believe that art, science, philosophy, the idea of right, the history of right, the historic method—all things, in short, require renovation; but we believe that analysis has already led us too far astray to allow us to dream of making it the instrument of our undertaking. Synthesis alone can create those great regenerating movements which transform peoples into nations. It is therefore necessary to awaken men's minds through the action of an Unitarian principle; the impulse once given, logic, the force of things, and the peoples will do the rest.

What can I say to you, sir, in answer to the fear expressed in your letter, that by making war against the Papacy we do an injury to religion and to practical morality? It is not easy fitly to develop a question of such importance in a letter. It would require long and intimate conversations in order fully to explain to you the course of thought which has led us to that conviction, the consequences of which appear to you so dangerous.

Nevertheless, believe me, mine is no sentiment of anger or rebellion. Every individual tendency of my own mind would incline me to regard all great organic ideas or conceptions with respect; and there is no youthful illusion nor dream of the future in which I have not myself at one time indulged concerning the gigantic ruin which enfolds within it the history of a world.

Were it only from love of my own country, I could have wished that one ray of the rising sun of Young Europe might have illumined that ruin, to revive therein the spirit that once animated the soul of Gregory VII, without that idea of despotism which belonged to his own times, but not to ours.

I could have wished that the two great institutions of the middle ages—the Papacy and the Empire—now crumbling to pieces, and leaving neither honour, glory, nor legacy behind them, had been permitted to expire, represented by men inspired by the consciousness of a sublime mission fulfilled; and transmitting to the generations alike the formula of the epoch which had been governed by their own conceptions and the first words of the epoch to come.

But it is not so. Those ruins have but one source of poetry left—the poetry of expiation. The condemnation of the Papacy is decreed, not by us, but by God; by God, who now calls upon the People to arise and found a new unity, embracing the two spheres of temporal and spiritual power. We do but interpret the thought of the epoch, and the thought of the epoch rejects every intermediate between humanity and its source of life. It claims the right of humanity to stand in the presence of God, like Moses upon Mount Sinai, and to ask of Him the law of its destiny. In our epoch humanity will forsake the Pope, and have recourse to a general council of the Church—that is to say, of all believers—a council which will be alike council of the Church and Constituent Assembly; for it will unite what has hitherto been divided, and lay the foundation of that unity without which there can be neither true faith nor practical morality.

The Papacy is doomed to perish, because it has betrayed its mission and denied alike the Father and his children. By both the Father and his children it is condemned.

The Papacy has destroyed religious faith, through a materialism far more degrading and fatal than that of the eighteenth century; for that at least displayed the courage of negation, while papal materialism hides itself beneath the Jesuit's cloak. The Papacy has drowned our love in a sea of blood. The Papacy has attempted to drive Liberty out of the world, and by Liberty it is destined to be driven out.

And when, at the cry of the first people arising in insurrection with an European idea and aim, three centuries shall rise in accusation against the Papacy, expiring without faith, power, or mission,—what human power shall avail to save it? Great institutions never renew an existence once decayed; for they do but interpret to humanity one single line of God's law.

The Papacy and the Austrian Empire are both doomed to perish. The first for having, during three centuries, impeded the fulfilment of the *general* mission confided by God to Humanity; the second for having, during three centuries, impeded the fulfilment of the *special* mission confided by God to the distinct races of Humanity. Humanity will arise upon the ruins of the one; the Fatherland will arise upon the ruins of the other.

Think over this, sir. Do not be surprised at the boldness of my words: it is a proof of the greatness I recognise in you, and of the trust I feel in you. What would become of Europe if, during the last moments that precede the coming crisis, the men of true power and faith should persist in bidding mankind seek the law of practical morality from the Papacy? What link would remain to unite in celestial harmony the two immortal sisters, Country and Humanity, if on the eve of the new creation the believers should teach the people that the secret of the future Unity lay with the God of the middle ages?

Another of the ideas expressed in your letter caused me much sorrow. You say you are convinced that Italy is unable to achieve her political emancipation through her own efforts.

It is precisely this opinion, preached and diffused on every side, that has deprived our efforts towards emancipation of all energy and vigour. You thus condemn to impotence twenty-six millions of men, having the Alps, the Apennines, and the sea as their bases of defence, and three thousand years of glorious memories to inspire them with courage. You thus deprive Italy of all mission upon earth, for there is no mission without spontaneity; without the sentiment of liberty no true liberty can exist, and no true sentiment or consciousness of liberty is possible, save in those who have emancipated themselves through their own efforts.

Sir, Italy does not lack force. She has strength enough to overcome obstacles twice as serious as those now standing in her way. What Italy wants is faith; not faith in liberty and equality—that faith is manifested by her continual protests—but faith in the possibility of realising these ideas; faith in God, the protector of violated right; faith in her own latent strength, in her own sword. Italy has no faith in her own multitudes, who have never been called into the arena; she has no faith in that unity of mission, of sufferings, and desires, that convert one first victory into a lever powerful enough to raise the whole peninsula; she has no faith in the yet untried power of Principles, which have never been invoked nor displayed before the eyes of the people, but which will, I hope, direct our first enterprise for freedom.

But this faith—the sole thing wanting to Italy—is dawning upon her even now while we write; it is springing up, taught by the lessons of 1830 and 1831, upon which she now is meditating; it begins to reveal itself in our enlightened youth, and from them it will descend upon the multitudes, and must progress—you cannot doubt it—for it is assuming the character of a religious belief. Observe the revival of the spiritualist tendency amongst us, the enormous risks incurred to read our publications, the enthusiasm awakened by your own sublime pages; think of the constant renewal of patriotic attempts despite their ill-success; think of our apostles, our martyrs. Now this dawning faith in action, deriving its inspiration from on high, and seeking to penetrate the multitudes, has hitherto always been wanting in Italy; has never yet been cast into the balance of her revolutionary destinies. For two centuries past men have struggled and died in Italy from an

instinct of independence or rebellion, or from a vague and undefined presentiment of the future; but during the last two years, we
have seen men die in Savoy, Genoa, Turin, Alexandria, and
Naples, for the sake of the oath they had taken to the Italian
people; for the sake of their belief that Italy *is* able to redeem
herself through her own efforts. And when the insignia of this
new faith shall be emblazoned upon a banner at once Humanitarian and National, who shall declare it doomed to succumb?

Do not, sir, judge our future by our past. There is an abyss
between them. It is true that all our revolutionary attempts have
failed; but all of them were the work of an aristocratic or military
caste, and designed to benefit a caste: all of them shrank from
adopting the only motto powerful enough to create great revolutions, *God and the people*; all of them sacrificed the sublime
dogma of equality to some unworthy greed, and all of them were
suffocated by treason at the very outset.

And this treason, which disgusted and repelled the people, and
threw the youth of Italy back upon scepticism, was inevitable; for
treason had been placed at the very summit of the edifice, under
the form of some diplomatic design, some promise made by a
prince, some foreign protection substituted for the idea of doing
battle for the sake of a holy cause.

Men were still under the influence of some frigid school of
individualism, which chilled every grand synthetical conception,
all enthusiasm or sacrifice, by a materialist spirit of analysis. And
a false principle once accepted, all its fatal consequences necessarily followed. It was in virtue of this false principle that friends
and enemies alike declared to Italy: *Your own sons are unable to
save you.* None dared to say to her: *Arise in all the strength and
energy of self-devotion; your sole trust is in God and your own
sons.*

The true regeneration of Italy can never be accomplished
through the action of others. Regeneration demands faith; faith
demands action, and this action must be spontaneous and her
own; not a mere imitation of the action of others. Moreover, what
attachment can men feel for a liberty which has cost them no
sacrifice? How can liberty be strong and enduring, where there is
neither individual nor popular dignity? and can either individual
or popular dignity exist, where liberty bears the stamp of a favour
or benefit granted by others?

Action creates action. One single initiative *act* is more fruitful of moral progress among a fallen people than ten insurrections brought about by external influence, or diplomatic contrivance.

I endeavour to diffuse my own belief by every means in my power. I meet with serious difficulties, but I am not discouraged by them. For some years past I have renounced all that might cast a ray of happiness over my individual life. Far away from my mother, my sisters, and all that I hold dear; having lost the dearest friend of my early years in prison: for these and for other reasons known only to myself, I have despaired of all individual life, and said to myself: *Thou art doomed to die, persecuted and misunderstood, half-way upon thy course.* But I certainly should not have had strength to bear up against the tempest, and learn resignation, had not the grand idea of Italian regeneration achieved by Italian effort been to me the baptism of faith. Destroy this idea, and for whom or for what should I struggle? Why exert one's-self, if Italy *cannot* arise until after a French insurrection?

It has been to me a deep sorrow, sir, when, having both wept and smiled over the last paragraphs of your eighteenth chapter, and said to myself: *Here is one who will understand us*—I received from your lips, not the words of comfort I had hoped to convey to my fellow-countrymen, but the chilling counsels I have so often heard from diplomatists and false prophets, bidding us *wait in apathy and inertia; perhaps liberty may come to you from the north; perhaps from the west of Germany; perhaps from Spain.*

But I have learned from your own inspired pages that liberty would be ours so soon as *each* of us should dare to say to himself, I *will* be free; so soon as each of us shall be ready to sacrifice and endure all things for freedom.

Must I say that we are *not* ready to sacrifice and to suffer as we ought? I do admit it; but because our minds are still clouded by doubt, must we despair of ever reaching certainty? because faith is wanting amongst us now, must we despair of faith in the future? I did not ask of you the signal of battle: I asked of you what you have already given to Poland, a commentary upon the counsels I have quoted for your book.

Reprove us—prophet-like—for our vices, our weakness, our divisions, our want of daring; but tell us at the same time: *The day which sees you better men and better brothers will be the day of*

your emancipation. So soon as you truly WILL *your freedom, you
need no longer fear your enemies, nor ask the aid of your friends
to achieve it.*

Adieu, sir. Believe in my deep esteem. But for it, I should never
have dared to open my heart to you thus.

JOSEPH MAZZINI

19. Adam Mickiewicz: Prologue to *Pan Tadeusz*

Adam Mickiewicz (1798–1855) was born in Lithuania, a member of
the Polonized lesser nobility. He became Poland's greatest poet, the
poet of the century after partition, during which, as Lord Acton said,
"there was a nation demanding to be united in a state—and a soul . . .
wandering in search of a body." His writings blend sentiments of
intense nationalism with a Catholic Christianity that anticipates the
regeneration of Europe as a consequence of the sufferings of Poland.
Much of Mickiewicz's adult life was spent outside Poland proper. In
1823 he had joined a secret patriotic society while a student at Vilna.
He was imprisoned by the Russian government, then exiled to Russia,
after which he moved to Italy, and subsequently to that Paris of exiles
of the 1840's, where were gathered Heine, Marx, and others. He took
no part in the Polish risings of 1831. In Paris, Mickiewicz was appointed to the chair of Slav Literature at the Collège de France in 1840
and held it until 1844. His lectures brought him great notoriety and
contributed to the already prevalent belief of Parisian intellectuals that
some special affinity linked the French and the Poles, through their
common Catholicism, through Napoleon's Grand Duchy of Warsaw
(Mickiewicz saw Bonaparte as an emissary of God), and through their
common opposition to the territorial settlement of Europe. The tie was
expressed in the protests by the Radicals, who invaded the French
Chamber on May 15, 1848, to demand a statement in favor of Poland.
Mickiewicz himself was disappointed and disillusioned by the failure of
1848 to produce a free Poland, but he had great hopes for Louis Napoleon. He died in 1855, trying to form a Polish legion in Constantinople
to fight the Russians in the Crimea.

His nationalism is dreamy, impractical, moving—a sentiment of faith
far more than a program for action. His view of the Polish people
adopts the primitivist sense of a virtuous, unmaterialistic peasantry. His
slavophilism views the West and what came to be called Westerniza-
tion as the enemy—the expression of materialistic egoism. The director
of the nationalist underground, Mazzini, appears in comparison to
Mickiewicz as an eminently practical politician.

The following selection is the Epilogue (often published as a Pro-
logue) to Mickiewicz's masterpiece, *Pan Tadeusz*, translated by
George Rapall Noyes (Everyman's Library edition, New York, 1966),
pp. xvii–xxi. Reprinted by permission of E. P. Dutton & Co., Inc., in
the United States and of J. M. Dent & Sons Ltd., in the British
Commonwealth.

Prologue

WHAT CAN be my thoughts, here on the streets of Paris, when I
bring home from the city ears filled with noise, with curses and
lies, with untimely plans, belated regrets, and hellish quarrels?

Alas for us deserters, that in time of pestilence, timid souls, we
fled to foreign lands! For wherever we trod, terror went before us,
and in every neighbour we found an enemy; at last they have
bound us in chains, firmly and closely, and they bid us give up
the ghost quickly as may be.

But if this world has no ear for their sorrows, if at each moment
fresh tidings overwhelm them, reverberating from Poland like a
graveyard bell; if their jailers wish them an early doom and their
enemies beckon them from afar like grave-diggers; if even in
Heaven they see no hope—then it is no marvel that they loathe
men, the world, themselves, that, losing their reason from their long
tortures, they spit upon themselves and consume one another.

I longed to pass by in my flight, bird of feeble wing—to pass by
regions of storm and thunder, and to search out only pleasant
shade and fair weather—the days of my childhood, and my home
gardens.

One happiness remains: when in a grey hour you sit by the
fireside with a few of your friends and lock the door against the
uproar of Europe, and escape in thought to happier times, and
muse and dream of your own land.

But of that blood that was shed so lately, of the tears which
have flooded the face of all Poland, of the glory that not yet has
ceased resounding: of these to think we had never the heart! For
the nation is in such anguish that even Valour when he turns his
gaze on its torture, can do naught but wring the hands.

Those generations black with mourning—that air heavy with

so many curses—there—thought dared not turn its flight to a sphere dreadful even to the birds of thunder.

O Mother Poland! Thou wast so lately laid in the grave. No man has the strength to speak of thee!

Ah! whose lips can dare to fancy that to-day they will at last find the magic word that will soften marble-like despair, that will lift the stony lid from men's hearts, and will open eyes heavy with so many tears?

Some time—when the lions of vengeance shall cease to roar, when the blare of the trumpet shall be stilled, when the ranks shall be broken, when our eagles with a flight like lightning shall settle on the ancient boundaries of Boleslaw the Brave, and, eating their fill of corpses, shall be drenched with blood, and finally fold their wings to rest; when the last enemy shall give forth a cry of pain, become silent, and proclaim liberty to the world: then, crowned with oak leaves, throwing aside their swords, our knights will seat themselves unarmed, and deign to hear songs. When the world envies their present fortune they will have leisure to hear of the past! Then they will weep over the fate of their fathers, and then those tears will not soil their cheeks.

To-day, for us, unbidden guests in the world, in all the past and in all the future—to-day there is but one region in which there is a crumb of happiness for a Pole: the land of his childhood! That land will ever remain holy and pure as first love; undisturbed by the remembrance of errors, not undermined by the deceitfulness of hopes, and unchanged by the stream of events.

Gladly would I greet with my thoughts those lands where I rarely wept and never gnashed my teeth; lands of my childhood, where one roamed over the world as through a meadow, and among the flowers knew only those that were lovely and fair, throwing aside the poisonous, and not glancing at the useful.

That land, happy, poor, and narrow; as the world is God's, so that was our own! How everything there belonged to us, how I remember all that surrounded us, from the linden that with its magnificent crown afforded shade to the children of the whole village, down to every stream and stone; how every cranny of the land was familiar to us, as far as the houses of our neighbours— the boundary link of our realm!

And if at times a Muscovite made his appearance, he left behind him only the memory of a fair and glittering uniform, for we knew the serpent only by his skin.

And only the dwellers in these lands have remained true to me until now; some as faithful friends, some as trusty allies! For *who* dwelt there? Mother, brothers, kindred, good neighbours! When one of them passed away, how tenderly did they speak of him! How many memories, what long-continued sorrow, in that land where a servant is more devoted to his master than in other countries a wife to her husband; where the soldier sorrows longer over his weapons than here a son over his father; where they weep longer and more sincerely over a dog, than here the people weep for a hero!

And in those days my friends aided my speech and cast me word after word for my songs; like the fabled cranes on the wild island, which flew in spring over the enchanted palace and heard the loud lament of an enchanted boy: each bird threw the boy a single feather; he made him wings and returned to his own people.

O, if some time I might attain this joy that my book might find shelter beneath roofs of thatch, and that the village girls, as they spin and turn the wheel, humming the while their much-loved verses, of the girl who so loved to make music that while fiddling she lost her geese, or of the orphan, who, fair as the dawn, went to drive home the birds at eventide—if even those village girls might take into their hands this book, simple as their songs!

So in my own day, along with the village sports, they sometimes read aloud, under the linden tree on the green, the song of Justina, or the story of Wieslaw; and the bailiff, dozing at the table, or the steward, or even the master of the farm, did not forbid us to read; he himself would deign to listen, and would interpret the harder places to the younger folk; he praised the beauties and forgave the faults.

And the young folk envied the fame of the bards, which in their own land still echoes through the woods and in the fields; of bards to whom dearer than the laurel of the Capitol is a wreath plaited by the hands of a village girl, of blue cornflowers and green rue.

20. Richard Wagner: "The Revolution"

Richard Wilhelm Wagner (1813–1883) was one of Europe's great cultural revolutionaries—early convinced that the full expression of his art required a social and political revolution. Even after his political revolutionary days, when his art was supported by Ludwig II of Bavaria and he had become an immensely successful artist, he remained an artistic innovator of immense importance.

Most of Wagner's prose on artistic subjects stems from the period around 1850, and is suffused with the atmosphere of the later Romantic period. He wrote much less in his later career when his music began to attain greater success. His formal education and musical training were relatively scant. From 1833 to 1839 he was chorus master, then conductor at several German provincial opera houses. He worked in poverty in Paris, then, before the 1848 Revolution, he became royal music director at Dresden where he wrote and produced *Tannhäuser* (1845) and finished scoring *Lohengrin* (1848).

He had to flee because of his part in the May Revolution in Dresden in 1849; he returned to Germany under the patronage of the Bavarian king in the 1860's, and later established his theater at Bayreuth where his masterpiece, *The Ring of the Nibelungen*, was produced in full in 1876.

Wagner's aesthetic theory contains familiar themes presented in sometimes confusing form, for he was not given to clear prose expression. He was fascinated with the uses of myth and legend as a source of profound truths about existence; he came increasingly to depend upon a version of the *Volk*—a sort of primitive communal soul—as the inspiration of true art. He grounded his theories familiarly enough in history; he attacked the philistinism of the triumphant bourgeoisie, who at first preferred an art quite unlike the combination of music and drama that he expected he would develop and lead as the culmination of artistic progress.

The following document is one of his few political tracts. Since Wagner took an active part in the May uprising in Dresden with his anarchist friend Bakunin, there is no reason to doubt his sincerity; but, as in the case of Lamartine, there may be reason to doubt how realistic he was at this point in his career. His political thought was never a major pursuit. He had strong negative reactions to what he considered bourgeois plutocracy and bad taste, believing that art needed a community without class divisions, but with warm emotional ties. In this essay he is nationalistic and socialist. Nationalist he remained, and he became increasingly anti-Semitic and distinctly anti-democratic. In

1849, however, he could feel at one with the masses who were to produce his "Revolution."

The selection is from *Richard Wagner's Prose Works*, translated by William Arthur Ellis (London, 1899–1900), Vol. VIII, pp. 232–238.

IF WE peer across its lands and peoples, we find throughout the whole of Europe the effervescence of a mighty movement, whose first vibrations have already reached us, whose full weight threatens soon to crash upon us. Europe seems to us a huge volcano, from whose inside an ever-waxing fearsome roar resounds, from out whose crater columns of black smoke ascend to heaven big with storm, and mantle all the earth with darkness, while here and there a lava-stream, a fiery harbinger, breaks through the hard-set crust and bears destruction to the vale below.

A supernatural force seems clutching at our quarter of the globe, intent on lifting it from its old rut and hurling it to pathways new.

Ay, we behold it, the old world is crumbling, a *new* will rise therefrom; for the lofty goddess *Revolution* comes rustling on the wings of storm, her stately head ringed round with lightnings, a sword in her right hand, a torch in her left, her eye so stern, so punitive, so cold; and yet what warmth of purest love, what wealth of happiness streams forth toward him who dares to look with steadfast gaze into that eye! Rustling she comes, the e'er-rejuvenating mother of mankind; destroying and fulfilling, she fares across the earth; before her soughs the storm, and shakes so fiercely at man's handiwork that vasty clouds of dust eclipse the sky, and where her mighty foot steps falls in ruins what an idle whim had built for æons, and the hem of her robe sweeps its last remains away. But in her wake there opens out a ne'er-dreamt paradise of happiness, illumed by kindly sunbeams; and where her foot had trodden down, spring fragrant flowers from the soil, and jubilant songs of freed mankind fill full the air scarce silent from the din of battle.

Now turn and look below, around you. There you see one, the mightiest prince, with halting heart and catching breath, yet seeking to assume a tranquil, cool demeanour, to shut his eyes and those of others to what he clearly sees to be inevitable. There see another, his leathern face all ploughed by vices, exerting all those petty sharper's arts that have brought him in so many a

titlet, so many an order's crosslet; you see him with his diplomatic
smile and air of mystery among the teeth-nipped lordlings, the
ladylings all snatching at their smelling-salts, whom he tries to
reassure by half-official information that highest personages have
deigned to pay attention to this strange phenomenon, that
couriers have been sent already to various parts with Cabinet-
orders, that the advice of that wise government-artist Metternich
is even on the road from London, that the right authorities have
had instructions all around, and accordingly the interesting surprise is in preparation for high-born society, at the next Court-
ball, of taking a peep at this horrid vagrant Revolution—of course
in an iron cage and fetters.—There see a third man, speculating
on the approach of the apparition, running off to the Bourse,
minutely reckoning the rise and fall of bondlets, higgling and
haggling, alert to catch the least per-centlet, till all his plunder
scatters to the winds. There, behind the dusty office-desk, you see
one of those warped and rusted wheels of our present State-ma-
chine, scratching away with its stump of a quill, and doing its
unceasing best to add fresh lumber to a paper world. Between
these files of documents and contracts the hearts of live humanity
are pressed like gathered leaves, and fall to powder in these
modern torture-rooms. Here rules a strenuous activity, for the
web outspun across the continent is torn in many a corner, and
the startled spiders are busy knitting up fresh threads to rectify
the holes. Here not a ray of light breaks in, here reign eternal
night and darkness; and into night and darkness will the whole
dissolve.—But listen! from that side there sounds shrill warlike
music, swords flash and bayonets, heavy guns clatter past, and
serried ranks of troops unroll their length. The valiant host of
heroes has set out for its brush with Revolution. The General bids
march to right and left, here stations infantry, there cavalry, and
wisely parcels out his bristling columns and his dread artillery;
and Revolution comes apace, her head high in the clouds,—they
see her not, but wait for the foe; and she stands already in their
midst,—they see her not, still waiting for the foe; and she has
seized them in her mighty whirlwind, has scattered the ranks,
dispersed the force which craft had stolen,—but the General, he
sits there, absorbed in his map, and calculating from which side
the foe may be expected, and what his strength, and when he will
arrive!—Stay! there you see a troubled face: an upright, thrifty

burgher it belongs to. He has toiled and moiled his whole life long, has honestly cared for the weal of all, so far as lay within his power; no shame, no wrong attaches to the mite his useful diligence has earned, to keep *himself* in feeble age, to give *his sons* a footing in this joyless life. He feels indeed the advent of the storm, he knows full well that no force can withstand it; yet his heart is sad when he looks back upon his life of hardships, whose only fruit is destined to destruction. We cannot gird at him, if timidly he grapples to his hoard, if futilely he puts forth all his blindfold strength 'gainst the invader. Unhappy man! uplift thine eyes, look up to where a thousand thousands gather on the hills in joyous expectation of the dawn! Regard them, they are all thy brothers, sisters, the troops of those poor wights who hitherto knew *naught* of life but *suffering*, have been but strangers on this earth of Joy; they all are waiting for that Revolution which affrights thee, their redemptrix from this world of sorrow, creatrix of a new world blessing *all*! See there, there stream the legions from the factories; they've made and fashioned lordly stuffs,— themselves and children, they are naked, frozen, hungry; for not to *them* belongs the fruit of all their labour, but to the rich and mighty one who calls men and the earth his *own*. See, there they troop, from fields and farmyards; they've tilled the earth and turned it to a smiling garden, and fruits in plenty, enough for all who live, have paid their pains,—yet poor are they, and naked, starving; for not to them, or others who are needy, belongs earth's blessing, but solely to the rich and mighty one who calls men and the earth his *own*. They all, the hundred-thousands, millions, are camped upon the hills and gaze into the distance, where thickening clouds proclaim the advent of emancipating Revolution; they all, to whom nothing is left to grieve for, from whom men rob the sons to train them into sturdy gaolers of their fathers, whose daughters walk the city's streets with burden of their shame, an offering to the baser lusts of rich and mighty; they all, with the sallow, careworn faces, the limbs devoured by frost and hunger, they all who have *never* known joy, encamp there on the heights and strain their eyes in blissful expectation of her coming, and listen in rapt silence to the rustle of the rising storm, which fills their ears with Revolution's greeting: I am the e'er-rejuvenating, ever-fashioning Life; where *I* am not, is Death! I am the dream, the balm, the hope of sufferers! I bring to nothing what exists, and whither I turn there wells fresh life from the dead rock. I come to you, to break all fetters that oppress you, to redeem you from the arms of Death and pour young Life through all your veins. Whatever stands, must fall: such is the everlasting law of Nature, such the condition of Life; and I, the eternal destroyer, fulfil the law and fashion ever-youthful life. From its root up will I destroy the order of things in which ye live, for it is sprung from sin, its flower is misery and its fruit is crime; but the harvest is ripe, and *I* am the reaper. I will destroy each phantom (*Wahn*) that has rule o'er men. I will destroy the dominion of one over many, of the dead o'er the living, of matter over spirit; I will break the power of the mighty, of law, of property. Be *his own* will the lord of man, his *own* desire his only law, his strength his whole possession, *for the only Holiness is the* free man, *and naught higher there is than* he. Annulled be the fancy that gives One power over millions, makes millions subject to the will of one, the doctrine that One has power to bless all others. Like may not rule over like; like has no higher potence than its equal: *and as ye all are equal, I will destroy all rulership of one over other.*

Annulled be the fancy that gives Death power over Life, the Past o'er the Future. The law of the dead is *their own* law; it shares their lot, and dies with them; it shall not govern Life. *Life is law unto itself.* And since the Law is for the living, not the dead, and *ye* are living, with none conceivable above you, *ye yourselves are the law, your own free will the sole and highest law, and I will destroy all dominion of Death over Life.*

Annulled be the fancy that makes man bondslave to his handiwork, to property. Man's highest good is his fashioning force, the fount whence springs all happiness forever; and not in the *created*, in the *act of creation itself*, in the *exercise of your powers* lies your true highest enjoyment. Man's work is lifeless; the living shall not bind itself to what is lifeless, not make itself a thrall to that. So away with the bugbear that restrains enjoyment, that hems free force, that sets up Property outside of Man, and makes him thrall to his own work.

Look hence ye wretched ones, upon those blessed fields ye now flit through as thralls, as aliens. *Free* shall ye wander there, free from the yoke of the living, free from the chains of the dead. What Nature made, what men have tilled and turned into a fruitful garden, belongs to *men*, the *needy*, and none shall come and say: "To *me* alone belongs all this; ye others are but guests I tolerate so long as I may please and they shall yield me tribute, guests I drive forth when so inclined. To *me* belongs what Nature made, what Man has wrought, and the living needs." Away with that lie; *to Need alone, belongs what satisfies it,* and such is offered in abundance by Nature and your own strong arm. See there the houses in the cities, and all that gives delight to men, which ye must journey past as strangers; Man's mind and strength have made it, and therefore it belongs to *men,* the *living,* and *one* man shall not come and say: "To *me* belongeth all that toiling men have made. I alone have a right to it, and the others shall enjoy but what I please and they pay toll for." Destroyed be this lie, with the others; for what the strength of men hath made, belongs to mankind for its unrestricted use, as everything besides on earth.

I will destroy the existing order of things, which parts this one mankind into hostile nations, into powerful and weak, privileged and outcast, rich and poor; for it makes *unhappy* men of all. I will destroy the order of things that turns millions to slaves of a few, and these few to slaves of their own might, own riches. I will destroy this order of things, that cuts enjoyment off from labour, makes labour a load (*Last*), enjoyment a vice (*Laster*), makes *one* man wretched through want, *another* through overflow. I will destroy this order of things, which wastes man's powers in service of dead matter, which keeps the half of humankind in inactivity or useless toil, binds hundreds of thousands to devote their vigorous youth—in busy idleness as soldiers, placemen, speculators and money-spinners—to the maintenance of these depraved conditions, whilst the other half must shore the whole disgraceful edifice at cost of over-taxing all their strength and sacrificing every taste of life. Down to its memory will I destroy each trace of this mad state of things, compact of violence, lies, care, hypocrisy, want, sorrow, suffering, tears, trickery and crime, with seldom a breath of even impure air to quicken it, and all but never a ray of pure joy. Destroyed be all that weighs on you and makes you suffer, and from the ruins of this ancient world let rise a *new,* instinct with happiness undreamt! Nor hate, nor envy, grudge nor enmity, be hencecorth found among you; as *brothers* shall ye all who live know one another, and *free,* free in willing, *free* in doing, *free* in enjoying, shall ye attest the worth of life. So up, ye peoples of the earth! Up, ye mourners, ye oppressed, ye poor! And up, ye others, ye who strive in vain to cloak the inner desolation of your hearts by idle show of might and riches! Up, in miscellany follow my steps; for no distinction can I make 'twixt those who follow me. *Two* peoples, only, are there from henceforth: the one, that follows me, the other, that withstands me. The one I lead to happiness; over the other grinds my path: for I am *Revolution*, I am the ever-fashioning Life, I am the only God, to whom each creature testifies, who spans and gives both life and happiness to all that is!

And lo! the legions on the hills, voiceless they fall to their knees and listen in mute transport; and as the sunbaked soil drinks up the cooling drops of rain, so their sorrow-parching hearts drink in the accents of the rustling storm, and new life courses through their veins. Nearer and nearer rolls the storm, on its wings Revolution; wide open now the quickened hearts of those awaked to life, and victrix Revolution pours into their brains, their bones, their flesh, and fills them through and through. In godlike ecstasy they leap from the ground; the poor, the hungering, the bowed by misery, are they no longer; proudly they raise themselves erect, inspiration shines from their ennobled faces, a radiant light streams from their eyes, and with the heaven-shaking cry *I am a Man!* the millions, the embodied Revolution, the God become Man, rush down to the valleys and plains, and proclaim to all the world the new gospel of Happiness.

Part IV: *History*

21. Sir Walter Scott: Dedicatory Epistle, *Ivanhoe*

Sir Walter Scott (1771–1832) was born in Edinburgh, and studied at its university, preparing for the bar, to which he was called in 1792. But he soon turned to literary pursuits, publishing *Minstrelsy of the Scottish Border* in 1802–1803 and *The Lay of the Last Minstrel* in 1805, maintaining himself by holding legal offices that demanded little labor. In the next few years he attained immense popularity as a poet, especially for *Marmion* and *The Lady of the Lake*. In 1814 came his first novel, *Waverly*. Again, success was instantaneous. Thereafter he published about two long novels a year, and his style of life came to match his expanding income, for he lived in a manner suitable to the re-creator of the feudal barony. His poems as well as his novels revived the past, not merely the Middle Ages, but, even more, of the Scottish border country he knew so well. And his knowledge was the product of assiduous search for remnants of the past, into which he sought to breathe life by his art—thereby outlining the new task of the historian as well as of the historical novelist. His efforts matched the influence and served the same end as the developing German historicist philosophy. G. M. Trevelyan wrote of him:

Gibbon was scarcely in the grave when a genius arose in Scotland who once and probably for ever transformed mankind's conception of itself from the classical to the romantic, from the uniform to the variegated . . . to Scott each age, each profession, each country, each province had its own manners, its own dress, its own way of thinking, talking and fighting. To Scott a man is not so much a human being as a type produced by special environment whether it be a border-farmer, a mediaeval abbot, a cavalier, a covenanter, a Swiss pikeman, or an Elizabethan statesman . . . it was he who first perceived that the history of mankind is not simple but complex, that history never repeats itself but ever creates new forms differing according to time and place.

The selection below is an introduction to *Ivanhoe*, Scott's most famous medieval romance, in the form of a letter from the imaginary author to an imaginary antiquarian.

From the *Works of Sir Walter Scott* (Thomas Nelson & Sons, London, 1905), Vol. IX, pp. xviii–xxxi.

Dedicatory Epistle to The Rev. Dr. Dryasdust, F.A.A., Residing in the Castle-Gate, York

MUCH ESTEEMED AND DEAR SIR,

It is scarcely necessary to mention the various and concurring reasons which induce me to place your name at the head of the following work. Yet the chief of these reasons may perhaps be refuted by the imperfections of the performance. Could I have hoped to render it worthy of your patronage, the public would at once have seen the propriety of inscribing a work designed to illustrate the domestic antiquities of England, and particularly of our Saxon forefathers, to the learned author of the Essays upon the Horn of King Ulphus, and on the lands bestowed by him upon the patrimony of St. Peter. I am conscious, however, that the slight, unsatisfactory, and trivial manner in which the result of my antiquarian researches has been recorded in the following pages, takes the work from under that class which bears the proud motto, *Detur digniori*. On the contrary, I fear I shall incur the censure of presumption in placing the venerable name of Dr. Jonas Dryasdust at the head of a publication, which the more grave antiquary will perhaps class with the idle novels and romances of the day. I am anxious to vindicate myself from such a charge; for although I might trust to your friendship for an apology in your eyes, yet I would not willingly stand convicted in those of the public of so grave a crime, as my fears lead me to anticipate my being charged with.

I must therefore remind you, that when we first talked over together that class of productions, in one of which the private and family affairs of your learned northern friend, Mr. Oldbuck of Monkbarns, were so unjustifiably exposed to the public, some discussion occurred between us concerning the cause of the popularity these works have attained in this idle age, which, whatever other merit they possess, must be admitted to be hastily written, and in violation of every rule assigned to the epopeia. It seemed then to be your opinion, that the charm lay entirely in the art with which the unknown author had availed himself, like a second M'Pherson,[1] of the antiquarian stores which lay scattered around him, supplying his own indolence or poverty of invention, by the incidents which had actually taken place in his country at no distant period, by introducing real characters, and scarcely suppressing real names. It was not above sixty or seventy years, you observed, since the whole north of Scotland was under a state of government nearly as simple and as patriarchal as those of our good allies the Mohawks and Iroquois. Admitting that the author cannot himself be supposed to have witnessed those times, he must have lived, you observed, among persons who had acted and suffered in them; and even within these thirty years, such an infinite change has taken place in the manners of Scotland, that men look back upon the habits of society proper to their immediate ancestors, as we do on those of the reign of Queen Anne, or even the period of the Revolution. Having thus materials of every kind lying strewed around him, there was little, you observed, to embarrass the author, but the difficulty of choice. It was no wonder, therefore, that, having begun to work a mine so plentiful, he should have derived from his works fully more credit and profit than the facility of his labours merited.

Admitting (as I could not deny) the general truth of these conclusions, I cannot but think it strange that no attempt has been made to excite an interest for the traditions and manners of Old England, similar to that which has been obtained in behalf of those of our poorer and less celebrated neighbors. The Kendal green, though its date is more ancient, ought surely to be as dear to our feelings as the variegated tartans of the north. The name of Robin Hood, if duly conjured with, should raise a spirit as soon as that of Rob Roy; and the patriots of England deserve no less their renown in our modern circles, than the Bruces and Wallaces of Caledonia. If the scenery of the south be less romantic and sublime than that of the northern mountains, it must be allowed to possess in the same proportion superior softness and beauty; and upon the whole, we feel ourselves entitled to exclaim with the

---

[1] James MacPherson (1736–96), Scottish poet who published *Fingal* in 1761, which he declared to be a translation from the ancient Gaelic poet, Ossian. The subsequent controversy over the poem's authenticity gave it great notoriety. (Ed.)

patriotic Syrian—"Are not Pharpar and Abana, rivers of Damascus, better than all the rivers of Israel?"

Your objections to such an attempt, my dear Doctor, were, you may remember, twofold. You insisted upon the advantages which the Scotsman possessed, from the very recent existence of that state of society in which his scene was to be laid. Many now alive, you remarked, well remembered persons who had not only seen the celebrated Roy M'Gregor, but had feasted, and even fought with him. All those minute circumstances belonging to private life and domestic character, all that gives verisimilitude to a narrative, and individuality to the persons introduced, is still known and remembered in Scotland; whereas in England, civilization has been so long complete, that our ideas of our ancestors are only to be gleaned from musty records and chronicles, the authors of which seem perversely to have conspired to suppress in their narratives all interesting details, in order to find room for flowers of monkish eloquence, or trite reflections upon morals. To match an English and a Scottish author in the rival task of embodying and reviving the traditions of their respective countries, would be, you alleged, in the highest degree unequal and unjust. The Scottish magician, you said, was, like Lucan's witch, at liberty to walk over the recent field of battle, and to select for the subject of resuscitation by his sorceries a body whose limbs had recently quivered with existence, and whose throat had but just uttered the last note of agony. . . . The English author, on the other hand, without supposing him less of a conjurer than the Northern Warlock, can, you observed, only have the liberty of selecting his subject amidst the dust of antiquity, where nothing was to be found but dry, sapless, mouldering, and disjointed bones, such as those which filled the valley of Jehoshaphat. You expressed, besides, your apprehension that the unpatriotic prejudices of my countrymen would not allow fair play to such a work as that of which I endeavoured to demonstrate the probable success. And this, you said, was not entirely owing to the more general prejudice in favour of that which is foreign, but that it rested partly upon improbabilities, arising out of the circumstances in which the English reader is placed. If you describe to him a set of wild manners, and a state of primitive society existing in the Highlands of Scotland, he is much disposed to acquiesce in the truth of what is asserted. And reason good. If he be of the ordinary class of readers, he has either never seen those remote districts at all, or he has wandered through those desolate regions in the course of a summer tour, eating bad dinners, sleeping on truckle-beds, stalking from desolation to desolation, and fully prepared to believe the strangest things that could be told him of a people wild and extravagant enough to be attached to scenery so extraordinary. But the same worthy person, when placed in his own snug parlour, and surrounded by all the comforts of an Englishman's fireside, is not half so much disposed to believe that his own ancestors led a very different life from himself; that the shattered tower, which now forms a vista from his window, once held a baron who would have hung him up at his own door without any form of trial; that the hinds, by whom his little pet-farm is managed, a few centuries ago would have been his slaves; and that the complete influence of feudal tyranny once extended over the neighbouring village, where the attorney is now a man of more importance than the Lord of the manor.

While I own the force of these objections, I must confess, at the same time, that they do not appear to me to be altogether insurmountable. The scantiness of materials is indeed a formidable difficulty; but no one knows better than Dr. Dryasdust, that to those deeply read in antiquity, hints concerning the private life of our ancestors lie scattered through the pages of our various historians, bearing, indeed, a slender proportion to the other matters of which they treat, but still, when collected together, sufficient to throw considerable light upon the *vie privée* of our forefathers; indeed, I am convinced that, however I myself may fail in the ensuing attempt, yet, with more labour in collecting, or more skill in using, the materials within his reach, illustrated as they have been by the labours of Dr. Henry, of the late Mr. Strutt, and, above all, of Mr. Sharon Turner, an abler hand would have been successful; and therefore I protest, beforehand, against any argument which may be founded on the failure of the present experiment.

On the other hand I have already said, that if anything like a true picture of old English manners could be drawn, I would trust to the good-nature and good sense of my countrymen for insuring its favourable reception.

Having thus replied, to the best of my power, to the first class of your objections, or at least having shown my resolution to overleap the barriers which your prudence has raised, I will be brief in noticing that which is more peculiar to myself. It seems to be your opinion that the very office of an antiquary, employed in grave, and, as the vulgar will sometimes allege, in toilsome and minute research, must be considered as incapacitating him from successfully compounding a tale of this sort. But permit me to say, my dear Doctor, that this objection is rather formal than substantial. It is true, that such slight compositions might not suit the severer genius of our friend Mr. Oldbuck. Yet Horace Walpole wrote a goblin tale which has thrilled through many a bosom; and George Ellis could transfer all the playful fascination of a humour, as delightful as it was uncommon, into his Abridgment of the Ancient Metrical Romances. So that, however I may have occasion to rue my present audacity, I have at least the most respectable precedents in my favour.

Still the severer antiquary may think that, by thus intermingling fiction with truth, I am polluting the well of history with modern inventions, and impressing upon the rising generation false ideas of the age which I describe. I cannot but in some sense admit the force of this reasoning, which I yet hope to traverse by the following considerations.

It is true that I neither can nor do pretend to the observation of complete accuracy, even in matters of outward costume, much less in the more important points of language and manners. But the same motive which prevents my writing the dialogue of the piece in Anglo-Saxon or in Norman-French, and which prohibits my sending forth to the public this essay printed with the types of Caxton or Wynken de Worde, prevents my attempting to confine myself within the limits of the period in which my story is laid. It is necessary, for exciting interest of any kind, that the subject assumed should be, as it were, translated into the manners, as well as the language, of the age we live in. No fascination has ever been attached to Oriental literature equal to that produced by Mr. Galland's first translation of the Arabian Tales; in which, retaining on the one hand the spendour of Eastern costume, and on the other the wildness of Eastern fiction, he mixed these with just so much ordinary feeling and expression as rendered them interesting and intelligible, while he abridged the long-winded narratives, curtailed the monotonous reflections, and rejected the endless repetitions of the Arabian original. The tales, therefore, though less purely Oriental than in their first concoction, were eminently better fitted for the European market, and obtained an unrivalled degree of public favour, which they certainly would never have gained had not the manners and style been in some degree familiarized to the feelings and habits of the Western reader.

In point of justice, therefore, to the multitudes who will, I trust, devour this book with avidity, I have so far explained our ancient manners in modern language, and so far detailed the characters and sentiments of my persons, that the modern reader will not find himself, I should hope, much trammelled by the repulsive dryness of mere antiquity. In this, I respectfully contend, I have in no respect exceeded the fair license due to the author of a fictitious composition. The late ingenious Mr. Strutt, in his romance of Queen-Hoo-Hall, acted upon another principle; and in distinguishing between what was ancient and modern, forgot, as it appears to me, that entensive neutral ground, the large proportion, that is, of manners and sentiments which are common to us and to our ancestors, having been handed down unaltered from them to us, or which, arising out of the principles of our common nature, must have existed alike in either state of society. In this manner, a man of talent, and of great antiquarian erudition, limited the popularity of his work, by excluding from it everything which was not sufficiently obsolete to be altogether forgotten and unintelligible.

The license which I would here vindicate, is so necessary to the execution of my plan, that I will crave your patience while I illlustrate my argument a little further.

He who first opens Chaucer, or any other ancient poet, is so much struck with the obsolete spelling, multiplied consonants, and antiquated appearance of the language, that he is apt to lay the work down in despair, as encrusted too deep with the rust of antiquity, to permit his judging of its merits or tasting its beauties. But if some intelligent and accomplished friend points out to him that the difficulties by which he is startled are more in appearance than reality, if, by reading aloud to him or by reducing the ordinary words to the modern orthography, he satisfies his proselyte that only about one-tenth part of the words employed are in fact obsolete, the novice may be easily persuaded to approach the "well of English undefiled," with the certainty that a slender degree of patience will enable him to enjoy both the humour and the pathos with which old Geoffrey delighted the age of Cressy and of Poictiers.

To pursue this a little further. If our neophyte, strong in the new-born love of antiquity, were to undertake to imitate what he had learned to admire, it must be allowed he would act very injudiciously, if he were to select from the Glossary the obsolete words which it contains, and employ those exclusively of all phrases and vocables retained in modern days. This was the error of the unfortunate Chatterton. In order to give his language the appearance of antiquity, he rejected every word that was modern, and produced a dialect entirely different from any that had ever been spoken in Great Britain. He who would imitate an ancient language with success, must attend rather to its grammatical character, turn of expression, and mode of arrangement, than labour to collect extraordinary and antiquated terms, which, as I have already averred, do not in ancient authors approach the number of words still in use, though perhaps somewhat altered in sense and spelling, in the proportion of one to ten.

What I have applied to language, is still more justly applicable to sentiments and manners. The passions, the sources from which these must spring in all their modifications, are generally the same in all ranks and conditions, all countries and ages; and it follows, as a matter of course, that the opinions, habits of thinking, and actions, however influenced by the peculiar state of society, must still, upon the whole, bear a strong resemblance to each other. Our ancestors were not more distinct from us, surely, than Jews are from Christians; they had "eyes, hands, organs, dimensions, senses, affections, passions"; were "fed with the same food, hurt with the same weapons, subject to the same diseases, warmed and cooled by the same winter and summer," as ourselves. The tenor, therefore, of their affections and feelings must have borne the same general proportion to our own.

It follows, therefore, that of the materials which an author has to use in a romance, or fictitious composition such as I have ventured to attempt, he will find that a great proportion, both of language and manners, is as proper to the present time as to those in which he has laid his time of action. The freedom of choice which this allows him is therefore much greater, and the difficulty of his task much more diminished, than at first appears. To take an illustration from a sister art, the antiquarian details may be said to represent the peculiar features of a landscape under delineation of the pencil. His feudal tower must arise in due majesty; the figures which he introduces must have the costume and character of their age; the piece must represent the peculiar features of the scene which he has chosen for his subject, with all its appropriate elevation of rock, or precipitate descent of cataract. His general colouring, too, must be copied from Nature: the sky must be clouded or serene, according to the climate, and the general tints must be those which prevail in a natural landscape. So far the painter is bound down, by the rules of his art, to a precise imitation of the features of Nature; but it is not required that he should descend to copy all her more minute features, or represent with absolute exactness the very herbs, flowers, and trees with which the spot is decorated. These, as well as all the more minute points of light and shadow, are attributes proper to scenery in general, natural to each situation, and subject to the artist's disposal, as his taste or pleasure may dictate.

It is true that this license is confined in either case within legitimate bounds. The painter must introduce no ornament inconsistent with the climate or country of his landscape; he must not plant cypress trees upon Inch-Merrin, or Scottish firs among the ruins of Persepolis; and the author lies under a corresponding restraint. However far he may venture in a more full detail of passions and feelings than is to be found in the ancient compositions which he imitates, he must introduce nothing inconsistent with the manners of the age; his knights, squires, grooms, and yeomen may be more fully drawn than in the hard, dry delineations of an ancient illuminated manuscript, but the character and costume of the age must remain inviolate; they must be the same figures, drawn by a better pencil, or, to speak more modestly, executed in an age when the principles of art were better understood. His language must not be exclusively obsolete and unintelligible; but he should admit, if possible, no word or turn of phraseology betraying an origin directly modern. It is one thing to make use of the language and sentiments which are common to ourselves and our forefathers, and it is another to invest them with the sentiments and dialect exclusively proper to their descendants.

This, my dear friend, I have found the most difficult part of my task; and, to speak frankly, I hardly expect to satisfy your less partial judgment, and more extensive knowledge of such subjects, since I have hardly been able to please my own.

I am conscious that I shall be found still more faulty in the tone of keeping and costume, by those who may be disposed rigidly to examine my Tale, with reference to the manners of the exact period in which my actors flourished. It may be that I have introduced little which can positively be termed modern; but, on the other hand, it is extremely probable that I may have confused the manners of two or three centuries, and introduced, during the reign of Richard the First, circumstances appropriated to a period either considerably earlier or a good deal later than that era. It is my comfort that errors of this kind will escape the general class of readers, and that I may share in the ill-deserved applause of those architects who, in their modern Gothic, do not hesitate to introduce, without rule or method, ornaments proper to different styles and to different periods of the art. Those whose extensive researches have given them the means of judging my backslidings with more severity, will probably be lenient in proportion to their knowledge of the difficulty of my task. My honest and neglected friend, Ingulphus, has furnished me with many a valuable hint; but the light afforded by the Monk of Croydon, and Geoffrey de Vinsauff, is dimmed by such a conglomeration of uninteresting and unintelligible matter, that we gladly fly for relief to the delightful pages of the gallant Froissart, although he flourished at a period so much more remote from the date of my history. If, therefore, my dear friend, you have generosity enough to pardon the presumptuous attempt, to frame for myself a minstrel coronet, partly out of the pearls of pure antiquity, and partly from the Bristol stones and paste with which I have endeavoured to imitate them, I am convinced your opinion of the difficulty of the task will reconcile you to the imperfect manner of its execution.

Of my materials I have but little to say. They may be chiefly found in the singular Anglo-Norman MS., which Sir Arthur Wardour preserves with such jealous care in the third drawer of his oaken cabinet, scarcely allowing any one to touch it, and being himself not able to read one syllable of its contents. I should never have got his consent, on my visit to Scotland, to read in those precious pages for so many hours, had I not promised to designate it by some emphatic mode of printing, as *The Wardour*

Manuscript; giving it, thereby, an individuality as important as the Bannatyne MS., the Auchinleck MS., and any other monument of the patience of a Gothic scrivener. I have sent, for your private consideration, a list of the contents of this curious piece, which I shall perhaps subjoin, with your approbation, to the third volume of my Tale, in case the printer's devil should continue impatient for copy, when the whole of my narrative has been imposed.

Adieu, my dear friend. I have said enough to explain, if not to vindicate, the attempt which I have made, and which, in spite of your doubts, and my own incapacity, I am still willing to believe has not been altogether made in vain.

I hope you are now well recovered from your spring fit of the gout, and shall be happy if the advice of your learned physician should recommend a tour to these parts. Several curiosities have been lately dug up near the wall, as well as at the ancient station of Habitancum. Talking of the latter, I suppose you have long since heard the news, that a sulky churlish boor has destroyed the ancient statue, or rather bas-relief, popularly called Robin of Redesdale. It seems Robin's fame attracted more visitants than was consistent with the growth of the heather upon a moor worth a shilling an acre. Reverend as you write yourself, be revengeful for once, and pray with me that he may be visited with such a fit of the stone, as if he had all the fragments of poor Robin in that region of his viscera where the disease holds its seat. Tell this not in Gath, lest the Scots rejoice that they have at length found a parallel instance among their neighbours to that barbarous deed which demolished Arthur's Oven. But there is no end to lamentation, when we betake ourselves to such subjects. My respectful compliments attend Miss Dryasdust. I endeavoured to match the spectacles agreeable to her commission, during my late journey to London, and hope she has received them safe, and found them satisfactory. I send this by the blind carrier, so that probably it may be some time upon its journey. The last news which I hear from Edinburgh is, that the gentleman who fills the situation of Secretary of the Society of Antiquaries of Scotland, is the best amateur draftsman in that kingdom, and that much is expected from his skill and zeal in delineating those specimens of national antiquity, which are either mouldering under the slow touch of time, or swept away by modern taste, with the same besom of destruction which John Knox used at the Reformation. Once more adieu; *vale tandem, non immemor mei.* Believe me to be,

Reverend, and very dear Sir,
Your most faithful humble Servant,
Laurence Templeton

Toppingwold, near Egremont,
   Cumberland, Nov. 17, 1817

22. Thomas Carlyle: *Past and Present*

Thomas Carlyle (1795–1881) was second only to Coleridge as a spokesman for German Romanticism, introducing English intellectuals to the new German thought,—in Carlyle's case, the introduction was to German culture as a whole. Carlyle's devotion to things German is clear in his first major work—the verbose, often confusing, yet powerful *Sartor Resartus* (1833–34)—and in his later *History of Frederick the Great* (1858–65). He knew the idealist philosophers, though less preceptively than Coleridge did. But it would be a mistake to view Carlyle as a mere imitator or popularizer. While not a very profound thinker and certainly unsystematic, he served as one of England's greatest social critics of the age—in the earlier part of his life as a kind of conscience, who wrote in the tones of Hebrew prophecy. He had been trained for the Calvinist ministry, but lost his faith and his oratorical prose is a finer version of the hortatory sermons his countrymen relished. His *Past and Present* (from which a selection follows) and *Chartism* were tracts attacking the egoism and materialism of an age that allowed the poor to suffer; and these texts bespoke his typically Romantic demand for a heroic faith and for faith in natural heroes and leaders, for discipline and an ethic of work to replace the moral atrophy he saw around him. His opposition to dominant currents of his age, in politics and in society, became stronger as he grew older, especially in such conservative works as *Shooting Niagara*, which opposed the Reform Bill of 1867.

    Our selection from *Past and Present* is chosen not to show Carlyle the social critic or moralist, but to show him in what will probably remain his most memorable guise, as an historian. We have noted how central to the aesthetics and religion of the Romantic era the new historical mentality of the age was. Such historians as Carlyle made major contributions to the knowledge of and the sentiment about the past. Carlyle's philosophy of history is by no means very clear (he sought to evoke the spirit of the past quite as much as he sought to portray its heroes—see his *On Heroes, Hero-Worship and the Heroic in History*, 1841, as well as parts of *The French Revolution*, 1837), but his history itself is a significant and conscious effort to place the reader in the past and to make him feel like a participant. The extract that follows asserts the possibility of such a re-creation. The work as a whole presents a sharp contrast between an era of faith and social unity and the atomized society of his own time.

The selection is from Carlyle's *Works* Vol. XIII *Past and Present*, (London, 1843), pp. 51–59, 62–64, 79–82.

WE WILL, in this Second Portion of our Work, strive to penetrate a little, by means of certain confused Papers, printed and other, into a somewhat remote Century; and to look face to face on it, in hope of perhaps illustrating our own poor Century thereby. It seems a circuitous way; but it may prove a way nevertheless. For man has ever been a striving, struggling, and, in spite of wide-spread calumnies to the contrary, a veracious creature: the Centuries too are all lineal children of one another; and often, in the portrait of early grandfathers, this and the other enigmatic feature of the newest grandson shall disclose itself, to mutual elucidation. This Editor will venture on such a thing.

Besides, in Editors' Books, and indeed everywhere else in the world of Today, a certain latitude of movement grows more and more becoming for the practical man. Salvation lies not in tight lacing, in these times;—how far from that, in any province what-soever! Readers and men generally are getting into strange habits of asking all persons and things, from poor Editors' Books up to Church Bishops and State Potentates, not, By what designation art thou called; in what wig and black triangle dost thou walk abroad? Heavens, I know thy designation and black triangle well enough! But, in God's name, what *art* thou? Not Nothing, sayest thou! Then, How much and what? This is the thing I would know; and even *must* soon know, such a pass am I come to!—
—What weather-symptoms,—not for the poor Editor of Books alone! The Editor of Books may understand withal that if, as is said, 'many kinds are permissible,' there is one kind not permissi-ble, 'the kind that has nothing in it, *le genre ennuyeux;*' and go on his way accordingly.

A certain Jocelinus de Brakelonda, a natural-born Englishman, has left us an extremely foreign Book,[1] which the labours of the Camden Society have brought to light in these days. Jocelin's Book, the 'Chronicle,' or private Boswellean Notebook, of Jocelin, a certain old St. Edmundsbury Monk and Boswell, now seven centuries old, how remote is it from us; exotic, extraneous; in all ways, coming from far abroad! The language of it is not foreign only but dead: Monk-Latin lies across not the British Channel, but the ninefold Stygian Marshes, Stream of Lethe, and one knows not where! Roman Latin itself, still alive for us in the Elysian Fields of Memory, is domestic in comparison. And then the ideas, life-furniture, whole workings and ways of this worthy Jocelin; covered deeper than Pompeii with the lava-ashes and inarticulate wreck of seven hundred years!

Jocelin of Brakelond cannot be called a conspicuous literary character; indeed few mortals that have left so visible a work, or footmark, behind them can be more obscure. One other of those vanished Existences, whose work has not yet vanished;—almost a pathetic phenomenon, were not the whole world full of such! The builders of Stonehenge, for example:—or, alas, what say we, Stonehenge and builders? The writers of the *Universal Review* and *Homer's Iliad;* the paviors of London streets;—sooner or later, the entire Posterity of Adam! It is a pathetic phenomenon; but an irremediable, nay, if well meditated, a consoling one.

By his dialect of Monk-Latin, and indeed by his name, this Jocelin seems to have been a Norman Englishman; the surname *de Brakelonda* indicates a native of St. Edmundsbury itself, *Brakelond* being the known old name of a street or quarter in that venerable Town. Then farther, sure enough, our Jocelin was a Monk of St. Edmundsbury Convent; held some '*obedientia*,' subaltern officiality there, or rather, in succession several; was, for one thing, 'chaplain to my Lord Abbot, living beside him night and day for the space of six years;'—which last, indeed, is the grand fact of Jocelin's existence, and properly the origin of this present Book, and of the chief meaning it has for us now. He was, as we have hinted, a kind of born *Boswell*, though an infinitesi-

---

[1] *Chronica Jocelini de Brakelonda, de rebus gestis Samsonis Abbatis Monasterii Sancti Edmundi: nunc primum typis mandata, curante Johanne Gage Rokewood.* (Camden Society, London, 1810.)

mally small one; neither did he altogether want his *Johnson* even there and then. Johnsons are rare; yet, as has been asserted, Boswells perhaps still rarer,—the more is the pity on both sides! This Jocelin, as we can discern well, was an ingenious and ingenuous, a cheery-hearted, innocent, yet withal shrewd, noticing, quick-witted man; and from under his monk's cowl has looked out on that narrow section of the world in a really *human* manner; not in any *simial*, canine, ovine, or otherwise *in*human manner,— afflictive to all that have humanity! The man is of patient, peaceable, loving, clear-smiling nature; open for this and that. A wise simplicity is in him; much natural sense; a *veracity* that goes deeper than words. Veracity: it is the basis of all; and, some say, means genius itself; the prime essence of all genius whatsoever. Our Jocelin, for the rest, has read his classical manuscripts, his Virgilius, his Flaccus, Ovidius Naso; of course still more, his Homilies and Breviaries, and if not the Bible, considerable extracts of the Bible. Then also he has a pleasant wit; and loves a timely joke, though in mild subdued manner: very amiable to see. A learned grown man, yet with the heart as of a good child; whose whole life indeed has been that of a child,—St. Edmundsbury Monastery a larger kind of cradle for him, in which his whole prescribed duty was to *sleep* kindly, and love his mother well! This is the Biography of Jocelin; 'a man of excellent religion,' says one of his contemporary Brother Monks. . . .

For one thing, he had learned to write a kind of Monk or Dog-Latin, still readable to mankind; and, by good luck for us, had bethought him of noting down thereby what things seemed notablest to him. Hence gradually resulted a *Chronica Jocelini;* new Manuscript in the *Liber Albus* of St. Edmundsbury. Which Chronicle, once written in its childlike transparency, in its innocent good-humour, not without touches of ready pleasant wit and many kinds of worth, other men liked naturally to read: whereby it failed not to be copied, to be multiplied, to be inserted in the *Liber Albus;* and so surviving Henry the Eighth, Putney Cromwell, the Dissolution of Monasteries, and all accidents of malice and neglect for six centuries or so, it got into the *Harleian Collection,*—and has now therefrom, by Mr. Rokewood of the Camden Society, been deciphered into clear print; and lies before us, a dainty thin quarto, to interest for a few minutes whomsoever it can.

Here too it will behove a just Historian gratefully to say that Mr. Rokewood, Jocelin's Editor, has done his editorial function well. Not only has he deciphered his crabbed Manuscript into clear print; but he has attended, what his fellow editors are not always in the habit of doing, to the important truth that the Manuscript so deciphered ought to have a meaning for the reader. Standing faithfully by his text, and printing its very errors in spelling, in grammar or otherwise, he has taken care by some note to indicate that they are errors, and what the correction of them ought to be. Jocelin's Monk-Latin is generally transparent, as shallow limpid water. But at any stop that may occur, of which there are a few, and only a very few, we have the comfortable assurance that a meaning does lie in the passage, and may by industry be got at; that a faithful editor's industry had already got at it before passing on. A compendious useful Glossary is given; nearly adequate to help the uninitiated through: sometimes one wishes it had been a trifle larger; but, with a Spelman and Ducange at your elbow, how easy to have made it far too large! Notes are added, generally brief; sufficiently explanatory of most points. Lastly, a copious correct Index; which no such Book should want, and which unluckily very few possess. And so, in a word, the *Chronicle of Jocelin* is, as it professes to be, unwrapped from its thick cerements, and fairly brought forth into the common daylight, so that he who runs, and has a smattering of grammar, may read.

We have heard so much of Monks; everywhere, in real and fictitious History, from Muratori Annals to Radcliffe Romances, these singular two-legged animals, with their rosaries and breviaries, with their shaven crowns, hair-cilices, and vows of poverty, masquerade so strangely through our fancy; and they are in fact so very strange an extinct species of the human family,—a veritable Monk of Bury St. Edmunds is worth attending to, if by chance made visible and audible. Here he is; and in his hand a magical speculum, much gone to rust indeed, yet in fragments still clear; wherein the marvellous image of his existence does still shadow itself, though fitfully, and as with an intermittent light! Will not the reader peep with us into this singular *camera lucida*, where an extinct species, though fitfully, can still be seen alive? Extinct species, we say; for the live specimens which still go about under that character are too evidently to be classed as spurious in Natural History: the Gospel of Richard Arkwright once promulgated, no Monk of the old sort is any longer possible in this world. But fancy a deep-buried Mastodon, some fossil Megatherion, Ichthyosaurus, were to begin to *speak* from amid its rock-swathings, never so indistinctly! The most extinct fossil species of Men or Monk can do, and does, this miracle,—thanks to the Letters of the Alphabet, good for so many things.

Jocelin, we said, was somewhat of a Boswell; but unfortunately, by Nature, he is none of the largest, and distance has now dwarfed him to an extreme degree. His light is most feeble, intermittent, and requires the intensest kindest inspection; otherwise it will disclose mere vacant haze. It must be owned, the good Jocelin, spite of his beautiful childlike character, is but an altogether imperfect 'mirror' of these old-world things! The good man, he looks on us so clear and cheery, and in his neighbourly soft-smiling eyes we see so well our *own* shadow,—we have a longing always to cross-question him, to force from him an explanation of much. But no; Jocelin, though he talks with such clear familiarity, like a next-door neighbour, will not answer any question: that is the peculiarity of him, dead these six hundred and fifty years, and quite deaf to us, though still so audible! The good man, he cannot help it, nor can we.

But truly it is a strange consideration this simple one, as we go on with him, or indeed with any lucid simple-hearted soul like him: Behold therefore, this England of the Year 1200 was no chimerical vacuity or dreamland, peopled with mere vaporous Fantasms, Rymer's Fœdera, and Doctrines of the Constitution; but a green solid place, that grew corn and several other things. The Sun shone on it; the vicissitude of seasons and human fortunes. Cloth was woven and worn; ditches were dug, furrow-fields ploughed, and houses built. Day by day all men and cattle rose to labour, and night by night returned home weary to their several lairs. In wondrous Dualism, then as now, lived nations of breathing men; alternating, in all ways, between Light and Dark; between joy and sorrow, between rest and toil,—between hope, hope reaching high as Heaven, and fear deep as very Hell. Not vapour Fantasms, Rymer's Fœdera at all! Cœur-de-Lion was not a theatrical popinjay with greaves and steel-cap on it, but a man living upon victuals,—*not* imported by Peel's Tariff. Cœur-de-Lion came palpably athwart this Jocelin at Edmundsbury; and had almost peeled the sacred gold '*feretrum*,' or St. Edmund Shrine itself, to ransom him out of the Danube Jail.

These clear eyes of neighbour Jocelin looked on the bodily presence of King John; the very John *Sansterre*, or Lackland, who signed *Magna Charta* afterwards in Runnymead. Lackland, with a great retinue, boarded once, for the matter of a fortnight, in St. Edmundsbury Convent; daily in the very eyesight, palpable to the very fingers of our Jocelin: O Jocelin, what did he say, what did he do; how looked he, lived he;—at the very lowest, what coat or breeches had he on? Jocelin is obstinately silent. Jocelin marks down what interests *him*; entirely deaf to *us*. With Jocelin's eyes we discern almost nothing of John Lackland. As through a glass darkly, we with our own eyes and appliances, intensely looking, discern at most: A blustering, dissipated human figure, with a kind of blackguard quality air, in cramoisy velvet, or other uncertain texture, uncertain cut, with much plumage and fringing; amid numerous other human figures of the like; riding abroad with hawks; talking noisy nonsense;—tearing out the bowls of St. Edmundsbury Convent (its larders namely and cellars) in the most ruinous way, by living at rack and manger there. Jocelin notes only, with a slight subacidity of manner, that the King's Majesty, *Dominus Rex*, did leave, as gift for our St. Edmund Shrine, a handsome enough silk cloak,—or rather pretended to leave, for one of his retinue borrowed it of us, and *we* never got sight of it again; and, on the whole, that the *Dominus Rex*, at departing, gave us 'thirteen *sterlingii*,' one shilling and one penny, to say a mass for him; and so departed,—like a shabby Lackland as he was! 'Thirteen pence sterling,' this was what the Convent got from Lackland, for all the victuals he and his had made away with. We of course said our mass for him, having covenanted to do it,—but let impartial posterity judge with what degree of fervour!

And in this manner vanishes King Lackland; traverses swiftly our strange intermittent magic-mirror, jingling the shabby thirteen pence merely; and rides with his hawks into Egyptian night again. It is Jocelin's manner with all things; and it is men's manner and men's necessity. How intermittent is our good Jocelin;

marking down, without eye to *us*, what *he* finds interesting! How much in Jocelin, as in all History, and indeed in all Nature, is at once inscrutable and certain; so dim, yet so indubitable; exciting us to endless considerations. For King Lackland *was* there, verily he; and did leave these *tredecim sterlingii*, if nothing more, and did live and look in one way or the other, and a whole world was living and looking along with him! There, we say, is the grand peculiarity; the immeasurable one; distinguishing, to a really infinite degree, the poorest historical Fact from all Fiction whatsoever. Fiction, 'Imagination,' 'Imaginative Poetry,' &c. &c., except as the vehicle for truth, or *fact* of some sort,—which surely a man should first try various other ways of vehiculating, and conveying safe,—what is it? Let the Minerva and other presses respond!—

But it is time we were in St. Edmundsbury Monastery, and Seven good Centuries off. If indeed it be possible, by any aid of Jocelin, by any human art, to get thither, with a reader or two still following us? . . .

Another world, truly: and this present poor distressed world might get some profit by looking wisely into it, instead of foolishly. But at lowest, O dilettante friend, let us know always that it *was* a world, and not a void infinite of gray haze with fantasms swimming in it. These old St. Edmundsbury walls, I say, were not peopled with fantasms; but with men of flesh and blood, made altogether as we are. Had thou and I then been, who knows but we ourselves had taken refuge from an evil Time, and fled to dwell here, and meditate on an Eternity, in such fashion as we could? Alas, how like an old osseous fragment, a broken blackened shin-bone of the old dead Ages, this black ruin looks out, not yet covered by the soil; still indicating what a once gigantic Life lies buried there! It is dead now, and dumb; but was alive once, and spake. For twenty generations, here was the earthly arena where painful living men worked out their life-wrestle,—looked at by Earth, by Heaven and Hell. Bells tolled to prayers; and men, of many humours, various thoughts, chanted vespers, matins; —and round the little islet of their life rolled forever (as round ours still rolls, though we are blind and deaf) the illimitable Ocean, tinting all things with *its* eternal hues and reflexes; making strange prophetic music! How silent now; all departed, clean gone. The World-Dramaturgist has written: *Exeunt.* The devouring Time-Demons have made away with it all: and in its stead, there is either nothing; or what is worse, offensive universal dust-clouds, and gray eclipse of Earth and Heaven, from 'dry rubbish shot here!'—

Truly it is no easy matter to get across the chasm of Seven Centuries, filled with such material. But here, of all helps, is not a Boswell the welcomest; even a small Boswell? Veracity, true simplicity of heart, how valuable are these always! He that speaks what *is* really in him, will find men to listen, though under never such impediments. Even gossip, springing free and cheery from a human heart, this too is a kind of veracity and *speech;*—much preferable to pedantry and inane gray haze! Jocelin is weak and garrulous, but he is human. Through the thin watery gossip of our Jocelin, we do get some glimpses of that deep-buried Time; discern veritably, though in a fitful intermittent manner, these antique figures and their life-method, face to face! Beautifully, in our earnest loving glance, the old centuries melt from opaque to partially translucent, transparent here and there; and the void black Night, one finds, is but the summing-up of innumerable peopled luminous *Days.* Not parchment Chartularies, Doctrines of the Constitution, O Dryasdust; not altogether, my erudite friend!—

Readers who please to go along with us into this poor *Jocelini Chronica* shall wander inconveniently enough, as in wintry twilight, through some poor stript hazel-grove, rustling with foolish noises, and perpetually hindering the eyesight; but across which, here and there, some real human figure is seen moving: very strange; whom we could hail if he would answer;—and we look into a pair of eyes deep as our own, *imaging* our own, but all unconscious of us; to whom we, for the time, are become as spirits and invisible! . . .

Dim, as through a long vista of Seven Centuries, dim and very strange looks that monk-life to us; the ever-surprising circumstance this, That it is a *fact* and no dream, that we see it there, and gaze into the very eyes of it! Smoke rises daily from those culinary chimney-throats; there are living human beings there, who chant, loud-braying, their matins, nones, vespers; awakening *echoes*, not to the bodily ear alone. St. Edmund's Shrine, perpetually illuminated, glows ruddy through the Night, and through the Night of Centuries withal; St. Edmundsbury Town paying yearly Forty pounds for that express end. Bells clang out; on great occasions, all the bells. We have Processions, Preachings, Festivals, Christmas Plays, *Mysteries* shown in the Churchyard, at which latter the Townsfolk sometimes quarrel. Time was, Time is, as Friar Bacon's Brass Head remarked; and withal Time will be. There are three Tenses, *Tempora*, or Times; and there is one Eternity; and as for us,

'We are such stuff as Dreams are made of!'

Indisputable, though very dim to modern vision, rests on its hillslope that same *Bury, Stow,* or Town of St. Edmund; already a considerable place, not without traffic, nay manufactures, would Jocelin only tell us what. Jocelin is totally careless of telling: but, through dim fitful apertures, we can see *Fullones,* 'Fullers,' see cloth-making; looms dimly going, dye-vats, and old women spinning yarn. We have Fairs, too, *Nundinae,* in due course; and the Londoners give us much trouble, pretending that they, as a metropolitan people, are exempt from toll. Besides there is Fieldhusbandry, with perplexed settlement of Convent rents: corn-ricks pile themselves within burgh, in their season; and cattle depart and enter; and even the poor weaver has his cow,—'dungheaps' lying quiet at most doors (*ante foras,* says the incidental Jocelin), for the Town has yet no improved police. Watch and ward nevertheless we do keep, and have Gates,—as what Town must not; thieves so abounding; war, *werra,* such a frequent thing! Our thieves, at the Abbot's judgment-bar, deny; claim wager of battle; fight, are beaten, and *then* hanged. 'Ketel, the thief,' took this course; and it did nothing for him,—merely brought us, and indeed himself, new trouble!

Everyway a most foreign Time. What difficulty, for example, has our *Cellerarius* to collect the *repselver,* 'reaping silver,' or penny, which each householder is by law bound to pay for cutting down the Convent grain! Richer people pretend that it is commuted, that it is this and the other; that, in short, they will not pay it. Our *Cellerarius* gives up calling on the rich. In the houses of the poor, our *Cellerarius* finding, in like manner, neither penny nor good promise, snatches, without ceremony, what *vadium* (pledge, *wad*) he can come at: a joint-stool, kettle, nay the very house-door, '*hostium*,' and old women, thus exposed to the unfeeling gaze of the public, rush out after him with their distaffs and the angriest shrieks: '*vetulæ exibant cum colis suis*,' says Jocelin, '*minantes et exprobrantes*.'

What a historical picture, glowing visible, as St. Edmund's Shrine by night, after Seven long Centuries or so! *Vetulæ cum colis:* My venerable ancient spinning grandmothers,—ah, and ye too have to shriek, and rush out with your distaffs; and become Female Chartists, and scold all evening with void doorway;—and in old Saxon, as we in modern, would fain demand some Five-point Charter, could it be fallen-in with, the Earth being too tyrannous!—Wise Lord Abbots, hearing of such phenomena, did in time abolish or commute the reap-penny, and one nuisance was abated. But the image of these justly offended old women, in their old wool costumes, with their angry features, and spindles brandished, lives forever in the historical memory. Thanks to thee, Jocelin Boswell. Jerusalem was taken by the Crusaders, and again lost by them; and Richard Cœur-de-Lion 'veiled his face' as he passed in sight of it: but how many other things went on, the while!

Thus, too, our trouble with the Lakenheath eels is very great. King Knut namely, or rather his Queen who also did herself honour by honouring St. Edmund, decreed by authentic deed yet extant on parchment, that the Holders of the Town Fields, once Beodric's, should, for one thing, go yearly and catch us four thousand eels in the marshpools of Lakenheath. Well, they went, they continued to go; but, in later times, got into the way of returning with a most short account of eels. Not the due six-score apiece; no, Here are two-score, Here are twenty, ten,—sometimes, Here are none at all; Heaven help us, we *could* catch no more, they were not there! What is a distressed *Cellerarius* to do? We agree that each Holder of so many acres shall pay one penny yearly, and let-go the eels as too slippery. But, alas, neither is this quite effectual: the Fields, in my time, have got divided among so many hands, there is no catching of *them* either; I have known our Cellarer get seven-and-twenty pence formerly, and now it is much if he get ten pence farthing (*vix decem denarios et obolum*). And then their sheep, which they are bound to fold nightly in our pens, for the manure's sake; and, I fear, do not always fold: and their *aver-pennies*, and their *avragiums*, and their *fodercorns,* and mill-and-market dues! Thus, in its undeniable but dim manner, does old St. Edmundsbury spin and till, and laboriously keep its pot boiling, and St. Edmund's Shrine lighted, under such conditions and averages as it can.

23. Jules Michelet: Preface to *Historical View* of *the French Revolution*

Jules Michelet (1798–1874) regarded himself as one of "the people" he glorified. His *History of France* (1833–43; 1855–67) portrayed the development of the French people, most tellingly in his pictures of medieval France and his justly famous treatment of Joan of Arc. His *Historical View of the French Revolution* (1847–53), made the Revolution—personified or represented as the activity of the virtuous people—the focal moment of all French history. His history had a hero, the people itself. He had offered a separate study called *The People,* published in 1846, in praise of his hero.

His empathy was genuine, for he was son of a poor printer who had suffered under Napoleon, and he himself had known poverty and hard work throughout his life, even though he managed to obtain a university education. He served as tutor and teacher at the École Normale and the Collège de France, and his writings have been highly influential in shaping historical education in French schools. He was director of the Historical Section of the National Archives, and he conscientiously pursued primary sources, impressionistic as his works came to be.

He was influenced by his discovery of Vico, whose work he translated, to see history as the product of the people. He really sought to bring his readers to relive, as he considered himself to have relived, the passions and pains of the past. He was an intense nationalist (never forgiving the English for Waterloo) and an ardent egalitarian, a passionate anti-cleric, and for a half century he was France's most noted republican historian.

The following selection is the Preface to *Historical View of the French Revolution from Its Earliest Indications to the Flight of the King,* translated by C. Cocks (London, 1860.) pp. 1–12.

Preface

EVERY YEAR, when I descend from my chair, at the close of my academic labours, when I see the crowd disperse,—another generation that I shall behold no more,—my mind is lost in inward contemplation.

Summer comes on; the town is less peopled, the streets are less noisy, the pavement grows more sonorous around my Pantheon. Its large black and white slabs resound beneath my feet.

I commune with my own mind. I interrogate myself as to my teaching, my history, and its all-powerful interpreter,—the spirit of the Revolution.

It possesses a knowledge of which others are ignorant. It contains the secret of all bygone times. In it alone France was conscious of herself. When, in a moment of weakness, we may appear forgetful of our own worth, it is to this point we should recur in order to seek and recover ourselves again. Here, the inextinguishable spark, the profound mystery of life, is ever glowing within us.

The Revolution lives in ourselves,—in our souls; it has no outward monument. Living spirit of France, where shall I seize thee, but within myself? The governments that have succeeded each other, hostile in all other respects, appear at least agreed in this, to resuscitate, to awaken remote and departed ages. But thee they would have wished to bury. Yet why? Thou, thou alone dost live.

Thou livest! I feel this truth perpetually impressed upon me at the present period of the year, when my teaching is suspended, —when labour grows fatiguing, and the season becomes oppressive. Then I wander to the Champ de Mars, I sit me down on the parched grass, and inhale the strong breeze that is wafted across the arid plain.

The Champ de Mars! This is the only monument that the Revolution has left. The Empire has its Column, and engrosses almost exclusively the arch of Triumph; royalty has its Louvre, its Hospital of Invalids; the feudal church of the twelfth century is still enthroned at Notre Dame: nay, the very Romans have their Imperial Ruins, the Thermae of the Caesars!

And the Revolution has for her monument—empty space.

Her monument is this sandy plain, flat as Arabia. A tumulus on either hand, resembling those which Gaul was accustomed to erect,—obscure and equivocal testimonial to her heroes' fame.

The Hero! do you mean him who founded the bridge of Jena? No, there is one here greater even than he, more powerful and more immortal, who fills this immensity.

"What God? We know not. But here a God doth dwell."

Yes, though a forgetful generation dares to select this spot for the theatre of its vain amusements, borrowed from a foreign land, —though the English race-horse may gallop insolently over the plain, a mighty breath yet traverses it, such as you nowhere else perceive; a soul, and a spirit omnipotent.

And though that plain be arid, and the grass be withered, it will, one day, renew its verdure.

For in that soil is profoundly mingled the fruitful sweat of their brows who, on a sacred day, piled up those hills,—that day when, aroused by the cannon of the Bastille, France from the North and France from the South came forward and embraced; that day when three millions of heroes in arms rose with the unanimity of one man, and decreed eternal peace.

Alas! poor Revolution. How confidingly on thy first day didst thou invite the world to love and peace. "O my enemies," didst thou exclaim, "there are no longer any enemies!" Thou didst stretch forth thy hand to all, and offer them thy cup to drink to the peace of nations—But they would not.

And even when they advanced to inflict a treacherous wound, the sword drawn by France was the sword of peace. It was to deliver the nations, and give them true peace—liberty, that she struck the tyrants. Dante asserts Eternal Love to be the founder of the gates of hell. And thus the Revolution wrote *Peace* upon her flag of war!

Her heroes, her invincible warriors, were the most pacific of human beings. Hoche, Marceau, Desaix, and Kleber, are deplored by friends and foes, as the champions of peace; they are mourned by the Nile, and by the Rhine, nay, by war itself,—by the inflexible Vendée.

France had so completely identified herself with this thought, that she did her utmost to restrain herself from achieving conquests. Every nation needing the same blessing—liberty,—and pursuing the same right, whence could war possibly arise? Could the Revolution, which, in its principle, was but the triumph of right, the resurrection of justice, the tardy reaction of thought against brute force,—could it without provocation, have recourse to violence?

This utterly pacific, benevolent, loving character of the Revolution seems today a paradox:—so unknown is its origin, so misunderstood its nature, and so obscured its tradition, in so short a time!

The violent, terrible efforts which it was obliged to make, in order not to perish in a struggle with the conspiring world, has been mistaken for the Revolution itself by a blind, forgetful generation.

And from this confusion has resulted a serious, deeply-rooted evil, very difficult to be cured among this people; the adoration of force.

The force of resistance, the desperate effort to defend unity, '93. They shudder, and fall on their knees.

The force of invasion and conquest, 1800; the Alps brought low, and the thunder of Austerlitz. They fall prostrate, and adore.

Shall I add, that, in 1815, with too much tendency to overvalue force, and to mistake success for a judgment of God, they found at the bottom of their hearts, in their grief and their anger, a miserable argument for justifying their enemy. Many whispered to themselves, "they are strong, therefore they are just."

Thus, two evils, the greatest that can afflict a people, fell upon France at once. Her own tradition slipped away from her, she forgot herself. And, every day more uncertain, paler, and more fleeting, the doubtful image of Right flitted before her eyes.

Let us not take the trouble to inquire why this nation continues to sink gradually lower, and becomes more weak. Attribute not its decline to outward causes; let it not accuse either heaven or earth; the evil is in itself.

The reason why an insidious tyranny was able to render it a prey to corruption is, that it was itself corruptible. Weak and unarmed, and ready for temptation, it had lost sight of the idea by which alone it had been sustained; like a wretched man deprived of sight, it groped its way in a miry road; it no longer saw its star. What! the star of victory? No, the sun of Justice and of the Revolution.

That the powers of darkness should have laboured throughout the earth to extinguish the light of France, and to smother Right, was natural enough. But, in spite of all their endeavours, success was impossible. The wonder is, that the friends of light should help its enemies to veil and extinguish it.

The party who advocate liberty have evinced, of late, two sad and serious symptoms of an inward evil. Let them permit a friend, a solitary writer, to tell them his entire mind.

A perfidious, an odious hand,—the hand of death,—has been offered and stretched out to them, and they have not withdrawn their own. They believed the foes of religious liberty might become the friends of political freedom. Vain scholastic distinctions, which obscured their view! Liberty is liberty.

And to please their enemy, they have proved false to their friend—nay, to their own father, the grand eighteenth century. They have forgotten that that century had founded liberty on the enfranchisement of the mind—till then bound down by the flesh, bound by the material principle of the double incarnation, theological and political, kingly and sacerdotal. That century, that of the spirit, abolished the gods of flesh in the state and in religion, so that there was no longer any idol, and there was no god but God.

Yet why have sincere friends of liberty formed a league with the party of religious tyranny? Because they had reduced themselves to a feeble minority. They were astonished at their own insignificance, and durst not refuse the advances of a great party which seemed to make overtures to them.

Our fathers did not act thus. They never counted their number. When Voltaire, a child, in the reign of Louis XIV entered upon the perilous career of religious contention, he appeared to be alone. Rousseau stood alone, in the middle of the century, when, in the dispute between the Christians and the philosophers, he ventured to lay down the new dogma. He stood alone. On the morrow the whole world was with him.

If the friends of liberty see their numbers decreasing, they are themselves to blame. Not a few have invented a system of progressive refinement, of minute orthodoxy, which aims at making a party a sect,—a petty church. They reject first this, and then that; they abound in restrictions, distinctions, exclusions. Some new heresy is discovered every day.

For heaven's sake, let us dispute less about the light of Tabor, like besieged Byzantium—Mahomett II is at our gates.

When the Christian sects became multiplied, we could find Jansenists, Molinists, etc., in abundance, but no longer any Christians; and so, the sects which are the offspring of the Revolution annul the Revolution itself; people became Constituants, Girondists, Montagnards, but the Revolutionists ceased to exist.

Voltaire is but little valued, Mirabeau is laid aside, Madame Roland is excluded, even Danton is not orthodox. What! must none remain but Robespierre and Saint-Just?

Without disowning what was in these men, without wishing to anticipate their sentence, let one word be sufficient here: If the Revolution rejects, condemns their predecessors, it rejects the very persons who gave it a hold upon mankind,—the very men who for a time imbued the whole world with a revolutionary spirit. If, on the other hand, it declares to the world its sympathy with their characters, and shews no more than the image of these two Apostles upon its altar, the conversion to its tenets will be slow, the French Propaganda will not have much to fear, and absolute governments may repose in peace.

Fraternity! fraternity! It is not enough to re-echo the word—to attract the world to our cause, as was the case at first. It must acknowledge in us a fraternal heart. It must be gained over by the fraternity of love, and not by the guillotine.

Fraternity! Why who, since the creation, has not pronounced that word? Do you imagine it was first coined by Robespierre of Mably?

Every state of antiquity talked of fraternity; but the word was addressed only to citizens,—to men; the slave was but a thing. And in this case fraternity was exclusive and inhuman.

When slaves or freed-men govern the Empire,—when they are named Terence, Horace, Phedrus, Epictetus, it is difficult not to extend fraternity to the slave. "Let us be brethren," cries Christianity. But to be a brother, one must first exist; man had no being; right and liberty alone constitute life. A theory from which these are excluded, is but a speculative fraternity between nought and nought.

"Fraternity, *or death*," as the reign of Terror subsequently exclaimed. Once more a brotherhood of slaves. Why, by atrocious derision, impart to such an union the holy name of liberty?

Brethren who mutually fly from one another, who shudder when they meet, who extend, who withdraw a dead and icy hand. O odious and disgusting sight! Surely, if anything ought to be free, it is the fraternal sentiment.

Liberty alone, as founded in the last century, has rendered fraternity possible. Philosophy found man without right, or rather a nonentity, entangled in a religious and political system, of which despotism was the base. And she said, "Let us create man, let him *be*, by liberty." No sooner was he created than he loved.

It is by liberty moreover, that our age, awakened and recalled to its true tradition, may likewise commence its work. It will no longer inscribe amongst its laws, "Be my brother, *or die!*" But by a skilful culture of the best sentiments of the human soul, it will attain its ends in such a manner that all, without compulsion, shall wish to be brothers indeed. The state will realise its destiny, and be a fraternal initiation, an education, a constant exchange of the spontaneous ideas of inspiration and faith, which are common to us all, and of the reflected ideas of science and meditation, which are found among thinkers.

Such is the task for our age to accomplish. May it at last set about the work in earnest!

It would indeed be a melancholy reflection, if, instead of achieving something great for itself, its time were wasted in censuring that age—so renowned for its labours, and to which it is so immensely indebted. Our fathers, we must repeat, did all that it was necessary then to do,—began precisely as it was incumbent on them to begin.

They found despotism in heaven and on earth, and they instituted law. They found individual man disarmed, bare, unprotected, confounded, lost in a system of apparent unity, which was no better than common death. And in order that he might have no appeal, even to the supreme tribunal, the religious dogma of the day held him bound for the penalty of a transgression which he had not committed; this eminently carnal dogma supposed that injustice is transmitted with our blood from father to son.

It was necessary, above all things, to vindicate the rights of man, which were thus so cruelly outraged, and to reestablish this truth, which, though obscured, was yet undeniable: "Man has rights, he is something; he cannot be disowned or annulled, even in the name of God; he is a responsible creature but for his own actions alone, for whatever good or evil he himself commits."

Thus does this false liability for the actions of others disappear from the world. The *unjust transmission of good*, perpetuated by the rights of the nobility; *the unjust transmission of evil*, by original sin, or the civil brand of being descended from sinners, are effaced by the Revolution.

O men of the present age, is this the creed you tax with individualism—is this what you term an egotistical law? But, remember, that without these rights of the individual, by which alone man was constituted, he really had no existence, was incapable of action, and man, therefore, could not fraternize. It was actually necessary to abolish the fraternity of death to found that of life.

Speak not of egotism. History will answer here, quite as strongly as logic. It was at the first moment of the Revolution, at the moment she was proclaiming the rights of the individual, it was then that the soul of France, far from shrinking, extended, embraced the whole world in sympathetic thought: then did she offer peace to all, and wish to participate with all her treasure, —liberty.

The moment of birth, the entrance upon a still dubious life, seems to justify a feeling of egotism in every being. We may observe that the newly-born infant, above all things, wishes to live, to prolong its existence. Yet, in the case before us, it was far otherwise. When young French Liberty first opened her eyes to the light, and uttered that earliest cry which transports every new creature,—"I am!" even in that moment her thoughts were not confined to *self;* she did not indulge in a selfish joy, she extended to mankind her life and her hope; her first impulse, in her cradle, was to open her affectionate arms. "I am!" she exclaimed to all nations; "O my brethren, you shall be also!"

In this lay her glorious error, her touching and sublime weakness: the Revolution, it must be confessed, commenced by loving everything.

She loved even her enemy,—England.

She loved, and long she strove to save, royalty—the key-stone of the abuses which she had just demolished. She wanted to save the Church; she endeavoured to remain Christian, being wilfully blind to the contradiction of the old principle,—Arbitrary Grace, and of the new one,—Justice.

This universal sympathy which, at first, made her adopt, and indiscreetly mingle so many contradictory elements, led her to inconsistency—to wish and not to wish, to do and undo, at the same time. Such is the strange result of our early assemblies.

The world has smiled at that work of hers: but let it not forget, that whatever was discordant in it, was partly owing to the too easy sympathy, to the indiscriminate benevolence which was the first feature in our Revolution.

Genius utterly humane! I love to follow and watch its progress, in those admirable fêtes wherein a whole people, at once the actors and spectators, gave and received the impulse of moral enthusiasm; wherein every heart expanded with all the sublimity of France,—of a country which, for its law, proclaimed the rights of humanity.

At the festival of the 14th of July, 1792, among the sacred images of Liberty and the Law,—in the civic procession,—in which figured, together with the magistrates, the representatives, the widows and orphans of those killed at the Bastille,—were seen divers emblems,—those of trades useful to men, instruments of agriculture, ploughs, sheaves, branches loaded with fruits; and the bearers were crowned with ears of corn and green vine-leaves. But others also were seen in mourning, crowned with cypress; they were carrying a table covered with crape, and, under the crape, a veiled sword,—that of the law! A touching image! Justice, showing her sword in mourning, was no longer distinguished from Humanity herself.

A year after, the 10th of August, 1793, a very different festival was celebrated. This one was heroic and gloomy. But the law had been mutilated; the legislative power had been violated; the judiciary power, unguaranteed and annulled, was the slave of violence. They durst no longer show the sword; it was no longer that of Justice; the eye could have bourne it no longer.

A thing to be told to everybody, and which it is but too easy to prove, is, that the humane and benevolent period of our Revolution had for its actors the very people, the whole people,—everybody. And the period of violence, the period of sanguinary deeds, into which danger afterwards thrust it, had for actors but an inconsiderable, an extremely small number of men.

That is what I have found established and verified, either by written testimony, or by such as I have gathered from the lips of old men.

The remarkable exclamation of a man who belonged to the Faubourg Saint-Antoine will never die: "We were all of us at the 10th of August, and not one at the 2nd of September."

Another thing which this history will render most conspicuous, and which is true of every party, is, that the people were generally much better than their leaders. The further I have searched, the more generally have I found that the more deserving class was ever underneath, buried among the utterly obscure. I have also found that those brilliant, powerful speakers, who expressed the thoughts of the masses, are usually but wrongfully considered as the sole actors. The fact is, that they rather received than communicated the impulse. The chief actor is the people. In order to find and restore the latter to its proper position, I have been obliged to reduce to their proportions those ambitious puppets whom they had set in motion, and in whom, till now, people fancied they saw, and have sought for, the secret transactions of history.

This sight, I must confess, struck me with astonishment. In proportion as I entered more deeply into this study, I observed that the mere party leaders, those heroes of the prepared scene neither foresaw nor prepared anything, that they were never the first proposers of any grand measure,--more particularly of those which were the unanimous work of the people in the outset of the Revolution.

Left to themselves, at those decisive moments, by their pretended leaders, they found out what was necessary to be done, and did it.

Great, astonishing results! But how much greater was the heart which conceived them! The deeds themselves are as nothing in comparison. So astonishing, indeed, was that greatness of heart, that the future may draw upon it for ever, without fearing to exhaust its resources. No one can approach its contemplation, without retiring a better man. Every soul dejected, or crushed with grief, every human or national heart has but to look there in order to find comfort: it is a mirror wherein humanity, in beholding itself, becomes once more heroic, magnanimous, disinterested; a singular purity, shrinking from the contamination of lucre as from filth, appears to be the characteristic glory of all.

I am endeavouring to describe to-day that epoch of unanimity, that holy period, when a whole nation, free from all party distinction, as yet a comparative stranger to the opposition of classes, marched together under a flag of brotherly love. Nobody can behold that marvellous unanimity, in which the selfsame heart beat together in the breasts of twenty millions of men, without returning thanks to God. These are the sacred days of the world —thrice happy days for history. For my part, I have had my reward, in the mere narration of them. Never, since the composition of my Maid of Orleans, have I received such a ray from above, such a vivid inspiration from Heaven.

But as "our thread of life is of a mingled yarn," whilst I enjoyed so much happiness in reviving the annals of France, my own peace has been disturbed for ever. I have lost him who so often

narrated the scenes of the Revolution to me, him whom I revered
as the image and venerable witness of the Grand Age, that is, of
the eighteenth century. I have lost my father, with whom I had
lived all my life,—forty-eight years.

When that blow fell upon me, I was lost in contemplation. I
was elsewhere, hastily realizing this work, so long the object of
my meditation. I was at the foot of the Bastille, taking that for-
tress, and planting our immortal banner upon its towers. That
blow came upon me, unforeseen, like a shot from the Bastille.

Many of these important questions, which have obliged me to
fathom deeply the foundations of my faith, have been investigated by me during the most awful circumstances that can attend
human life, between death and the grave,—when the survivor,
himself partly dead, has been sitting in judgment between two
worlds. Then I resumed my course, even to the conclusion of this
work, whilst death and life had equal claims upon my mind. I
struggled to keep my heart in the closest communion with justice,
strengthening myself in the faith by my very bereavements and
my hopes; and, in proportion as my own household gods were
shattered, I clung to the home of my native land.

24. Alphonse de Lamartine: *History of the Revolution of* 1848

Alphonse de Lamartine (1790–1869) was a poet in politics. A product
of the old French nobility, he was one of France's leading Romantic
poets. He held diplomatic positions before 1830; but he was already a
liberal and was elected to the Chamber of Deputies of the July Monarchy in 1834. There he stood alone, joining none of the parties and
coalitions until, in the monarchy's last years, when he became more
and more of a democrat, he supported the banquet campaign of 1847
and 1848, which ended in the Revolution of 1848. Lamartine's political
position had been enhanced by his support of popular causes in the
Chamber, by his publication in 1847 of the *History of the Girondins*
(an enthusiastic presentation of the virtues of a "moderate" left-wing
position), and through his newspaper *Le Bien Public*.

His failure to support a regency upon Louis-Philippe's abdication
may have been a crucial turning point promoting the success of the

revolution, and he became the leading figure and foreign minister of the Provisional Government. The following selection from his history of the Revolution of 1848 gives his description of the early moments of that government's life. He did succeed in mediating among the demands of radical democrats and socialists and the desires of the more moderate liberal groups who had brought about the revolution. But his foreign policy was conservative, and in domestic affairs he became associated with the failures of the policy of concessions to the left, which had produced the "make work" program of the National Workshops. The closing of the workshops set off the civil war of the June Days, and marked the end of Lamartine's period of dominance in the Second Republic. He was badly defeated in the presidential election by Louis Napoleon. After the *coup d'état* of December, 1851, he retired from public life.

The objectivity and accuracy of the selections offered here are clearly subject to doubt; they do, however, reveal the tone and quality of the rhetoric of Romantic politics and history, and they suggest the importance many could attach to the role of the individual leader, the hero at the heroic moment. That this importance was attached by the "hero" to himself exemplifies the self-adulation that seems one of Lamartine's most unattractive traits—and perhaps a source of some of his unrealistic interpretations of the facts he faced.

The text is from the translation by Francis A. Durivage and William S. Chase of *History of the French Revolution of 1848* (Boston, 1851), pp. 150–151, 153–155, 158–166.

XI.

THE REPUBLIC once proclaimed, the government and the Hôtel de Ville seemed to draw a moment's breath, as if a new vital air from heaven had breathed upon this furnace of men. Uncertainty is the wind of popular passions, as it is, in the pains and labor of existence, half the weight upon the human heart.

A part of the people seemed to retire to go and spread the great news in their dwellings. With the exception of Lamartine and Marie, the greater part of the members of the government who were at the same time ministers successively left the Hôtel de Ville, and went to their departments; Ledru Rollin to the Interior, Arago to the Navy. The new ministers, strangers to government, —such as Goudchaux, of Finance, General Subervie, of War, Carnot, of Public Instruction, and Bethmont, of Commerce,— retired to go and establish subordination in their administration. Some returned, at intervals, to assist the government council in permanent session.

These first hours of the night were a tumult rather than a council. They were obliged to rise at every noise without; to sustain, by the weight of their shoulders, doors burst by blows from the butts of muskets, or arms impatient of resistance; to make way through naked weapons to harangue, implore, and subdue these detachments of the multitude; to bear them back, partly by eloquence, partly by force, always by a calm brow, cordial gesture, and energetic attitude, thus detaching one party to combat another; then, the tumult repressed, to reenter amidst applause which deafened the ear, shaking of hands that paralyzed the members, embraces which choked the respiration; to dry the perspiration, to resume their places coolly at the council-table, to digest proclamations and decrees, until some new assault jarred the ceilings, shook the doors, drove back the sentinels, twisted the bayonets, and recalled the citizens collected round the government, and its members themselves, to the same harangues, the same efforts, and the same dangers.

Lamartine was almost always summoned by name. His tall figure and sonorous voice rendered him most fitted for these conflicts with the crowd. His clothes were in tatters, his neck bare, his hair reeking with perspiration, and soiled with dust and smoke. He went out and returned, rather carried than escorted by groups of citizens, National Guards, and pupils of the schools who had attached themselves to his steps without his knowing them, like a volunteer staff to a leader in the field of a revolution.

Among them was noticed a young professor of the college of France, Payer, whose very name Lamartine did not know, but whose cool ascendency in the face of danger, and collectedness in the midst of tumult, characteristics of the men of crises, he admired. There was noted, also, a young man with blue eyes, light hair, and stentorian voice, whose gestures were imperious, whose stature was athletic, ruling, hectoring, and breaking up the masses, sabre in hand, and who, from the first day, both within and without the chateau, on foot or on horseback, assumed a magnetic empire over the multitude. This was Château Renaud.

There were, a young pupil of the Polytechnic School, handsome, calm, and mute, but always on his feet, like a statue of reflection in action,—a figure which recalled the silent Bonaparte of Vendémiaire; Dr. Sanson, placed in charge of the wounded, and the arrangement of the bodies heaped up in the courts and lower halls; Faivre, a young physician, his features excited by the whirl of action and the idea which he believed he saw bursting forth like a revelation of the people; Ernest Grégoire, an orator, diplomatist, and soldier of the masses, fitted for everything in those extreme moments when the division of faculties ceases, and the thought, word, and hand of intrepidity and address must be united in an instinct as rapid as the movements, as manifold as the faces, of a revolution; and a great number of others, whose names will be found in the explanatory notes to this history.

XIII.

MEANWHILE NIGHT had fallen. The deep hum of the quarters in the vicinity of the centre sank with it. The citizens, satisfied with the existence of an active and firm government, recalled to their houses by the hour of rest, and the necessity of quieting their families, began to drop away. There only remained upon the place de Grève bivouacs, the rear-guards of the revolution, combatants exhausted and tottering with cold and wine, who were watching, with lighted matches, round four pieces of artillery, charged with grape-shot, and the excited, feverish and tenacious mass, insatiable in agitation and action, which encamped, floated, or created disturbances, in the courts and halls or on the staircases of the Hôtel de Ville.

These masses were especially composed of old members of secret societies; an army of conspirators of all dates, from 1815; restless revolutionists, deceived in their hopes in 1830, by the revolution which they had created only to baffle them; and combatants of the three days, directed by committees of *La Réforme* newspaper, who had hoped that the government would belong exclusively to those who had so large a share of the bloodshed and victory.

To these three or four thousand men, animated by resentment and political ambition, were united, but still in small numbers, a few socialist and communist adepts, who saw in the explosion of the day the dawn of a loaded mine beneath the very foundations of ancient society, and who thought they held in their muskets the guarantee of their system, and of the renovation of humanity. The remainder was composed of those madmen who have no political system in their minds, nor social chimeras in their hearts, but who only receive a revolution on account of the disorder it perpetuates, the blood it sheds, and the terror it inspires. Writers and cold-blooded demagogues had nurtured them, for twenty years, on ferocious admiration for the grandeurs of crime, the sacrifices and massacres of the former reign of terror. Few in number, they were still men decided to recognize no republic but by the scaffold, and no government but by the axe it would lend them to decimate the citizens.

Finally, the tide of the day had cast, and the night had left at the Hôtel de Ville, a portion of the ragged scum of the vicious population of great capitals, which commotions raise and keep afloat for a few days on the surface, until they sink again into their natural sewers; men always between two seas, of wine and blood, who scent carnage on quitting debauch, and who never cease to besiege the ear of the people till they have thrown them a carcass, or swept them into prison, as a disgrace to all parties. They were the drainings of the jails and galleys.

XIV.

WHILE THE government was profiting by these first moments of quiet in the streets, to multiply its orders, regulate its relations with the different quarters, and send its decrees to the departments and the armies, these men, repudiated by the true people in other parts of this vast edifice, wavered, at the voice of speech-making demagogues, between the acceptance of the new government, and the installation of as many governments as they had chimeras, ambition, fury or crimes in their hearts. Tremendous vociferations rose at intervals, from the bottom of the court-yards, to the ears of the provisional government; discharges of musketry applauded the most incendiary motions. Here they spoke of planting the red flag, the symbol of blood that was to flow until terror had subdued all the enemies of disorder; there, of display-ing the black flag, the sign of misery and degradation of the prole-tary race, or the mourning of a suffering society, which ought not to declare itself at peace until after having wreaked its vengeance on the *bourgeoisie* and property.

Some wished the government to be chosen by nocturnal ballot, and that the members should only be selected from among the combatants of the barricades; others, that the leaders of the most unbridled socialist schools should be alone raised by the votes of

the victorious working-men of different parties. These demanded
that the government, whatever it might be, should deliberate in
the presence and under the bayonets of delegates chosen by them
as censors and avengers of all its acts; those, that the people
should declare itself in permanence at the Hôtel de Ville, and
should be itself its own government in an uninterrupted assembly, where all measures should be voted by acclamation.

Fanaticism, delirium, fever and intoxication, uttered these sin-
ister or absurd notions at random, sustained here and there by
confused acclamations, then instantly falling under the disgust of
the multitude, who, like good citizens, treated them with horror
or contempt.

XVI.

THE INSURGENTS came several times and knocked at the doors of
the retreat where the provisional government was sitting, threatening to turn it out, and refusing all obedience to its decrees.
Crémieux first, and Marie afterwards, had succeeded, by dint of
firmness mingled with skilful supplications, to make these bands
retire to the court-yards of the palace. They had won back the
moral authority of the government. Seven times since nightfall
had Lamartine left his pen to rush into the corridors, upon the
landing-places, and even the steps of the Hôtel de Ville, followed
by a few faithful citizens, to ask of these disorderly masses obedience or death. Each time, though received at first with imprecations and murmurs, he had ended by removing to the right or left
sabres, poinards, and bayonets, brandished by drunken and unsteady hands; making a tribune of a window, a balustrade, or a
flight of steps; causing weapons to sink, cries to cease, applause to
burst forth, and tears of enthusiasm and reason to fall.

The last time, a phrase of happy coolness and audacity, involving a reproach in a pleasantry, had saved him. An irritated mass
covered the steps of the Hôtel de Ville. Musket-shots, directed
against the windows, threatened to exterminate the feeble posts
of volunteers who opposed this new invasion, with which the
palace was going to be choked to suffocation. All voices were
hushed, all arms weary, all supplication lost. They went in search
of Lamartine: he came out once more; he came upon the landing-
place of the first story, where some National Guards, some pupils

of the Polytechnic School, and some intrepid citizens, were struggling hand to hand with the invaders. At his name and appearance the strife ceased for a moment, and the crowd opened. Lamartine saw the steps of the great staircase covered to the right and left with combatants, who formed a hedge of steel as far as the courts, and even out upon the square;—some, friendly and respectful, shaking his hand and loading him with blessings; the greater number irritated and frowning, their brows loaded with doubt, their looks full of suspicion, their gestures threatening, and their mutterings bitter. He feigned not to perceive these signs of anger. He descended to a level with the great interior court, where they had deposited the corpses, and where a forest of steel was waving over the heads of thousands of armed men. Thence a broad staircase leads down to the left, towards the great gate of Henry IV, which opens on the place de Grève, and where the people were half swallowed up. It was here that the tide of invasion, meeting the tide of defenders, produced the greatest confusion, tumult and shouting. "Lamartine is a traitor!" "Do not hear Lamartine!" "Down with the beguiler!" "To the lamp-post with traitors!" "The head—the head of Lamartine!" cried some madmen, against whose weapons he pressed in passing. Lamartine paused a moment on the first flight, and looking on the vociferators with a steady eye, and a slightly sarcastic but not irritating smile, replied: "My head, citizens? Would to God that you all had it at this moment on your shoulders; you would be calmer, and wiser, and the work of your revolution would be better done." At these words the imprecations changed into shouts of laughter, and the threats of death into shaking of hands. Lamartine vigorously pushed away one of the leaders who opposed his going to speak to the people in the square. "We know that thou art brave and honest," said the young man, "with a seductive figure and tragic gestures; but thou art not made to measure thyself with the people. Thou wilt lull its victory to sleep; thou art but a lyre—go and sing." "Leave me," replied Lamartine, without being irritated by his apostrophe; "the people have my head in pledge; if I betray them, I first betray myself. You shall see whether I have the soul of a poet, or that of a citizen." And violently disengaging the collar of his coat from the hands which detained him, he went down, harangued the people in the square, brought them back to reason, and raised them to enthusiasm. The applauses of the square resounded even under the arches of the palace; and these shouts of ten thousand voices intimidated the insurgents within. They felt that the people were for Lamartine. Lamartine reentered, and went up stairs again, applauded and stifled with the embraces of the very men who demanded his head as he went down.

XVII.

BUT WHILE this agitation was subsiding on one side of the Hôtel de Ville, it was fermenting on the other. Hardly had Lamartine reentered the cabinet of council when a new storm broke forth, and an assault more terrible than the preceding ones threatened to sweep away the government.

After having for a long time undulated hither and thither, from court to court, from square to square, and from tribune to tribune, in search of a place for deliberation, the crowd ended by collecting in the vast hall of Saint Jean, a kind of common forum for the great gatherings of the capital, and in the hall of council prepared for solemn deliberations.

There, on an estrade converted into a tribune, by the light of lamps and lustres lit up as in the theatre of a real drama, orators succeeded and surpassed each other in violence, one after another. They were agitating the question of a choice of government. "Who are these men, unknown to the people, who glide from the bosom of a vanquished Chamber to the head of a victorious people? Where are their titles—their wounds? What names do their hands show? Are they black with powder, like our own? Are they calloused, like yours, brave workmen, by handling tools of labor? By what right do they make their decrees? In the name of what principle, of what government, do they promulgate them? Are they republicans? and of what kind of republic? Are they masked accomplices of the monarchy, introduced by it into our ranks, in order to stifle our just vengeance, and to bring us back, seduced and enchained, to the yoke of their barbarous society? Let us send these men back to their source: they wear different clothes from ours; they speak a different language; they have different manners: these working-jackets, or these rags of misery, are the uniform of the people. Our leaders must be chosen among ourselves. Let us go and drive those away whom surprise and perfidy have given us."

Others, more moderate and more numerous, said: "Let us listen to them before judging and proscribing them. Let us call them hither and permit them to explain their designs."

Inexpressible tumults responded within and without the hall, to these opposing motions. The Hôtel de Ville seemed threatened with an explosion.

XVIII.

ALREADY BANDS detached from this centre of agitation had rushed forward upon the stairways; they had overturned and trampled under foot the sentinels, attacked the guards, invaded the narrow corridor which led to the double door of the cabinet of the government. Intrepid citizens, prodigal of their lives for the protection of order, had preceded them; they came to warn the council of the peril henceforth impossible to conjure down. But Garnier Pagès, Carnot, Crémieux, Marrast, Lamartine, aided by the secretaries and some of the citizens, among whom figured in the first rank the impassible Bastide and the headstrong Ernest Grégoire, barricade the door; they pile against it, in order to increase its resistance, sofas and furniture, heavy with the weight of several men standing on the chairs and arm-chairs. All in the room press their shoulders against this fragile rampart, so as to sustain the assault and the weight of the assailants.

Scarcely had they taken these desperate precautions, when they heard the tumult, the shouts, the clashing of arms, the defiances, the imprecations, the steps, the heavy movements, of the column in the outer corridor. Those who defend it are thrust aside or trampled upon. Butt-ends of muskets, pommels of sabres, blows of the fist, sound against the first door. The panes of glass over its upper part shake, crack, and jingle upon the slabs of the pavement, in the passage between the two folding-doors. The cracking of wood shows the pressure of the crowd. The first door yields and bursts into splinters; the second is about to be forced in the same manner. A low and hurried dialogue ensues between the assailants and the members of the government. Marie, Crémieux, Garnier Pagès, their colleagues, their friends, refuse obstinately to obey the commands of the invaders. A sort of capitulation follows; the furniture is half removed; Ernest Grégoire, well known to both camps, partially opens the door; he announces that

Lamartine is going to confer with the people, that he is going forth to harangue it, and to convince it of the intentions of the government.

Upon the name of Lamartine, at that time a charm over the people, curses changed into acclamations of confidence and love. Lamartine glides in the steps of Grégoire, of Payer, and yields himself, half stifled by the crowd, to the ebb and flow of this multitude. It becomes calm, and gradually suspends its convulsions before him. His lofty stature permits his head to tower above it; his serene countenance pacifies it; his voice, his gestures, make it open or recede. A counter-current sets in and bears him along through the obscure and unknown labyrinth of corridors and flights of stairs, as far as the entrance to the hall of popular deliberations. The provisional government, thus momentarily freed, recloses its doors, stations guards and sentinels, and fortifies itself against fresh assaults, uncertain all the while whether Lamartine would rise victor, or remain vanquished, in his struggle between two peoples and two governments.

XIX.

THE HALL overflowed with crowds and tumult. A dismal light, gusts of warm breath exhaling from this furnace of men, clamors, now smothered, anon harsh and loud, issued from it. A long time was required before it could be penetrated by Lamartine and the group which accompanied him.

On the threshold he heard the voices of some orators, who were announcing him to the multitude. Those voices were now covered with applause, now repulsed by terms of defiance, of wrath and disdain.—Yes, yes!—No, no!—Let us listen to Lamartine!—Let's not listen to Lamartine!—*Vive Lamartine!*—Down with Lamartine! These outcries, accompanied by undulations, gestures, stamping with the feet, lifting of arms above the head, blows with the butt-ends of muskets striking the floor, almost equally contended for mastery in the audience.

During this tumult Lamartine made his way with difficulty through the dense crowd at the door; he was lifted forward by vigorous arms as far as the foot of the little inner staircase, which led to the top of an estrade, serving as a kind of tribune, from which the people were addressed. The shades of night, imperfectly dispersed by a few gleams of light at the centre of the hall, the gas of lighted lamps at his feet, thickening the air, the smoke of musket-shots fired all day in the courts, and penetrating thence by the windows, the species of mist which the feverish perspiration and panting breath of a thousand men diffused throughout the hall, prevented him from clearly discovering, and have ever since prevented him from distinctly retracing, that scene. He only remembers that he rose above an agitated crowd at his feet; their countenances, pale with emotion, and blackened with powder, were lit up only at the foot of the estrade, and were turned towards him with various expressions. With the exception of two of those countenances, all were unknown to him; one was the face, strongly marked with resolution, of an old aid-de-camp of Lafayette, Sarrans, at once the writer, soldier and orator of liberty: the other was that of Coste, former editor of the journal *Le Temps*, whom Lamartine had previously known at Rome; this face appeared, after ten years, as that of an impassioned auditor of a new forum below these new rostra.

Beyond the first ranks of the spectators who stood around, the glimmering light, fading away into shadow, revealed on the floor at the further end, around and upon the steps that rose against the walls of the hall, nothing but agitated and numberless shadows, which moved about in the obscurity. Only the sabres, the barrels of muskets, the bayonets reflecting here and there the brightness of the lamps on the polished metal, flashed like fireworks over the heads of the multitude at each shuddering emotion of the audience.

Contradictory cries, feverish, frantic, were uttered at every movement by these thousands of mouths; a real storm of men, where every wind of opinion that passed over the crowd drew from each fresh wave a roaring of voices.

Lamartine, cast as it were upon the estrade as on a cape, advanced into the midst of this swelling sea, contemplated it, uncertain whether it would sustain him or engulf him. Many orators, pressing round him to the right and left, and up to the steps of this sort of tribune, disputed his speaking by word and act. They uttered, confusedly, addresses and short incendiary inquiries to the assembly; but Lamartine, having succeeded in removing these oratorical rivals by the exertion of hand and shoulder, and appearing at last alone and free before the eyes of the people, a silence, broken by murmurs, vociferations, and bitter apostrophes, was finally established by degrees. He attempted to speak.

XX.

"CITIZENS," CRIED he, with the full power of a voice whose energy the danger of the country doubled, "behold me here ready to reply to you. Why have you summoned me?"

"To know by what right you constitute yourself a government of the people, and to understand whether we have to do with traitors, tyrants, or citizens worthy of the soul of the revolution," replied some voices from the midst of the auditory.

"By what right we constitute ourselves a government?" replied Lamartine, advancing and uncovering himself boldly to eyes, arms and murmurs, like a man who surrenders by laying down his weapons. "By right of the blood that flows, the fire which devours your edifices, the people without guides, and to-morrow perhaps without bread! the right of the most devoted and the most courageous! nay, since it must be spoken, citizens, the right of those who were the first to surrender their hearts to suspicion, their blood to the scaffold, their heads to the vengeance of people or kings, to save their nation. Do you envy us this right? You all possess it—assume it as we do! We do not contest it with you. You are all worthy of devoting yourselves to the common safety. We have no title but that derived from our consciences and your dangers. But the people, falling from a government into an interregnum, require chiefs. The voices of this people, victorious and trembling for their victory in the very heart of battle, have designated us, called us by name, and we have obeyed the summons. Would you, then, prolong an election, terrible and impossible, in the midst of fire and blood,—you are the masters; but the fire and blood will be upon your heads, and the nation will curse you."

"No! no!" cried voices already touched and recalled by this abandonment of all legal right, and by this invocation to the sole right of devotion. "Yes! yes!" replied other and more obstinate voices, "they have no right to rule us. They do not belong to the people; they do not come from the barricades. They came out of that venal assembly, where they have breathed an atmosphere poisoned by corruption." "They have protested against corruption," said some. "They defended the cause of the people there," said others. "Well, let them declare, at least, what sort of a government they pretend to give us," cried the most moderate. "We have overthrown the monarchy—we have won a republic; let Lamartine explain whether or no he will give us the republic."

At this interrogatory, which came from every part of the throng assembled in the hall, Lamartine assumed that half smile which has the air of retaining a slightly sceptical indecision on the lips, an expression of countenance which seems to provoke an audience to extract the last secret of the listener's heart.

"The republic, citizens," said he, at last, in a tone of solemn interrogation,—"who has uttered the word republic?"—"Every one! every one!" replied hundreds of voices, and thousands of hands waving their weapons over their heads, in token of their wishes and their joy.—"The republic, citizens!" resumed Lamartine, with a more pensive and almost melancholy gravity. "Know you what you demand? Do you know what a republican government is?"—"Tell us, tell us," was the answer on all hands.—"The republic!" continued Lamartine. "Do you know that it is the government of the universal mind, and do you feel yourself ripe enough to have no other masters than yourselves, and no other government than your own reason?—"Yes, yes," said the people.—"The republic! Do you know that it is the government of justice, and do you feel sufficiently just to do right even to your enemies?"

"Yes! yes! yes!" repeated the people, with an accent of self-esteem and consciousness in their voice.—"The republic!" resumed Lamartine. "Do you know that it is the government of virtue, and do you feel yourselves virtuous enough, magnanimous enough, clement enough, to sacrifice yourself for others; to forget injuries, to look without envy on the happy, to forgive your enemies; to disarm your hearts of these sentences of death, these proscriptions, these scaffolds, which have dishonored this name under the popular tyranny that was called by the false name of the republic half a century ago, and to reconcile France with this name at the present day?—Question yourselves, search yourselves, and yourselves pronounce your own sentence or your own glory!"

"Yes, yes, yes! we feel ourselves capable of all these virtues," cried, with unanimous enthusiasm, these voices, which united in an almost religious tone at the voice of the orator.—"Do you feel it? Do you swear it? Do you invoke as a witness that God who manifests himself, in hours like this, by the cry and the instinct of the people?" continued Lamartine, pausing as if waiting a reply. A thunder of affirmation responds to his gesture. "Ah! well," said he, "it is you who have said it. You shall have a republic! if you are as worthy to preserve it as you have been heroic in gaining it." The hall, the courts, the arches, which extend under the vestibules, tremble with the prolonged echo of the applause.

"—But let us understand ourselves," continues Lamartine; "we desire the republic; but we should be unworthy the name of republicans, if we designed to commence liberty by tyranny, or to deprive the government of liberty, equality, justice, religion, and virtue, as it were, by theft in a night of sedition and confusion like this. We have but one right, that of declaring our opinion, our wishes, to the people of Paris; that of taking the glorious initiative in the government of liberty brought about by the age, and of saying to the country and to the world, that we take upon ourselves the responsibility of proclaiming a provisional republic as the government of the country; but leaving to the country, to its thirty-six millions of souls, who are not here present, and who have the same right as ourselves to consent, to prefer or to repudiate, this or that form of constitution; reserving to them, I say, that which belongs to them, as our preferences belong to ourselves, namely, the expression of their sovereign will by universal suffrage, the first truth and only foundation of every national republic!"

"Yes, yes, it is right! it is right!" reply the people. "France is not here. Paris is the head; but Paris ought to guide, and not oppress, the members."

"*Vive la république! Vive le gouvernement provisoire! Vive Lamartine!* Let the provisional government save us; it is worthy of its command. To choose another would divide the people, and offer an opportunity for tyranny to return."

At these cries, Lamartine descends in triumph from the estrade, in the midst of unanimous applause. He reestablished order; he stationed the posts, sentinels, and cannon in the courts; he ascended, assured of the confidence of the people, and the unity of the provisional government.

Part V: *Personal Ideals*

25. Johann Wolfgang von Goethe: *The Sorrows of Young Werther*

Johann Wolfgang von Goethe (1749–1832) helped initiate the *Sturm und Drang* period of German letters with his play *Götz von Berlichingen*, and through the 1770's he promoted the building of a German literature no longer dependent upon the French. Well before the Romantic school took shape at the Schlegels' behest, Goethe had become a dominant figure in German and European letters, and had contributed to a number of the themes and tendencies that came to be identified with Romanticism, such as a medieval setting, a more sensitively apprehended Hellas, and the need for a national literature. His *Sorrows of Young Werther*, portions of which appear below, was published in 1774. The artistic hero, his hopeless love, and his suicide appear in the context that touches major Romantic themes: the glorification of children, the emotional impact of contact with nature, the artist's sense of separation from his society. Like the Rousseau of the *Confessions*, like Chateaubriand's René, like the Byronic hero, a model was established that is said to have been influential in contributing to a fad of suicides by young people who considered themselves insufficiently understood.

In his later works, Goethe repudiated or went beyond his Romanticism, and his *Faust*, Part I (1808), can be taken as a commentary upon the insatiable Romantic hero (see the brief final selections). Besides his prolific literary output of poems, plays, and prose, Goethe long held the position of Minister of State in Weimar. He was also an acute and original scientist, retaining a view of nature as a process of constant transformation that had been visible in his work as early as the 1770's.

The selection, translated by R. D. Boylan, is from *Novels and Tales* by Goethe (London, 1890), pp. 249, 254–255, 268–269, 282–287.

May 10th

A WONDERFUL serenity has taken possession of my entire soul, like these sweet mornings of Spring which I enjoy with my whole heart. I am alone, and feel the charm of existence in this spot, which was created for the bliss of souls like mine. I am so happy, my dear friend, so absorbed in the exquisite sense of mere tranquil existence, that I neglect my talents. I should be incapable of drawing a single stroke at the present moment, and yet I feel that I never was a greater artist than now. When the lovely valley teems with vapour around me, and the meridian sun strikes the upper surface of the impenetrable foliage of my trees, and but a few stray gleams steal into the inner sanctuary, then I throw myself down in the tall grass by the trickling stream, and as I lie close to the earth, a thousand unknown plants discover themselves to me. When I hear the buzz of the little world among the stalks, and grow familiar with the countless indescribable forms of the insects and flies, then I feel the presence of the Almighty, who formed us in His own image, and the breath of that universal love which bears and sustains us, as it floats round us in an eternity of bliss; and then, my friend, when darkness overspreads my eyes, and heaven and earth seem to dwell in my soul, and absorb its power, like the idea of a beloved mistress, then I often long and think: O! that you could describe these conceptions, that you could impress upon paper all that lives so full and warm within you, that it might be the mirror of your soul, as your soul is the mirror of the infinite God! O, my friend—but it is too much for my strength—I sink under the weight of the grandeur of these visions.

May 26th

You know of old my ways of finding amusement; how I select a little cottage in some sequestered spot, and there put up with every inconvenience. I have just discovered such a spot here, which possesses peculiar charms for me.

About a league from the town is a place called Walheim. It is delightfully situated on the side of a hill, and by proceeding along one of the footpaths which lead out of the village, you can have a view of the whole valley. A good old woman lives there, who keeps a small inn. She sells wine, beer, and coffee, and is cheerful and pleasant notwithstanding her age. The chief charm of this spot consists in two linden-trees, which spread their enormous branches over the little green before the church, which is entirely surrounded by peasants' cottages, with their barns and homesteads. I have seldom seen a place so retired and peaceable, and I often have my table and chair brought out from the little inn, and there I drink my coffee and read my Homer. Accident brought me to the spot one fine afternoon, and I found it perfectly deserted. Everybody was in the fields, except a little boy about four years old, who was sitting on the ground and held between his knees a child about six months old; he pressed it to his bosom with both arms, which thus formed a sort of arm-chair, and notwithstanding the liveliness which sparkled in its black eyes, it remained perfectly still. The sight charmed me. I sat down upon a plough opposite, and sketched with great delight this little picture of brotherly tenderness. I added the neighbouring hedge, the barn-door, and some broken cart-wheels, just as they happened to lie; and I found in about an hour that I had made a very correct and interesting drawing, without putting in the slightest thing of my own. This confirmed me in my resolution of adhering for the future entirely to nature. She alone is inexhaustible, and capable of forming the greatest masters. Much may be alleged in favour of rules, as much may be likewise advanced in favour of the laws of society; an artist formed upon them will never produce anything absolutely bad or disgusting, as a man who observes the laws and obeys decorum, can never be an absolutely intolerable neighbour, nor a decided villain; but yet say what you will of rules, they destroy the genuine feeling of nature as well as its true expression. Do not tell me "that this is too hard, that they only restrain and prune superfluous branches, &c." My good friend, I will illustrate this by an analogy. These things resemble love. A warm-hearted youth becomes strongly attached to a maiden, he spends every hour of the day in her company, wears out his health, and lavishes his fortune, to afford continual proof that he is wholly devoted to her. Then comes a man of the world, a man of place and respectability, and addresses him thus:—"My good young friend, love is natural, but you must love within bounds. Divide your time, devote a portion to business, and give the hours of recreation to your mistress. Calculate your fortune, and out of the superfluity you may make her a present, only not too often, on her birthday and such occasions." Pursuing this advice, he may

become a useful member of society, and I should advise some
prince to give him an appointment; but his love is annihilated,
and if he be an artist, his genius is fled. Oh, my friends, why is
it that the torrent of genius so seldom bursts forth, so seldom
rolls in full flowing stream, overwhelming your wondering soul?
Because, on either side of this stream, cold and respectable persons have taken up their abodes, and forsooth their summer-
houses and tulip-beds would suffer from the torrent, wherefore
they dig trenches and raise embankments betimes, in order to
avert the impending danger.

June 29th

The day before yesterday, the physician came from the town to
pay a visit to the Judge. He found me on the floor playing with
Charlotte's children. Some of them were scrambling over me, and
others romped with me, and as I caught and tickled them they
made a great noise. The Doctor is a formal sort of personage; he
adjusts the plaits of his ruffles, and continually settles his frill
whilst he speaks with you, and he thought my conduct beneath
the dignity of a sensible man. I could perceive this by his countenance. But I did not suffer myself to be disturbed. I allowed him
to continue his wise conversation whilst I rebuilt the children's
card-houses for them as fast as they threw them down. He went
about the town, afterwards, complaining that the Judge's children
were spoiled enough before, but that now Werther was completely ruining them.

Nothing on this earth, my dear Wilhelm, affects my heart so
much as children. When I consider them, when I mark in the
little creatures the seeds of all those virtues and qualities which
they will one day find so indispensable; when I behold in the
obstinate all the future firmness and constancy of a noble character; in the capricious, that levity and gaiety of temper which will
carry them lightly over the dangers and troubles of life, their
whole nature simple and unpolluted; then I call to mind the
golden words of the Great Teacher of mankind, "If you become
not like one of these!" And now, my friend, these children, who
are our equals, whom we ought to consider as our models, we
treat them as subjects. They are allowed no will of their own! And
have we then none ourselves? Whence comes our exclusive right?
Is it because we are older and more experienced? Great God!
from the height of thy heaven, thou beholdest great children and

little children, and no others; and thy Son has long since declared which afford Thee greatest pleasure. But they believe in Him, and hear Him not,—that too is an old story; and they train their children after their own image, &c.

Adieu, Wilhelm, I will not further bewilder myself with this subject.

August 12th

Certainly Albert is the best fellow in the world. I had a strange scene with him yesterday. I went to take leave of him, for I took it into my head to spend a few days in these mountains, from whence I now write to you. As I was walking up and down his room, my eye fell upon his pistols. "Lend me those pistols," said I, "for my journey." "By all means," he replied, "if you will take the trouble to load them, for they only hang there for form." I took down one of them, and he continued: "Ever since I was near suffering for my extreme caution, I have had nothing to do with such things." I was curious to hear the story. "I was staying," said he, "some three months ago, at a friend's house in the country. I had a brace of pistols with me unloaded, and I slept without any anxiety. One rainy afternoon I was sitting by myself, doing nothing, when it occurred to me—I do not know how—that the house might be attacked—that we might require the pistols—that we might—in short, you know how we go on fancying, when we have nothing better to do. I gave the pistols to the servant to clean and load. He was playing with the maid, and trying to frighten her, when the pistol went off—God knows how!—the ramrod was in the barrel, and it went straight through her right hand, and shattered the thumb. I had to endure all the lamentation and the surgeon's bill to pay; so since that time I have kept all my weapons unloaded. But, my dear friend, what is the use of prudence? We can never be on our guard against all possible dangers. However,"—now you must know I can tolerate all men till they come to "however," for it is self-evident that every universal rule must have its exceptions. But he is so exceedingly accurate, that if he only fancies he has said a word too precipitate, or too general, or only half true, he never ceases to qualify, to modify, and extenuate, till at last he appears to have said nothing at all. Upon this occasion Albert was deeply immersed in his subject; I ceased to hear him, and became lost in reverie. With a sudden motion I pointed the mouth of the pistol to my forehead, over the right eye. "What do you mean?" cried Albert, turning back the pistol. "It is not loaded," said I. "And even if not," he answered with impatience, "what can you mean? I cannot comprehend how a man can be so mad as to shoot himself, and the bare idea of it shocks me."

"But why should any one," said I, "in speaking of an action, venture to pronounce it mad, or wise, or good, or bad? What is the meaning of all this? Have you carefully studied the secret motives of our actions? Do you understand—can you explain the causes which occasion them, and make them inevitable? If you can, you will be less hasty with your decision."

"But you will allow," said Albert, "that some actions are criminal, let them spring from whatever motives they may." I granted it, and shrugged my shoulders.

"But still, my good friend," I continued, "there are some exceptions here too. Theft is a crime, but the man who commits it from extreme poverty, with no design but to save his family from perishing, is he an object of pity or of punishment? Who shall throw the first stone at a husband, who, in the heat of just resentment, sacrifices his faithless wife and her perfidious seducer? or at the young maiden, who in her weak hour of rapture, forgets herself in the impetuous joys of love? Even our laws, cold and cruel as they are, relent in such cases, and withhold their punishment."

"That is quite another thing," said Albert; "because a man under the influence of violent passion, loses all power of reflection, and is regarded as intoxicated or insane."

"O! you people of sound understandings," I replied, smiling, "are ever ready to exclaim, 'Extravagance and madness, and intoxication!' You moral men are so calm and so subdued! You abhor the drunken man, and detest the extravagant; you pass by like the Levite, and thank God, like the Pharisee, that you are not like one of them. I have been more than once intoxicated, my passions have always bordered on extravagance; I am not ashamed to confess it, for I have learnt, by my own experience, that all extraordinary men, who have accomplished great and astonishing actions, have ever been decried by the world as drunken or insane. And in private life, too, is it not intolerable that no one can undertake the execution of a noble or generous deed, without giving rise to the exclamation that the doer is intoxicated or mad? Shame upon you, ye sages!"

"This is another of your extravagant humours," said Albert; "you always exaggerate a case, and in this matter you are undoubtedly wrong, for we were speaking of suicide, which you compare with great actions, when it is impossible to regard it as anything but a weakness. It is much easier to die than to bear a life of misery with fortitude."

I was on the point of breaking off the conversation, for nothing puts me so completely out of patience as the utterance of a wretched common-place, when I am talking from my inmost heart. However, I composed myself, for I had often heard the same observation with sufficient vexation, and I answered him, therefore, with a little warmth: "You call this a weakness—beware of being led astray by appearances. When a nation which has long groaned under the intolerable yoke of a tyrant, rises at last and throws off its chains,—do you call that weakness? The man, who to rescue his house from the flames, finds his physical strength redoubled, so that he lifts burdens with ease, which in the absence of excitement he could scarcely move; he who under the rage of an insult attacks and puts to flight half a score of his enemies—are such persons to be called weak? My good friend, if resistance be strength, how can the highest degree of resistance be a weakness?"

Albert looked steadfastly at me, and said, "Pray forgive me, but I do not see that the examples you have adduced bear any relation to the question." "Very likely," I answered, "for I have often been told that my style of illustration borders a little on the absurd. But let us see if we cannot place the matter in another point of view, by inquiring what can be a man's state of mind, who resolves to free himself from the burden of life,—a burden often so pleasant to bear,—for we cannot otherwise reason fairly upon the subject.

"Human nature," I continued, "has its limits. It is able to endure a certain degree of joy, sorrow, and pain, but becomes annihilated as soon as this measure is exceeded. The question, therefore, is, not whether a man is strong or weak, but whether he is able to endure the measure of his sufferings? The suffering may be moral or physical; and in my opinion it is just as absurd to call a man a coward who destroys himself as to call a man a coward who dies of a malignant fever."

"Paradox, all paradox!" exclaimed Albert. "Not so paradoxical as you imagine," I replied. "You allow that we designate a disease as mortal, when nature is so severely attacked, and her strength so far exhausted, that she cannot possibly recover her former condition, under any change that may take place.

"Now, my good friend, apply this to the mind; observe a man in his natural isolated condition, consider how ideas work, and how impressions fasten upon him, till at length a violent passion seizes him, destroying all his powers of calm reflection, and provoking his utter ruin.

"It is in vain that a man of sound mind and cool temper understands the condition of such a wretched being, in vain he counsels him! He can no more communicate his own wisdom to him than a healthy man can instil his strength into the invalid, by whose bedside he is seated."

Albert thought this too general. I reminded him of a girl who had drowned herself a short time previously, and I related her history.

She was a good creature, who had grown up in the narrow sphere of household industry and weekly-appointed labour; one who knew no pleasure beyond indulging in a walk on Sundays, arrayed in her best attire, accompanied by her friends, or perhaps joining in the dance now and then at some festival, and chatting away her spare hours with a neighbour, discussing the scandal or the quarrels of the village—trifles sufficient to occupy her heart. At length the warmth of her nature is influenced by certain new and unknown wishes. Inflamed by the flatteries of men, her former pleasures became by degrees insipid, till at length she meets with a youth to whom she is attracted by an indescribable feeling: upon him she now rests all her hopes; she forgets the world around her; she sees, hears, desires nothing but him, and him only. He alone occupies all her thoughts. Uncorrupted by the idle indulgence of an enervating vanity, her affection moving steadily towards its object, she hopes to become his, and to realise in an everlasting union with him, all that happiness which she sought, all that bliss for which she longed. His repeated promises confirm her hopes; embraces and endearments, which increase the ardour of her desires, overmaster her soul. She floats in a dim delusive anticipation of her happiness, and her feelings become excited to their utmost tension. She stretches out her arms finally to embrace the object of all her wishes—and her lover forsakes her. Stunned and bewildered, she stands upon a precipice. All is darkness around her. No prospect, no hope, no consolation—forsaken by him in whom her existence was centred! She sees nothing of the wide world before her, thinks nothing of the many individuals who might supply the void in her heart; she feels herself deserted, forsaken by the world; and blinded and impelled by the agony which wrings her soul, she plunges into the deep, to end her sufferings in the broad embrace of death. See here, Albert, the history of thousands, and tell me, is not this a case of physical infirmity? Nature has no way to escape from the labyrinth, her powers are exhausted, she can contend no longer, and the poor soul must die.

Shame upon him who can look on calmly and exclaim, "The foolish girl! she should have waited; she should have allowed time to wear off the impression; her despair would have been softened, and she would have found another lover to comfort her." One might as well say, "The fool, to die of a fever!—why did he not wait till his strength was restored, till his blood became calm?—all would then have gone well, and he would have been alive now."

Albert, who could not see the justice of the comparison, offered some further objections, and amongst others, urged that I had taken the case of a mere ignorant girl. But how any man of sense, of more enlarged views and experience, could be excused, he was unable to comprehend. "My friend," I exclaimed, "man is but man, and whatever be the extent of his reasoning powers, they are of little avail when passion rages within, and he feels himself confined by the narrow limits of nature. It were better, then—But we will talk of this some other time," I said, and caught up my hat. Alas! my heart was full; and we parted without conviction on either side. How rarely in this world do men understand each other!

26. Jean-Jacques Rousseau: *Confessions*

Jean Jacques Rousseau (1712–1778) has been accused of as well as credited with causing both the Romantic movement and the French Revolution (or whatever was good or evil in each). He certainly was one of the most influential thinkers of modern times, and his works have been used as sources of stimulation or authority for an immense variety of social, political, and aesthetic positions. He was born in Geneva: the opening pages of his *Confessions* which appear below, describe his family circumstances. He had to make his own way and did so largely as a copier of music, spending considerable time in Paris, moving among the *philosophes* but remaining solitary in consequence of his irascible and sensitive nature. His works contain a whole range of themes that were to become the staples of Romanticism. Like Goethe's *Werther*, it is a misunderstood young genius who appears in the *Confessions*. His *Emile* expressed his opposition to the conventionality and formality of prevalent modes of child-rearing and education, and an untheological religion stressing the benignity of nature appeared in the "Confession of Faith of the Savoyard Vicar." His *Discourse on the Arts and Sciences* has strong primitivist implications, and his *Social Contract* proposes a kind of religious nationalism, emphasizes the need for emotional participation in civic affairs, and seems to laud the political virtues of a simple peasantry. His works are difficult and diffuse, but it can be asserted that he was no simple-minded primitivist. He was in many respects a critic of democracy and a proponent of the cultivation of reason in order that men might possess a freedom that was not mere bestiality. Yet his emotionality and praise of the natural were already promoting a sentimental democratic outlook before the Revolution; his doctrine of the general will was later drawn upon to produce a doctrine of democratic despotism by Robespierre.

The selection here is included to suggest a model of the image of themselves that the Romanticists adopted.

The text is taken from the English translation of *The Confessions of Jean Jacques Rousseau* (Oliver and Boyd, Edinburgh, 1904), pp. 1–11.

PART THE FIRST

Book I [1712–1719]

I AM commencing an undertaking, hitherto without precedent, and which will never find an imitator. I desire to set before my fellows the likeness of a man in all the truth of nature, and that man myself.

Myself alone! I know the feelings of my heart, and I know men. I am not made like any of those I have seen; I venture to believe that I am not made like any of those who are in existence. If I am not better, at least I am different. Whether Nature has acted rightly or wrongly in destroying the mould in which she cast me, can only be decided after I have been read.

Let the trumpet of the Day of Judgment sound when it will, I will present myself before the Sovereign Judge with this book in my hand. I will say boldly: "This is what I have done, what I have thought, what I was. I have told the good and the bad with equal frankness. I have neither omitted anything bad, nor interpolated anything good. If I have occasionally made use of some immaterial embellishments, this has only been in order to fill a gap caused by lack of memory. I may have assumed the truth of that which I knew might have been true, never of that which I knew to be false. I have shown myself as I was: mean and contemptible, good, high-minded and sublime, according as I was one or the other. I have unveiled my inmost self even as Thou hast seen it, O Eternal Being. Gather round me the countless host of my fellow-men; let them hear my confessions, lament for my unworthiness, and blush for my imperfections. Then let each of them in turn reveal, with the same frankness, the secrets of his heart at the foot of the Throne, and say, if he dare, *'I was better than that man!'* "

I was born at Geneva, in the year 1712, and was the son of Isaac Rousseau and Susanne Bernard, citizens. The distribution of a very moderate inheritance amongst fifteen children had reduced my father's portion almost to nothing; and his own means of livelihood was his trade of watchmaker, in which he was really very clever. My mother, a daughter of the Protestant minister Bernard, was better off. She was clever and beautiful, and my father had found difficulty in obtaining her hand. Their affection for each other had commenced almost as soon as they were born. When only eight years old, they walked every evening upon the Treille; at ten, they were inseparable. Sympathy and union of soul strengthened in them the feeling produced by intimacy. Both, naturally full of tender sensibility, only waited for the moment when they should find the same disposition in another—or, rather, this moment waited for them, and each abandoned their heart to the first which opened to receive it. Destiny, which appeared to oppose their passion, only encouraged it. The young lover, unable to obtain possession of his mistress, was consumed by grief. She advised him to travel, and endeavour to forget her. He travelled, but without result, and returned more in love than ever. He found her whom he loved still faithful and true. After this trial of affection, nothing was left for them but to love each other all their lives. This they swore to do, and Heaven blessed their oath.

Gabriel Bernard, my mother's brother, fell in love with one of my father's sisters, who only consented to accept the hand of the brother, on condition that her own brother married the sister. Love arranged everything, and the two marriages took place on the same day. Thus my uncle became the husband of my aunt, and their children were doubly my first cousins. At the end of a year, a child was born to both, after which they were again obliged to separate.

My uncle Bernard was an engineer. He took service in the Empire and in Hungary, under Prince Eugène. He distinguished himself at the siege and battle of Belgrade. My father, after the birth of my only brother, set out for Constantinople, whither he was summoned to undertake the post of watchmaker to the Sultan. During his absence, my mother's beauty, intellect and talents gained for her the devotion of numerous admirers. M. de la Closure, the French Resident, was one of the most eager to offer his. His passion must have been great, for, thirty years later, I saw him greatly affected when speaking to me of her. To enable her to resist such advances, my mother had more than her virtue: she loved her husband tenderly. She pressed him to return; he left all, and returned. I was the unhappy fruit of this return. Ten months later I was born, a weak and ailing child; I cost my mother her life, and my birth was the first of my misfortunes.

I have never heard how my father bore this loss, but I know that he was inconsolable. He believed that he saw his wife again in me, without being able to forget that it was I who had robbed him of her; he never embraced me without my perceiving, by his sighs and the convulsive manner in which he clasped me to his breast, that a bitter regret was mingled with his caresses, which were on that account only the more tender. When he said to me, "Jean Jacques, let us talk of your mother," I used to answer, "Well, then, my father, we will weep!"—and this word alone was sufficient to move him to tears. "Ah!" said he, with a sigh, "give her back to me, console me for her loss, fill the void which she has left in my soul. Should I love you as I do, if you were only my son?" Forty years after he had lost her, he died in the arms of a second wife, but the name of the first was on his lips and her image at the bottom of his heart.

Such were the authors of my existence. Of all the gifts which Heaven had bestowed upon them, a sensitive heart is the only one they bequeathed to me; it had been the source of their happiness, but for me it proved the source of all the misfortunes of my life.

I was brought into the world in an almost dying condition, little hope was entertained of saving my life. I carried within me the germs of a complaint which the course of time has strengthened, and which at times allows me a respite only to make me suffer more cruelly in another manner. One of my father's sisters, an amiable and virtuous young woman, took such care of me that she saved my life. At this moment, while I am writing, she is still alive, at the age of eighty, nursing a husband younger than herself, but exhausted by excessive drinking. Dear aunt, I forgive you for having preserved my life; and I deeply regret that, at the end of your days, I am unable to repay the tender care which you lavished upon me at the beginning of my own. My dear old nurse Jacqueline is also still alive, healthy and robust. The hands which opened my eyes at my birth will be able to close them for me at my death.

I felt before I thought: this is the common lot of humanity. I experienced it more than others. I do not know what I did until I was five or six years old. I do not know how I learned to read; I only remember my earliest reading, and the effect it had upon me; from that time I date my uninterrupted self-consciousness. My mother had left some romances behind her, which my father and I began to read after supper. At first it was only a question of practising me in reading by the aid of amusing books; but soon the interest became so lively, that we used to read in turns without stopping, and spent whole nights in this occupation. We were unable to leave off until the volume was finished. Sometimes, my father, hearing the swallows begin to twitter in the early morning, would say, quite ashamed, "Let us go to bed; I am more of a child than yourself."

In a short time I acquired, by this dangerous method, not only extreme facility in reading and understanding what I read, but a knowledge of the passions that was unique in a child of my age. I had no idea of things in themselves, although all the feelings of actual life were already known to me. I had conceived nothing, but felt everything. These confused emotions, which I felt one after the other, certainly did not warp the reasoning powers which I did not as yet possess; but they shaped them in me of a peculiar stamp, and gave me odd and romantic notions of human life, of which experience and reflection have never been able wholly to cure me.

[1719-1723]—The romances came to an end in the summer of 1719. The following winter brought us something different. My mother's library being exhausted, we had recourse to the share of her father's which had fallen to us. Luckily, there were some good books in it; in fact, it could hardly have been otherwise, for the library had been collected by a minister, who was even a learned man according to the fashion of the day, and was at the same time a man of taste and intellect. The "History of the Empire and the Church," by Le Sueur; Bossuet's "Treatise upon Universal History"; Plutarch's "Lives of Famous Men"; Nani's "History of Venice"; Ovid's "Metamorphoses"; La Bruyère; Fontenelle's "Worlds"; his "Dialogues of the Dead"; and some volumes of Molière—all these were brought over into my father's room, and I read to him out of them while he worked. I conceived a taste for them that was rare and perhaps unique at my age. Plutarch, especially, became my favourite author. The pleasure I took in reading him over and over again cured me a little of my taste for romance, and I soon preferred Agesilaus, Brutus and Aristides to Orondates, Artamenes, and Juba. This interesting reading, and the conversations between my father and myself to which it gave rise, formed in me the free and republican spirit, the proud and indomitable character unable to endure slavery or servitude, which has tormented me throughout my life in situations the least fitted to afford it scope. Unceasingly occupied with thoughts of Rome and Athens, living as it were amongst their great men, myself by birth the citizen of a republic and the son of a father whose patriotism was his strongest passion, I was fired by his example; I believed myself a Greek or a Roman; I lost my identity in that of the individual whose life I was reading; the recitals of the qualities of endurance and intrepidity which arrested my attention made my eyes glisten and strengthened my voice. One day, while I was relating the history of Scaevola at table, those present were alarmed to see me come forward and hold my hand over a chafing-dish, to illustrate his action.

I had a brother seven years older than myself, who was learning my father's trade. The excessive affection which was lavished upon myself caused him to be somewhat neglected, which treatment I cannot approve of. His education felt the consequences of this neglect. He took to evil courses before he was old enough to be a regular profligate. He was put with another master, from whom he was continually running away, as he had done from home. I hardly ever saw him; I can scarcely say that I knew him; but I never ceased to love him tenderly, and he loved me as much as a vagabond can love anything. I remember that, on one occasion, when my father was chastising him harshly and in anger, I threw myself impetuously between them and embraced him closely. In this manner I covered his body with mine, and received the blows which were aimed at him; I so obstinately maintained my position that at last my father was obliged to leave off, being either disarmed by my cries and tears, or afraid of hurting me more than him. At last, my brother turned out so badly that he ran away and disappeared altogether. Some time afterwards we heard that he was in Germany. He never once wrote to us. From that time nothing more has been heard of him, and thus I have remained an only son.

If this poor boy was carelessly brought up, this was not the case with his brother; the children of kings could not be more carefully looked after than I was during my early years—worshipped by all around me, and, which is far less common, treated as a beloved, never as a spoiled child. Till I left my father's house, I was never once allowed to run about the streets by myself with the other children; in my case no one ever had to satisfy or check any of those fantastic whims which are attributed to Nature, but are all in reality the result of education. I had the faults of my age: I was a chatterbox, a glutton, and, sometimes, a liar. I would have stolen fruits, bonbons, or eatables; but I have never found pleasure in doing harm or damage, in accusing others, or in tormenting poor dumb animals. I remember, however, that I once made water in a saucepan belonging to one of our neighbours, Madame Clot, while she was at church. I declare that, even now, the recollection of this makes me laugh, because Madame Clot, a

good woman in other respects, was the most confirmed old grum-
bler I have ever known. Such is the brief and true story of all my
childish offences.

How could I become wicked, when I had nothing but examples
of gentleness before my eyes, and none around me but the best
people in the world? My father, my aunt, my nurse, my relations,
our friends, our neighbours, all who surrounded me, did not, it is
true, obey me, but they loved me; and I loved them in return. My
wishes were so little excited and so little opposed, that it did not
occur to me to have any. I can swear that, until I served under a
master, I never knew what a fancy was. Except during the time I
spent in reading or writing in my father's company, or when my
nurse took me for a walk, I was always with my aunt, sitting or
standing by her side, watching her at her embroidery or listening
to her singing; and I was content. Her cheerfulness, her gentleness and her pleasant face have stamped so deep and lively an
impression on my mind that I can still see her manner, look, and
attitude; I remember her affectionate language: I could describe
what clothes she wore and how her head was dressed, not forgetting the two little curls of black hair on her temples, which she
wore in accordance with the fashion of the time.

I am convinced that it is to her I owe the taste, or rather
passion, for music, which only became fully developed in me a
long time afterwards. She knew a prodigious number of tunes and
songs which she used to sing in a very thin, gentle voice. This
excellent woman's cheerfulness of soul banished dreaminess and
melancholy from herself and all around her. The attraction which
her singing possessed for me was so great, that not only have
several of her songs always remained in my memory, but even
now, when I have lost her, and as I grew older, many of them,
totally forgotten since the days of my childhood, return to my
mind with inexpressible charm. Would anyone believe that I, an
old dotard, eaten up by cares and troubles, sometime find myself
weeping like a child, when I mumble one of those little airs in a
voice already broken and trembling? One of them, especially, has
come back to me completely, as far as the tune is concerned; the
second half of the words, however, has obstinately resisted all my
efforts to recall it, although I have an indistinct recollection of the
rhymes. Here is the beginning, and all that I can remember of the
rest:

Tircis, je n'ose
Ecouter ton chalumeau
Sous l'ormeau:
Car on en cause
Déjà dans notre hameau.
. . . .
. . . . . un berger
. . . . s'engager
. . . . . sans danger
Et toujours l'épine est sous la rose.

I ask, where is the affecting charm which my heart finds in this song? it is a whim, which I am quite unable to understand; but, be that as it may, it is absolutely impossible for me to sing it through without being interrupted by my tears. I have intended, times without number, to write to Paris to make inquiries concerning the remainder of the words, in case anyone should happen to know them; but I am almost certain that the pleasure which I feel in recalling the air would partly disappear, if it should be proved that others besides my poor aunt Suson have sung it.

Such were my earliest emotions on my entry into life; thus began to form or display itself in me that heart at once so proud and tender, that character so effeminate but yet indomitable, which, ever wavering between timidity and courage, weakness and self-control, has throughout my life made me inconsistent, and has caused abstinence and enjoyment, pleasure and prudence equally to elude my grasp.

This course of education was interrupted by an accident, the consequences of which have exercised an influence upon the remainder of my life. My father had a quarrel with a captain in the French army, named Gautier, who was connected with some of the members of the Common Council. This Gautier, a cowardly and insolent fellow (whose nose happened to bleed during the affray), in order to avenge himself, accused my father of having drawn his sword within the city walls. My father, whom they wanted to send to prison, persisted that, in accordance with the law, the accuser ought to be imprisoned as well as himself. Being unable to have his way in this, he preferred to quit Geneva and expatriate himself for the rest of his life, than to give way on a

point in which honour and liberty appeared to him to be com-
promised.

I remained under the care of my uncle Bernard, who was at the
time employed upon the fortifications of Geneva. His eldest
daughter was dead, but he had a son of the same age as myself.
We were sent together to Bossey, to board with the Protestant
minister Lambercier, in order to learn, together with Latin, all
the sorry trash which is included under the name of education.

Two years spent in the village in some degree softened my
Roman roughness and made me a child again. At Geneva, where
no tasks were imposed upon me, I loved reading and study, which
were almost my only amusements; at Bossey, my tasks made me
love the games which formed a break in them. The country was
so new to me, that my enjoyment of it never palled. I conceived
so lively an affection for it, that it has never since died out. The
remembrance of the happy days I have spent there filled me with
regretful longing for its pleasures, at all periods of my life, until
the day which has brought me back to it. M. Lambercier was a
very intelligent person, who, without neglecting our education,
never imposed excessive tasks upon us. The fact that, in spite of
my dislike to restraint, I have never recalled my hours of study
with any feeling of disgust—and also that, even if I did not learn
much from him, I learnt without difficulty what I did learn and
never forgot it—is sufficient proof that his system of instruction
was a good one.

The simplicity of this country life was of inestimable value to
me, in that it opened my heart to friendship. Up to that time I
had only known lofty, but imaginary sentiments. The habit of
living peacefully together with my cousin Bernard drew us together in tender bonds of union. In a short time, my feelings
towards him became more affectionate than those with which I
had regarded my brother, and they have never been effaced. He
was a tall, lanky, weakly boy, as gentle in disposition as he was
feeble in body, who never abused the preference which was
shown to him in the house as the son of my guardian. Our tasks,
our amusements, our tastes were the same: we were alone, we
were of the same age, each of us needed a companion: separation
was to us, in a manner, annihilation. Although we had few opportunities of proving our mutual attachment, it was very great; not
only were we unable to live an instant apart, but we did not

imagine it possible that we could ever be separated. Being, both of us, ready to yield to tenderness, and docile, provided compulsion was not used, we always agreed in everything. If, in the presence of those who looked after us, he had some advantage over me in consequence of the favour with which they regarded him, when we were alone I had an advantage over him which restored the equilibrium. When we were saying our lessons, I prompted him if he hesitated; when I had finished my exercise, I helped him with his; and in our amusements, my more active mind always led the way. In short, our two characters harmonised so well, and the friendship which united us was so sincere, that, in the five years and more, during which, whether at Bossey or Geneva, we were almost inseparable, although I confess that we often fought, it was never necessary to separate us, none of our quarrels ever lasted longer than a quarter of an hour, and neither of us ever made any accusation against the other. These observations are, if you will, childish, but they furnish an example which, since the time that there have been children, is perhaps unique.

The life which I led at Bossey suited me so well that, had it only lasted longer, it would have completely decided my character. Tender, affectionate and gentle feelings formed its foundation. I believe that no individual of our species was naturally more free from vanity than myself. I raised myself by fits and starts to lofty flights, but immediately fell down again into my natural languor. My liveliest desire was to be loved by all who came near me. I was of a gentle disposition; my cousin and our guardians were the same. During two whole years I was neither the witness nor the victim of any violent feeling. Everything nourished in my heart those tendencies which it received from Nature. I knew no higher happiness than to see all the world satisfied with me and with everything. I shall never forget how, if I happened to hesitate when saying my catechism in church, nothing troubled me more than to observe signs of restlessness and dissatisfaction on Mademoiselle Lambercier's face. That alone troubled me more than the disgrace of failing in public, which, nevertheless, affected me greatly: for, although little susceptible to praise, I felt shame keenly; and I may say here that the thought of Mademoiselle's reproaches caused me less uneasiness than the fear of offending her.

27. Friedrich Schleiermacher: *Soliloquies*

Earlier we offered some of Friedrich Schleiermacher's views of religion. The following selection is taken from his *Soliloquies*, written in 1800, shortly after the *Speeches on Religion*. The *Soliloquies* were chiefly intended to pursue issues in ethics that were raised in the earlier work.

Once again, Schleiermacher focused his attention on the free development of the individual, stressing the freedom of the conscience and the self-expression of the ego. The Soliloquy that follows suggests some of these ideas while pursuing the Romantic theme of the need to maintain youthful idealism into old age.

The text is from an English translation of Schleiermacher's *Monologen*, with a critical Introduction and Appendix by Horace Leland Friess, pp. 89–103, reprinted with the permission of The Open Court Publishing Company, La Salle, Illinois.

Youth and Age

As THE stroke of the clock tolls the hours, and the sun's course measures out the years, my life, as I am well aware, draws ever nearer the hour of death. But does it also approach old age, weak and broken old age, of which everyone bitterly complains, when without warning the zest of joyous youth has slipped away, and all health of spirit, all exuberance is gone? Why do men permit life's golden years to pass, and sighing bend their necks beneath a self-imposed yoke? There was a time when I myself believed the privileges of youth did not befit manhood; I thought to conduct myself quietly and prudently, preparing for years more drab by a wise resolve of renunciation. My spirit however, would not content itself within such narrow bounds, and I soon repented this life of bare economy. At the very first summons joyous youth returned, and ever since has held me in its protecting embrace. Were I now convinced that youth would escape me with the flight of years, I should voluntarily hasten to meet an early death, lest fear of certain misery to come embitter every good of the present, and incapacitate my life until finally I deserved an even worse end.

But I know that this cannot be true, because it should not be. Shall the free and immeasurable life of the spirit be spent before the life of the flesh is ended, which contains the seeds of death in its very first pulsations? Shall not my imagination always contemplate beauty with its full and wonted strength? Can I not always count on bouyancy of spirit, responsiveness to good, and warmth of heart? Am I to listen with dread to the waves of time, and see them grind and channel me until I give way? Tell me, O heart, how many times the time just now spent upon this wretched thought may I still expect to live before these horrors come to pass? Could I count them, I should think a thousand times as brief as one. But be not a fool, to prophecy the spirit's strength in terms of time, for time can never be its measure! The stars in their courses do not traverse equal distances in equal times; you must seek a higher calculus to comprehend their motion. And should the spirit follow meaner laws than they? No, nor does it do so. Old age, soured, bare, and hopeless, fetches many prematurely, and some evil spirit breaks off the bud of their youth before it has scarcely blossomed; others keep their vigor long; though white, their heads are unbowed, a fire still animates their eyes, and happy laughter graces their lips. Why should I not successfully fight off the death that lurks in hiding for me, even longer than he who has maintained his prime the longest? Ignoring the toll of years and the body's decay, why should I not by sheer force of will cling to youth's dear divinity until my last breath is drawn? For what is to explain this difference in ageing, if not force of will? Is the spirit forsooth of a finite size and measure, which can be spent and exhausted? Is its strength used up by action and dissipated in every movement? Is it only misers who have been chary of their deeds that enjoy long life? If it be so, let shame and scorn smite all whose old age wears a fresh and happy look; for he deserves scorn who has been miserly with his youth.

Were time actually the measure of man's life and destiny, I should rather realize all my spiritual possibilities in a brief span; I should want to live a short life that I might keep young and vital while it lasted! What good are rays of light thinly diffused over a wide surface? There can be no revelation of power in them, no effective accomplishment. Of what avail is it to economize and conserve action, if you must weaken its inner content, and if finally you have nothing left anyway? Rather spend your life in a few years with brilliant prodigality, so that you may enjoy the sense of your strength, and be able to survey what you have amounted to. But man's measure and his destiny are not temporal; the spirit will not submit to such empirical delimitation. For what is there to break its power? What can it lose of its being by activity and by pouring itself out to others? What is there to consume it? I feel myself enriched and clarified by every action, stronger, and more sound; for in every act I receive some nourishment from humanity's common store, and in the process of growth my nature assumes a more definite character. Is this true only because I am still climbing up the hill of life? Perhaps, but when will this happy condition suddenly be reversed? When shall I begin to decline instead of growing by activity? And how will this great transformation be announced? If it comes, I can not help but recognize it, and if I recognize it, I shall rather choose to die, than to live in protracted misery, beholding in myself the impotence of human existence.

The decline of vigor and of strength is an ill that man inflicts upon himself; old age is but an idle prejudice, an ugly fruit of the mad delusion that the spirit is dependent on the body! But I know this madness, and its evil fruit shall not succeed in poisoning my healthy life. Does the spirit inhabit the fibres of my flesh, or are the two identical, that it needs must stiffen like a mummy when they are petrified? Let the body have its due. If the senses grow dull, and our impressions of reality's earthly images grow faint, then surely memory too will be dimmed, and many pleasures and delights will fade. But is this the life of the spirit? Is this the everlasting youth that I worship? If such things had power to weaken the spirit, how long had I already been old age's slave! How long ago should I have bade my youth a last farewell! But nothing that has hitherto been unable to disturb my energetic life, shall ever succeed in doing so. Am I not surrounded by others who have sharper senses and stronger bodies? Will they not always be about me as they are now to offer the service of their love? To lament my physical decline is of all things furthest from my mind! Why should that trouble me? Would it be such a misfortune, if I did forget the events of yesterday? Are the day's minutia the world in which I live? Is the sphere of my inner life limited to the impressions I get of those particular things that happen to exist within the narrow confines of my immediate physical environment? Whoever has loved youth only because it excelled in these immediate physical advantages, and whose inferior perception cannot grasp a higher calling, may justly complain of old age and its misery. But who will dare maintain that the presence of those great and sublime thoughts which the spirit produces out of its own depths is dependent on the body, and that a sense for true reality hinges on the functioning of one's frame? In order to contemplate humanity do I need this eye, the nerve of which already begins to weaken when my life is but half over? Or must my blood, which even now begins to flow slowly, rush more impetuously through my narrow veins, if I am to love all who deserve my love? Does the power of my will depend on the strength of my muscles, or on the marrow of my bones? Does courage depend upon my feeling in good health? Those who are thus physically favored are often enough deceived; death lurks in hidden corners, and suddenly springs upon them with sardonic laughter. What harm, then, if I already know, where my own death lies waiting? But perhaps repeated pain, or manifold sufferings, can so depress the spirit as to incapacitate it for its own unique and proper functions? Why! to resist such pains is also a function of the spirit; they too call forth sublime thoughts for their relief. And the spirit can find no evil in anything that merely changes its activity from one form to another.

Yes, in my advanced years I shall still have the same strength of spirit, and I shall never lose my keen zest for life. That which now rejoices me, shall ever give me joy; my will shall remain strong, and my imagination active, and nothing shall wrest from me the magic key which opens the mysterious portals of the higher world; nor shall love's ardent flame ever be quenched. I will not see the dread infirmities of old age; I vow a mighty scorn of all adversity that does not touch the aim of my existence, and I pledge myself to an eternal Youth.

But am I not repudiating good along with evil? Is old age sheer weakness when compared with youth? Why then is it that mankind honors a grey head, even though it shows no trace of this eternal youth, freedom's finest fruit? Alas, often it is only because some people lead their lives in an atmosphere like that of a cellar, which will for a long time preserve a corpse from decay, and such men are popularly venerated as sacred bodies. People think of the soul as like a grape-vine; be it even of poor quality, it improves and is more highly prized when it grows old. Nay more! they talk much of virtues peculiar to life's riper years, of sober wisdom, cool self-possession, a rich experience, a poised and unassailable perfection is one's understanding of this variegated world. Youth's charm, they say, is only the evanescent blossom of human nature, but the mature fruit is old age and what it brings the soul. Then only are the innermost depths of human nature ripe for enjoyment when they have been completely purified by air and sun, and brought to some significant and beautiful perfection. O ye northern barbarians, who do not know the happier clime, where fruit and blossom burst forth together, and race side by side in all their glory to a joint fulfillment! Is the world so cold and unfriendly that the human spirit may not emulate this higher beauty and perfection? Of course, everyone cannot have all that is good and beautiful, but diverse gifts are given to diverse persons and not apportioned to the different seasons of life. Each man is a plant of unique growth, but he can continually bear fruit and flower at the same time according to his kind. Whatever can be harmoniously realized in a single individual, he can cultivate simultaneously and possess permanently; he not only can but should.

How does man acquire discreet wisdom and ripe experience? Are they granted him from on high, and is it foreordained that he shall not receive them until he can prove that youth is passed? I am conscious of acquiring them at this very moment; it is precisely the urge of youth and the quickened life of the spirit that brings them forth. To inspect all things, to absorb them in the innermost sense, to master the force of random emotions lest tears either of joy or grief dim the spirit's vision or cloud its impressions, to proceed readily from one thing to another, and being of insatiable energy to assimilate even the experience of others by rehearsing their deeds in imagination, such is the active life of youth, and such too is the process by which wisdom and experience come into being. The livelier the imagination, the more active the spirit, the more is their growth hastened and prospered. And when they have been acquired, is the vigorous life that produced them no longer appropriate? Are then these supreme virtues ever perfected? If they were born in youth and by reason of youth, will they not always require the same energy to maintain and further their growth? Mankind, however, is deceived by a hypocritical vanity in respect to this its greatest blessing, and its hypocrisy is rooted in depths of narrowest ignorance. Youth's restlessness is supposed to imply the urge of a seeker, and seeking is not thought becoming to one who has reached the end of life; such a one should clothe himself in the repose of idleness, that respected symbol of life's fulfillment, and in emptiness of desire, the sign of complete understanding. Such should be the deportment of old age, they say, lest seeming still to be seeker, man descend into the grave amid laughter mocking his vain efforts. But only those who have sought what is cheap and vulgar may pride themselves on having found all they desire! What I aspire to know and make my own is infinite, and only in an infinite series of attempts can I completely fashion my own being. The spirit that drives man forward, and the constant appeal of new goals, that can never be satisfied by past achievements, shall never depart from me. It is man's peculiar pride, to know that his goal is infinite, and yet never to halt on his way, to know that at some point on his journey he will be engulfed, and yet when he sees that point, to make no change either in himself or in his circumstances, nor in any wise to slacken his pace. Hence it is fitting that he should ever pursue his way in the carefree buoyancy of youth. I shall never consider myself old until I am perfect, and I shall never be perfect, because I know and desire what I should. Furthermore, the excellences of old age cannot conflict with those of youth, for not only do the qualities esteemed in old age develop in youth, but old age in its turn nourishes the young and tender life. It is generally conceded that youth fares better when ripe old age takes an interest in it, and in the same way a man's own inner youth is enhanced, if he acquires in early life the spiritual qualities of maturity. A practiced eye surveys its field more quickly, and a person of experience grasps a situation more readily, and that love which springs from a higher level of self-development must needs be more intense. Wherefore I shall preserve my youthful vigor and I shall enjoy its zest unto the last. Unto the last I shall gain in strength and in vitality with every act, and with each step in my self-development I shall become more capable of love. I shall marry my youth to my old age, that the latter too may enjoy exuberance and be permeated with vivifying warmth. For what is it, after all, of which men complain in old age? not of consequences that necessarily follow from experience, wisdom, and self-development. Does a treasury of accumulated ideas make a man less sensitive, so that nothing either old or new interests him? Do established words of wisdom at last give way to disquieting doubts that vitiate all action? Is self-development a consuming fire that leaves the soul an inert mass? The general complaint is only that youth has fled. And why does youth fail man? Because in his youth he has lacked maturity. Let there be a double marriage. Let the strength of years enter into your robust spirit at once to preserve its youth, that in later years youth may protect you against the weakness of old age. The usual division of life into youth and age ought never to be made. He debases himself who wishes first to be young, and then old, who allows himself to be controlled first by what is called the spirit of youth, and only afterwards wishes to follow what is considered the counsel of maturity. Life cannot bear this separation of its elements. There is a two-fold activity of the spirit that should exist in its entirety at every time of life, and it is the perfection of human development ever to become more intimately and more clearly conscious of both its aspects, assigning to each its own peculiar and proper function.

The individual existence of a plant is perfected in its blossom, but the world attaches supreme value to its fruit, which serves as protection to the seed of future generations, and is a gift which every creature must offer in order that the rest of nature may receive his life. So too, the supreme thing for a human being is the spirited life of youth, and woe to him whom it forsakes, but the world desires him to grow old, that his life may bear fruit, the sooner the better. Wherefore set your life in accord with this fact once and for all. It is a lesson which old age teaches men all too late, when time has dragged them thither in its chains, but by a firm resolution of your free will you may at once make it your rule in all matters upon which the world has a claim. Wherever fruit appears as the spontaneous result of your life's free flowering, let it develop to the world's advantage, and may there be hidden in it a fertile seed destined to unfold one day into a new life of its own. But let whatever you offer to the world be fruit. Do not sacrifice the least part of your being itself in mistaken generosity! Let no bud be broken off, nor the smallest leaf plucked, through which you receive nourishment from the surrounding world! On the other hand, do not put forth mere foliage, unpruned and unpleasing, in which some poisonous insect may hide and sting

you. If it is not part of your own proper development, or the
growth of new members, let it be genuine fruit, engendered
within the heart of the spirit, a free act testifying to its youthful
creative energy. But when it is once conceived, such fruit should
emerge from the province of the inner life:then let its further
development conform to the laws of outward behavior. Then let
shrewdness and sober wisdom and cool discretion take it in
charge, that what your love generously intended for the world
may actually prove to its benefit. Then weigh means and end with
care, take heed and be circumspect with cautious misgiving, seek
counsel of work and power, despise no pains, and wait for propitious moments with untiring patience.

Woe unto me, if my youth, with its vitality that brooks no
restraint and its restless imagination, should ever meddle with the
affairs of old age, and failing to succeed in the realm of action,
which is not its proper province, should thereby waste the
strength of its inner life! Only such as are ignorant of inner energies may perish thus, those who, misunderstanding the spiritual
urge, wish to be young in their outward behavior. They expect
fruit to ripen in a moment even as a blossom opens in a night;
each of their projects crowds upon the heels of another, and none
matures. Every enterprise, which they commence, is destroyed in
the rapid alternation of their conflicting plans. And when they
have thus wasted the loveliest half of life in vain attempts, doing
and achieving nought, because to do and to accomplish was their
only aim, then they condemn the free imagination and the
youthful life. Nought but old age is left them, weak and miserable
as it must be, wherever youth has been used up and driven out.
Lest it flee from me also, I shall not abuse it; I shall not expect its
service in matters that are not its proper sphere; I shall keep it
within the limits of its own domain, that it may meet with no
injury. But there in truth it shall have full sway, now and forever
in unmolested freedom, nor shall any law, the proper sphere of
which is to govern external actions, cramp my inner life.

May my inner activity and all that affects it, in so far as the
world has no claim upon it and it concerns only my own growth,
bear youth's colors everlastingly, and may it proceed wholly from
an inner impulse with a gracious and perfect joy. O my soul, let
no rule be imposed on your coming in and going out, your hours
of meditation and reflection! Heartily despise such alien legislation and banish the thought which would put the free movement

of your life under the sign of a dead letter. Let no one persuade you that one thing must wait upon the completion of another! Proceed, if you like, with buoyant step; what you have done lives on in you, and you will find it again when you return. Do not anxiously ponder what to begin and what will come of it! You alone are in the making, and whatever you can will, is also part of you. Shun frugal behavior! Let life be unconfined: no power is ever lost, unless you repress it within yourself, and leave it unused. Let not your will for today be determined by your wish for tomorrow! Take shame, free spirit that you are, if ought within you should become subservient to the rest; no part of your being may be mere means to an end, for one is as precious as another. Wherefore whatever you become, let it be for its own sake. A stupid self-deception to think that you ought to want what you do not want! Let not the world tell you how you should serve it and when! Laugh to scorn its silly pretensions, spirited youth, and do not brook restraint. Whatever you give is a gift of your freedom, for the resolve to benefit the world must issue from within you. Attempt nothing unless it proceeds freely from a love and desire within your soul. And let no limit be set upon your love, no measure whether of kind or of duration! If it is your own, who can demand it of you? Is not its law entirely within you? Then who may command it in any respect? Be ashamed to depend on other's opinions in such matters of holiest import. Blush for that false shame which fears lest people may not understand you when you reply to the questioner: "Such is the reason of my love." Let not yourself be troubled in the fullness and joy of your inner life by anything external whatsoever! Who would choose to combine within himself elements that are incompatible, and thus be soured in his soul? Grieve not for what you cannot be or do! Who would be ever gazing toward the impossible in empty aspiration and turning covetous eyes upon goods that are not his?

Thus is my inner life joyous and untrammelled! And how should time and destiny ever teach me another philosophy? I give the world its due; in my outward behavior I strive for order and wisdom, discretion and proportion. Indeed, what reason have I to disdain anything that proceeds so readily and freely and happily from my inner being and its activity? By observing the world one will gain all this in rich measure without effort. But in beholding himself, man triumphs over discouragement and weakness, for from the consciousness of inner freedom there blossoms eternal youth and joy. On these have I laid hold, nor shall I ever give them up, and so I can see with a smile my eyes growing dim, and my blond locks turning white. Nought can happen to affright my heart, and the pulse of my inner life will beat with vigor until death.

28. Lord Byron: *Childe Harold's Pilgrimage* and *Manfred*

Byronism was a phenomenon produced by the life and notoriety as well as by the poetry of George Gordon, Lord Byron (1788-1824). After the publication of the first part of *Childe Harold's Pilgrimage* Byron became famous, then notorious. Beginning in 1812, he had a series of dramatic social and poetic triumphs in London society. The young nobleman had been lionized in part for his charm and good looks, in part for his earlier travels through the Mediterranean, and for the melancholy and suffering contemporaries saw in him. These years of success included publication, among other works, of two pieces reflecting Byron's travels, *The Giaour* (1813) and *The Corsair* (1814), which presented early portraits of the Byronic heroes—men at odds with their worlds, men unable to mix effectively with their fellows, men with secret sorrows or secret crimes. Yet these were men in some ways more admirable than any of those around them, men who could lead because of their aura of strength. Such depictions helped build the image of their author. The Byron who set out for the Continent in 1816 left behind him marital scandal and the consequent opposition of much of polite London society. The heroes of *Childe Harold's Pilgrimage* in Canto III (after 1816) and of *Manfred* (1817) reveal a still more profoundly felt sense of difference and separation from society. The autobiographical character of *Childe Harold* helps to make clear how closely Byron himself may be identified with the Byronic hero.

Byron lived most of his last years in Italy until, having first aided Carbonarists there, he left in 1824 for Greece to support the Greek Revolution. There he died at Missolonghi, adding still further to what was to become the legendary image, now given a final touch of true heroic dedication. The figure of Byron, as he appeared in his life and his poetry was probably second only to that of Napoleon as a model for Romantic youth; for this reason, it seems suitable to include Byron's judgment on Napoleon. The selections also echo typical Romantic themes, like the beneficence of nature and the praise of peasantry in a medieval setting.

The texts are from "Childe Harold's Pilgrimage," *The Works of Lord Byron*. (London, 1899), Vol. II, pp. 217–225, 237–243, 257–264, 270–273 and "Manfred," *The Works of Lord Byron* (London, 1901), Vol. VI, pp. 99–100, 119–126.

Childe Harold's Pilgrimage: Canto III

III.

In my youth's summer I did sing of One,
   The wandering outlaw of his own dark mind;
   Again I seize the theme, then but begun,
   And bear it with me, as the rushing wind
   Bears the cloud onwards: in that Tale I find
   The furrows of long thought, and dried-up tears,
   Which, ebbing, leave a sterile track behind,
   O'er which all heavily the journeying years
Plod the last sands of life,—where not a flower appears.

IV.

Since my young days of passion—joy, or pain—
   Perchance my heart and harp have lost a string—
   And both may jar: it may be, that in vain
   I would essay as I have sung to sing:
   Yet, though a dreary strain, to this I cling;
   So that it wean me from the weary dream
   Of selfish grief or gladness—so it fling
   Forgetfulness around me—it shall seem
To me, though to none else, a not ungrateful theme.

V.

He, who grown agèd in this world of woe,
   In deeds, not years, piercing the depths of life,
   So that no wonder waits him—nor below
   Can Love or Sorrow, Fame, Ambition, Strife,
   Cut to his heart again with the keen knife
   Of silent, sharp endurance—he can tell
   Why Thought seeks refuge in lone caves, yet rife
   With airy images, and shapes which dwell
Still unimpaired, though old, in the Soul's haunted cell.

VI.

'Tis to create, and in creating live
  A being more intense that we endow
  With form our fancy, gaining as we give
  The life we image, even as I do now—
  What am I? Nothing: but not so art thou,
  Soul of my thought! with whom I traverse earth,
  Invisible but gazing, as I glow
  Mixed with thy spirit, blended with thy birth,
And feeling still with thee in my crushed feelings' dearth.

VII.

Yet must I think less wildly:—I *have* thought
  Too long and darkly; till my brain became,
  In its own eddy boiling and o'erwrought,
  A whirling gulf of phantasy and flame:
  And thus, untaught in youth my heart to tame,
  My springs of life were poisoned. 'Tis too late:
  Yet am I changed; though still enough the same
  In strength to bear what Time can not abate,
And feed on bitter fruits without accusing Fate.

VIII.

Something too much of this:—but now 'tis past,
  And the spell closes with its silent seal—
  Long absent HAROLD re-appears at last;
  He of the breast which fain no more would feel,
  Wrung with the wounds which kill not, but ne'er heal;
  Yet Time, who changes all, had altered him
  In soul and aspect as in age: years steal
  Fire from the mind as vigour from the limb;
And Life's enchanted cup but sparkles near the brim.

IX.

His had been quaffed too quickly, and he found
  The dregs were wormwood; but he filled again,
  And from a purer fount, on holier ground,
  And deemed its spring perpetual—but in vain!
  Still round him clung invisibly a chain
  Which galled for ever, fettering though unseen,

And heavy though it clanked not; worn with pain,
Which pined although it spoke not, and grew keen,
Entering with every step he took through many a scene.

X.

Secure in guarded coldness, he had mixed
Again in fancied safety with his kind,
And deemed his spirit now so firmly fixed
And sheathed with an invulnerable mind,
That, if no joy, no sorrow lurked behind;
And he, as one, might 'midst the many stand
Unheeded, searching through the crowd to find
Fit speculation—such as in strange land
He found in wonder-works of God and Nature's hand.

XI.

But who can view the ripened rose, nor seek
To wear it? who can curiously behold
The smoothness and the sheen of Beauty's cheek,
Nor feel the heart can never all grow old?
Who can contemplate Fame through clouds unfold
The star which rises o'er her steep, nor climb?
Harold, once more within the vortex, rolled
On with the giddy circle, chasing Time,
Yet with a nobler aim than in his Youth's fond prime.

XII.

But soon he knew himself the most unfit
Of men to herd with Man, with whom he held
Little in common; untaught to submit
His thoughts to others, though his soul was quelled
In youth by his own thoughts; still uncompelled,
He would not yield dominion of his mind
To Spirits against whom his own rebelled,
Proud though in desolation—which could find
A life within itself, to breathe without mankind.

XIII.

Where rose the mountains, there to him were friends;
Where rolled the ocean, thereon was his home;
Where a blue sky, and glowing clime, extends,

He had the passion and the power to roam;
The desert, forest, cavern, breaker's foam,
Were unto him companionship; they spake
A mutual language, clearer than the tome
Of his land's tongue, which he would oft forsake
For Nature's pages glassed by sunbeams on the lake.

XIV.

Like the Chaldean, he could watch the stars,
  Till he had peopled them with beings bright
  As their own beams; and earth, and earth-born jars,
  And human frailties, were forgotten quite:
  Could he have kept his spirit to that flight
  He had been happy; but this clay will sink
  Its spark immortal, envying it the light
  To which it mounts, as if to break the link
That breaks us from yon heaven which woos us to its
    brink.

XV.

But in Man's dwellings he became a thing
  Restless and worn, and stern and wearisome,
  Drooped as a wild-born falcon with clipt wing,
  To whom the boundless air alone were home:
  Then came his fit again, which to o'ercome,
  As eagerly the barred-up bird will beat
  His breast and beak against his wiry dome
  Till the blood tinge his plumage—so the heat
Of his impeded Soul would through his bosom eat.

XVI.

Self-exiled Harold wanders forth again,
  With nought of Hope left—but with less of gloom;
  The very knowledge that he lived in vain,
  That all was over on this side the tomb,
  Had made Despair a smilingness assume,
  Which, though 'twere wild,—as on the plundered wreck
  When mariners would madly meet their doom
  With draughts intemperate on the sinking deck,—
Did yet inspire a cheer, which he forbore to check.

. . . .

XXXV.

The Psalmist numbered out the years of man:
　　They are enough; and if thy tale be *true*,
　　Thou, who didst grudge him even that fleeting span,
　　More than enough, thou fatal Waterloo!
　　Millions of tongues record thee, and anew
　　Their children's lips shall echo them, and say—
　　"Here, where the sword united nations drew,
　　Our countrymen were warring on that day!"
And this is much—and all—which will not pass away.

XXXVI.

There sunk the greatest, nor the worst of men,
　　Whose Spirit, antithetically mixed,
　　One moment of the mightiest, and again
　　On little objects with like firmness fixed;
　　Extreme in all things! hadst thou been betwixt,
　　Thy throne had still been thine, or never been;
　　For Daring made thy rise as fall: thou seek'st
　　Even now to re-assume the imperial mien,
And shake again the world, the Thunderer of the
　　　　scene!

XXXVII.

Conqueror and Captive of the Earth art thou!
　　She trembles at thee still, and thy wild name
　　Was ne'er more bruited in men's minds than now
　　That thou art nothing, save the jest of Fame,
　　Who wooed thee once, thy Vassal, and became
　　The flatterer of thy fierceness—till thou wert
　　A God unto thyself; nor less the same
　　To the astounded kingdoms all inert,
Who deemed thee for a time whate'er thou didst assert.

XXXVIII.

Oh, more or less than man—in high or low—
　　Battling with nations, flying from the field;
　　Now making monarchs' necks thy footstool, now
　　More than thy meanest soldier taught to yield;
　　An Empire thou couldst crush, command, rebuild,
　　But govern not thy pettiest passion, nor,

However deeply in men's spirits skilled,
Look through thine own, nor curb the lust of War,
Nor learn that tempted Fate will leave the loftiest Star.

XXXIX.

Yet well thy soul hath brooked the turning tide
With that untaught innate philosophy,
Which, be it Wisdom, Coldness, or deep Pride,
Is gall and wormwood to an enemy.
When the whole host of hatred stood hard by,
To watch and mock thee shrinking, thou hast smiled
With a sedate and all-enduring eye;—
When Fortune fled her spoiled and favorite child,
He stood unbowed beneath the ills upon him piled.

XL.

Sager than in thy fortunes; for in them
Ambition steeled thee on too far to show
That just habitual scorn, which could contemn
Men and their thoughts; 'twas wise to feel, not so
To wear it ever on thy lip and brow,
And spurn the instruments thou wert to use
Till they were turned unto thine overthrow:
'Tis but a worthless world to win or lose;
So hath it proved to thee, and all such lot who choose.

XLI.

If like a tower upon a headlong rock,
Thou hadst been made to stand or fall alone,
Such scorn of man had helped to brave the shock;
But men's thoughts were the steps which paved thy throne,
Their admiration thy best weapon shone;
The part of Philip's son was thine, not then
(Unless aside thy Purple had been thrown)
Like stern Diogenes to mock at men—
For sceptered Cynics Earth were far too wide a den.

XLII.

But Quiet to quick bosoms is a Hell,
And *there* hath been thy bane; there is a fire
And motion of the Soul which will not dwell

In its own narrow being, but aspire
Beyond the fitting medium of desire;
And, but once kindled, quenchless evermore,
Preys upon high adventure, nor can tire
Of aught but rest; a fever at the core,
Fatal to him who bears, to all who ever bore.

XLII.

This makes the madmen who have made men mad
By their contagion; Conquerors and Kings,
Founders of sects and systems, to whom add
Sophists, Bards, Statesmen, all unquiet things
Which stir too strongly the soul's secret springs,
And are themselves the fools to those they fool;
Envied, yet how unenviable! what stings
Are theirs! One breast laid open were a school
Which would unteach Mankind the lust to shine or rule:

XLIV.

Their breath is agitation, and their life
A storm whereon they ride, to sink at last,
And yet so nursed and bigoted to strife,
That should their days, surviving perils past,
Melt to calm twilight, they feel overcast
With sorrow and supineness, and so die;
Even as a flame unfed, which runs to waste
With its own flickering, or a sword laid by,
Which eats into itself, and rusts ingloriously.

XLV.

He who ascends to mountain-tops, shall find
The loftiest peaks most wrapt in clouds and snow;
He who surpasses or subdues mankind,
Must look down on the hate of those below.
Though high *above* the Sun of Glory glow,
And far *beneath* the Earth and Ocean spread,
Round him are icy rocks, and loudly blow
Contending tempests on his naked head,
And thus reward the toils which to those summits led.

. . . .

LXVIII.

Lake Leman woos me with its crystal face,
  The mirror where the stars and mountains view
  The stillness of their aspect in each trace
  Its clear depth yields of their far height and hue:
  There is too much of Man here, to look through
  With a fit mind the might which I behold;
  But soon in me shall Loneliness renew
  Thoughts hid, but not less cherished than of old,
Ere mingling with the herd had penned me in their fold.

LXIX.

To fly from, need not be to hate, mankind:
  All are not fit with them to stir and toil,
  Nor is it discontent to keep the mind
  Deep in its fountain, lest it overboil
  In the hot throng, where we become the spoil
  Of our infection, till too late and long
  We may deplore and struggle with the coil,
  In wretched interchange of wrong for wrong
Midst a contentious world, striving where none are
    strong.

LXX.

There, in a moment, we may plunge our years
  In fatal penitence, and in the blight
  Of our own Soul turn all our blood to tears,
  And colour things to come with hues of Night;
  The race of life becomes a hopeless flight
  To those that walk in darkness: on the sea
  The boldest steer but where their ports invite—
  But there are wanderers o'er Eternity
Whose bark drives on and on, and anchored ne'er
    shall be.

LXXI.

Is it not better, then, to be alone,
  And love Earth only for its earthly sake?
  By the blue rushing of the arrowy Rhone,
  Or the pure bosom of its nursing Lake,

Which feeds it as a mother who doth make
A fair but froward infant her own care,
Kissing its cries away as these awake;—
Is it not better thus our lives to wear,
Than join the crushing crowd, doomed to inflict or bear?

LXXII.

I live not in myself, but I become
  Portion of that around me; and to me
  High mountains are a feeling, but the hum
  Of human cities torture: I can see
  Nothing to loathe in Nature, save to be
  A link reluctant in a fleshly chain,
  Classed among creatures, when the soul can flee,
  And with the sky—the peak—the heaving plain
Of Ocean, or the stars, mingle—and not in vain.

LXXIII.

And thus I am absorbed, and this is life:—
  I look upon the peopled desert past,
  As on a place of agony and strife,
  Where, for some sin, to Sorrow I was cast,
  To act and suffer, but remount at last
  With a fresh pinion; which I feel to spring,
  Though young, yet waxing vigorous as the Blast
  Which it would cope with, on delighted wing,
Spurning the clay-cold bonds which round our being
      cling.

LXXIV.

And when, at length, the mind shall be all free
  From what it hates in this degraded form,
  Reft of its carnal life, save what shall be
  Existent happier in the fly and worm,—
  When Elements to Elements conform,
  And dust is as it should be, shall I not
  Feel all I see less dazzling but more warm?
  The bodiless thought? the Spirit of each spot?
Of which, even now, I share at times the immortal lot?

LXXV.

Are not the mountains, waves, and skies, a part
  Of me and of my Soul, as I of them?
  Is not the love of these deep in my heart
  With a pure passion? should I not contemn
  All objects, if compared with these? and stem
  A tide of suffering, rather than forego
  Such feelings for the hard and worldly phlegm
  Of those whose eyes are only turned below,
Gazing upon the ground, with thoughts which dare not
    glow?
. . . .

LXXXVIII.

Ye Stars! which are the poetry of Heaven!
  If in your bright leaves we would read the fate
  Of men and empires,—'tis to be forgiven,
  That in our aspirations to be great,
  Our destinies o'erleap their mortal state,
  And claim a kindred with you; for ye are
  A Beauty and a Mystery, and create
  In us such love and reverence from afar,
That Fortune,—Fame,—Power,—Life, have named themselves
    a Star.

LXXXIX.

All Heaven and Earth are still—though not in sleep,
  But breathless, as we grow when feeling most,
  And silent, as we stand in thoughts too deep:—
  All Heaven and Earth are still: From the high host
  Of stars, to the lulled lake and mountain-coast,
  All is concentrated in a life intense,
  Where not a beam, nor air, nor leaf is lost,
  But hath a part of Being, and a sense
Of that which is of all Creator and Defence.

XC.

Then stirs the feeling infinite, so felt
  In solitude, where we are *least* alone;
  A truth, which through our being then doth melt,

And purifies from self: it is a tone,
The soul and source of Music, which makes known
Eternal harmony, and sheds a charm
Like to the fabled Cytherea's zone,
Binding all things with beauty;—'twould disarm
The spectre Death, had he substantial power to harm.

XCI.

Not vainly did the early Persian make
His altar the high places, and the peak
Of earth-o'ergazing mountains, and thus take
A fit and unwalled temple, there to seek
The Spirit, in whose honour shrines are weak
Upreared of human hands. Come, and compare
Columns and idol-dwellings—Goth or Greek—
With Nature's realms of worship, earth and air—
Nor fix on fond abodes to circumscribe thy prayer!

Manfred

ACT II

SCENE I—*A Cottage among the Bernese Alps*—MANFRED *and the*
CHAMOIS HUNTER

C. Hun. No—no—yet pause—thou must not yet go forth:
Thy mind and body are alike unfit
To trust each other, for some hours, at least;
When thou art better, I will be thy guide—
But whither?
    Man.   It imports not: I do know
My route full well, and need no further guidance.
    C. Hun. Thy garb and gait bespeak thee of high lineage—
One of the many chiefs, whose castled crags
Look o'er the lower valleys—which of these
May call thee lord? I only know their portals;
My way of life leads me but rarely down
To bask by the huge hearths of those old halls,
Carousing with the vassals; but the paths,
Which step from out our mountains to their doors,

I know from childhood—which of these is thine?
Man. No matter.
C. Hun.   Well, Sir, pardon me the question,
And be of better cheer. Come, taste my wine;
'Tis of an ancient vintage; many a day
'T has thawed my veins among our glaciers, now
Let it do thus for thine—Come, pledge me fairly!
Man. Away, away! there's blood upon the brim!
Will it then never—never sink in the earth?
C. Hun. What dost thou mean? they senses wander from thee.
Man. I say 'tis blood—my blood! the pure warm stream
Which ran in the veins of my fathers, and in ours
When we were in our youth, and had one heart;
And loved each other as we should not love,
And this was shed: but still it rises up,
Colouring the clouds, that shut me out from Heaven,
Where thou art not—and I shall never be.
C. Hun. Man of strange words, and some half-maddening sin,
Which makes thee people vacancy, whate'er
Thy dread and sufferance be, there's comfort yet—
The aid of holy men, and heavenly patience—
Man. Patience—and patience! Hence—that word was made
For brutes of burthen, not for birds of prey!
Preach it to mortals of a dust like thine,—
I am not of thine order.
C. Hun.   Thanks to Heaven!
I would not be of thine for the free fame
Of William Tell; but whatsoe'er thine ill,
It must be borne, and these wild starts are useless.
Man. Do I not bear it?—Look on me—I live.
C. Hun. This is convulsion, and no healthful life.
Man. I tell thee, man! I have lived many years,
Many long years, but they are nothing now
To those which I must number: ages—ages—
Space and eternity—and consciousness,
With the fierce thirst of death—and still unslaked!
C. Hun. Why on thy brow the seal of middle age
Hath scarce been set; I am thine elder far.
Man. Think'st thou existence doth depend on time?
It doth; but actions are our epochs: mine
Have made my days and nights imperishable,

Endless, and all alike, as sands on the shore,
Innumerable atoms; and one desert,
Barren and cold, on which the wild waves break,
But nothing rests, save carcasses and wrecks,
Rocks, and the salt-surf weeds of bitterness.
 C. Hun. Alas! he's mad—but yet I must not leave him.
 Man. I would I were—for then the things I see
Would be but a distempered dream.
 C. Hun.   What is it
That thou dost see, or think thou look'st upon?
 Man. Myself, and thee—a peasant of the Alps—
Thy humble virtues, hospitable home,
And spirit patient, pious, proud, and free;
Thy self-respect, grafted on innocent thoughts;
Thy days of health, and nights of sleep; thy toils,
By danger dignified, yet guiltless; hopes
Of cheerful old age and a quiet grave,
With cross and garland over its green turf,
And thy grandchildren's love for epitaph!
This do I see—and then I look within—
It matters not—my Soul was scorched already!
 C. Hun. And would'st thou then exchange thy lot for mine?
 Man. No, friend! I would not wrong thee, nor exchange
My lot with living being: I can bear—
However wretchedly, 'tis still to bear—
In life what others could not brook to dream,
But perish in their slumber.
 C. Hun.   And with this—
This cautious feeling for another's pain,
Canst thou be black with evil?—say not so.
Can one of gentle thoughts have wreaked revenge
Upon his enemies?
 Man.   Oh! no, no, no!
My injuries came down on those who loved me—
On those whom I best loved: I never quelled
An enemy, save in my just defence—
But my embrace was fatal.
 C. Hun.   Heaven give thee rest!
And Penitence restore thee to thyself;
My prayers shall be for thee.

Man.   I need them not,
But can endure thy pity. I depart—
'Tis time—farewell!—Here's gold, and thanks for thee—
No words—it is thy due.—Follow me not—
I know my path—the mountain peril's past:
And once again I charge thee, follow not!

> [*Exit* MANFRED

SCENE II—*A lower Valley in the Alps—A Cataract*

Enter MANFRED

It is not noon—the Sunbow's rays still arch
The torrent with the many hues of heaven,
And roll the sheeted silver's waving column
O'er the crag's headlong perpendicular,
And fling its lines of foaming light along,
And to and fro, like the pale courser's tail,
The Giant steed, to be bestrode by Death,
As told in the Apocalypse. No eyes
But mine now drink this sight of loveliness;
I should be sole in this sweet solitude,
And with the Spirit of the place divide
The homage of these waters.—I will call her.

> [MANFRED *takes some of the water into the palm of his hand and
> flings it into the air, muttering the adjuration. After a pause,
> the* WITCH OF THE ALPS *rises beneath the arch of the sun-
> bow of the torrent.*

Beautiful Spirit! with thy hair of light,
And dazzling eyes of glory, in whose form
The charms of Earth's least mortal daughters grow
To an unearthly stature, in an essence
Of purer elements; while the hues of youth,—
Carnationed like a sleeping Infant's cheek,
Rocked by the beating of her mother's heart,
Or the rose tints, which Summer's twilight leaves
Upon the lofty Glacier's virgin snow,
The blush of earth embracing with her Heaven,—
Tinge thy celestial aspect, and make tame
The beauties of the Sunbow which bends o'er thee.

Beautiful Spirit! in thy calm clear brow,
Wherein is glassed serenity of Soul,
Which of itself shows immortality,
I read that thou wilt pardon to a Son
Of Earth, whom the abstruser powers permit
At times to commune with them—if that he
Avail him of his spells—to call thee thus,
And gaze on thee a moment.
    Witch.   Son of Earth!
I know thee, and the Powers which give thee power!
I know thee for a man of many thoughts,
And deeds of good and ill, extreme in both,
Fatal and fated in thy sufferings.
I have expected this—what would'st thou with me?
    Man. To look upon thy beauty—nothing further.
The face of the earth hath maddened me, and I
Take refuge in her mysteries, and pierce
To the abodes of those who govern her—
But they can nothing aid me. I have sought
From them what they could not bestow, and now
I search no further.
    Witch.   What could be the quest
Which is not in the power of the most powerful,
The rulers of the invisible?
    Man.   A boon;—
But why should I repeat it? 'twere in vain.
    Witch. I know not that; let thy lips utter it.
    Man. Well, though it torture me, 'tis but the same;
My pang shall find a voice. From my youth upwards
My Spirit walked not with the souls of men,
Nor looked upon the earth with human eyes;
The thirst of their ambition was not mine,
The aim of their existence was not mine;
My joys—my griefs—my passions—and my powers,
Made me a stranger; though I wore the form,
I had no sympathy with breathing flesh,
Nor midst the Creatures of Clay that girded me
Was there but One who—but of her anon.
I said with men, and with the thoughts of men,
I held but slight communion; but instead,

My joy was in the wilderness,—to breathe
The difficult air of the iced mountain's top,
Where the birds dare not build—nor insect's wing
Flit o'er the herbless granite; or to plunge
Into the torrent, and to roll along
On the swift whirl of the new-breaking wave
Of river-stream, or Ocean, in their flow.
In these my early strength exulted; or
To follow through the night the moving moon,
The stars and their development; or catch
The dazzling lightnings till my eyes grew dim;
Or to look, list'ning, on the scattered leaves,
While Autumn winds were at their evening song.
These were my pastimes, and to be alone;
For if the beings, of whom I was one,—
Hating to be so,—crossed me in my path,
I felt myself degraded back to them,
And was all clay again. And then I dived,
In my lone wanderings, to the caves of Death,
Searching its cause in its effect; and drew
From withered bones, and skulls, and heaped up dust,
Conclusions most forbidden. Then I passed
The nights of years in sciences untaught,
Save in the old-time; and with time and toil,
And terrible ordeal, and such penance
As in itself hath power upon the air,
And spirits that do compass air and earth,
Space, and the peopled Infinite, I made
Mine eyes familiar with Eternity,
Such as, before me, did the Magi, and
He who from out their fountain-dwellings raised
Eros and Anteros, at Gadara,
As I do thee;—and with my knowledge grew
The thirst of knowledge, and the power and joy
Of this most bright intelligence, until—
    Witch. Proceed.
    Man.   Oh! I but thus prolonged my words,
Boasting these idle attributes, because
As I approach the core of my heart's grief—
But—to my task. I have not named to thee

Father or mother, mistress, friend, or being,
With whom I wore the chain of human ties;
If I had such, they seemed not such to me—
Yet there was One—
    Witch.   Spare not thyself—proceed.
    Man. She was like me in lineaments—her eyes—
Her hair—her features—all, to the very tone
Even of her voice, they said were like to mine;
But softened all, and tempered into beauty:
She had the same lone thoughts and wanderings,
The quest of hidden knowledge, and a mind
To comprehend the Universe: nor these
Alone, but with them gentler powers than mine,
Pity, and smiles, and tears—which I had not;
And tenderness—but that I had for her;
Humility— and that I never had.
Her faults were mine—her virtues were her own—
I loved her, and destroyed her!
    Witch.   With thy hand?
    Man. Not with my hand, but heart, which broke her heart;
It gazed on mine, and withered. I have shed
Blood, but not hers—and yet her blood was shed;
I saw—and could not stanch it.
    Witch.   And for this—
A being of the race thou dost despise—
The order, which thine own would rise above,
Mingling with us and ours,—thou dost forego
The gifts of our great knowledge, and shrink'st back
To recreant mortality—Away!
    Man. Daughter of Air! I tell thee, since that hour—
But words are breath—look on me in my sleep,
Or watch my watchings—Come and sit by me!
My solitude is solitude no more,
But peopled with the Furies;—I have gnashed
My teeth in darkness till returning morn,
Then cursed myself till sunset;—I have prayed
For madness as a blessing—'tis denied me.
I have affronted Death—but in the war
Of elements the waters shrunk from me,
And fatal things passed harmless; the cold hand

Of an all-pitiless Demon held me back,
Back by a single hair, which would not break.
In Fantasy, Imagination, all
The affluence of my soul—which one day was
A Crœsus in creation—I plunged deep,
But, like an ebbing wave, it dashed me back
Into the gulf of my unfathomed thought.
I plunged amidst Mankind—Forgetfulness
I sought in all, save where 'tis to be found—
And that I have to learn—my Sciences,
My long pursued and superhuman art,
Is mortal here: I dwell in my despair—
And live—and live for ever.
    Witch.   It may be
That I can aid thee.
    Man.   To do this thy power
Must wake the dead, or lay me low with them.
Do so—in any shape—in any hour—
With any torture—so it be the last.
    Witch. That is not in my province; but if thou
Wilt swear obedience to my will, and do
My bidding, it may help thee to thy wishes.
    Man. I will not swear—Obey! and whom? the Spirits
Whose presence I command, and be the slave
Of those who served me—Never!
    Witch.   Is this all?
Hast thou no gentler answer?—Yet bethink thee,
And pause ere thou rejectest.
    Man.   I have said it.
    Witch. Enough! I may retire then—say!
    Man.   Retire!
                      [*The* WITCH *disappears*
    Man. (alone) We are the fools of Time and Terror: Days
Steal on us, and steal from us; yet we live,
Loathing our life, and dreading still to die.
In all the days of this detested yoke—
This vital weight upon the struggling heart,
Which sinks with sorrow, or beats quick with pain,
Or joy that ends in agony or faintness—
In all the days of past and future—for

In life there is no present—we can number
How few—how less than few—wherein the soul
Forbears to pant for death, and yet draws back
As from a stream in winter, though the chill
Be but a moment's. I have one resource
Still in my science—I can call the dead,
And ask them what it is we dread to be:
The sternest answer can but be the Grave,
And that is nothing: if they answer not—
The buried Prophet answered to the Hag
Of Endor; and the Spartan Monarch drew
From the Byzantine maid's unsleeping spirit
An answer and his destiny—he slew
That which he loved, unknowing what he slew,
And died unpardoned—though he called in aid
The Phyxian Jove, and in Phigalia roused
The Arcadian Evocators to compel
The indignant shadow to depose her wrath,
Or fix her term of vengeance—she replied
In words of dubious import, but fulfilled.
If I had never lived, that which I love
Had still been living; had I never loved,
That which I love would still be beautiful,
Happy and giving happiness. What is she?
What is she now?—a sufferer for my sins—
A thing I dare not think upon—or nothing.
Within few hours I shall not call in vain—
Yet in this hour I dread the thing I dare:
Until this hour I never shrunk to gaze
On spirit, good or evil—now I tremble,
And feel a strange cold thaw upon my heart.
But I can act even what I most abhor,
And champion human fears.—The night approaches.

                                                          [*Exit*

ACT III

SCENE I—*A Hall in the Castle of Manfred*—MANFRED *and* HERMAN
  Man. What is the hour?
  Her.   It wants but one till sunset,

And promises a lovely twilight.
Man.   Say,
Are all things so disposed of in the tower
As I directed?
Her.   All, my Lord are ready:
Here is the key and casket.
Man.   It is well:
Thou mayst retire.   [*Exit* HERMAN
Man. (Alone)   There is a calm upon me—
Inexplicable stillness! which till now
Did not belong to what I knew of life.
If that I did not know Philosophy
To be of all our vanities the motliest,
The merest word that ever fooled the ear
From out the schoolman's jargon, I should deem
The golden secret, the sought "Kalon," found,
And seated in my soul. It will not last,
But it is well to have known it, though but once:
It hath enlarged my thoughts with a new sense,
And I within my tablets would note down
That there is such a feeling. Who is there?
                    Re-enter HERMAN
Her. My Lord, the Abbot of St. Maurice craves
To greet your presence.
            Enter the ABBOT OF ST. MAURICE
Abbot.   Peace be with Count Manfred!
Man. Thanks, holy father! welcome to these walls;
Thy presence honours them, and blesseth those
Who dwell within them.
    Abbot.   Would it were so, Count!—
But I would fain confer with thee alone.
Man. Herman, retire.—What would my reverend guest?
    Abbot. Thus, without prelude:—Age and zeal—my office—
And good intent must plead my privilege;
Our near, though not acquainted neighbourhood,
May also be my herald. Rumours strange,
And of unholy nature, are abroad,
And busy with thy name—a noble name
For centuries: may he who bears it now
Transmit it unimpaired!

Man.   Proceed,—I listen.

Abbot. 'Tis said thou holdest converse with the things
Which are forbidden to the search of man;
That with the dwellers of the dark abodes,
The many evil and unheavenly spirits
Which walk the valley of the Shade of Death,
Thou communest. I know that with mankind,
Thy fellows in creation, thou dost rarely
Exchange thy thoughts, and that thy solitude
Is as an Anchorite's—were it but holy.

Man. And what are they who do avouch these things?

Abbot. My pious brethren—the scaréd peasantry—
Even thy own vassals—who do look on thee
With most unquiet eyes. Thy life's in peril!

Man. Take it.

Abbot.   I come to save, and not destroy:
I would not pry into thy secret soul;
But if these things be sooth, there still is time
For penitence and pity: reconcile thee
With the true church, and through the church to Heaven.

Man. I hear thee. This is my reply—whate'er
I may have been, or am, doth rest between
Heaven and myself—I shall not choose a mortal
To be my mediator—Have I sinned
Against your ordinances? prove and punish!

Abbot. My son! I did not speak of punishment,
But penitence and pardon;—with thyself
The choice of such remains—and for the last,
Our institutions and our strong belief
Have given me power to smooth the path from sin
To higher hope and better thoughts; the first
I leave to Heaven,—"Vengeance is mine alone!"
So saith the Lord, and with all humbleness
His servant echoes back the awful word.

Man. Old man! there is no power in holy men,
Nor charm in prayer, nor purifying form
Of penitence, nor outward look, nor fast,
Nor agony—nor, greater than all these,
The innate tortures of that deep Despair,
Which is Remorse without the fear of Hell,

But all in all sufficient to itself
Would make a hell of Heaven—can exorcise
From out the unbounded spirit the quick sense
Of its own sins—wrongs—sufferance—and revenge
Upon itself; there is no future pang
Can deal that justice on the self-condemned
He deals on his own soul.
  Abbot.   All this is well;
For this will pass away, and be succeeded
By an auspicious hope, which shall look up
With calm assurance to that blessed place,
Which all who seek may win, whatever be
Their earthly errors, so they be atoned:
And the commencement of atonement is
The sense of its necessity. Say on—
And all our church can teach thee shall be taught;
And all we can absolve thee shall be pardoned.
  Man. When Rome's sixth Emperor was near his last,
The victim of a self-inflicted wound,
To shun the torments of a public death
From senates once his slaves, a certain soldier,
With show of loyal pity, would have stanched
The gushing throat with his officious robe;
The dying Roman thrust him back, and said—
Some empire still in his expiring glance—
"It is too late—is this fidelity?"
  Abbot. And what of this?
  Man.   I answer with the Roman—
"It is too late!"
  Abbot.   It never can be so,
To reconcile thyself with thy own soul,
And thy own soul with Heaven. Hast thou no hope?
'Tis strange—even those who do despair above,
Yet shape themselves some fantasy on earth,
To which frail twig they cling, like drowning men.
  Man. Aye—father! I have had those early visions,
And noble aspirations in my youth,
To make my own the mind of other men,
The enlightener of nations; and to rise
I knew not whither—it might be to fall;

But fall, even as the mountain-cataract,
Which having leapt from its more dazzling height,
Even in the foaming strength of its abyss,
(Which casts up misty columns that become
Clouds raining from the re-ascended skies,)
Lies low but mighty still.—But this is past,
My thoughts mistook themselves.
    Abbot.   And wherefore so?
    Man. I could not tame my nature down; for he
Must serve who fain would sway; and soothe, and sue,
And watch all time, and pry into all place,
And be a living Lie, who would become
A mighty thing amongst the mean—and such
The mass are; I disdained to mingle with
A herd, though to be leader—and of wolves.
The lion is alone, and so am I.
    Abbot. And why not live and act with other men?
    Man. Because my nature was averse from life;
And yet not cruel; for I would not make,
But find a desolation. Like the Wind,
The red-hot breath of the most lone Simoom,
Which dwells but in the desert, and sweeps o'er
The barren sands which bear no shrubs to blast,
And revels o'er their wild and arid waves,
And seeketh not, so that it is not sought,
But being met is deadly,—such hath been
The course of my existence; but there came
Things in my path which are no more.
    Abbot.   Alas!
I 'gin to fear that thou art past all aid
From me and from my calling; yet so young,
I still would—
    Man.   Look on me! there is an order
Of mortals on the earth, who do become
Old in their youth, and die ere middle age,
Without the violence of warlike death;
Some perishing of pleasure—some of study—
Some worn with toil, some of mere weariness,—
Some of disease—and some insanity—
And some of withered, or of broken hearts;

For this last is a malady which slays
More than are numbered in the lists of Fate,
Taking all shapes, and bearing many names.
Look upon me! for even of all these things
Have I partaken; and of all these things,
One were enough; then wonder not that I
Am what I am, but that I ever was,
Or having been, that I am still on earth.
    Abbot. Yet, hear me still—
    Man.   Old man! I do respect
Thine order, and revere thine years; I deem
Thy purpose pious, but it is in vain:
Think me not churlish; I would spare thyself,
Far more than me, in shunning at this time
All further colloquy—and so—farewell.

                              [*Exit* MANFRED

    Abbot. This should have been a noble creature: he
Hath all the energy which would have made
A goodly frame of glorious elements,
Had they been wisely mingled; as it is,
It is an awful chaos—Light and Darkness—
And mind and dust—and passions and pure thoughts
Mixed, and contending without end or order,—
All dormant or destructive. He will perish—
And yet he must not—I will try once more,
For such are worth redemption; and my duty
Is to dare all things for a righteous end.
I'll follow him—but cautiously, though surely.

                                [*Exit* ABBOT

29. Alfred de Musset: *The Confession of a Child of the Century*

Alfred de Musset 1810–1857) captured in his *The Confession of a Child of the Century* the mood of many younger Romantics who found themselves without hope of attaining the heroic careers their fathers had experienced and saw themselves forced to wait and restrict their talents in an age that seemed devoted to the safe, to the moderate, and to material things. The distress he evokes in the chapter given below is much the same as that of other young men of earlier eras who believed the world did not fit their talents, or vice versa—Rousseau is the most obvious example. But it is a special trait of the era of the Bourbon restoration to find so many who believed that the times, not just social arrangements or human qualities, were out of joint.

Musset himself, a product of the French aristocracy, was quite unappreciated as a dramatist, and ended by writing plays for reading rather than production. Only after 1848 did he gain fame; he was elected to the Académie Française in 1852.

The reader will note the typical concern over the loss of faith on the part of the people, who are treated in terms much like those used by Lammenais and Michelet, and the rhetorical apostrophe to the farmers of the future, which may seem out of place from the pen of a Parisian dandy, yet is fully characteristic of the sentiments of the era.

The extract is from *The Complete Writings*, translated by Kendall Warren (New York, 1892–1908), Vol. VIII, pp. 2–24.

Chapter II

DURING THE wars of the Empire, while the husbands and brothers were in Germany, the anxious mothers brought forth an ardent, pale, nervous generation. Conceived between two battles, educated amidst the noises of war, thousands of children looked about them with a somber eye while testing their puny muscles. From time to time their blood-stained fathers would appear, raise them on their gold-laced bosoms, then place them on the ground and remount their horses.

The life of Europe was centered in one man; all were trying to fill their lungs with the air which he had breathed. Every year France presented that man with three hundred thousand of her youth; it was the tax paid to Cæsar, and, without that troop behind him, he could not follow his fortune. It was the escort he needed that he might traverse the world, and then perish in a little valley in a deserted island, under the weeping willow.

Never had there been so many sleepless nights as in the time of that man; never had there been seen, hanging over the ramparts of the cities, such a nation of desolate mothers; never was there such a silence about those who spoke of death. And yet there was never such joy, such life, such fanfares of war, in all hearts. Never was there such pure sunlight as that which dried all this blood. God made the sun for this man, they said, and they called it the Sun of Austerlitz. But he made this sunlight himself with his ever-thundering cannons which dispelled all clouds but those which succeed the day of battle.

It was this air of the spotless sky, where shone so much glory, where glistened so many swords, that the youth of the time breathed. They well knew that they were destined to the hecatomb; but they regarded Murat as invulnerable, and the emperor had been seen to cross a bridge where so many bullets whistled that they wondered if he could die. And even if one must die, what did it matter? Death itself was so beautiful, so noble, so illustrious, in his battle-scarred purple! It borrowed the color of hope, it reaped so many ripening harvests that it became young, and there was no more old age. All the cradles of France, as all its tombs, were armed with shield and buckler; there were no more old men, there were corpses or demi-gods.

Nevertheless, the immortal emperor stood one day on a hill watching seven nations engaged in mutual slaughter; as he did not know whether he would be master of all the world or only half, Azrael passed along, touched him with the tip of his wing, and pushed him into the Ocean. At the noise of his fall, the dying powers sat up in their beds of pain; and stealthily advancing with furtive tread, all the royal spiders made the partition of Europe, and the purple of Cæsar became the frock of Harlequin.

Just as the traveler, sure of his way, hastens night and day through rain and sunlight, regardless of vigils or of dangers; but when he has reached his home and seated himself before the fire, he is seized upon by a feeling of extreme lassitude and can hardly drag himself to his bed: thus France, the widow of Cæsar, suddenly felt her wound. She fell through sheer exhaustion, and lapsed into a sleep so profound that her old kings, believing her dead, wrapped about her a white shroud. The old army, its hair whitened in service, returned exhausted with fatigue, and the hearths of deserted castles sadly flickered into life.

Then the men of the Empire, who had been through so much, who had lived in such carnage, kissed their emaciated wives and spoke of their first love; they looked into the fountains of their natal prairies and found themselves so old, so mutilated, that they bethought themselves of their sons, in order that they might close their eyes in peace. They asked where they were; the children came from the schools, and seeing neither sabers, nor cuirasses, neither infantry nor cavalry, they asked in turn where were their fathers. They were told that the war was ended, that Cæsar was dead, and that the portraits of Wellington and of Blücher were suspended in the antechambers of the consulates and the embassies, with these two words beneath: *Salvatoribus mundi.*

Then there seated itself on a world in ruins an anxious youth. All the children were drops of burning blood which had inundated the earth; they were born in the bosom of war, for war. For fifteen years they had dreamed of the snows of Moscow and of the sun of the pyramids. They had not gone beyond their native towns; but they were told that through each gate of these towns lay the road to a capital of Europe. They had in their heads all the world; they beheld the earth, the sky, the streets and the highways; all these were empty, and the bells of parish churches resounded faintly in the distance.

Pale fantoms shrouded in black robes, slowly traversed the country; others knocked at the doors of houses, and when admitted, drew from their pockets well-worn documents with which they drove out the tenants. From every direction came men still trembling with the fear which had seized them when they fled twenty years before. All began to urge their claims, disputing loudly and crying for help; it was strange that a single death should attract so many crows.

The king of France was on his throne, looking here and there to see if he could perchance find a bee in the royal tapestry. Some held out their hats, and he gave them money; others showed him a crucifix, and he kissed it; others contented themselves with pronouncing in his ear great names of powerful families, and he replied to these by inviting them into his *grand' salle,* where the echoes were more sonorous; still others showed him their old cloaks, when they had carefully effaced the bees, and to these he gave new apparel.

The children saw all this, thinking that the spirit of Cæsar would soon land at Cannes and breathe upon this larva; but the silence was unbroken and they saw floating in the sky only the paleness of the lily. When these children spoke of glory, they were answered: "Become priests"; when they spoke of hope, of love, of power, of life: "Become priests."

And yet there mounted the rostrum a man who held in his hand a contract between the king and the people; be began by saying that glory was a beautiful thing; and ambition and war as well; but there was something still more beautiful, and it was called liberty.

The children raised their heads and remembered that their grandfathers had spoken thus. They remembered having seen in certain obscure corners of the paternal home mysterious marble busts with long hair and a Latin inscription; they remembered seeing their grandsires shake their heads and speak of a stream of blood more terrible than that of the emperor. There was something in that word liberty that made their hearts beat with the memory of a terrible past and the hope of a glorious future.

They trembled at the word; but returning to their homes they encountered on the street three panniers which were being borne to Clamart; there were, within, three young men who had pronounced that word liberty too distinctly.

A strange smile hovered on their lips at that sad sight; but other speakers, mounted on the rostrum, began to publicly estimate what ambition had cost and how very dear was glory; they pointed out the horror of war and called the hecatombs butcheries. And they spoke so often and so long that all human illusions, like the trees in autumn, fell leaf by leaf about them, and those who listened passed their hands over their foreheads as though awakened from a feverish dream.

Some said: "The emperor has fallen because the people wished no more of him"; others added: "The people wished the king; no, liberty; no, reason; no, religion; no, the English constitution; no, absolutism"; and the last one said: "No, none of these things, but repose."

Three elements entered into the life which offered itself to

these children: behind them a past forever destroyed, moving un-
easily on its ruins with all the fossils of centuries of absolutism;
before them the aurora of an immense horizon, the first gleams of
the future; and between these two worlds—something like the
Ocean which separates the old world from Young America, something vague and floating, a troubled sea filled with wreckage,
traversed from time to time by some distant sail or some ship
breathing out a heavy vapor; the present, in a word, which separates the past from the future, which is neither the one nor the
other, which resemble both, and where one can not know
whether, at each step, one is treading on a seed or a piece of
refuse.

It was in this chaos that the choice must be made; this was the
aspect presented to children full of spirit and of audacity, sons of
the Empire and grandsons of the Revolution.

As for the past, they would none of it, they had no faith in it;
the future, they loved it, but how? As Pygmalion loved Galatea:
it was for them a lover in marble and they waited for the breath
of life to animate that breast, for the blood to color those veins.

There remained then, the present, the spirit of the time, angel
of the dawn who is neither night nor day; they found him seated
on a lime sack filled with bones, clad in the mantle of egoism, and
shivering in terrible cold. The anguish of death entered into the
soul at the sight of that specter, half mummy and half fetus; they
approached it as the traveler who is shown at Strasburg the
daughter of an old count of Sarvenden, embalmed in her bride's
dress: that childish skeleton makes one shudder, for her slender
and livid hand wears the wedding-ring and her head falls into
dust in the midst of orange blossoms.

As upon the approach of a tempest there passes through the
forests a terrible sound which makes all the trees shudder, to
which profound silence succeeds, thus had Napoleon, in passing,
shaken the world; kings felt their crowns vacillate in the storm
and, raising their hands to steady them, they found only their
hair, bristling with terror. The pope had traveled three hundred
leagues to bless him in the name of God and to crown him with
the diadem; but Napoleon had taken it from his hands. Thus
everything trembled in that dismal forest of old Europe; then
silence succeeded.

It is said that when you meet a mad dog if you keep quietly on
your way without turning, the dog will merely follow you a short

distance growling and showing his teeth; but if you allow yourself to be frightened into a movement of terror, if you but make a
sudden step, he will leap at your throat and devour you; when the
first bite has been taken there is no escaping him.

In European history it has often happened that a sovereign has
made that movement of terror and his people have devoured him;
but if one had done it, all had not done it at the same time, that is
to say, one king had disappeared, but not all royal majesty. Before the sword of Napoleon majesty made this movement, this
gesture which loses everything, and not only majesty, but religion, nobility, all power both human and divine.

Napoleon dead, human and divine power were re-established,
but belief in them no longer existed. A terrible danger lurks in the
knowledge of what is possible, for the mind always goes farther.
It is one thing to say: "That may be" and another thing to say:
"That has been"; it is the first bite of the dog.

The deposition of Napoleon was the last flicker of the lamp of
despotism; it destroyed and it parodied kings as Voltaire the Holy
Scripture. And after him was heard a great noise: it was the stone
of St. Helena which had just fallen on the ancient world. Immediately there appeared in the heavens the cold star of reason, and
its rays, like those of the goddess of the night, shedding light
without heat, enveloped the world in a livid shroud.

There had been those who hated the nobles, who cried out
against priests, who conspired against kings; abuses and prejudices had been attacked; but all that was not so great a novelty as
to see a smiling people. If a noble or a priest or a sovereign
passed, the peasants who had made war possible began to shake
their heads and say: "Ah! when we saw this man at such a time
and place he wore a different face." And when the throne and
altar were mentioned, they replied: "They are made of four
planks of wood; we have nailed them together and torn them
apart." And when some one said: "People, you have recovered
from the errors which led you astray; you have recalled your
kings and your priests," they replied: "We have nothing to do
with those prattlers." And when some one said: "People, forget
the past, work and obey," they arose from their seats and a dull
rumbling could be heard. It was the rusty and notched saber in
the corner of the cottage chimney. Then they hastened to add:
"Then keep quiet, at least; if no one harms you, do not seek to
harm." Alas! they were content with that.

But youth was not content. It is certain that there are in man two occult powers engaged in a death struggle: the one, clear-sighted and cold, is concerned with reality, calculation, weight, and judges the past; the other is thirsty for the future and eager for the unknown. When passion sways man, reason follows him weeping and warning him of his danger; but when man listens to the voice of reason, when he stops at her request and says: "What a fool I am; where am I going?" passion calls to him: "And must I die?"

A feeling of extreme uneasiness began to ferment in all young hearts. Condemned to inaction by the powers which governed the world, delivered to vulgar pendants of every kind, to idleness and to ennui, the youth saw the foaming billows which they had prepared to meet, subside. All these gladiators, glistening with oil, felt in the bottom of their souls an insupportable wretched-ness. The richest became libertines; those of moderate fortune followed some profession and resigned themselves to the sword or to the robe. The poorest gave themselves up with cold enthusiasm to great thoughts, plunged into the frightful sea of aimless effort. As human weakness seeks association and as men are herds by nature, politics became mingled with it. There were struggles with the *garde du corps* on the steps of the legislative assembly; at the theater, Talma wore a peruke which made him resemble Cæsar; every one flocked to the burial of a liberal deputy.

But of the members of the two parties there was not one who, upon returning home, did not bitterly realize the emptiness of his life and the feebleness of his hands.

While life outside was so colorless and so mean, the interior life of society assumed a somber aspect of silence; hypocrisy ruled in all departments of conduct; English ideas of devotion, gaity even, had disappeared. Perhaps Providence was already preparing new ways, perhaps the herald angel of future society was already sow-ing in the hearts of women the seeds of human independence. But it is certain that a strange thing suddenly happened; in all the salons of Paris the men passed to one side and the women to the other; and thus, the one clad in white like a bride and the other in black like an orphan began to take measurements with the eye.

Let us not be deceived: that vestment of black which the men of our time wear is a terrible symbol; before coming to this, the armor must have fallen piece by piece and the embroidery flower by flower. Human reason has overthrown all illusions; but it bears in itself sorrow, in order that it may be consoled.

The customs of students and artists, those customs so free, so beautiful, so full of youth, began to experience the universal change. Men in taking leave of women whispered the word which wounds to the death: contempt. They plunged into the dissipation of wine and courtesans. Students and artists did the same; love was treated as glory and religion: it was an old illusion. The grisette, that class so dreamy, so romantic, so tender, and so sweet in love, abandoned herself to the counting-house and to the shop. She was poor and no one loved her; she wanted dresses and hats and she sold herself. O, misery! the young man who ought to love her, whom she loved, who used to take her to the woods of Verrieres and Romainville, to the dances on the lawn, to the suppers under the trees; he who used to talk with her as she sat near the lamp in the rear of the shop on the long winter evenings; he who shared her crust of bread moistened with the sweat of her brow, and her love at once sublime and poor; he, that same man, after having abandoned her, finds her after a night of orgie, pale and leaden, forever lost, with hunger on her lips and prostitution in her heart.

About this time two poets, whose genius was second only to that of Napoleon, consecrated their lives to the work of collecting all the elements of anguish and of grief scattered over the universe. Goethe, the patriarch of a new literature, after having painted in *Werther* the passion which leads to suicide, traced in his *Faust* the most somber human character which has ever represented evil and unhappiness. His writings began to pass from Germany into France. From his studio, surrounded by pictures and statues, rich, happy and at ease, he watched with a paternal smile, his gloomy creations marching in dismal procession across the frontiers of France. Byron replied to him by a cry of grief which made Greece tremble, and suspended *Manfred* over the abyss as if nothingness had been the answer of the hideous enigma with which he enveloped him.

Pardon me! O, great poets! who are now but ashes and who sleep in peace! Pardon me; you are demi-gods and I am only a child who suffers. But while writing all this I can not help cursing you. Why did you not sing of the perfume of flowers, of the voices of nature, of hope and of love, of the vine and the sun, of the azure heavens and of beauty. You must have understood life, you must have suffered, and the world was crumbling to pieces about you, you wept on its ruins and you despaired; and your mistresses were false; your friends caluminated, your compatriots misunderstood; and your heart was empty; death was in your eyes, and you were the very Colossi of grief. But tell me, you noble Goethe, was there no more consoling voice in the religious murmur of your old German forests? You, for whom beautiful poesy was the sister of science, could you with their aid find in immortal nature no healing plant for the heart of their favorite? You, who were a pantheist, and antique poet of Greece, a lover of sacred forms, could you not put a little honey in the beautiful vases you made; you, who had only to smile and allow the bees to come to your lips? And thou, thou Byron, hadst thou not near Ravenna, under thy orange trees of Italy, under thy beautiful Venetian sky, near thy dear Adriatic, hadst thou not thy well beloved? O, God! I who speak to you and who am only a feeble child, I have perhaps known sorrows that you have never suffered, and yet I believe and I hope, and yet I bless God.

When English and German ideas passed thus over our heads there ensued disgust and mournful silence, followed by a terrible convulsion. For to formulate general ideas is to change saltpeter into powder, and the Homeric brain of the great Goethe had sucked up, as an alembic, all the juice of the forbidden fruit. Those who did not read him did not believe it, knew nothing of it. Poor creatures! The explosion carried them away like grains of dust into the abyss of universal doubt.

It was a degeneration of all things of heaven and of earth that might be termed disenchantment or if you preferred, despair; as if humanity in lethargy had been pronounced dead by those who held its place. Like a soldier who was asked: "In what do you believe?" and who replied: "In myself." Thus the youth of France, hearing that question, replied: "In nothing."

Then they formed into two camps: on one side the exalted spirits, sufferers, all the expansive souls who had need of the infinite, bowed their heads and wept; they wrapt themselves in unhealthy dreams and there could be seen nothing but broken reeds on an ocean of bitterness. On the other side the men of the flesh remained standing, inflexible in the midst of positive joys, and cared for nothing except to count the money they had acquired. It was only a sob and a burst of laughter, the one coming from the soul, the other from the body.

This is what the soul said:

"Alas! Alas! religion has departed; the clouds of heaven fall in rain; we have no longer either hope or expectation, not even two little pieces of black wood in the shape of a cross before which to clasp our hands. The star of the future is loath to rise; it can not get above the horizon; it is enveloped in clouds, and like the sun in winter its disk is the color of blood, as in '93. There is no more love, no more glory. What heavy darkness over all the earth! And we shall be dead when the day breaks."

This is what the body said:

"Man is here below to satisfy his senses, he has more or less of white or yellow metal to which he owes more or less esteem. To eat, to drink and to sleep, that is life. As for the bonds which exist between men, friendship consists in loaning money; but one rarely has a friend whom he loves enough for that. Kinship determines inheritance; love is an exercise of the body; the only intellectual joy is vanity."

Like the Asiatic plague exhaled from the vapors of the Ganges, frightful despair stalked over the earth. Already Chateaubriand, prince of poesy, wrapping the horrible idol in his pilgrim's mantle, had placed it on a marble altar in the midst of perfumes and holy incense. Already the children were tightening their idle hands and drinking in their bitter cup the poisoned brewage of doubt. Already things were drifting toward the abyss, when the jackals suddenly emerged from the earth. A cadaverous and infected literature which had no form but that of ugliness, began to sprinkle with fetid blood all the monsters of nature.

Who will dare to recount what was passing in the colleges? Men doubted everything: the young men denied everything. The poets sung of despair; the youth came from the schools with serene brow, their faces glowing with health and blasphemy in their mouths. Moreover, the French character, being by nature gay and open, readily assimilated English and German ideas; but hearts too light to struggle and to suffer withered like crushed flowers. Thus the principle of death descended slowly and without shock from the head to the bowels. Instead of having the enthusiasm of evil we had only the negation of the good; instead of despair, insensibility. Children of fifteen seated listlessly under flowering shrubs, conversed for pastime on subjects which would have made shudder with terror the motionless groves of Versailles. The Communion of Christ, the host, those wafers that stand as the eternal symbol of divine love, were used to seal letters; the children spit upon the bread of God.

Happy they who escaped those times! Happy they who passed over the abyss while looking up to Heaven. There are such, doubtless, and they will pity us.

It is unfortunately true that there is in blasphemy a certain discharge of power which solaces the burdened heart. When an atheist, drawing his watch, gave God a quarter of an hour in which to strike him dead, it is certain that it was a quarter of an hour of wrath and of atrocious joy. It was the paroxysm of despair, a nameless appeal to all celestial powers; it was a poor wretched creature squirming under the foot that was crushing him; it was a loud cry of pain. And who knows? In the eyes of Him who sees all things, it was perhaps a prayer.

Thus these youth found employment for their idle powers in a fondness of despair. To scoff at glory, at religion, at love, at all the world, is a great consolation for those who do not know what to do; they mock at themselves and in doing so prove the correctness of their view. And then it is pleasant to believe oneself unhappy when one is only idle and tired. Debauchery, moreover, the first conclusion of the principle of death, is a terrible millstone for grinding the energies.

The rich said: "There is nothing real but riches, all else is a dream; let us enjoy and then let us die." Those of moderate fortune said: "There is nothing real but oblivion, all else is a dream; let us forget and let us die." And the poor said: "There is nothing real but unhappiness, all else is a dream; let us blaspheme and die."

This is too black? It is exaggerated? What do you think of it? Am I a misanthrope? Allow me to make a reflection.

In reading the history of the fall of the Roman Empire, it is impossible to overlook the evil that the Christians, so admirable in the desert, did the state when they were in power. "When I think," said Montesquieu, "of the profound ignorance into which

the Greek clergy plunged the laity, I am obliged to compare them
to the Scythians of whom Herodotus speaks, who put out the eyes
of their slaves in order that nothing might distract their attention
from their work. . . . No affair of state, no peace, no truce, no
negotiation, no marriage could be transacted by any one but the
clergy. The evils of this system were beyond belief."

Montesquieu might have added: Christianity destroyed the
emperors but it saved the people. It opened to the barbarians the
palaces of Constantinople, but it opened the doors of cottages to
the ministering angels of Christ. It had much to do with the great
ones of earth. And what is more interesting than the death-rattle
of an empire corrupt to the very marrow of its bones, than the
somber galvanism under the influence of which the skeleton of
tyranny danced upon the tombs of Heliogabalus and Caracalla!
What a beautiful thing that mummy of Rome, embalmed in the
perfumes of Nero and swathed in the shroud of Tiberius! It had
to do, messieurs the politicians, with finding the poor and giving
them life and peace; it had to do with allowing the worms and
tumors to destroy the monuments of shame, while drawing from
the ribs of this mummy a virgin as beautiful as the mother of the
Redeemer, hope, the friend of the oppressed.

That is what Christianity did; and now, after many years, what
have they who destroyed it done? They saw that the poor allowed
themselves to be oppressed by the rich, the feeble by the strong,
because of that saying: "The rich and the strong will oppress me
on earth; but when they wish to enter paradise, I shall be at the
door and I will accuse them before the tribunal of God." And so,
alas! they were patient.

The antagonists of Christ therefore said to the poor: "You wait
patiently for the day of justice: there is no justice; you wait for
the life eternal to achieve your vengeance: there is no life eternal;
you gather up your tears and those of your family, the cries of
children and the sobs of women, to place them at the feet of God
at the hour of death: there is no God."

Then it is certain that the poor man dried his tears, that he told
his wife to check her sobs, his children to come with him, and
that he stood upon the earth with the power of a bull. He said to
the rich: "Thou who oppressest me, thou art only man"; and to
the priest: "Thou who hast consoled me, thou hast lied." That was

just what the antagonists of Christ desired. Perhaps they thought this was the way to achieve man's happiness, sending him out to the conquest of liberty.

But, if the poor man, once satisfied that the priests deceive him, that the rich rob him, that all men have rights, that all good is of this world, and that misery is impiety; the poor man, believing in himself and in his two arms, says to himself some fine day: "War on the rich! for me, happiness here in this life, since there is no other! for me, the earth, since heaven is empty! for me and for all, since all are equal." Oh! reasoners sublime who have led him to this, what will you say to him if he is conquered?

Doubtless you are philanthropists, doubtless you are right about the future, and the day will come when you will be blessed; but thus far, we have not blessed you. When the oppressor said: "This world for me!" the oppressed replied: "Heaven for me!" Now what can he say?

All the evils of the present come from two causes: the people who have passed through 1793 and 1814, nurse wounds in their hearts. That which was is no more; what will be, is not yet. Do not seek elsewhere the cause of our malady.

Here is a man whose house falls in ruins; he has torn it down in order to build another. The rubbish encumbers the spot, and he waits for fresh materials for his new home. At the moment he has prepared to cut the stone and mix the cement, while standing, pick in hand, with sleeves rolled up, he is informed that there is no more stone, and is advised to whiten the old material and make the best possible use of that. What can you expect this man to do who is unwilling to build his nest out of ruins? The quarry is deep, the tools too weak to hew out the stones. "Wait!" they say to him, "we will draw out the stones one by one; hope, work, advance, withdraw." What do they not tell him? And in the meantime he has lost his old house, and has not yet built the new; he does not know where to protect himself from the rain, or how to prepare his evening meal, nor where to work, nor where to sleep, nor where to die; and his children are newly born.

I am much deceived if we do not resemble that man. O, people of the future! when on a warm summer day you bend over your plows in the green fields of your native land; when you see, in the pure sunlight under a spotless sky, the earth, your fruitful mother, smiling in her matutinal robe on the workman, her well-beloved child; when drying on your brow the holy baptism of sweat, you cast your eye over the vast horizon, when there will not be one blade higher than another in the human harvest, but only violets and marguerites in the midst of ripening sheafs. Oh! free men! when you thank God that you were born for that harvest, think of those who are no more, tell yourself that we have dearly purchased the repose which you enjoy; pity us more than all your fathers, for we have suffered the evil which entitled them to pity and we have lost that which consoled them.

30. Selections from Goethe, Novalis, and William Blake

There follow brief selections from three authors that seem to me to epitomize most tellingly some of the themes exemplified in this book. The speeches from Goethe's *Faust*, Part, I offer another view of the Romantic personality in the greatly influential Faust figure, insatiable for knowledge and experience, like Manfred, quite unsatisfied with the limits of human existence. The selections are from the translation by Bayard Taylor, 1870.

Novalis's philosophy as it appeared apart from his poetry is largely contained in aphorisms and fragments such as those below. They are from Novalis, *Hymns to the Night and Other Selected Writings*, translated by Charles E. Passage, copyright © 1960, The Liberal Arts Press, Inc., reprinted by permission of the Liberal Arts Press Division of the Bobbs-Merrill Company, Inc.

Finally, a few lines from William Blake (1757–1827). Blake lived as an engraver in London. He was a mystic and an ardent opponent of Enlightenment thought but also a great supporter of the Revolution. He saw reason as a destructive analytic power that must be opposed by the spiritual powers of imagination, genius, inspiration, and energy. He glorified the senses, love, and creativity.

Faust, Part I
Goethe

Mephisto and Faust on knowing and feeling

Mephisto: He who would study organic existence,
First drives out the soul with rigid persistence;

Then the parts in his hand he may hold and class,
But the spiritual link is lost, alas! . . .

Faust: Call it Bliss! Heart! Love! God!
I have no name to give it!
Feeling is all in all:
The Name is sound and smoke,
Obscuring Heaven's clear glow. . . .

MEPHISTO DESCRIBES FAUST TO GOD

Mephisto: Forsooth! He serves you after strange devices:
No earthly meat or drink the fool suffices:
His spirit's ferment far aspireth;
Half conscious of his frenzied, crazed unrest,
The fairest stars from Heaven he requireth,
From Earth the highest raptures and the best,
And all the near and far that he desireth
Fails to subdue the tumult of his breast. . . .

FAUST DESCRIBES HIMSELF

Faust: One impulse art thou conscious of, at best:
O, never seek to know the other!
Two souls, alas! reside within my breast,
And each withdraws from, and repels, its brother;
One with tenacious organs holds in love
And clinging lust the world in its embraces;
The other strongly sweeps, this dust above,
Into the high ancestral spaces.
If there be airy spirits near,
'Twixt Heaven and Earth on potent errands fleeing,
Let them drop down the golden atmosphere,
And bear me forth to new and varièd being!
Yea, if a magic mantle once were mine,
To waft me o'er the world at pleasure,
I would not for the costliest stores of treasure—
Not for a monarch's robe—the gift resign. . . .

Faust: But thou hast heard, tis not of joy we're talking.
I take the wildering whirl, enjoyment's keenest pain,

Enamored hate, exhilarant disdain.
My bosom, of its thirst for knowldege sated,
Shall not, henceforth, from any pang be wrested,
And all of life for all mankind created
Shall be within mine inmost being tested:
The highest, lowest forms my soul shall borrow,
Shall heap upon itself their bliss and sorrow,
And thus, my own sole self to all their selves expanded
I too, at last, shall with them all be stranded! . . .

From Aphorisms,
Novalis

Where children are, there is the Golden Age.

Describing human beings has hitherto been impossible because it was not known what a human being was. Once it is known what a human being is, it will be possible to describe individuals in genuine genetic fashion. Anyone who holds fragments of this sort to the letter may be an honorable man—only he shouldn't call himself a poet. Must we always be circumspect? He who is too old for enthusiasm, let him avoid youthful fatherings. Now there are literary saturnalia. The more motley life is, the better.

From "Miscellaneous Fragments,"
Novalis

The raw discursive thinker is a scholastic. The true scholastic is a mystical subtilizer. Out of logical atoms he builds his universe— he annihilates all living nature in order to put an artifice of thought in its place. His objective is an infinite automaton. Opposed to him is the raw intuitive thinker. He is a mystical macrologue. He hates rules and fixed forms. A wild, violent life prevails in Nature— everything is alive. No laws—arbitrariness and miracles everywhere. He is purely dynamic.

Lessing saw too sharply and in so doing lost the feeling for the unclear totality, the magical view of objects together in multiple lighting and shadow.

The artist stands on mankind like a statue on its pedestal.

Only an artist can divine the meaning of life.

Anyone seeking God will find him everywhere.

The more personal, local, temporal, particularized a poem is, the nearer it stands to the *centrum* of poetry. A poem must be completely inexhaustible, like a human being or a good proverb.

From "Proverbs of Hell,"
William Blake

The road of excess leads to the palace of wisdom.
He who desires but acts not, breeds pestilence.
No bird soars too high, if he soars with his own wings.
Excess of sorrow laughs. Excess of joy weeps.
What is now proved was once only imagined.
Everything possible to be believed is an image of truth.
The tygers of wrath are wiser than the horses of instruction.
Expect poison from the standing water.
Improvement makes strait roads, but the crooked roads without improvement are roads of Genius.

From "Annotations to Sir Joshua Reynold's Discourses,"
William Blake

To Generalize is to be an Idiot. To Particularize is the Alone Distinction of Merit. General Knowledges are those Knowledges that Idiots possess.
Minute Discrimination is Not Accidental. All Sublimity is founded on Minute Discrimination.
I do not believe that Rafael taught Mich. Angelo, or that Mich. Angelo taught Rafael, any more than I believe that the Rose teaches the Lilly how to grow, or the Apple tree teaches the Pear tree how to bear Fruit. I do not believe the tales of Anecdote writers when they militate against Individual Character.
Knowledge of Ideal Beauty is Not to be Acquired. It is Born with us. Innate Ideas are in Every Man, Born with him; they are truly Himself. The Man who says that we have No Innate Ideas must be a Fool & Knave, Having no Con-Science or Innate Science.
God Forbid that Truth should be Confined to Mathematical Demonstration.

Chronology

1760–63–MacPherson, Ossian poems
  1765–Walpole, *Castle of Otranto*
  1774–Goethe, *Sorrows of Young Werther*
1781–88–Rousseau, *Confessions*
  1790–Burke, *Reflections on the Revolution in France*
  1791–Burke, *Appeal from the New to the Old Whigs*
1793–94–The Terror
  1796–Lewis, *The Monk*
  1798–Wordsworth and Coleridge, *Lyrical Ballads*
      Schlegel brothers founded the *Athenaeum*
  1799–Novalis, "Christendom or Europe"
      Schleiermacher, *Speeches on Religion to Its Cultured Despisers*
  1802–Chateaubriand, *Genius of Christianity*
  1804–Napoleon made Emperor
  1808–Goethe, *Faust*, Part I
1808–09–De Maistre, *Essay on the Generative Principle of Political Constitutions*
1812–19–Byron, *Childe Harold*
  1814–Scott, *Waverley*
  1815–Savigny, *Of the Vocation of Our Age for Legislation and Jurisprudence*
  1815–Waterloo
  1817–Coleridge, *Biographia Literaria;* Byron, *Manfred*
  1819–Carlsbad Decrees; Scott, *Ivanhoe;* Géricault, "Raft of the Medusa"
  1822–Delacroix, "Dante and Virgil"
  1825–Saint-Simon, *The New Christianity*
  1827–Hugo, Preface to *Cromwell*
  1830–Hugo, *Hernani; Berlioz, Symphonie Fantastique*
      Stendhal, *The Red and the Black*
  1834–Lammenais, *Words of a Believer*
  1836–Musset, *Confession of a Child of the Century;* Heine, *The Romantic School*
  1837–Hegel, *Philosophy of History*
  1840–Shelley, *Defence of Poetry*
  1841–Carlyle, *On Heroes, Hero-Worship, and the Heroic in History*
1847–53–Michelet, *History of the French Revolution*
  1848–Revolutions in Europe's major cities
  1851–*Coup d'etat* of Louis Napoleon Bonaparte

Suggestions for Additional Reading

A. Collections of Documents:

George R. Creeger and Joseph W. Reed, Jr., *Selected Prose and Poetry of the Romantic Period* (New York, 1964).

Elizabeth Gilmore Holt, *From the Classicists to the Impressionists: A Documentary History of Art and Architecture in the Nineteenth Century*, (New York, 1966).

Howard E. Hugo, *The Viking Portable Romantic Reader* (New York, 1957).

Morse Peckham, *Romanticism, The Culture of the Nineteenth Century* (New York, 1966).

Louis L. Snyder, *The Dynamics of Nationalism* (Princeton, N.J., 1964).

Fritz Stern, *The Varieties of History* (New York, 1956).

Eugen Weber, *Paths to the Present, Aspects of European Thought from Romanticism to Existentialism* (New York, 1960).

Carl R. Woodring, *Prose of the Romantic Period* (Boston, 1961).

B. Secondary Studies:

Reinhold Aris, *A History of Political Thought in Germany from 1789 to 1815* (London, 1936).

Irving Babbitt, *Rousseau and Romanticism* (Boston, 1919).

Jacques Barzun, *Classic, Romantic, and Modern* (Garden City, N.Y., 1961).

Walter Jackson Bate, *From Classic to Romantic* (Cambridge, Mass., 1946).

Crane Brinton, *The Political Thought of the English Romanticists* (Oxford, 1926).

R. G. Collingwood, *The Idea of History* (Oxford, 1946).

Frederick Engel-Janosi, *Four Studies in French Historical Writing* (Baltimore, 1955).

Robert Ergang, *Herder and the Foundations of German Nationalism* (New York, 1931).

Hoxie Neale Fairchild, *The Noble Savage, A Study in Romantic Naturalism* (New York, 1928).

Reginald A. Foakes, *The Romantic Assertion* (London and New Haven, Conn., 1958).

Albert Joseph George, *The Development of French Romanticism: The Impact of the Industrial Revolution on Literature* (New York, 1956).

Robert Gleckner and Gerald Enscoe, eds., *Romanticism, Points of View* (Englewood Cliffs, N.J., 1962).

G. P. Gooch, *History and Historians in the Nineteenth Century* (London, 1913).

Arnold Hauser, *The Social History of Art* (London, 1958).

C. J. H. Hayes, *Essays on Nationalism* (New York, 1941).

Hans Kohn, *Panslavism* (New York, 1960).

Leonard Krieger, *The German Idea of Freedom* (Boston, 1957).

Arthur O. Lovejoy, *Essays in the History of Ideas* (Baltimore, 1948).

Frank E. Manuel, *The Prophets of Paris* (New York, 1965).

G. H. Mead, *Movements of Thought in the Nineteenth Century* (Chicago, 1936).

Emery Neff, *The Poetry of History* (New York, 1961).

Morse Peckham, *Beyond the Tragic Vision* (New York, 1962).

Mario Praz, *The Romantic Agony* (London, 1933).

Boyd Shafer, *Nationalism: Myths and Reality* (New York, 1955).

Louis L. Snyder, *The Meaning of Nationalism* (New Brunswick, N.J., 1054).

J. L. Talmon, *Political Messianism: The Romantic Phase* (London, 1960).

R. Tymms, *German Romantic Literature* (London, 1055).

Peter Viereck, *Metapolitics: From the Romantics to Hitler* (New York, 1041).

René Wellek, *A History of Modern Criticism* (New Haven, Conn., 1055).

L. A. Willoughby, *The Romantic Movement in Germany* (London, 1930).

Index

DOCUMENTARY HISTORY OF WESTERN CIVILIZATION
Edited by Eugene C. Black and Leonard W. Levy

ANCIENT AND MEDIEVAL HISTORY OF THE WEST

Morton Smith: ANCIENT GREECE

A. H. M. Jones: A HISTORY OF ROME THROUGH THE FIFTH CENTURY
Vol. I: The Republic
Vol. II: The Empire

Deno Geanakopolos: BYZANTINE EMPIRE

Marshall W. Baldwin: CHRISTIANITY THROUGH THE CRUSADES

Bernard Lewis: ISLAM THROUGH SULEIMAN THE MAGNIFICENT

David Herlihy: HISTORY OF FEUDALISM

William M. Bowsky: RISE OF COMMERCE AND TOWNS

David Herlihy: MEDIEVAL CULTURE AND SOCIETY

EARLY MODERN HISTORY

Hannah Gray: CULTURAL HISTORY OF THE RENAISSANCE

Florence Edler De Roover: MONEY, BANKING & COMMERCE, 13TH-16TH CENTURIES

V. J. Parry: THE OTTOMAN EMPIRE

Ralph E. Giesey: EVOLUTION OF THE DYNASTIC STATE

J. H. Parry: THE EUROPEAN RECONNAISSANCE

Hans J. Hillerbrand: THE PROTESTANT REFORMATION

John C. Olin: THE CATHOLIC COUNTER-REFORMATION

Orest Ranum: THE CENTURY OF LOUIS XIV

Thomas Hegarty: RUSSIAN HISTORY THROUGH PETER THE GREAT

Marie Boas-Hall: THE SCIENTIFIC REVOLUTION

Barry E. Supple: HISTORY OF MERCANTILISM

_____: IMPERIALISM, WAR & DIPLOMACY, 1550-1763

Herbert H. Rowen: THE LOW COUNTRIES

C. A. Macartney: THE EVOLUTION OF THE HABSBURG & HOHENZOLLERN DYNASTIES

Lester G. Crocker: THE ENLIGHTENMENT

Robert Forster: EIGHTEENTH CENTURY EUROPEAN SOCIETY